lg

Psychological Foundations of Sport and Exercise, 3rd Edition

Institute of Sport & Exercise Science

University of Worcester

prepared by:

Dr P Castle, J West, A Faull and D Mycock

McGraw-Hill

A Division of The McGraw-Hill Companies

McGraw-Hill Custom Publishing

ISBN 13:   9780390148629

Texts:

Text:

Professor Upload

Sport Psychology: Concepts and
Applications, Sixth Edition
Cox

Understanding Psychology, Ninth Edition
Feldman

Writing, Reading, and Researching in the
Disciplines: Student Guides
Melzer

The Psychology of Physical Activity
Carron-Hausenblas-Estabrooks

Pathways to Psychology: A Modular
Approach
Feldman

The Science of Psychology: An Appreciative
View
King

Guide to Writing, Third Edition
Wells

and others . . .

McGraw-Hill Custom Publishing

http://www.primisonline.com

This McGraw−Hill Primis text may include materials submitted to McGraw−Hill for publication by the instructor of this course. The instructor is solely responsible for the editorial content of such materials.

Printed in Great Britain by Bell & Bain Ltd., Glasgow

ISBN: 9780390148629

Contents

Introduction   **1**

King • *The Science of Psychology: An Appreciative View*

      1. What is Psychology?   **10**
      Text   **10**

Cox • *Sport Psychology: Concepts and Applications, Sixth Edition*

      I. Understanding Sport Psychology   **36**
      1. Foundations of Sport Psychology   **36**

King • *The Science of Psychology: An Appreciative View*

      11. Personality   **54**
      Text   **54**

Feldman • *Understanding Psychology, Ninth Edition*

      XIII. Personality   **91**
      41. Trait, Learning, Biological and Evolutionary, and Humanistic
            Approaches to Personality   **91**

Cox • *Sport Psychology: Concepts and Applications, Sixth Edition*

      II. Motivation in Sport and Exercise   **103**
      6. Goal Perspective Theory   **103**

Feldman • *Pathways to Psychology: A Modular Approach*

      Feeling and Experiencing the World   **120**
      Motivation and Emotion   **120**

Williams • *Applied Sport Psychology: Personal Growth to Peak Performance, Sixth Edition*

II. Mental Training for Performance Enhancement   **135**

12. Arousal–Performance Relationships   **135**

Carron–Hausenblas–Estabrooks • *The Psychology of Physical Activity*

I. Introduction to the Psychology of Physical Activity and Exercise   **161**

1. The Psychology of Physical Activity   **161**

II. The Individual and Physical Activity   **172**

4. Physical Activity and Mood   **172**

IV. Models for Involvement in Physical Activity   **184**

15. The Transtheoretical Model and Physical Activity   **184**
16. Motivational Theories of Exercise and Physical Activity   **196**

Cox • *Sport Psychology: Concepts and Applications, Sixth Edition*

V. Social Psychology of Sport   **208**

15. Team Cohesion in Sport   **208**

Williams • *Applied Sport Psychology: Personal Growth to Peak Performance, Sixth Edition*

I. Learning, Motivation, and Social Interaction   **226**

7. The Sport Team as an Effective Group   **226**

Melzer • *Writing, Reading, and Researching in the Disciplines: Student Guides*

Student Guides   **243**

Writing, Reading, and Researching in the Social Sciences   **243**

Wells • *Guide to Writing, Third Edition*

1. In–Class Writing   **272**

Text   **272**

Psychological Foundations of Sport and Exercise

Introduction

This textbook has been compiled in order to provide the reader with an appropriate context for Psychological Foundations of Sport and Exercise. It offers background information on the disciplines of sport and exercise psychology today. The module upon which this text is based enables the student to recognise and explain the individual and social characteristics that influence behaviour in sport and exercise. It introduces the nature of psychological approaches to the study of sport and exercise and their associated techniques. This textbook covers three broad issues: sport psychology; physical activity and exercise psychology; and finally effective learning techniques.

With tutor guidance and support from this text, students should be able to achieve the following learning outcomes, by the end of the module:

On successful completion of the module, students should be able to meet the following learning outcomes:

1. Develop familiarity with a range of psychological approaches relevant to the study of sport and exercise;
2. Evaluate selected psychological factors that influence an individual's behaviour in sport and exercise;
3. Establish an approach to learning, which promotes independence.

Setting the Scene: 'Perspectives' (LO1)

The Introductory chapter of this compilation will provide an overview of the science of psychology and an appreciation of each perspective in psychology. A 'perspective' is one's own viewpoint upon which evaluation and intervention is based (Hill, 2001). This means that the type of assistance one provides is coloured by one's theoretical approach. An understanding of perspectives will help students when considering the themes contained within this module.

Which Perspective Should I Adopt?

There is no correct answer to this question. The choice is based on your own judgement. In order to help guide you, in selecting a particular perspective to adopt, you should reflect on each one and consider the following questions.

- How has it been/ may be applied to sport, both in general and in relation to specific sports?
- To what extent do you agree with each perspective?
- What are the strengths and weaknesses of each perspective?
- Using each perspective, how would you conduct a consultation with an athlete?

Why Is The 'Perspectives' Issue Important Anyway?

The 'perspectives' issue is important because it signifies YOUR approach to sports performance psychology. During your career, a single perspective may guide you, or you may adopt a combination of perspectives, as your expertise grows. Nevertheless, your perspective will define your parameters, i.e., what is/is not appropriate for whatever you are doing. It will underpin your thinking as you explore the wide variety of themes within sport psychology.

To read more about these topics see chapter by:
King – What is Psychology?

Cox – Foundations of Sport Psychology.

The Next Step: Factors Influencing Performance in Sport Psychology (LO2).

Having identified your perspective in sport psychology, it is possible to explore various factors that contribute to performance. In this module we explore such factors as personality, motivation and arousal. Any combination of these factors will undoubtedly influence performance either in a positive or negative way. The Sport Psychologist's role is to understand the relationship between these factors and to offer solutions to challenges associated with fluctuations between them. We outline each of these factors below.

Personality.

In general terms personality is defined as an individual's unique psychological make-up and denotes consistent characteristics of individual differences in behaviour (Gill, 2000). Defining and understanding personality more specifically depends upon which perspective you choose to adopt. For example, behaviourists suggest that the individual is conditioned to respond in certain ways whereas, social learning theorists suggest one learns from observing others succeeding in particular environments. Personality is seen as a relatively stable response to a variety of situations. This response is a consequence of what the individual thinks, how they interpret the situation and their subsequent decision, which, in turn, is influenced by beliefs, the social environment and past experience of similar situations.

Personality can be measured in a variety of ways. One of the most common is Eysenck's Personality Inventory (EPI, Sanderson, 1988). This measure categorises individuals into 4 personality types:

- stable introvert;
- unstable introvert;
- stable extrovert;
- unstable extrovert.

Introversion, extraversion and neuroticism are three of the Big Five personality factors which is also a popular measure for personality traits.

To read more about this topic, see chapters by King – The science of Psychology; and Feldman – Understanding Psychology.

Motivation.

Motivation is responsible for: the *selection* and *preference* for an *activity*, the *persistence* at the activity, the *intensity* and *effort* put into performance. There are many theories of motivation including:

- need achievement theory;
- goal achievement theory;
- hierarchy of needs;
- cognitive evaluation theory;
- self-determination theory.

One of the most recent theoretical developments for motivation is the hierarchical model of motivation (Vallerand in Roberts, 2001) which derives from self determination theory and looks at intrinsic motivation, extrinsic motivation and amotivation across three levels, global, contextual and situational. Motivation is possibly one of the most vital psychological components for performance as it determines participation or dropout. It has an integrated effect on mood, confidence, anxiety and competence and without motivation for an activity participation would not take place. Novice performers tend to focus their motivation around internal factors including effort and enjoyment whilst at the more elite level, athletes value the feedback from peers and significant others (Halliburton and Weiss, 2002).

Motivation is measured by self-report, either through psychometric measures derived from specific theories, or through interviews/ focus groups, to ascertain the reasons 'why' performance manifests itself in the way it does. It is such an intangible concept that using other forms of measurement is extremely difficult and often unreliable, lacking validity and credibility.

To read more about this topic, see chapters by Feldman – Pathways to Psychology;

Cox – Sports Psychology.

Arousal and Anxiety

The concepts of arousal and anxiety are pervasive in both modern life and in sport. There are many examples of athletes succeeding in sport, yet others choke under the pressure and stress of competition. It is important to understand both concepts as they are closely related.

Arousal is a general term regarding the physiological components of the intensity of alertness and readiness of an individual. It can vary on a continuum from extremely low (e.g. sleep), to extremely high (e.g. excitement) (Weinberg, 1989). Changes in arousal levels can occur in different sporting environments and relate to the individual's perception of the situation. Moreover, an individual will have an optimum level of arousal required for

producing their optimum sports performance. Different levels of arousal are also required for different sports and different activities within a sport. For example, compare the optimum level of arousal required for archery (low) to rugby (high). Furthermore, within the sport of rugby, consider the difference in arousal required for tackling or the scrum (high) compared to taking penalty kicks (lower).

Anxiety is generally considered as a consequence of higher states of physiological arousal, which produce feelings of discomfort and worry (Weinberg, 1989). In sport, it is commonplace for athletes to experience the negative effects of anxiety (Castle, 2008).

In line with personality theory, anxiety can be categorised into trait and state anxiety. Consequently, individuals with a high level of trait anxiety will be prone to experience more frequent and more intense levels of state anxiety in certain situations. The extent of the state anxiety reaction will also depend upon the individual's interpretation and appraisal of the situation, as illustrated in the example below.

Consider two athletes both competing in County level ladies hockey trials.

- Athlete A has a very high expectation of performance and has set a very high goal for herself. However, she does not feel that her previous performances are at a high enough level and does not feel quite ready for the trials.

- Athlete B has also set high goals for herself, but feels that she has been very successful in performances running up to the trials, is really focused and ready for the event.

It is likely that athlete A will experience and exhibit a greater state anxiety reaction than athlete B. This reaction is based on the athlete's assessment of a variety of factors including:

- performance expectations;
- ability;
- previous performances;
- perceived readiness for the event;
- information regarding the opposition.

To read more about this topic, see chapter by Williams - Arousal-Performance Relationships

Physical Activity and Exercise Psychology (LO1, LO2).

Psychological foundations of sport and exercise could be construed as being 'two sides of a coin'. Whereas some Chartered or Accredited Sport and Exercise Psychologists work solely with sports performers, others work in the area of physical activity and/or exercise. Students will begin to understand what is meant by the term physical activity and suggested guidelines associated with being 'physically active'. Students will explore the benefits of physical activity/ exercise and how it impacts upon mood and motivation. It is important to be aware of the link between physical activity and lifestyle change. The Transtheoretical Model of physical activity will be introduced and complemented with Self-Determination Theory and personal investment Theory, both of which consider the motivation for involvement in physical activity and exercise.

To read more about these topics, see chapters by:
Carron, Hausenblas and Estabrooks
– Introduction to the Psychology of Physical Activity.
- Physical Activity and Mood.

- **The Transtheoretical Model and Physical Activity.**
- **Motivational Theories of Exercise and Physical Activity.**

Team Cohesion.

Team cohesion is an important ingredient in the development and creation of any successful team. The concept of team cohesion can be expressed in many different ways with some viewing it as "chemistry" or a "bond" that a team possesses. It is the presence or the absence of this chemistry which is believed to contribute to, or detract from, team success. Individuals are believed to be attracted to a team for a variety of different reasons and when these reasons are common, greater team cohesion is believed to exist and has a role to play in the success of a team. Two distinct attractions exist namely; task and social cohesion. Task cohesion is the degree in which a group of individuals will work together in order to achieve a common goal or task. Whereas social cohesion is more associated with the individual group member's attraction to the group for personal satisfaction reasons and the enjoyment of being part of the group.

A number of inventories have been designed to measure team cohesion including the Sport Cohesiveness Questionnaire (SCQ; Martens & Peterson, 1971) and the Team Cohesion Questionnaire (TCQ; Gruber & Gray, 1981) but the most widely used is the Group Environment Questionnaire (GEQ; Widmeyer, Brawley & Carron, 1985).

To read more about this topic, see chapters by:

Cox
- Team Cohesion in Sport.
Williams
-The Sport Team as an Effective Group.

The Effective Learner Programme (ELP) (LO3).

The higher education environment encourages students to think in a wider, broader, creative and more critical way in developing an independent approach to learning. It is acknowledged that students both can and do think in this way; however, many individuals then struggle to express their thinking or the results of their thinking at this or any other level. The philosophy of this module (and indeed the ELP) is to develop opportunities for students to practise both their learning skills and their subsequent communication from using these skills.

Reading, writing and referencing the wide and varied sources of information are crucial in demonstrating unique and progressive higher education processes. Do you struggle to read difficult articles? Do you know where to start when writing essays or indeed how to start?

Those students who manage their time well, submit coherent, reflective and fully justified pieces of work are more likely to demonstrate their understanding within their university degree programme, at an appropriate level of competence. Whilst the chapters in this book are useful they are only indicators and should not be seen to replace tutorial support. Indeed this material used in conjunction with individual or small group tutorials may help enhance academic work and provide a greater level of student satisfaction.

To read more about this topic, see chapters by Melzer: Writing, Reading and Researching in the Social Sciences; and Wells et al: In-Class writing.

Dr Paul Castle, Julia West, Andrea Faull & David Mycock
Summer 2009

References

Castle, P.C. (2008). Psychology of Motorsport Success: How to improve your performance with mental skills training. Yeovil: Haynes Publishing.

Halliburton, A.L. and Weiss, M.R. (2002). Sources of competence information and perceived motivational climate among adolescent female gymnasts varying in skill level. *Journal of Sport and Exercise Psychology*. **24** (4), 396-419.

Hill, K. (2000). *Framework For Sport Psychologists: Enhancing Sport Performance*. Champaign: Human Kinetics

Jones, J.G., Swain, A. and Hardy, L. (1993). Intensity and direction dimensions of competitive state anxiety and relationships with performance. *Journal of Sports Sciences,* **11,** 525-532.

Maslow, A.H. (1970). *Motivation and Personality (2nd ed)*. New York: Harper and Row.

Roberts, G.C. (Ed). (2001). *Advances in Motivation in Sport and Exercise*. Champaign: Human Kinetics.

Sanderson, F. (1988). Your Squash Personality. *Squash Player International*. **16**.

Watson, J.B. (1913). Psychology as a Behaviourist Views it. *Psychological Review,* **20**, 158-177.

Weinberg, R. (1989). Anxiety, arousal and motor performance; theory, research and applications. In *Anxiety in Sports: An International Perspective* (edited by D. Hackfort & C.D. Spielberger), pp. 95-116, New York: Hemisphere Publishing Corporation.

CHAPTER 1

CHAPTER OUTLINE

1 Defining Psychology

2 The Roots and Early Scientific Approaches of Psychology

3 Contemporary Approaches to Psychology

4 Areas of Specialization and Careers in Psychology

5 Psychology and Health and Wellness

WHAT IS PSYCHOLOGY?

Experiencing Psychology

THE MYSTERY THAT IS YOU

Do you have a hero? When you think about someone you truly admire, does a high-achieving celebrity or sports figure come to mind? If so, you are in good company, because individuals such as Tiger Woods, Oprah Winfrey, and Mother Teresa show up on many lists of most admired people. In a December 2006 Gallup poll, the most admired man was George W. Bush, followed by Bill Clinton, Jimmy Carter, Barack Obama, Colin Powell, and the Reverend Billy Graham (Jones, 2006). The most admired women were Hillary Clinton, Oprah Winfrey, Condoleezza Rice, Laura Bush, former British prime minister Margaret Thatcher, and Angelina Jolie. These are individuals who have made significant contributions in public life, many of them throughout long careers.

But at the right moment, an ordinary individual can become a hero. Jabbar Gibson was a teenager when Hurricane Katrina struck New Orleans, leaving him among the masses of people ravaged and stranded by the storm ("Editorial," 2005). After 2 days of wading alone in the filthy flood waters, he made a drastic move to save himself. He broke into a school, took the keys to a yellow school bus parked outside, and set off for Houston. Once on the way, Gibson's desperate act of self-preservation turned into something quite different: heroism. As he drove along Highway 10 (he never had driven a bus before), Gibson started picking up people stranded by the road. Soon his bus carried dozens of frightened but thankful individuals from all walks of life, including new babies with their mothers, as well as elderly people, all relying on young Gibson to get them to safety. The harrowing 8-hour, 300-mile journey included a stop for gas, paid for with spare change the passengers collected. When Gibson and his weary riders arrived in Houston, it occurred to him that he might be in trouble for taking the bus. But true to the spirit of the hero he had become, Gibson concluded, "I don't care if I get blamed for it so long as I saved my people" ("Editorial," 2005). In the aftermath of Katrina, Gibson was hardly the only hero to emerge; many doctors, nurses, and other citizens rode out the tempest and stayed to help others. Every catastrophe has its heroes.

Does it take a disaster to be a hero? The answer is no, because even in more ordinary daily circumstances, people make choices that might reasonably be called heroic. People are kind to individuals in need when they could be thoughtless or cruel. They are generous when they might be selfish. They work hard when they could slack off. When we think about the admirable people we encounter every day, we can see how ordinary human behavior can be extraordinary if viewed in the right light.

Similarly, many other aspects of human life take on extraordinary dimensions when looked at with a close lens. Scientists bring such powerful observations to their efforts. Consider astronomers, who wonder at the stars, and zoologists, who marvel at the varied creatures that populate the earth. As scientists, psychologists too are passionate about what they study, and what they study is you. Right now, as you are reading this book, thousands of dedicated scientists are studying things about you that you might have never considered, such as how your brain responds to a picture flashed on a screen or how your eyes adjust to a sunny day. It is hard to imagine a single thing about you that is not fascinating to some psychologist somewhere. As a human being you have been endowed with remarkable gifts—from the capacities to see, hear, smell, think, reason, and remember to the abilities to fall in love, strive for goals, and become someone's hero. As you interact with the world every day, you manifest these gifts in a variety of ways that psychologists find fascinating to study.

So, although psychology shares many similarities with other sciences, especially in how it studies the world, it is different from other sciences because of what it studies: the many facets of you. As you learn more about psychology, you will also be learning about more aspects of yourself than you ever imagined existed. Throughout this book and your introductory psychology class, you will join in the passionate scientific inquiry that seeks to unravel the mystery that is you. ▨

PREVIEW

This chapter begins by defining psychology more formally, and then gives context to that definition by reviewing the history and the intellectual underpinnings of the field. We next examine a number of contemporary approaches to the subject, as well as areas of specialization and potential careers. Our introduction to this dynamic, practical field closes by looking into how psychology can play a key role in human health and wellness.

1 Defining Psychology

Explain what psychology is and describe the positive psychology movement.

What is psychology? When asked this question, if you are like most people, you think of therapy. You probably imagine a situation where a clinical psychologist, be it Sigmund Freud or Dr. Phil, sees clients and tries to help them deal with a variety of mental problems. Yet formally defined, **psychology** is the scientific study of behavior and mental processes. There are three key terms in this definition: *science, behavior,* and *mental processes.*

psychology The scientific study of behavior and mental processes.

Behavior includes the observable act of two people kissing; mental processes include their unobservable thoughts about kissing.

As a **science,** psychology uses the systematic methods of science to observe human behavior and draw conclusions. The goals of psychological science are to describe, predict, and explain behavior. Researchers might be interested in knowing whether individuals will help a stranger who has fallen down. The researchers could devise a study in which they observe people walking past a person who needs help. Through many observations, the researchers could come to describe helping behavior by counting how many times it occurs in particular circumstances. The researchers may also try to *predict* who will help, and when, by examining characteristics of the individuals studied. Are happy people more likely to help? Are women or men more likely to help? What circumstances promote helping? After psychologists have analyzed their data, they also will want to *explain* why helping behavior occurred when it did.

Behavior is everything we do that can be directly observed—two people kissing, a baby crying, a college student riding a motorcycle. **Mental processes** are the thoughts, feelings, and motives that each of us experiences privately but that cannot be observed directly. Although we cannot directly see thoughts and feelings, they are nonetheless real. They include *thinking* about kissing someone, a baby's *feelings* when its mother leaves the room, and a college student's *memory* of a motorcycle ride.

science In psychology, the use of systematic methods to observe, describe, predict, and explain behavior.

behavior Everything we do that can be directly observed.

mental processes The thoughts, feelings, and motives that each of us experiences privately but that cannot be observed directly.

Psychology Versus Common Sense: What Don't You Already Know About Psychology?

One of the challenges facing teachers and practitioners of the science of psychology is overcoming the sense that everybody "knows" everything there is to know about psychology because we are all people. Of course, we all have brains—but we do not necessarily know how they work! So, it is worthwhile to ask the question, How is psychology different from our common knowledge about ourselves and one another?

You may think that psychology is the same as simple common sense about people. But, in fact, researchers often turn up the unexpected in human behavior. For example, it may seem obvious that couples who live together (cohabit) before marriage have a better chance of making the marriage last. After all, practice makes perfect, doesn't it? However, researchers have found a higher rate of success for couples who marry before living together (Liefbroer & Dourleijn, 2006; Popenoe & Whitehead, 2005; Seltzer, 2004). It also might seem obvious that we would experience

career woman—report more satisfaction with their lives than women who perform a single role or fewer roles, such as wife or wife and mother (Barnett & Hyde, 2001; Bennett & McDaniel, 2006).

As you read this book, you will encounter some findings that fit well with what you already know about people, but other conclusions will seem counterintuitive. Keep in mind that "what everybody knows" is a category that is influenced by historical and cultural context. Although it is shocking and incredible from our present-day perspective, there was a time when "everybody knew" that African Americans were innately intellectually inferior to Whites and that women were morally inferior to men. As you will see, psychology does not accept assumptions at face value. Psychology is a rigorous discipline that tests assumptions, bringing scientific data to bear on the questions of central interest to human beings (McBurney & White, 2007; Stanovich, 2007).

Thinking Like a Psychologist Means Thinking Like a Scientist

Psychologists approach human behavior as scientists. As scientific thinkers, they examine the available evidence about some aspect of mind and behavior, evaluate how strongly the data (information) support their hunches, analyze disconfirming evidence, and carefully consider whether they have explored all of the possible factors and explanations (Sternberg, Roediger, & Halpern, 2007). It is important to underscore how critical it is that psychologists look for biases in the way people think and behave. Consider, for example, a person who expresses wild enthusiasm about the remarkable effects of exercise on health when responding to survey questions about health awareness. It would be crucial for a researcher to uncover the fact that this particular individual sells exercise videos on the side and thus perhaps is communicating a biased perspective.

Psychologists, like other scientists, rely on critical thinking. **Critical thinking** is the process of thinking reflectively and productively and evaluating the evidence. Thinking critically means asking ourselves how we know something. Too often we have a tendency to recite, define, describe, state, and list rather than to analyze, infer, connect, synthesize, criticize, create, evaluate, think, and rethink (Brooks & Brooks, 2001). Thinking critically is an important aspect of psychology, as it is in all disciplines (Sternberg, 2007; Sternberg, Roediger, & Halpern, 2007). The ability to evaluate information critically is also essential to all areas of daily life (Halpern, 2003, 2007). For example, if you are planning to buy a car, you might want to collect information about different makes and models and evaluate their features and costs before deciding which one(s) to test drive. This is an exercise in critical thinking.

Critical thinking is not a spectator sport. It means actively engaging with ideas and not settling for easy answers. Critical thinking means being open-minded, curious, and careful.

As you will see throughout this book, psychologists do not agree on everything. Instead, psychology, like any science, is filled with debate and controversy. How might psychology benefit from these controversies? Psychology has advanced as a field because it does not accept simple explanations and because psychologists do not always concur with one another about why mind and behavior work the way they do. Psychologists have reached a more accurate understanding of mind and behavior *because* psychology fosters controversies and *because* psychologists think deeply and reflectively and examine the evidence on all sides.

What are some of psychology's controversies? Here is a brief sample:

- Are memories of sexual abuse real or imagined?
- Can personality change?
- Is self-esteem always a good thing?
- Should the psychological disorders of children be treated with drugs?

critical thinking The process of thinking reflectively and productively, as well as evaluating evidence.

Because it is important for you to think critically about controversies, each chapter of this book has a Critical Controversy feature that presents an issue of disagreement or debate in contemporary psychology. Psychology is a science that is alive and constantly changing. Reviewing these controversies gives you a chance to see how scientists grapple with the ever-changing questions presented by their continuously emerging knowledge about human behavior.

One controversy in psychology centers on the growing popularity of a new approach to the field. That new perspective is called positive psychology.

Positive Psychology

So, psychology is the science of human behavior. As you consider this general definition of psychology, you might be thinking, Okay, where's the couch? Where's the mental illness? The science of psychology certainly includes the study of therapy and psychological disorders, but by definition psychology is a much more general science (Ash & Sturm, 2007). This discrepancy between popular beliefs and the reality of psychology was one motivating factor behind the debate in the discipline that began at the beginning of the twenty-first century. A number of scholars noted that psychology had become far too negative, focusing on what can go wrong in people's lives rather than on what they can do competently and what can go right (Seligman & Csikszentmihalyi, 2000). Too often, they said, psychology has characterized people as passive and victimized. The desire to study the full range of human experience motivated the **positive psychology movement:** the push for a stronger emphasis on research involving the experiences that people value (such as hope, optimism, and happiness), the traits associated with optimal capacities for love and work, and positive group and civic values (such as responsibility, civility, and tolerance) (Csikszentmihalyi & Csikszentmihalyi, 2006; Diener, 2000; Emmons, 2007; Peterson, Park, & Seligman, 2006; Rathunde & Csikszentmihalyi, 2006; Snyder & Lopez, 2006).

To get a sense of why positive psychology is a valuable perspective, imagine that you have been asked to create a science of "watchology." You have two watches that have both had the unfortunate trauma of being left in the pocket of a pair of jeans as they churned and tumbled through the washer and dryer. One watch has suffered the worst possible fate—it no longer tells time. The other has emerged from the traumatic event still ticking. Which watch will you want to use in developing your theory of watchology? You quite reasonably conclude that the working watch will help you understand watches better than the broken one.

What does watchology have to do with psychology? When they think of psychology, many people think of Sigmund Freud. Certainly, Freud has had a lasting impact on the field and on the larger society. (As recently as March 2006, on the occasion of his 150th birthday, Freud was featured on the cover of *Newsweek*.) But it is important to keep in mind that Freud based his ideas about human nature on the patients that he saw in his clinical practice—individuals who were struggling with psychological problems. His experiences with these individuals colored his outlook on all of humanity. Freud (1918/1996) once wrote, "I have found little that is 'good' about human beings on the whole. In my experience most of them are trash."

This negative view of human nature has crept into general perceptions of what psychology is all about. Imagine, for example, that you are seated on a plane, having a pleasant conversation with the stranger sitting next to you. At some point you ask your seatmate what she does for a living, and she informs you she is a psychologist. You might think to yourself, "Uh-oh. What have I already told this person? What secrets does she know about me that I don't know about myself? Has she been analyzing me this whole time?" Would you be surprised to discover that this psychologist studies happiness? Or intelligence? Or the processes related to the experience of vision? The study of abnormal problems is a very important aspect of psychology, but to equate the science of psychology entirely with the study of abnormal problems is like equating biology with the field of medicine or a cellular biologist with a medical doctor (which, as any pre-med major will assure you, is a mistake). As you read further, you will discover that psychology is a diverse field and that psychologists have wide-ranging interests. Psychologists have made extraordinary advances

positive psychology movement The push for a stronger emphasis on research involving the experiences that people value, the traits associated with optimal capacities for love and work, and positive group and civic values.

The murder in 2006 of five Amish schoolgirls evoked feelings in the community not of hatred and revenge but of forgiveness.

in understanding psychological disorders and treatment, and these topics are essential to an understanding of the science of psychology. At the same time, the field of psychology is broader than these topics.

In this book, we consider the full range of human behavior, including strengths and capacities as well as disorders and dysfunction. Psychology is interested in understanding the rich truths of human life in all its dimensions, including people's best and worst experiences. Psychologists acknowledge that, as in the heroism of Jabbar Gibson, sometimes individuals' best moments emerge amid the most difficult circumstances.

Research on the human capacity for forgiveness demonstrates this point (Cohen & others, 2006; Legaree, Turner, & Lollis, 2007; McCullough, Bono, & Root, 2007; Ross, Hertenstein, & Wrobel, 2007). Forgiveness is the act of letting go of our anger and resentment toward someone who has done something harmful to us. With forgiveness we cease seeking revenge or avoiding the person who did us harm, and we might even wish that person well. Most world religions place value on the sometimes challenging act of forgiveness. In October 2006, after Charles Carl Roberts IV took 10 young Amish girls hostage in a one-room schoolhouse in Pennsylvania, eventually killing 5 of them and wounding 5 others before killing himself, the grief-stricken Amish community focused not on hatred and revenge but on forgiveness. As funds were being set up for the victims' families, the Amish insisted that one be established for the murderer's family. As they prepared simple funerals for the dead girls, the community invited the wife of the killer to attend.

The willingness of the Amish people to forgive this horrible crime is both remarkable and puzzling. Can we scientifically understand the human ability to forgive even what might seem to be unforgivable? A number of psychologists have taken up the topic of forgiveness in research and clinical practice (Bono & McCullough, 2006; Cohen & others, 2006). Michael McCullough and his colleagues (2007) have shown that the capacity to forgive is an unfolding process that often takes time. Furthermore, sometimes forgiveness is a dynamic process—we might forgive someone for an offense immediately but then later return to thoughts of revenge or punishment. For the Amish, their deep religious faith led them to embrace forgiveness, where many people might have been motivated to seek revenge and retribution. Researchers also have explored the relation between religious commitment and forgiveness (Cohen & others, 2006; McCullough, Bono, & Root, 2007; Tsang, McCullough, & Hoyt, 2005).

The positive psychology movement is certainly not without controversy and critics (Lazarus, 2003). As already noted, however, controversy is a part of any science. Healthy debate characterizes the field of psychology, and a new psychological perspective has sometimes arisen when one scientist questions the views of another. Such ongoing debate and controversy are signs of a vigorous, vital discipline. Indeed, the very birth of the field was itself marked with controversy and debate. As we will see, great minds do not always think alike, especially when they are thinking about psychology.

REVIEW AND SHARPEN YOUR THINKING

1 Explain what psychology is and describe the positive psychology movement.

- Define psychology and discuss how psychology differs from our common knowledge about ourselves and others.
- Discuss the role of critical thinking in scientific thought.
- Outline the objectives of positive psychology and discuss why they are important.

The human capacity for forgiveness is a topic that interests psychologists. What is an important strength of your own that you think should be included in psychology's research agenda? Why?

2 The Roots and Early Scientific Approaches of Psychology

Discuss the roots and early scientific foundations of psychology.

Psychology seeks to answer questions that people have been asking for thousands of years. For example:

- How do our senses perceive the world?
- How do we learn?
- What is memory?
- Why does one person grow and flourish, whereas another person struggles in life?
- Do dreams matter?
- Can people learn to be happier and more optimistic?

Wilhelm Wundt (1832–1920)
Wundt founded the first psychology laboratory (with his co-workers) in 1879 at the University of Leipzig in Germany.

The notion that these questions might be answered by scientific inquiry is a relatively new idea. From the time human language included the word *why* and became rich enough to let people talk about the past, we have been creating myths to explain why things are the way they are. Ancient myths attributed most important events to the pleasure or displeasure of the gods: When a volcano erupted, the gods were angry; if two people fell in love, they had been struck by Cupid's arrows. Gradually, myths gave way to philosophy—the rational investigation of the underlying principles of being and knowledge. People attempted to explain events in terms of natural rather than supernatural causes (Viney & King, 2003).

Western philosophy came of age in ancient Greece in the fourth and fifth centuries B.C.E. Socrates, Plato, Aristotle, and others debated the nature of thought and behavior, including the possible link between the mind and the body. Later philosophers, especially René Descartes, argued that the mind and body were completely separate and focused their attention on the mind. Psychology grew out of this tradition of thinking about the mind and body. The influence of philosophy on contemporary psychology persists today, as researchers who study emotion still talk about Descartes, and scientists who study happiness refer back to Aristotle.

Philosophy was not the only discipline from which psychology emerged. Psychology also has roots in the natural sciences of biology and physiology (Johnson, 2008; Kalat, 2007). Indeed, it was Wilhelm Wundt (1832–1920), a German philosopher-physician, who put the pieces of the philosophy–natural science puzzle together to create the academic discipline of psychology.

Some historians like to say that modern psychology was born in December 1879 at the University of Leipzig, when Wundt and two young students performed an experiment to measure the time lag between the instant at which a person heard a sound and the instant at which that person actually pressed a telegraph key to signal that he had heard. The experiment was one of many attempts to measure human behavior through physiological measurement.

What was so special about this experiment? Wundt's experiment was about the workings of the brain: He was trying to measure the time it took the human brain and nervous system to translate information into action. At the heart of this experiment was the idea that mental processes could be studied quantitatively—that is, that they could be measured. This focus ushered in the new science of psychology.

Structuralism

The main research conducted by Wundt and his collaborators focused on trying to discover basic elements, or "structures," of mental processes. For example, they described three different dimensions of *feeling*: pleasure/displeasure, tension/relaxation, and excitement/depression. A student of Wundt's, E. B. Titchener (1867–1927), gave Wundt's approach the label of **structuralism** because of its focus on identifying the structures of the human mind.

structuralism An early school of psychology that attempted to identify the structures of the human mind.

William James (1842–1910)
James's approach became known as functionalism.

The method used in the study of mental structures was *introspection* (literally, "looking inside"). For this type of experiment, a person was placed in a laboratory setting and was asked to think (introspect) about what was going on mentally as various events took place. For example, the individual might be subjected to a sharp, repetitive clicking sound and asked to report whatever conscious feelings the clicking produced. What made this method scientific was the systematic, detailed self-reports required of the person in the controlled laboratory setting.

These studies focused mainly on sensation and perception because they were the easiest processes to break down into component parts. For example, Titchener used the introspective method to study taste. He trained participants to identify and record their taste sensations. The outcome was the identification of four components of taste: bitter, sweet, salty, and sour. In the long run, though, conscious introspection was not a very productive method of exploring the basic elements of human behavior. You might be able to describe to someone how you solved a math problem using introspection, but could you explain the process by which you remember, say, your own phone number? It seems to pop into consciousness without your awareness of the operations that must be involved. Where did it come from? Where was it stored? How did you find it?

Functionalism

Although Wundt is most often regarded as the founding father of modern psychology, it was William James (1842–1910), perhaps more than any other person, who gave the field an American stamp. James's approach to psychology developed out of his interest in the school of philosophy called *pragmatism*, which essentially holds that to find out the meaning of an idea, you must determine its consequences. So, an idea is evaluated based on how useful it is. From a pragmatic perspective, then, the question is not so much what the mind is (that is, its structures) as what it is for (its purpose or functions). This interest in the outcome of mental processes led James to emphasize cause and effect, prediction and control, and the important interaction of the environment and behavior. James's view was eventually named *functionalism*.

In contrast to structuralism, which emphasized the components of the mind, **functionalism** was concerned with the functions and purposes of the mind and behavior in individuals' adaptation to the environment. Structuralists were not interested in an individual's interaction with the environment, but this activity was a major functionalist theme. Whereas the structuralists were looking *inside* the mind, searching for its structures, the functionalists were focusing more on what was going on in human interactions with the *outside* world. If structuralism is about the "what" of the mind, functionalism is about the "why."

Central to functionalism is the question of why it is adaptive that people think the way they do. James and other functionalists did not believe in the existence of elementary, rigid structures of the mind. Instead, James saw the mind as flexible and fluid, characterized by constant change and adaptation in response to a continuous flow of information. James objected to the tendency of structuralists to break mental processes down into minute, separate components. Not surprisingly then, he called the natural flow of thought a *stream of consciousness*.

Functionalism meshed well with another important intellectual development at the time, the work of British naturalist Charles Darwin (1809–1882). In 1859, Darwin published his ideas in *On the Origin of Species*. He proposed the principle of **natural selection,** an evolutionary process that favors organisms' traits or characteristics that are best adapted to reproduce and survive. He believed that organisms reproduce at rates that would cause enormous increases in the population of most species, yet noted that populations remain nearly constant. Darwin reasoned that an intense, constant struggle for food, water, and resources must occur among the young born in each generation, because many of the young do not survive. Those that do survive to adulthood pass their genes on to the next generation. Darwin concluded that organisms with biological features that led to more successful reproduction were better represented in subsequent generations. Over many generations, organisms with these characteristics would constitute a larger percentage of the population. Eventually this process could modify a whole population. If environmental

functionalism An early school of psychology that was concerned with the functions and purposes of the mind and behavior in individuals' adaptation to the environment.

natural selection An evolutionary process that favors organisms' traits or characteristics that are best adapted to reproduce and survive.

conditions changed, however, other characteristics might become favored by natural selection, moving the process in a different direction.

If you are unfamiliar with Darwin's theory of evolution, it might be useful to review these ideas through a simple example. Consider the question, Why do giraffes have long necks? An early explanation of this characteristic might be that giraffes live in places where the trees are very high, and so the giraffes must stretch their necks to get to their favorite food—leaves. Lots of stretching might lead to giraffes with longer necks. The problem with this explanation is that it does not tell us why giraffes are born with long necks. A characteristic cannot be passed from one generation to the next unless it is recorded in the genes. According to evolutionary theory, species change through random genetic mutation, so that presumably long, long ago, some giraffes were genetically predisposed to have longer necks, and some giraffes were genetically predisposed to have shorter necks. Only those with the long necks survived to reproduce, giving us the giraffes we see today. The survival of the giraffes with long necks is a product of natural selection. Natural selection favors organisms' traits or characteristics that are best adapted to survive in a particular environment. Evolutionary theory fits well with the functionalist perspective since it emphasizes the survival function of characteristics. Evolutionary theory implies that the way we are, at least partially, is the way that is best suited to surviving in our environment (Kardong, 2008). James was certainly influenced by Darwin's work (Myers, 1986). The influence of functionalism on psychology is apparent today in the application of the psychology to areas such as business and education (Kreitner & Kinicki, 2007; Santrock, 2008).

Wundt and James were each generally unimpressed with the other's perspective. Wundt famously compared James's masterwork *The Principles of Psychology* to literature: "It is beautiful but it is not psychology" (Fancher, 1996, p. 266). In turn, James wrote that Wundt's structuralist school of thought had "plenty of school, but no thought" (James, 1904, p.1). Nonetheless, although these two great minds did not agree, each had a profound influence on the science of psychology. Indeed, if you trace the intellectual history of any living psychologist, the academic family tree will end with one of these notable figures.

The survival of giraffes with long necks (and not giraffes with short necks) vividly illustrates natural selection at work.

2 Discuss the roots and early scientific foundations of psychology.
  • Summarize the roots of psychology and the view of psychology called structuralism.
  • Define functionalism and explain the differing emphases of structuralists and functionalists.

List some questions about your mind and behavior that a deeper understanding of psychology might help you to answer.

3 Contemporary Approaches to Psychology

Summarize the main themes of seven approaches to psychology.

If structuralism won the battle to be the birthplace of psychology, it is safe to say that functionalism won the war. Today most psychologists talk about the adaptiveness of behavior and mental processes and rely on methods beyond introspection to understand the complex processes of the human mind (Strack & Schwarz, 2007). In the century since Wundt and James debated the best way to think about psychology, a number of broad approaches have emerged. In this section we briefly survey seven different approaches that represent the intellectual backdrop of psychological science: biological, behavioral, psychodynamic, humanistic, cognitive, evolutionary, and sociocultural.

The Biological Approach

biological approach A psychological perspective that examines behavior and mental processes through a focus on the body, especially the brain and nervous system.

neuroscience The scientific study of the structure, function, development, genetics, and biochemistry of the nervous system.

behavioral approach A psychological perspective emphasizing the scientific study of observable behavioral responses and their environmental determinants.

psychodynamic approach A psychological perspective emphasizing unconscious thought, the conflict between biological instincts and society's demands, and early family experiences.

humanistic approach A psychological perspective that emphasizes a person's positive qualities, capacity for positive growth, and the freedom to choose any destiny.

cognitive approach A psychological perspective that focuses on the mental processes involved in knowing: how we direct our attention, perceive, remember, think, and solve problems.

Some psychologists examine behavior and mental processes through the **biological approach,** which is a focus on the body, especially the brain and nervous system. For example, researchers might investigate the way your heart races when you are afraid or how your hands sweat when you tell a lie. Although a number of physiological systems may be involved in thoughts and feelings, perhaps the largest contribution to physiological psychology has come through the emergence of neuroscience (Bosel, 2007; Hagner, 2007).

   Neuroscience is the scientific study of the structure, function, development, genetics, and biochemistry of the nervous system. Neuroscience emphasizes that the brain and nervous system are central to understanding behavior, thought, and emotion. Neuroscientists believe that thoughts and emotions have a physical basis in the brain. Electrical impulses zoom throughout the brain's cells, releasing chemical substances that enable us to think, feel, and behave. Our remarkable human capabilities would not be possible without the brain and nervous system, which constitute the most complex, intricate, and elegant system imaginable. Although biological approaches might sometimes seem to reduce complex human experience into simple physical structures, developments in neuroscience have allowed psychologists to understand the brain as an amazingly complex organ, perhaps just as complex as the psychological processes linked to its functioning.

The Behavioral Approach

The **behavioral approach** emphasizes the scientific study of observable behavioral responses and their environmental determinants. In other words, the behavioral approach focuses on interactions with the environment that can be seen and measured. The principles of the behavioral approach also have been widely applied to help people change their behavior for the better (Martin & Pear, 2007; Watson & Tharp, 2007). The psychologists who adopt this approach are called *behaviorists.* Under the intellectual leadership of John B. Watson (1878–1958) and B. F. Skinner (1904–1990), behaviorism dominated psychological research during the first half of the twentieth century.

   Many studies with a behavioral approach take place in experimental laboratories under carefully controlled conditions. When behaviorism was in its infancy, virtually all behavioral studies were conducted in the laboratory, although today many take place outside the laboratory in natural settings such as schools and homes.

   Skinner emphasized that what we *do* is the ultimate test of who we are. He believed that rewards and punishments determine our behavior. For example, a child might behave in a well-mannered fashion because her parents have rewarded this behavior. An adult might work hard at a job because of the money he gets for his effort. We do these things, say behaviorists, not because of an inborn motivation to be competent people but rather because of the environmental conditions we have experienced and continue to experience (Skinner, 1938).

   Contemporary behaviorists still emphasize the importance of observing behavior to understand an

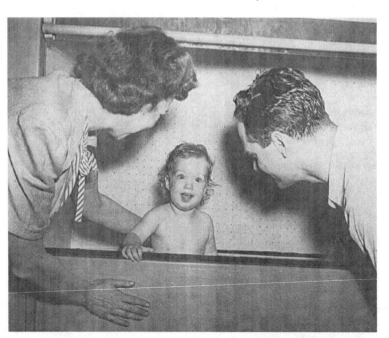

B. F. Skinner was a tinkerer who liked to make new gadgets. The younger of his two daughters, Deborah, was raised in Skinner's enclosed Air-Crib. Some critics accused Skinner of monstrous experimentation with his children; however, the early controlled environment has not had any noticeable harmful effects. Deborah, shown here as a child with her parents, is today a successful artist whose work strongly reflects her unique early childhood experience.

individual, and they continue to use the rigorous sorts of experimental methods advocated by Watson and Skinner (Cooper, Heron, & Heward, 2007). They also continue to stress the importance of environmental determinants of behavior (DeSantis-Moniaci & Altshuler, 2007). However, not every behaviorist today accepts the earlier behaviorists' rejection of thought processes (often called *cognition*) (Kushner, 2007).

The Psychodynamic Approach

The **psychodynamic approach** emphasizes unconscious thought, the conflict between biological instincts and society's demands, and early family experiences. This approach argues that unlearned biological instincts, especially sexual and aggressive impulses, influence the way people think, feel, and behave. These instincts, buried deep within the unconscious mind, are often at odds with society's demands. Although Sigmund Freud (1856–1939), the founding father of the psychodynamic approach, saw much of psychological development as instinctual, he theorized that early relationships with parents are the chief forces that shape an individual's personality. Freud's (1917) theory was the basis for the therapeutic technique that he called *psychoanalysis*. His approach was controversial when he introduced it in Vienna at the beginning of the twentieth century. However, his ideas flourished, and many clinicians still find value in his insights into human behavior.

Sigmund Freud (1856–1939)
Freud was the founding father of the psychodynamic approach.

Unlike the behavioral approach, the psychodynamic approach focuses almost exclusively on clinical applications rather than on experimental research. For this reason, psychodynamic theories always have been controversial and difficult to validate. Nonetheless, they are an important part of psychology. Today's psychodynamic theories tend to place less emphasis on sexual instincts and more on cultural experiences as determinants of behavior.

The Humanistic Approach

The **humanistic approach** emphasizes a person's positive qualities, the capacity for positive growth, and the freedom to choose any destiny. Humanistic psychologists stress that people have the ability to control their lives and avoid being manipulated by the environment (Maslow, 1971; Rogers, 1961). They theorize that, rather than being driven by unconscious impulses (as the psychodynamic approach dictates) or by external rewards (as the behavioral approach emphasizes), people can choose to live by higher human values, such as altruism—unselfish concern for other people's well-being—and free will. Humanistic psychologists also think that people have a tremendous potential for self-understanding and that the way to help others achieve self-understanding is by being warm and supportive. Many aspects of this optimistic approach appear in research on motivation, emotion, and personality, and in many ways the humanistic perspective provides a foundation for positive psychology (Diaz-Laplante, 2007; Patterson & Joseph, 2007).

According to humanistic psychologists, warm, supportive behavior toward others helps us to realize our tremendous capacity for self-understanding.

The Cognitive Approach

According to cognitive psychologists, your brain hosts or embodies a "mind" whose mental processes allow you to remember, make decisions, plan, set goals, and be creative (Gluck & others, 2007; Sternberg, 2008). The **cognitive approach,** then, emphasizes the mental processes involved in knowing: how we direct our attention, how we perceive, how we remember, and how we think and solve problems. For example, cognitive psychologists want to know how we solve algebraic equations, why we remember some things for

F-Minus: © United Feature Syndicate, Inc.

only a short time but remember others for a lifetime, and how we can use imagery to plan for the future.

Cognitive psychologists view the mind as an active and aware problem-solving system (Plessner, Betsch, & Betsch, 2007). This positive view contrasts with the behavioral view, which portrays behavior as controlled by external environmental forces. The cognitive view also contrasts with pessimistic views (such as those of Freud) that see human behavior as being controlled by instincts or other unconscious forces. In the cognitive view, an individual's mental processes are in control of behavior through memories, perceptions, images, and thinking.

The Evolutionary Approach

Although arguably all of psychology emerges out of evolutionary theory, some psychologists emphasize an **evolutionary approach** that uses evolutionary ideas such as adaptation, reproduction, and "survival of the fittest" as the basis for explaining specific human behaviors. David Buss (1995, 2008) argues that just as evolution shapes our physical features, such as body shape, it also influences our decision making, level of aggressiveness, fears, and mating patterns. Thus, evolutionary psychologists argue, the way we adapt can be traced to problems animals and early humans faced in adapting to their environments (Dunbar & Barrett, 2007).

Evolutionary psychologists believe that their approach provides an umbrella that unifies the diverse fields of psychology (Bjorklund, 2007; Geary, 2006). Not all psychologists agree with this conclusion. For example, some critics stress that the evolutionary approach provides an inaccurate account of why men and women have different social roles and does not adequately account for cultural diversity and experiences (Wood & Eagly, 2007). But the evolutionary approach is young, and its future may be fruitful.

The Sociocultural Approach

The **sociocultural approach** examines the ways in which the social and cultural environments influence behavior. Socioculturalists argue that a full understanding of a person's behavior requires knowing about the cultural context in which the behavior occurs (Kagitcibasi, 2007; Shiraev & Levy, 2007). For example, in some cultures, including the United States, it may be entirely acceptable for a woman to be assertive, but in other cultures, such as in Iran, the same behavior may be considered inappropriate.

We find an example of the sociocultural approach in recent research examining motivation in Western versus Eastern cultures. Imagine that you are in a psychological study in which you are asked to solve a number of puzzles. Some of the puzzles are quite easy, and you complete them with no problem. The other puzzles are more difficult; try as you might, you cannot figure them out. After the study you are left alone with the puzzles, and the researcher informs you that if you like, you can keep playing with the puzzles while she prepares the rest of the study materials. Which puzzles would you be likely to work on?

If you are like most U.S. college students, you will gravitate toward the easy puzzles, choosing to work on what you know you are already good at. However, if you are like most Asian students, you will pick up the difficult puzzles and keep working on those that you have not yet solved (Heine, 2005; Norenzayan & Heine, 2005). These cultural differences are thought to emerge out of differing views of the self, goals, and learning. It has been suggested that Asian students show a particularly adaptive response to task difficulty and failure and that U.S. students might benefit from looking at failure as an opportunity to learn rather than as something to avoid.

evolutionary approach A psychological perspective that uses evolutionary ideas such as adaptation, reproduction, and "survival of the fittest" as the basis for explaining specific human behaviors.

sociocultural approach A psychological perspective that examines the ways in which the social and cultural environments influence behavior.

King: The Science of
Psychology: An
Appreciative View

1. What is Psychology?

Text

© The McGraw–Hill
Companies, 2008

23

Critical Controversy   Can Humans Really Be Altruistic?

If there was a silver lining in the dark cloud of September 11, 2001, it was that firefighters, police officers, emergency medical personnel, and many ordinary individuals altruistically risked their own lives to help people caught in the collapse of the twin towers of the World Trade Center in New York City. Other heroes of 9/11 included the passengers aboard United Flight 93 who selflessly forced the plane to crash in a field instead of allowing it to hit the intended target.

Altruistic behavior is often defined as voluntary behavior that is intended to benefit others and is not motivated by any expectation of personal gain. The most extreme form of altruism is giving one's life to save someone else, as did many responding to the attacks of September 11.

Altruism poses an important problem for the evolutionary approach to psychology (Van Lange & others, 2007). According to Darwin's theory of evolution, behaviors that favor an organism's reproductive success are likely to be passed on to future generations. In fact, altruistic behavior *reduces* a person's chances of reproductive success, to the extent that it means providing one's resources to another with no apparent gain. Therefore, altruists should be at a clear evolutionary disadvantage compared to those who act more selfishly and thereby ensure the propagation of their own genes. Over many generations, selfish behavior should be favored and altruistic behavior should die out, according to the evolutionary view.

Seen in this way through the Darwinian lens of the survival of the fittest, human altruism is hard to understand. The concept of *kin selection*, however, provides one way to reconcile altruism with evolutionary theory. According to this concept, our genes survive not just when we reproduce but also when our relatives reproduce. Kin selection includes the idea of *inclusive fitness*, which means that a gene may be considered successfully adaptive if it benefits not only the individual who possesses it but also anyone who is genetically related to that person (Caporael, 2007). Indeed, from an evolutionary perspective, the individuals who carry our genes—our children—have a special place in the domain of altruism. Natural selection favors parents who care for their children and improve their probability of surviving. Human parents who feed their young are performing a biologically altruistic act because feeding increases their offsprings' chances of survival. So is a mother bird that altruistically tries to drive predators away from the fledglings in her nest. She is willing to sacrifice herself so that three or four of her young offspring will have the chance to survive, thus preserving her genes.

The theory of kin selection can explain why some

Firefighters helping victims of the September 11, 2001, terrorist attack on the World Trade Center in New York City.

people forgo having their own children and choose instead to care for relatives and relatives' children. What this theory cannot explain is altruism directed toward people outside the family—and especially toward strangers. However, evolutionary psychologists believe that tremendous benefits can come to individuals who form cooperative, reciprocal relationships (Bernhard, Fischbacher, & Fehr, 2006; Wenseleers & Ratnieks, 2006). By being good to someone now, individuals increase the likelihood that they will receive a benefit from the other person in the future. Through this reciprocal process, both gain something beyond what they could have gained by acting alone.

In contrast to the evolutionary interpretation, the sociocultural approach attempts to explain altruistic behavior as being the result of social and cultural experiences. According to the sociocultural approach, each of us is a product of many culturally and socially derived relationships, which continually unfold over time (Newson, Richerson, & Boyd, 2007; Shiraev & Levy, 2007). Because our relationships within our culture are open-ended and adaptable rather than rigidly determined by our genes, genuine acts of altruism

(continued)

are possible. Simply put, if our culture teaches us to be kind without regard for our own gain, then we can become true altruists.

By providing a theory that emphasizes the importance of adaptation and natural selection in explaining all behavior, the evolutionary approach has much to recommend it (Fletcher & Zwick, 2006; Freeman & Herron, 2007). It forces us to look at our capacity for selfishness and to refine our notions of kindness and altruism. Yet the sociocultural approach also is attractive, because it stresses that people can be genuinely altruistic (Eisenberg, Fabes, & Spinrad, 2006). This possibility is what comes to mind when we think about the firefighters, police officers, and passengers who sacrificed their lives on September 11, 2001. In the end, this contrast in views may well sharpen our understanding of what it is to be fully human.

What Do You Think?

- Are people ever truly altruistic? Or are they operating according to selfish motives?
- Have you ever acted in a genuinely altruistic fashion? If so, when and how? Could your behavior be explained instead by theories of kin selection?
- What kind of research might settle the question of whether humans are capable of genuine altruism?

The sociocultural approach focuses not only on comparisons of behavior across countries but also on the behavior of individuals from different ethnic and cultural groups within a country (Berry, 2007). Thus there is increasing interest in the behavior of African Americans, Latinos, and Asian Americans, especially in terms of the factors that have restricted or enhanced their ability to adapt and cope with living in a predominantly White society (Banks, 2008; Bennett, 2007).

These seven approaches to understanding psychology provide different and often complementary views of the same behavior. Think about a simple event you might experience—say, seeing a cute puppy. Seeing that puppy involves physical processes in the eyes, nervous system, and brain. But the moment you spot that puppy, you might smile without thinking. You might feel the cuteness of the puppy give your heart a little squeeze. Such an emotional reaction might be a response to your past learning experiences with animals, or to your unconscious memories of a childhood dog, or even to evolutionary processes that promoted cuteness as a way for helpless offspring to survive. You might find yourself tempted to pick up and cuddle the little guy. Sociocultural factors might play a role in your decision about whether to ask the owner if holding the puppy would be okay, whether to share those warm feelings about the puppy with others, and even whether (as in some cultures) to view that puppy as food.

The sociocultural approach especially contrasts with the evolutionary approach. To read about how these two approaches view altruism, see the Critical Controversy.

REVIEW AND SHARPEN YOUR THINKING

3 Summarize the main themes of seven approaches to psychology.
- Describe the biological approach.
- Discuss the behavioral approach.
- Summarize the psychodynamic approach.
- Explain the humanistic approach.
- Provide an overview of the cognitive approach.
- Review the evolutionary approach.
- Recap the sociocultural approach.

Suppose you could talk with a psychologist specializing in each of the seven approaches. Think about the members of your family and other people you know. Write down at least one question you might want to ask about the thoughts and behaviors of these people.

4 Areas of Specialization and Careers in Psychology

Evaluate areas of specialization and careers in psychology.

If you were to go to graduate school to earn an advanced degree in psychology, you would be required to specialize in a particular area. Here we review the major areas of psychology that are the focus of this book. It is important to keep in mind that these specializations are not mutually exclusive. Indeed, the boundaries that separate these areas are quite fuzzy, and psychologists in one field may collaborate with researchers in another. Throughout this book, in a feature called Intersection (see page 21 of this chapter for the first example), we highlight areas where different fields of psychology come together to address important and often intriguing research questions.

Richard J. Davidson of the University of Wisconsin, Madison, shown with the Dalai Lama, is a leading researcher in behavioral neuroscience.

Areas of Specialization

Psychology has many areas of specialization. In 2007, there were 56 divisions in the American Psychological Association, each focusing on a specific area of psychology. The most recent division to be added was trauma psychology. Here we describe some of the main specializations in the field of psychology.

Physiological Psychology and Behavioral Neuroscience Researchers who study physiological psychology are interested in the physical processes that underlie mental processes such as vision and memory. Physiological psychologists may use animal models (that is, they may use animals, such as rats, to study processes that are difficult or impossible to study in the same way in humans) to examine such topics as the development of the nervous system. The field of behavioral neuroscience also focuses on biological processes, especially the brain's role in behavior (Kolb & Whishaw, 2007). In Chapter 3 we examine the many ways that physiological processes relate to psychological experience.

Developmental Psychology *Developmental psychology* is concerned with how people become who they are, from conception to death. In particular, developmental psychologists concentrate on the biological and environmental factors that contribute to human development. For many years the major emphasis of developmentalists was child development. However, an increasing number of today's developmental psychologists show a strong interest in adult development and aging (Birren & Schaie, 2007; Schaie, 2007). Their inquiries range across the biological, cognitive, and social domains of life. Chapter 4 reviews the key findings in this fascinating area.

Sensation and Perception Researchers who study sensation and perception focus on the physical systems and psychological processes that allow us to experience the world—to smell the Thanksgiving turkey in the oven and to see the beauty of a sunset. These complex processes are the subject of Chapter 5.

The research of Carol S. Dweck of Stanford University spans the fields of developmental and social psychology. Her influential work looks at how our ideas of self play a role in motivation, self-regulation, and achievement.

Cognitive Psychology *Cognitive psychology* (addressed in Chapters 8 and 9) is the broad name given to the field of psychology that examines attention, consciousness, information processing, and memory. Cognitive psychologists are also interested in cognitive skills and abilities such as problem solving, decision making, expertise, and intelligence, topics covered in Chapter 9 (Gluck & others, 2007; Sternberg, 2006). Researchers in cognitive psychology and sensation perception are sometimes called experimental psychologists.

Learning *Learning* is the complex process by which behavior changes to adapt to changing circumstances. Learning has been addressed from the behavioral and cognitive perspectives, and this topic is covered in Chapter 7 (Bandura, 2007a, 2007b).

"Well, you don't look like an experimental psychologist to me."

Motivation and Emotion   Researchers from a variety of specializations are interested in these two important aspects of experience. Research questions addressed by scientists who study motivation include how individuals persist to attain a difficult goal and how rewards affect the experience of motivation (Fishbach & Ferguson, 2007). Emotion researchers delve into such topics as the physiological and brain processes that underlie emotional experience, the role of emotional expression in health, and the possibility that emotions are universal (Barrett & others, 2007; Frijda, 2007). These fascinating questions are examined in Chapter 10.

Personality Psychology   *Personality psychology* focuses on the relatively enduring characteristics of individuals. Personality psychologists study such topics as traits, goals, motives, genetics, personality development, and well-being (Cloninger, 2008). Researchers in personality psychology are interested in those aspects of your psychological makeup that make you uniquely you. The field of personality is explored fully in Chapter 11.

Social Psychology   *Social psychology* deals with people's social interactions, relationships, social perceptions, social cognition, and attitudes. Social psychologists are interested in the influence of groups on individuals' thinking and behavior and in the ways that the groups to which we belong influence our attitudes (Brewer, 2007). Some of the research questions that concern social psychologists include understanding and working to reduce racial prejudice, determining whether two heads really are better than one, and exploring how the presence of others influences performance (Mays, Cochran, & Barnes, 2007). Social psychologists believe that we can better understand mind and behavior if we know how people function in groups. Chapter 12 reviews the major research findings of social psychology.

Industrial and Organizational Psychology   *Industrial and organizational psychology (I/O psychology)* centers on the workplace—both on the workers and on the organizations that employ them. I/O psychology is often divided into industrial psychology and organizational psychology. Among the main concerns of industrial psychology are personnel matters and human resource management (Fouad, 2007). Thus, industrial psychology is increasingly referred to as *personnel psychology*. Organizational psychology examines the social and group influences of the organization (McShane & von Glinow, 2007). I/O psychology is the focus of Chapter 13.

Clinical and Counseling Psychology   *Clinical and counseling psychology* is the most widely practiced specialization in psychology. Clinical and counseling psychologists diagnose and treat people with psychological problems (Nolen-Hoeksema, 2007; Prochaska & Norcross, 2007). Counseling psychologists sometimes deal with people who have less serious problems (Santee, 2007). For example, counseling psychologists may work with students, advising them about personal problems and career planning.

A clinical psychologist typically has a doctoral degree in psychology, which requires 3 to 4 years of graduate work and 1 year of internship in a mental health facility. Clinical psychologists are different from psychiatrists, who study *psychiatry,* which is a branch of medicine. Psychiatrists are physicians with a doctor of medicine (MD) degree who subsequently specialize in abnormal behavior and psychotherapy. Despite their different training, clinical psychologists and psychiatrists are alike in sharing a common interest in improving the lives of people with mental health problems. One important distinction is that psychiatrists can prescribe

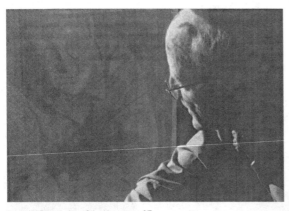

James W. Pennebaker of the University of Texas, Austin, is a distinguished social psychologist. His research probes the connections among traumatic life experience, expressive writing, physical and mental health, and work performance.

Social psychologists explore the powerful influence of groups (such as, clockwise, Chinese Americans, members of motorcycle clubs, gay dads, military families, and inner-city youths) on individuals' attitudes, thinking, and behavior.

drugs, whereas clinical psychologists generally cannot. Chapters 14 and 15 address the intriguing world of psychological disorders and treatment.

Health Psychology   *Health psychology* is a multidimensional approach to health that emphasizes psychological factors, lifestyle, and the nature of the healthcare delivery system (Taylor, 2007). Many health psychologists study the roles of stress and coping in people's lives (Stanton, Revenson, & Tennen, 2007). Health psychologists may work in physical or mental health areas. Some are members of multidisciplinary teams that conduct research or provide clinical services. Health psychology is examined in Chapter 16.

The psychology specialties that we have discussed so far are the main areas of psychology that we cover in this book. However, they do not represent an exhaustive list of the interests of the field. Other specializations in psychology include the following.

Community Psychology   *Community psychology* is concerned with providing accessible care for people with psychological problems. Community-based mental health centers are one means of delivering services such as outreach programs to people in need, especially those who traditionally have been underserved by mental health professionals (Dalton, Elias, & Wandersman, 2007). Community psychologists view human behavior in terms of adaptation to resources and the specific situation. They work to create communities that are more supportive of residents by pinpointing needs, providing needed services, and teaching people how to gain access to resources that are already available (Beeson & others, 2006). Community psychologists are also concerned with prevention. That is, they try to prevent mental health problems by identifying high-risk groups and then intervening with appropriate services and by stimulating new opportunities in the community.

"I thought we'd look at reducing your medication and replacing it with eight hugs a day before and after meals."

© CartoonStock.com

Howard Berenbaum of the University of Illinois, Urbana-Champaign, is a well-known clinical psychologist. His primary research delves into the roots of, and relationships among, various symptoms of mental disorders.

School and Educational Psychology *School and educational psychology* centrally concerns children's learning and adjustment in school. School psychologists in elementary and secondary school systems test children, make recommendations about educational placement, and work on educational planning teams. Educational psychologists work at colleges and universities, teach classes, and do research on teaching and learning (Alexander & Winne, 2006).

Environmental Psychology *Environmental psychology* is the study of the interactions between people and the physical environment. Environmental psychologists explore the effects of physical settings in most major areas of psychology, including perception, cognition, learning, development, abnormal behavior, and social relations (Israel & others, 2006; Sallis & Glanz, 2006). Topics that an environmental psychologist might study range from how different building and room arrangements influence behavior to what strategies might be used to reduce human behavior that harms the environment.

Psychology of Women The *psychology of women* studies psychological, social, and cultural influences on women's development and behavior. This field stresses the importance of integrating information about women with current psychological knowledge and beliefs and applying the information to society and its institutions (Hyde, 2007; Smith, 2007).

Forensic Psychology *Forensic psychology* is the field of psychology that applies psychological concepts to the legal system (Fradella, 2006). Social and cognitive psychologists increasingly conduct research on topics related to psychology and law. Forensic psychologists are hired by legal teams to provide input about many aspects of a trial, such as jury selection. Forensic psychologists with clinical training may also provide expert testimony in trials, particularly to add their expertise to the question of whether a criminal is likely to be a danger to society.

Sport Psychology *Sport psychology* applies psychology's principles to improving sport performance and enjoying sport participation (Cox, 2007; Williams, 2006). Sport psychology is a relatively new field, but it is rapidly gaining acceptance. It is now common to hear about elite athletes working with a sport psychologist to improve their games.

Cross-Cultural Psychology *Cross-cultural psychology* is the study of culture's role in understanding behavior, thought, and emotion (Kagitcibasi, 2007; Kitayama & Cohen, 2007). Cross-cultural psychologists compare the nature of psychological processes in different cultures with a special interest in whether psychological phenomena are universal or culture-specific. The International Association for Cross-Cultural Psychology promotes research on cross-cultural comparisons and awareness of culture's role in psychology. To read about some cross-cultural research on a topic of interest to almost everyone, see the Intersection on how culture influences happiness.

Careers

Psychologists do not pass all of their time in a laboratory, white-smocked with clipboard in hand, observing rats and crunching numbers. Some psychologists spend their days seeing individuals with problems; others teach at universities and conduct research. Still others work in business and industry, designing more efficient criteria for hiring. In short, psychology is a field with many areas of specialization.

Could you get passionate about psychology? Have you ever thought about majoring in psychology? Students who major in psychology often find the subject matter highly interesting (Kuther & Morgan, 2007; Landrum & Davis, 2007). In the remaining chapters of this book, you will encounter hundreds of truly fascinating inquiries in psychology.

Barbara L. Frederickson (right) of the University of North Carolina, Chapel Hill, is a leading specialist in social psychology, the psychology of women, and positive psychology. Her research investigates topics such as positive emotions and human flourishing.

King: The Science of
Psychology: An
Appreciative View

1. What is Psychology?

Text

© The McGraw–Hill
Companies, 2008

29

Cross-Cultural Psychology and Emotion: Are Some Cultures Happier Than Others?

When you think of all the things that might make a life good, you would probably include happiness. When asked to make three wishes for anything at all, many people wish for happiness (King & Broyles, 1997). And worldwide, people value being happy (Inglehart, 1990).

How do psychologists study happiness? Using the 1–7 scale, read the 5 statements below and indicate your agreement with each item.

7	6	5	4	3	2	1
Strongly Agree	Agree	Slightly Agree	Neither Agree Nor Disagree	Slightly Disagree	Disagree	Strongly Disagree

1. In most ways my life is close to my ideal.
2. The conditions of my life are excellent.
3. I am satisfied with my life.
4. So far I have gotten the important things I want in life.
5. If I could live my life over, I would change almost nothing.

You have just completed the Satisfaction with Life Scale (Diener & others, 1985), a commonly used questionnaire that measures how generally happy people are with their lives. To find out how happy you perceive yourself to be, add up your ratings and divide by 5. This average rating could be considered your level of general happiness. This scale and others like it have been used to measure happiness levels in a broad range of studies in many different countries.

Based on such research, Ed and Carol Diener (1996) have declared that "most people are pretty happy," scoring above the midpoint on the scale you just completed. These researchers concluded that being generally happy might be a characteristic of most people and that evolution may have endowed us with a propensity to be moderately happy most of the time. Still, research on happiness in various cultures has generally centered on relatively industrialized countries. What about truly nonindustrialized cultures?

> *When asked to make three wishes for anything at all, many people wish for happiness.*

In a recent study, levels of happiness were examined in groups of people who have not generally been included in psychological studies (Biswas-Diener, Vitterso, & Diener, 2005). The research included three groups: the Inuits of Greenland, the Masai of southern Kenya, and American Old Order Amish. All three groups completed measures essentially the same as the one you just did. The Inuit tribe studied (the Inughuit) live at 79 degrees latitude (very far north!), in the harshest climate inhabited by a traditional human society. The landscape consists of rocks, glaciers, and the sea. Farming is impossible. The Inughuits do have some modern conveniences, such as electricity and running water, but they generally adhere to a traditional hunting culture. It is not uncommon to find an Inughuit hunter carving a seal or caribou on the kitchen floor while children in the next room watch TV. Most of us might feel a little blue in the winter months when gloomy weather seems to stretch on, day after day. For the Inughuits,

however, the sun never rises at all throughout the winter months, and in the summer, it never sets. How happy could an individual be in such a difficult setting? Pretty happy, it turns out, as the Inughuits averaged a 5.0 on the Satisfaction with Life Scale.

The Masai are an indigenous African nomadic group who live in villages of about 20 people, with little exposure to the West. The Masai are known to be fierce warriors, and their culture has many traditional ceremonies built around a boy's passage from childhood to manhood. Boys are circumcised between the ages of 15 and 22, and they are forbidden from moving or making a sound during the procedure. Girls also experience circumcision as they enter puberty, a controversial rite that involves the removal of the clitoris and that makes childbirth extremely difficult. The Masai practice child marriage and polygamy, and each tribe has a "medicine man." Women in Masai culture have very little power and are generally expected to do most of the work. How happy could an individual be in this context? Masai men and women who completed the measure orally in their native tongue, Maa, averaged a 5.4 on the life satisfaction scale (Biswas-Diener, Vitterso, & Diener, 2005).

Finally, the Old Order Amish belong to a strict religious sect that explicitly rejects modern aspects of life. The Amish separate themselves from mainstream society and can be seen on horse and buggy in various areas of the midwestern and northeastern United States. The women wear bonnets, and the men sport beards, dark clothes, and old-fashioned brimmed hats. Children are schooled only to the 8th grade. The people farm without modern machinery and dedicate their lives to simplicity—without radios, TVs, CDs, DVDs, iPods, cell phones, washing machines, and cars. But the Amish are still relatively happy, averaging 4.4 on the 7-point happiness scale (Biswas-Diener, Vitterso, & Diener, 2005).

These results converge with the findings of a host of other studies on happiness indicating that most individuals are indeed happy. But there is evidence for national differences in happiness. In one study, levels of happiness were examined in over 100,000 people from 55 nations (Diener, Diener, & Diener, 1995). The happiest countries were Iceland, Sweden, Australia,

(continued)

21

Denmark, Canada, Switzerland, and the United States. The least happy nations were the Dominican Republic, Cameroon, China, Russia, and South Korea. What might account for national differences in general happiness? Among the factors that were found to relate to increased national well-being were income, civil rights, and social equality (including the number of girls enrolled in secondary school).

Research on cultural factors in well-being suggests that even if most people are indeed reasonably happy, the factors that affect happiness may be culture-specific (Tov & Diener, 2007). Researchers have distinguished individualistic cultures from collectivistic cultures (Triandis, 2007). *Individualistic cultures* (such as the United States and western European nations) emphasize the uniqueness of each individual and his or her thoughts, feelings, and choices. Individualistic cultures view the person as having an independent sense of self, separate from his or her social group. In contrast, *collectivistic cultures* (such as those in East Asia) emphasize the social group and the roles the individual plays in that larger group. Collectivistic cultures view the person as embedded in the social network or having an interdependent sense of self. Researchers have found that the individualism is associated with higher levels of personal happiness (Diener, 2000; Diener, Diener, & Diener, 1995).

This difference between individualistic and collectivistic cultures is all the more interesting when we consider that although individualistic cultures report higher levels of personal happiness, they also have higher suicide rates. Similarly, individualistic cultures are characterized by higher levels of marital satisfaction but also higher divorce rates (Diener, 2000).

It may be that individuals in collectivistic cultures are more likely to sacrifice personal happiness for the sake of duty—for instance, staying in an unsatisfying marriage. Indeed, personal happiness is higher for individuals in collectivistic cultures when their personal goals and values fit societal dictates (Lu, 2006).

One factor that differs across cultures in relation to happiness is the individual's level of consistency across various situations. Are you essentially the same person at work, at school, and in your interactions with friends, family members, and romantic partners? In the West, being consistent across different situations is often considered an aspect of psychological health and of living in a way that is "true to yourself." In addition, in the West, when individuals perceive themselves to be consistent across different situations, they report higher levels of happiness. However, in other cultures, among them Korea (a collectivistic culture), consistency is unrelated to well-being (Suh, 2002). In more collectivistic cultures, tailoring one's behavior to social situations and roles is not experienced as being fake but rather as pursuing the goal of harmony with others.

This research shows how putting the central questions of psychology in a cross-cultural context can illuminate not only general human characteristics (such as happiness) but also differences in the culture-bound processes that lead to these characteristics (such as individualism versus collectivism). Further, cross-cultural research can help us to identify important characteristics within members of the same culture that influence the process by which individuals define and lead happy lives (Cross, Gore, & Morris, 2003; Kagitcibasi, 2007; Shiraev & Levy, 2007; Tov & Diener, 2007).

Not only do you gain considerable knowledge and understanding of the mind and behavior, but majoring in psychology equips you with a rich and diverse portfolio of skills that serve you well in many different types of work, both practical and professional (Morgan & Korschgen, 2006). A psychology major helps you improve your skills in research, measurement and computing, problem solving, critical thinking, and writing. Integrating these skills, which span the arts and sciences, provides you with unique qualifications. And even if you are not a psychology major and do not plan to major in psychology, this course and others in psychology can give you a richer, deeper understanding of many areas of life.

FIGURE 1.1

Some Job Possibilities for Students with an Undergraduate Degree in Psychology A psychology degree opens the door to many possible careers in the realms of business, social and human services, and research.

Business
- personnel administrator
- public relations
- sales representative
- admissions recruiter
- textbook representative
- advertising
- insurance agent
- management trainee
- retail sales management
- loan officer

Social/Human Services
- case worker
- youth counselor
- employment counselor
- fund-raising specialist
- alumni affairs coordinator
- mental health aide
- parent educator
- drug abuse counselor

Research
- research assistant
- trainee for product research companies
- marketing researcher
- grant and report writer
- information specialist/ researcher
- mental health aide
- research analyst
- statistical assistant

PSYCHOLOGY AND LIFE

Is Psychology in Your Future?

Instructions

Students who are successful as psychology majors have a profile that is related to the questions below. Answer true or false to each item.

		True	False
1.	I often think about what makes people do what they do.		
2.	I like reading about new findings that scientists have discovered doing behavioral research.		
3.	I am often skeptical when someone tries to persuade me about behavioral claims unless there is evidence to back up the claim.		
4.	I like the prospect of measuring behavior and doing statistics to determine meaningful differences.		
5.	I can usually come up with multiple explanations to account for behavior.		
6.	I think I could come up with ideas to research to help explain behaviors I am curious about.		
7.	I am often approached by others who want me to listen to their problems and share my ideas about what to do.		
8.	I don't get especially frustrated if I can't get answers to my questions.		
9.	I am usually careful with details.		
10.	I enjoy writing and speaking about things I am learning.		
11.	I like to solve puzzles.		
12.	I feel comfortable that psychology can provide me with an education that will lead to a good job.		

Scoring and Interpretation

If you answered true to a majority of the items, psychology is a major that likely matches up well with your interests. Although the items are not a perfect predictor of whether you will enjoy majoring in and pursuing a career in psychology, they can give you an indication of whether you might benefit from finding out more about what psychologists do and what is involved in becoming a psychologist. Your psychology professor or a career counselor at your college likely can inform you about the best way to pursue a career in psychology.

Psychology also pays reasonably well. Psychologists earn well above the median salary in the United States. It is unlikely that you would live in a palatial mansion because you majored in psychology, but it is also unlikely that you would go broke. A psychology major enables you to improve people's lives, to understand yourself and others, possibly to advance the state of knowledge in the field, and to have an enjoyable time while you are doing these things.

An undergraduate degree in psychology can give you access to a variety of jobs. For a list of some of the job possibilities in business, social and human services, and research that are open to students with such a degree, see Figure 1.1. If you choose a career in psychology, you can greatly expand your opportunities (and your income) by getting a graduate degree, either a master's or a doctorate.

Where do psychologists work? Slightly more than one-third are teachers, researchers, or counselors at colleges or universities. Most other psychologists work in clinical and private practice settings (Figure 1.2). To reflect on whether a career in psychology might be in your future, see the Psychology and Life box.

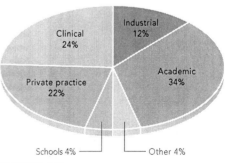

FIGURE 1.2

Settings in Which Psychologists Work More psychologists work in academic settings (34%), such as colleges and universities, than any other. However, clinical (24%) and private practice (22%) settings, both contexts in which many psychologists in the mental health professions work, together make up almost half of the total settings.

REVIEW AND SHARPEN YOUR THINKING

4 Evaluate areas of specialization and careers in psychology.
- Name and describe the various areas of specialization in psychology.
- Discuss career opportunities that are available to individuals who have an undergraduate degree in psychology.

Think of a career other than psychology that you might enter. In what ways might studying psychology be useful in that career?

5 Psychology and Health and Wellness

Describe the connections between the mind and the body.

psychopathology The study of mental illness.

One problem with the common tendency to equate the science of psychology with clinical psychology or with **psychopathology**—the study of mental illness—is that such a perspective limits the relevance of psychology to people with problems. This narrow way of viewing the field ignores the important question, What does psychology have to do with me and those around me? One of positive psychology's goals is to enhance general awareness of the role of psychological research in providing an understanding of "normal" people and their everyday lives. In this book, we seek to answer the question, What does psychology have to say about me? by tying research in psychology to your health and wellness. How better to show that psychology matters than to demonstrate how it matters to your ability to function as a healthy person every day?

How the Mind Impacts the Body

When you think of psychology, you might think first about the mind and its complex mental processes such as love, gratitude, hate, and anger. But psychology has come to recognize more and more that the mind we are studying is intricately connected to the body. As you will see when we examine neuroscience as an approach to psychology in Chapter 3, observations of the brain at work reveal that when mental processes change, so do physical processes (Hagner, 2007).

Health psychologists talk about "health behavior" as a subset of behaviors that are relevant to physical health. These behaviors might include eating well, exercising, not smoking, performing testicular and breast self-exams, brushing your teeth, and getting enough sleep. But think about your body for a moment. Are there really ever times when your behavior is not relevant to your body (and therefore your health)? Is there ever a time when you are doing anything—thinking, feeling, walking, running, singing—when your physical body is not present? As long as your body is there, with your heart, lungs, blood, and brain activated, your health is implicated. Everything we do, see, think, and feel is potentially important to our health and well-being.

It might be helpful to think about the ways the mind and body can relate to each other, even as they are united in the physical reality of a person. Let's say you experience a mental "event" such as seeing a "Buns of Steel" infomercial on TV. You decide to embark on a quest for these legendary buns of steel. Mental commitment, goal setting, and self-discipline will be the kinds of mental processes necessary to transform your body. The mind can work on the body, changing its shape and size.

How the Body Impacts the Mind

Similarly, the body can influence the mind in dramatic ways. Consider how fuzzy your thinking is after you stay out too late, and how much easier it is to solve life's problems when you have had a good night's sleep. Also consider your outlook on the first day of true recovery from a nagging cold: Everything just seems better. Your mood and your work improve. Clearly, physical states such as illness and health influence the way we think. So do physical conditions such as being hot or uncomfortable. Research has shown, for instance, that when people experience extreme heat, they can start to feel hostile and even act more aggressively than usual. A study by Doug Kenrick and Steve MacFarlane (1986) showed that during very hot weather, people without air conditioning in their cars were much more likely to honk their horns during a traffic jam.

FRANK & ERNEST: © Thaves/Dist. by Newspaper Enterprise Association, Inc.

The link between the mind and the body has fascinated philosophers for centuries. Psychology occupies the very spot where the mind and body meet. Throughout this book, we point out the ways that all of the various approaches to psychology matter to your well-being. Psychology is not only *about* you—it is *crucially about* you, essential to your understanding of your life, your goals, and the ways that you can use the insights of these thousands of scientists to make your life healthier and happier.

REVIEW AND SHARPEN YOUR THINKING

5 Describe the connections between the mind and the body.
- Summarize the ways that the mind can influence the body.
- Summarize the ways that the body can influence the mind.

Consider your activities last night. What was your body doing, and what was your mind doing? Think of the various ways that these two aspects of yourself affected each other in one evening.

34

King: The Science of
Psychology: An
Appreciative View

1. What is Psychology?

Text

© The McGraw–Hill
Companies, 2008

26   CHAPTER 1   What Is Psychology?

1 DEFINING PSYCHOLOGY

Explain what psychology is and describe the positive psychology movement.

Psychology Versus Common Sense: What Don't You Already Know About Psychology?

Psychology is the scientific study of behavior and mental processes. Science uses systematic methods to observe, describe, predict, and explain. Behavior includes everything organisms do that can be observed. Mental processes are thoughts, feelings, and motives. The science of psychology is different from common sense. Often, commonsense notions have been proven to be erroneous by sound scientific research.

Thinking Like a Psychologist Means Thinking Like a Scientist

Critical thinking involves thinking reflectively and productively and evaluating the evidence. It is important to maintain a healthy skepticism about anything that appears to be magical and wondrous. Psychology is full of controversies, and it is essential to think critically about these controversies. Most controversies are not completely resolved on one side or the other.

Positive Psychology

The positive psychology movement is a recent development, and the approach is not without controversy. Its proponents argue that psychology has been too negative and needs to focus more on the positive aspects of people, such as their optimism, creativity, and civic values. Positive psychology draws attention to what works, as a basis for understanding what *does not* work.

2 THE ROOTS AND EARLY SCIENTIFIC APPROACHES OF PSYCHOLOGY

Discuss the roots and early scientific foundations of psychology.

Structuralism

Structuralism emphasized the study of the conscious mind and its structures. Wilhelm Wundt founded the first laboratory in psychology in 1879, dedicated to searching for the mind's elemental structures, and E. B. Titchener named the approach "structuralism."

Functionalism

Functionalism focused on the functions of the mind in adapting to the environment. William James was the leading functionalist theorist. The functionalist emphasis on the adaptive character of the mind fit well with the emerging understanding of Darwin's theory of evolution.

3 CONTEMPORARY APPROACHES TO PSYCHOLOGY

Summarize the main themes of seven approaches to psychology.

The Biological Approach

The biological approach focuses on the body, especially the brain and nervous system. Technological advances in imaging the brain have allowed psychological researchers to examine the brain in all its complexity.

The Behavioral Approach

The behavioral approach emphasizes the scientific study of observable behavioral responses and their environmental determinants. John B. Watson and B. F. Skinner were important early behaviorists.

The Psychodynamic Approach

The psychodynamic approach emphasizes unconscious thought, the conflict between biological instincts and society's demands, and early family experiences. Sigmund Freud was the founding father of the psychodynamic approach.

The Humanistic Approach

The humanistic approach emphasizes a person's capacity for positive growth, freedom to choose a destiny, and positive qualities.

The Cognitive Approach

The cognitive approach emphasizes the mental processes involved in knowing. Cognitive psychologists study attention, thinking, problem solving, remembering, and learning.

The Evolutionary Approach

The evolutionary approach stresses the importance of adaptation, reproduction, and "survival of the fittest."

The Sociocultural Approach

The sociocultural approach focuses on the social and cultural determinants of behavior. This approach encourages us to attend to the ways that our behavior and mental processes are embedded in a social context.

4 AREAS OF SPECIALIZATION AND CAREERS IN PSYCHOLOGY

Evaluate areas of specialization and careers in psychology.

Areas of Specialization

Main areas of specialization in psychology include physiological psychology and behavioral neuroscience, developmental psychology, sensation and perception, cognitive psychology, learning, motivation and emotion, personality psychology, social psychology, industrial and organizational psychology, clinical and counseling psychology, and health psychology. Other specialties include community psychology, school and educational psychology, environmental psychology, the psychology of women, forensic psychology, sport psychology, and cross-cultural psychology.

Careers

Majoring in psychology can open up many career opportunities. Careers range from conducting therapy with people who have mental problems to teaching and conducting research at a university to working in advertising and public relations.

5 PSYCHOLOGY AND HEALTH AND WELLNESS

Describe the connections between the mind and the body.

How the Mind Impacts the Body

While philosophers have debated the relation between the mind and the body for centuries, psychologists have come to recognize that these two aspects of a human being are intricately related. The mind can influence the body. The way we think has implications for our nervous system and brain. Our motives and goals can influence our bodies as we strive to be physically fit and eat well.

How the Body Impacts the Mind

The body can have an influence over the mind. We think differently when our bodies are rested versus tired, healthy versus unhealthy, and hot versus comfortable.

King: The Science of
Psychology: An
Appreciative View

1. What is Psychology?

Text

© The McGraw–Hill
Companies, 2008

35

Summary   **27**

Key Terms

psychology, p. 4
science, p. 5
behavior, p. 5
mental processes, p. 5
critical thinking, p. 6

positive psychology
    movement, p. 7
structuralism, p. 9
functionalism, p. 10
natural selection, p. 10

biological approach, p. 12
neuroscience, p. 12
behavioral approach, p. 12
psychodynamic approach, p. 12
humanistic approach, p. 12

cognitive approach, p. 12
evolutionary approach, p. 14
sociocultural approach, p. 14
psychopathology, p. 24

Apply Your Knowledge

1. Why are psychology and philosophy considered different disciplines? Research some of the questions addressed by both fields and the approaches each discipline uses to answer these questions.

2. Ask 10 friends and family members to tell you the first thing that comes to mind when they think of a psychologist. Do their responses reflect the need for positive psychology? Why or why not?

3. Visit the website of a major book retailer (like Amazon.com) and enter *psychology* as a search term. Examine descriptions of the five to seven most popular psychology books listed. How well do the themes covered represent your perceptions of what

psychology is? How well do they represent the approaches to psychology discussed in the text? Are any perspectives over- or underrepresented? If so, why do you think that is?

4. In the faculty directory for your school (or for another institution), look up the psychology faculty. Select several faculty members and discover what the area of specialization is for each (be careful, it may not be the same as the classes they teach). How do you think their areas of academic training might affect the way they teach their classes?

5. Look at the health or science section of your local paper or favorite magazine. Evaluate the use of psychological research there. How are psychological studies presented in this publication?

CHAPTER 1

Foundations of Sport Psychology

KEY TERMS

Accreditation
Acculturation
Clinical/counseling sport
  psychologist
Cultural compatibility model
Cultural competence
Diversity
Educational sport psychologist
Enculturation
Feminism
Gay
Griffith, Coleman
Heterosexist behavior
Heterosexual
Homophobia
Homophobic behavior
Homosexual
Inclusiveness
Lesbian
Martens, Rainer
Multicultural training
Ogilvie, Bruce
Race thinking
Racist thinking
Research sport psychologist
Sexism
Sexual orientation
Sport Psychology Registry
Triplett, Norman
Universalistic model
USOC
White privilege

4   Part One   Understanding Sport Psychology

Hardly a subject associated with sport is more intriguing than the subject of sport psychology. Perhaps this is so because it is a subject coaches, athletes, and fans feel comfortable discussing. The average spectator does not usually venture to offer a biomechanical explanation for an athlete's achievement of a near-superhuman feat, yet the same spectator is often willing to give a psychological explanation (e.g., mental toughness, motivation, strength of character). Every four years, sport fans from all over North America become transfixed by the spectacle of the Summer or Winter Olympic Games. Throughout the television broadcasts of these games, viewers are exposed to frequent references to athletes who train with the aid of professional sport psychologists. Many times the sport psychologist will be identified as the camera zooms in on the individual athlete. It is also becoming somewhat common for television crews to identify professional golfers who employ the services of sport psychologists. Somewhat recently, a sport psychologist was given credit for the Indianapolis Colts' decision to select Peyton Manning over Ryan Leaf in the 1998 professional football draft (Carey, 1999). Manning went on to stardom in Indianapolis, while Leaf continued to struggle for several years with the San Diego Chargers. Over the years, selected professional baseball teams have acquired the services of applied sport psychologists. At the present time there are many young people seeking to earn a living providing sport psychology services to professional, Olympic, or even collegiate sports teams. Hopefully, these young people will acquire the knowledge, experience, and certification/licensure that will allow them to realize their dreams.

One wonders, however, who will provide sport psychology services to the coaches and players of millions of youth and high school sports teams that do not have the financial resources to employ a full- or even part-time sport psychologist. The goal of providing sport psychology services to every coach and athlete is unrealistic. A better goal might be to train coaches and athletes to serve as their own sport psychology consultants and to train one another. As advocated by Martin, Thomson, and McKnight (1998), the ultimate goal of a sport psychology consultant should be to teach clients to teach or counsel themselves.

Think of the marvelous example of coaching that was provided by UCLA's legendary John Wooden, and contrast that with the intimidation style of former Indiana and current Texas Tech coach Bob Knight. Either John Wooden was a great applied sport psychologist, or he had someone on his staff who was. Knight, on the other hand, has been an example of a coach in desperate need of a sport psychologist to help him relate in a positive way with his athletes and fellow coaches. Bill Walton said it best:

> With Coach Wooden, an Indiana native, life was always fun, always upbeat, always positive, always about the team, always about the greatness of the game. Sadly you don't get any sense of that from Knight. There's no joy. Even worse, there's no happiness on the faces of his players (Walton, 2000, p. 96).

As a student of sport psychology, you may not go on to become a consultant to a professional team, but hopefully you will be able to apply what you have learned from this book and to share it with others.

This text offers the prospective coach and scholar the opportunity to learn correct concepts and applications of sport psychology, even though sport psychology is not a perfect science. We have a great deal to learn about mental preparation for sport competition. We will always have a need for the scientist who is interested in discovering new knowledge. As you read this text, keep an open mind and become interested in sport psychology as a science.

In the paragraphs that follow, a number of peripheral issues will be discussed that provide background information for the study of sport and exercise psychology. Specifically, this chapter provides a definition of sport psychology; sketches a brief history of sport psychology in North America,

including development of professional organizations; discusses the issue of certification; reviews various roles of the sport psychologist; discusses ethics associated with applied sport psychology; broaches the issue of accreditation; and concludes with a discussion of multicultural issues that relate to race and gender.

Sport and Exercise Psychology Defined

Sport psychology is a science in which the principles of psychology are applied in a sport or exercise setting. These principles are often applied to enhance performance. However, the true sport psychologist is interested in much more than performance enhancement and sees sport as a vehicle for human enrichment. A win-at-all-costs attitude is inconsistent with the goals and aspirations of the best sport psychologist. The sport psychologist is interested in helping every sport participant reach his or her potential as an athlete. If helping a young athlete develop self-control and confidence results in superior athletic performance, this is good. However, it is also possible that a quality sport experience can enhance an athlete's intrinsic motivation without the athlete's necessarily winning. Taken as a whole, sport psychology is an exciting subject dedicated to the enhancement of both athletic performance and the social-psychological aspects of human enrichment.

Stated more simply, sport and exercise psychology is the study of the effect of psychological and emotional factors on sport and exercise performance, and the effect of sport and exercise involvement on psychological and emotional factors. This is an easy-to-understand definition that shows clearly the interactive relationship between sport and exercise involvement and psychological and emotional factors. It is upon this basic construct that this book is based. Athletic performance is influenced by psychological and emotional factors that can be fine-tuned and learned. Conversely, involvement in sport and exercise activities can

have a positive effect upon an individual's psychological and emotional makeup.

History of Sport Psychology in North America

Sport psychology as a distinct field of study is extremely young and is evolving. Perhaps the first clear historical example of research being conducted in the area of sport psychology was reported by **Norman Triplett** in 1897. Drawing upon field observations and secondary data, Triplett analyzed the performance of cyclists under conditions of social facilitation. He concluded from this "milestone" research that the presence of other competitors was capable of facilitating better cycling performance (Davis, Huss, & Becker, 1995).

While Triplett provided an example of one of the earliest recorded sport psychology research investigations, he was not the first person to systematically carry out sport psychology research over an extended period of time. This distinction is attributed to **Coleman Griffith,** often referred to as the "father of sport psychology in North America" (Gould & Pick, 1995). Griffith is credited with establishing the first sport psychology laboratory at the University of Illinois in 1925. Griffith, a psychologist, was selected by George Huff, head of the Department of Physical Education at the University of Illinois, to develop this new laboratory based on Huff's vision. Dr. Griffith's laboratory was devoted to solving psychological and physiological problems associated with sport and athletic performance. Over an extended period of time, Griffith studied the nature of psychomotor skills, motor learning, and the relationship between personality variables and physical performance. Thus, the historical trend for the next sixty years was established in this early event. Physical Education, a cross-disciplinary entity, would provide the academic home for the application of psychology to sport and athletics.

6   Part One   Understanding Sport Psychology

Along with developing the first sport psychology laboratory at the University of Illinois, Griffith was also the first psychologist hired by a professional sports team in the United States. In 1938, P. K. Wrigley, owner of the Chicago Cubs, hired him to be the team sport psychologist and to improve performance. Resisted by the team manager, Charlie Grimm, Griffith did not enjoy great success with the Chicago Cubs, but his scientific approach to the psychology of coaching has emerged as the current model for sport psychologists working with professional teams (Green, 2003).

While Coleman Griffith was credited with the development of the first sport psychology research laboratory, others would follow his lead. Following World War II, such notables as Franklin M. Henry at the University of California, John Lawther at Pennsylvania State University, and Arthur Slater-Hammel at Indiana University pioneered graduate-level courses and developed research laboratories of their own.

Many women were also instrumental in the early development of sport psychology in North America. Such notables as Dorothy Harris, Eleanor Metheny, Camille Brown, Celeste Ulrich, and Aileen Lockhart could all be considered the "mothers of sport psychology," with Dorothy Harris also being the "mother of applied sport psychology" (Gill, 1995; Granito, 2002; Oglesby, 2001). Women such as Diane Gill, Tara Scanlan, Jean Williams, Bonnie Berger, and Carole Oglesby not only made significant contributions to the development of modern sport psychology, but remain to this day leaders in the field (Gill, 1995).

Dan Landers (1995) referred to the period of time from 1950 to 1980 as the "formative years" for sport psychology. During this time, sport psychology began to emerge as a discipline somewhat distinct from exercise physiology and motor learning. This is especially true of "applied" sport psychology. Prior to the emergence of applied sport psychology, most research related to sport psychology was conducted within a laboratory setting and was referred to as motor learning research.

During the formative years, a number of important research initiatives and textbooks were published. These early sporadic initiatives paved the way for the emergence of sport psychology as an academic subdiscipline within physical education and psychology. Some of the early textbooks included *Psychology of Coaching,* by John D. Lawther (1951); *Problem Athletes and How to Handle Them,* by Bruce Ogilvie and Tom Tutko (1966); *Motor Learning and Human Performance,* by Robert Singer (1968); *Psychology of Motor Learning,* by Joseph B. Oxendine (1968); *Psychology and the Superior Athlete,* by Miroslaw Vanek and Bryant Cratty (1970); *Social Psychology and Physical Activity,* by Rainer Martens (1975); and *Social Psychology of Sport,* by Albert Carron (1980).

As mentioned earlier, the book titled *Problem Athletes and How to Handle Them* was authored in 1966 by Thomas Tutko and Bruce Ogilvie. This book and the authors' personality inventory for athletes—the Athletic Motivation Inventory (AMI)—caught on with coaches and athletes. Notwithstanding the popularity of the book and the inventory with the athletic community, Tutko and Ogilvie's work was not well received by the sport psychology community of scholars at the time. For reasons to be discussed in detail in the chapter on personality, the AMI and the book on how to handle problem athletes were deemed by the scientific community to be overly simplistic and not based on good science. Interestingly, Bruce Ogilvie's work as an applied sport psychologist is much better received by the scientific community today than it was in the 1960s. Because of his pioneering work with personality and applied sport psychology, **Bruce Ogilvie** is referred to as the father of applied sport psychology in North America.

If Coleman Griffith is the father of sport psychology in North America and Bruce Ogilvie the father of applied sport psychology, then the title "father of modern sport psychology" should go to **Rainer Martens,** former professor of sport psychology at the University of Illinois and founder of Human Kinetics Publishers. In modern times,

Baseball is an excellent game in which to observe sport psychology in action. Courtesy Ball State University Sports Information.

Rainer Martens has done more for the development of sport psychology in North America than any other single individual. This assessment is based upon his research initiatives while a professor at Illinois, and on the fact that the students that he mentored are now leaders in the field throughout the world.

Development of Professional Organizations

A number of professional sport psychology organizations have evolved since the 1960s. In 1965 the *International Society of Sport Psychology* (ISSP) was formed. Organized in Rome, the purpose of ISSP is to promote and disseminate information about the practice of sport psychology throughout the world. In North America a small group of sport psychologists from Canada and the

United States met in Dallas, Texas, to discuss the feasibility of forming a professional organization distinct from the American Alliance for Health, Physical Education, Recreation, and Dance (AAHPERD). The efforts of this small group came to fruition in 1966 when it was recognized by ISSP. The name of this new organization was the *North American Society for the Psychology of Sport and Physical Activity* (NASPSPA). The first annual meeting of NASPSPA was held prior to the 1967 AAHPER National Convention in Las Vegas. Since that time, NASPSPA has evolved into an influential academic society focusing on sport psychology in the broadest sense. NASPSPA provides a forum for researchers in the areas of sport psychology, sport sociology, motor learning, motor control, and motor development to meet and exchange ideas and research. Shortly after the emergence of NASPSPA in the United States, another significant professional organization came into existence in Canada in 1969. This organization was named the *Canadian Society for Psychomotor Learning and Sport Psychology* (CSPLSP). CSPLSP was originally organized under the auspices of the Canadian Association for Health, Physical Education, and Recreation (CAHPER), but became an independent society in 1977. Somewhat concurrent with the emergence of the Canadian society, the *Sports Psychology Academy* (SPA) emerged in the United States as one of six academies within the National Association for Sport and Physical Education (NASPE). NASPE is an association within AAHPERD. In order to better address the interests and needs of sport psychologists interested in applying the principles of psychology to sport and exercise, the *Association for the Advancement of Applied Sport Psychology* (AAASP) was formed in the fall of

1985 (Silva, 1989). AAASP emerged in the 1990s as the dominant association for the advancement of applied sport psychology as well as research in North America, and perhaps in the world.

In addition to the specialized organizations mentioned above, two significant North American–based associations created interest areas dedicated to sport psychology within their organizations. These include the American Psychological Association (APA) with its Division 47 (formed in 1986), and the American College of Sports Medicine (ACSM). Paralleling the emergence of professional sport psychology organizations are journals that provide an outlet and forum for research generated by members of these organizations.

As a summary, table 1.1 lists professional organizations partially or completely dedicated to sport and exercise psychology. This table also indicates the year each organization was formed. Table 1.2 provides an incomplete list of research

TABLE 1.1 | Summary of Major Professional Societies That Are Dedicated or Partially Dedicated to the Discipline/Profession of Sport Psychology

Genesis	Name of Association or Society
1954	American College of Sports Medicine (ACSM)
1965	International Society of Sport Psychology (ISSP)
1967	North American Society for the Psychology of Sport and Physical Activity (NASPSPA)
1977	Canadian Society for Psychomotor Learning and Sport Psychology (CSPLSP)
1977	Sport Psychology Academy (SPA) (Division within AAHPERD)
1985	Association for the Advancement of Applied Sport Psychology (AAASP)
1986	Division 47 of the American Psychological Association (APA)

TABLE 1.2 | Incomplete List of Journals Completely or Partially Dedicated to the Advancement/Application of Knowledge in Sport and Exercise Psychology

Journal Name	Affiliation
International Journal of Sport Psychology (IJSP)	ISSP
Journal of Applied Sport Psychology (JASP)	AAASP
Journal of Sport Behavior (JSB)	None
Journal of Sport & Exercise Psychology (JS&EP)	NASPSPA
Medicine and Science in Sports and Exercise (MSSE)	ACSM
Research Quarterly for Exercise and Sport (RQES)	AAHPERD
The Sport Psychologist (TSP)	None

journals that are partially or completely dedicated to sport and exercise psychology.

Issue of Certification

Historically, sport psychology emerged as a discipline from physical education. In recent years, however, a significant interest in the discipline has developed among individuals prepared in psychology and counseling. This has raised the issue among practicing sport psychologists as to which people are qualified to call themselves "sport psychologists" and to provide services to athletes.

Some have gone so far as to argue that only licensed psychologists should be allowed to call themselves sport psychologists, and suggest that the appropriate title for a nonlicensed "sport psychologist" would be "mental training consultant." Most agree, however, that even licensed psychologists should have significant academic training in the exercise and sport sciences before practicing applied sport psychology (Taylor, 1994).

A partial solution to the issue of professionalization of sport psychology was presented by the **United States Olympic Committee (USOC)** (1983) and clarified by May (1986). The USOC developed the **Sport Psychology Registry** to identify three categories in which a person can demonstrate competence. These categories correspond to three types of sport psychologists: the clinical/counseling sport psychologist, the educational sport psychologist, and the research sport psychologist. The purpose of the Sport Psychology Registry was to identify individuals in the area of sport psychology who could work with specific national teams within the Olympic movement. The registry was not meant to be a licensing or authorizing committee.

The AAASP took the issue of who is qualified to deliver sport psychology services one step further. It adopted a certification document outlining the process an individual must take to be given the title "Certified Consultant, Association for the Advancement of Applied Sport Psychology." As one of the certification criteria, the applicant is required to hold a doctorate in an area related to sport psychology (e.g., psychology, sport science, or physical education). In addition, numerous specific courses and experiences are identified. While this certification process adopted by the AAASP may not be the final one, it is a good beginning, since it recognizes that an individual needs specialized training in psychology and physical education (sport and exercise science) to be certified as a practicing sport psychologist.

It should be mentioned, however, that not all sport psychologists are in agreement about the merits of the AAASP certification process. Anshel (1993), for example, argued that the AAASP certification process is discriminatory and counterproductive. He argues that there is scant evidence that certified consultants make better consultants than noncertified consultants. Nevertheless, it appears that the AAASP certification initiative is a move in the right direction. It requires both licensed and unlicensed psychologists to meet minimum standards in order to be certified by AAASP.

The issue of what sport psychology is and who is qualified to practice applied sport psychology was addressed by the European Federation of Sport Psychology (FEPSAC, 1996). This body took the position that the term *sport psychology* was properly used in a broad sense, and included all qualified persons, independent of their specific academic fields. It did, however, acknowledge that different countries and different states within the U.S. may have restrictions on the use of the term *psychologist*.

What Does the Sport Psychologist Do?

In an effort to promote the virtues of sport psychology to coaches, athletes, and prospective students, many thoughtful professionals have suggested contributions that sport psychologists can make to sport. In the paragraphs that follow, different roles and functions of the sport psychologist are outlined. Generally, these roles and functions describe the sport psychologist in the categories of clinician, educator, and researcher.

The Clinical/Counseling Sport Psychologist

The clinical/counseling sport psychologist is a person trained in clinical or counseling psychology and may be a licensed psychologist. Generally, the clinical/counseling sport psychologist also has a deep interest in and understanding of the athletic experience. Training may also include coursework and experience in sport psychology from programs in physical education. Clinical/counseling sport psychologists are individuals who are prepared to deal with emotional and personality disorder problems that affect some athletes. The athletic experience can be very stressful to some athletes, and can negatively affect their performance or their ability to function as healthy human beings. In these cases, sport psychologists trained in counseling psychology or clinical psychology are needed.

The Educational Sport Psychologist

Most sport psychologists who received their academic training through departments of physical education (i.e., sport and exercise science) consider themselves to be educational sport psychologists. These individuals have mastered the knowledge base of sport psychology and serve as practitioners. They use the medium of education to teach correct principles of sport and exercise psychology to athletes and coaches. In general, their mission and role is to help athletes develop psychological skills for performance enhancement. They also help athletes, young and old, to enjoy sport and use it as a vehicle for improving their quality of life.

The Research Sport Psychologist

For sport and exercise psychology to be a recognized and respected science, the knowledge base must continue to grow. It is the scientist and scholar who serves this important role. For the practicing sport psychologist to enjoy professional credibility, there must exist a credible scientific body of knowledge.

Given the different roles that sport psychologists can play, it is of interest to note the kinds of jobs that recent graduates are placed in and their job satisfaction. For the years 1994 to 1999, a recent study reported that 73 percent of individuals who graduated with a doctoral degree in a sport psychology–related field found employment in academia. Almost half of the students with a master degree found jobs in sport psychology–related fields. A large portion of the remainder found jobs related to their academic training. Students who graduated during the indicated timeframe also reported improved job satisfaction and success in achieving career goals, as compared to those who graduated between the years 1989 and 1994 (Anderson, Williams, Aldridge & Taylor, 1997; Williams & Scherzer, 2003).

Ethics in Sport Psychology

While the ethical application of sport psychology principles is discussed throughout this text, and specifically in the chapter on psychological skills training, it is important to emphasize the topic. In recent years it has become clear that theories and techniques derived from the study of sport psychology can provide the winning edge for athletes and athletic teams. In this text, you will learn many of the psychological theories and techniques that can make you a more effective teacher and/or coach. This does not mean, however, that you will be qualified to provide psychological services to coaches and athletes. It takes much more than one course in sport psychology to become a consulting sport psychologist. This is true despite the fact that at the present time there are limited licensing procedures in sport psychology; almost anyone can claim to be a sport psychologist. However, without certain minimal qualifications this would be unethical. When one considers the dangers involved in the inappropriate application of psychological theory, personality assessment, and intervention strategies, it is no wonder that many professionals are concerned.

The practice of sport psychology, whether by a coach or by a licensed psychologist, involves two diverse components. The first has to do with teaching, while the second is clinical in nature.

For example, the sport psychologist uses teaching principles to help an athlete learn how to use imagery and/or relaxation techniques effectively. A well-trained and informed coach or teacher should be able to give such service. However, when the sport psychologist is called upon to provide clinical services such as crisis counseling, psychotherapy, or psychological testing, it is important that that person be specifically trained and licensed. To do otherwise would be unethical and irresponsible.

Accreditation Issues in Sport Psychology

The issue of who is qualified to deliver sport psychology services has been addressed to some degree by AAASP with its certification program and by the USOC with its classification of three different kinds of sports psychologists. The issue still remains, however, as to who is qualified to prepare or train sport and exercise psychologists. Silva, Conroy, and Zizzi (1999) have argued that AAASP should provide leadership for a movement to accredit university sport psychology programs. They argue that **accreditation** is the only way to ensure quality and consistency of academic training. Students graduating from accredited programs would be prepared to become certified AAASP consultants. Arguments in favor of accreditation are bolstered by research that shows that of 79 programs listed in the fifth edition of the *Directory of Graduate Programs in Applied Sport Psychology* (see the AAASP Web site), only 27 percent offer coursework in all of the 12 different content areas mandated by AAASP for certification (Van Raalte et al., 2000).

In response to arguments in favor of accreditation, Hale and Dannish (1999) respond that the issue of accreditation is premature and naive relative to the complex issues involved. They point out that unless an academic program is viewed as "critical" to the mission of a university, the university will be reluctant to pay the cost of accreditation.

Second, they point out that accreditation would certainly raise the issue of who is qualified to call himself or herself a "psychologist." The APA and departments of psychology would resist accreditation of programs that produce sport psychologists who are not licensable as psychologists. Third, the debate over accreditation standards within, AAASP would be costly, from both a monetary and an emotional perspective. Finally, they argue that the impact of accreditation upon university programs would be to reduce academic freedom and program flexibility. While it is true that most programs in sport psychology continue to be in departments of physical education (e.g., kinesiology, exercise and sport science, etc.), the trend is moving slowly toward having departments of psychology, and particularly counseling psychology, provide training in sport psychology. It would be difficult for faculty from such diverse program areas to agree upon accreditation standards that they could take back and sell to their university deans and department chairs.

Multicultural Issues That Relate to Race

In this section we talk first about why race is an issue in sport psychology, and then about different multicultural training models that can be developed. In a subsequent section we will address multicultural issues related to gender, but in this section the focus is upon racial issues. In the broad sense, multicultural issues go well beyond race to include the concepts of **diversity** and **inclusiveness** (Sue & Sue, 1999). Diversity implies that people from diverse cultural background are represented in any group; inclusiveness implies that individuals are not excluded from a group because of their race, ethnic background, gender, sexual orientation, or religion. Sport psychology clients include individuals of different races, different cultures, different sexual orientations, and they have different ways of thinking about sport and the world we live in.

The Issue of Race in Applied Sport Psychology

An important goal of applied sport psychology should be to attract into the field more individuals from different races. This is important because the vast majority of sport psychologists are Caucasians from a European background, while many college and professional athletes are African American blacks (Kontos & Breland-Noble, 2002). This not to say, however, that a white sport psychologist cannot provide excellent services to black or non-white athletes. Until more African Americans and members of other ethnic groups enter the discipline of sport psychology, those who are Caucasian must focus upon understanding and accepting cultural differences. Butryn (2002) addresses this difficult issue by reporting on a life history interview with a white male sport psychologist consultant and a male African American athlete, in which they discussed racial awareness and the notion of **white privilege** in North America, and particularly in the United States. Butryn argues that it is not enough to be "color blind." The white sport psychologist must also come to recognize the fact that he is privileged simply by having been born white. Butryn insists, "White people carry with them a host of unearned, largely unconscious privileges, which are conferred upon them simply because they were born with a white skin" (2002, p. 318). He goes on: ". . . white people may not recognize that the way whiteness is represented in the consciousness of many black people are [is] profoundly negative and intimately connected with the systematic and destructive oppression of African-Americans by white people throughout history" (p. 318).

What is the white sport psychologist to do? One cannot stop being white, but one can come to recognize why resentment and distrust may exist between white consultant and black athlete. Furthermore, it is important to recognize the difference between **race thinking,** which is not racist, and **racist thinking,** which is. For a white sport psychologist to work with a black athlete, she must engage in race thinking. A failure to engage in race thinking is illustrated in a study reported by Ram, Stareck, and Johnson (2004). In this study, the researchers reviewed 982 articles published in *The Sport Psychologist, Journal of Applied Sport Psychology,* and the *Journal of Sport & Exercise Psychology* from 1987 to 2000 inclusive, relative to reference to race/ethnicity or sexual orientation. Results of the study showed that only 20 percent made reference in any way to race/ethnicity, while only 2 percent made substantive reference to sexual orientation. The results were even worse relative to sexual orientation, where only 12 articles out of 982 made any reference at all to sexual orientation issues.

In a thoughtful article, Kontos and Breland-Noble (2002) discuss the meaning of **cultural competence** and the ways a person becomes culturally competent. Cultural competence means that the coach or sport psychologist understands his client's racial identity, his own racial identity, and the role that race and cultural ethnicity play in the athlete/consultant relationship. The distinction between acculturation and enculturation is made. An individual is encultured, or experiences **enculturation,** simply by being born and raised in a particular group or culture. Conversely, **acculturation** implies learning to look at the world through a multicultural lens. It involves assimilation, truly understanding the culture of other ethnic groups, developing a world view of multiculturalism, and focusing upon the individual and not the group.

Multicultural Training in Sport Psychology

An accreditation issue that must be addressed, either formally or informally, is the issue of **multicultural training.** Graduates of sport psychology programs should be adequately trained in issues that relate to culture and race. According to Martens, Mobley, and Zizzi (2000), multicultural counseling is defined as counseling that takes place among individuals from different cultural/racial backgrounds.

Sports competition brings out the best in athletes, regardless of racial background. Courtesy University of Missouri–Columbia Sports Information.

Multicultural training of sport psychology students should be provided in four domains. First, students should experience a heightened awareness of and sensitivity to cultural groups different from their own. Second, they should gain knowledge about people who belong to cultures different from their own. Third, students should learn helping and intervention skills through the process of role playing and simulated interaction. Finally, each prospective graduate should experience a supervised practicum to gain hands-on experience working with members of a different culture or race.

According to census reports, approximately 29 percent of all people in the United States belong to racial and/or ethnic minorities. Yet, in some National Collegiate Athletic Association sports, the proportion of racial minorities is much greater than 29 percent. For example, in men's basketball, it is estimated to be as high as 68 percent; in football, 57 percent; and in women's basketball, 43 percent. Contrast this to the fact that most sport psychologists are white, and you see a clear need for multicultural training. Martens et al. identified two basic strategies for addressing the cultural disparity between athletes and applied sport psychologists. The **universalistic model** endorses the concept of teaching prospective sport psychologists cultural sensitivity and how to be culturally competent. In the absence of more minority sport psychologists, this is the model that must be aggressively promoted. The **cultural compatibility model** proposes to address multicultural issues by matching the background of the counseling sport psychologist with that of the athlete. Given an increase in the number of minority sport psychologists, a combination of the two models would seem to be most appropriate. If sport psychologists are truly sensitive and educated relative to racial/cultural issues, it should not matter what race or culture the athlete and psychologist belong to.

A number of different multicultural training designs may be implemented. Four different designs are listed in table 1.3. They range from the least preferred design (workshop) to the most preferred (integrated model). Where there is no formal course or concentration for teaching multicultural issues, then workshops may be organized and provided. While a workshop is better than no training at all, this method of delivery does not assure that participants gain a desired level of

| 1.1 | CONCEPT & APPLICATION |

CONCEPT   It is the responsibility of the coach and team leaders to foster multiculturalism in sport teams with respect to accepting diversity and being inclusive when it comes to individuals from different racial and ethnic backgrounds.

APPLICATION   Acculturation must take place among the athletes and between athletes and coaches. This means that team members learn to look at the world through a multicultural lens. They do this by understanding themselves first, and then taking the time to learn and understand the cultures that other teammates belong to.

TABLE 1.3 | Multicultural Training Designs in Sport Psychology

Design	Design Characteristics
1. Workshop Model	One- or two-day workshops are provided as needed.
2. Separate Course Model	Free-standing semester-long course on multicultural issues is provided.
3. Area of Concentration	Several free-standing courses and experiences are provided as part of a program concentration.
4. Integrated Model	Multicultural training is provided through all of the above, as well as integrated within each course in the curriculum.

knowledge and sensitivity to issues. A separate semester-long course dedicated to multicultural issues would be much more likely to successfully enhance cultural sensitivity. An even better approach would be to provide students with an area of concentration that focuses upon different aspects of multicultural issues. Finally, the integrated model endorses the concept that multicultural issues be addressed in all courses within the sport psychology curriculum. In addition, the integrated model would use workshops, dedicated courses, and the area of concentration concept to make sure that all sport psychology students were thoroughly immersed in multicultural issues.

Multicultural Issues That Relate to Gender

In the previous section of this chapter, we talked about multicultural issues in sport psychology that relate to race. In this section we turn our attention to multicultural issues in sport that relate to gender and to sexual orientation within gender.

Gender and Feminist Issues in Sport Psychology

As pointed out by Oglesby (2001), women have been largely overlooked and unrecognized in any historical discussion of the development of sport psychology in North America. As defined by Bell (2000), **feminism** is "a movement to end sexism, sexist exploitation, and oppression" (p. viii). Leaving the contribution of women out of a historical description of the development of sport psychology in North America would be an example of unintentional **sexism.** Volume 15 (issue 4) of the 2001 edition of *The Sport Psychologist* is edited by Diane Gill and is dedicated to feminism in sport psychology. Gill (2001) identifies four themes drawn from feminist theory and sport psychologist scholarship:

1. Gender is relational rather than categorical.
2. Gender is inextricably linked with race/ethnicity, class and other social identities.
3. Gender and cultural relations involve power and privilege.
4. Feminism demands action.

Consistent with Diane Gill's item number two, Hall (2001) makes the inextricable connection between gender and race in this way:

> When we discuss women or feminism, the focus is on white women. Conversely, when we discuss athletes of color, the focus is on males, especially African-American males. As a result, women of color frequently feel isolated and are treated as if their race and/or gender are non-issues, or at the very least have little relevance to these respective groups. Consequently, women of color frequently feel alienated in the sport arena and in the sport psychology literature. (p. 391)

Past research and practice in sport psychology focused almost exclusively on a masculine perspective and utilized male participants to a large degree. This has changed a great deal in recent years, as university human subject committees require justification for excluding either male or female participants. The feminist movement has served as an effective reminder to researchers and practitioners to avoid sexist practices or sexist language in all aspects of sport psychology. When conducting research, sport psychologists can (a) include males and females, people of color, and people with diverse sexual orientations as participants; (b) include gender and race as categorical variables; (c) include references that address race and gender; and (d) include substantive discussions related to race and gender (Ram et al., 2004). We will return to this important topic throughout the text, as gender issues are woven into the fabric of every chapter in the book.

Sexual Orientation in Sport Psychology

The multicultural concepts of diversity and inclusiveness extend to the inclusion of individuals who have a **sexual orientation** that may be different from the traditional heterosexual one. By definition, males who embrace a homosexual sexual orientation describe themselves as **gay,** while women who embrace a homosexual sexual orientation describe themselves as **lesbian.** For an individual to describe him or herself as gay or lesbian is to indicate sexual attraction to members of his or her own sex. Thus, to be **heterosexual** is to be sexually attracted to members of the opposite sex, while to be **homosexual** is to be sexually attracted to members of the same sex. To be inclusive is to accept both heterosexual and homosexual individuals into a group.

Homophobic behavior is defined as harmful behavior directed at individuals who are believed to be gay or lesbian, or such behavior directed at organizations or groups that support gay and lesbian people (Morrow & Gill, 2003). Examples of homophobic behavior include, but are not limited to, name calling, physical assaults, and destruction of property. As it relates to gay and lesbian people, inclusive behavior is behavior that is accepting and non-prejudiced. **Homophobia** is defined as irrational fear and intolerance of homosexual individuals or organization (Roper, 2002). While not as directly harmful as homophobic behavior, **heterosexist behavior** is more insidious. Heterosexist behavior is behavior that implies that everyone in a group is heterosexual, or that everyone lives in a traditional family or is attracted to someone of the opposite sex (Morrow & Gill, 2003). In many ways, this is more damaging than homophobic behavior, because it marginalizes people and forces them into thinking of themselves as "other" (Krane, 2001).

In a study involving a sample of high school physical education teachers and college students asked to reflect on the high school experience, Morrow and Gill (2003) reported that (a) homophobic behavior is as common in physical education

| 1.2 | CONCEPT & APPLICATION |

CONCEPT   It is the responsibility of the coach and team leaders to foster multiculturalism in sports teams with respect to being accepting of homosexual individuals and being inclusive when it comes to sexual orientation.

APPLICATION   Coaches and team leaders can cultivate multiculturalism with respect to different sexual orientations by educating athletes about homophobic behavior and about what it means to practice heterosexist behavior. Once this is accomplished, the focus should be upon treating every athlete with respect and dignity and upon valuing the athletic abilities of each athlete, regardless of sexual orientation.

classes as in the wider school population; (b) homophobic and heterosexist behavior is a regular part of the secondary school experience; and (c) despite the high level of homophobic and heterosexist behavior that exists, few teachers or students regularly confront the behaviors. The researchers reported that the most dramatic finding of the study was the great disparity between teachers' perception and students' perception of the creation of a psychologically "safe environment" for the students by the teachers.

Research also shows that the media treat men and women differently when it comes to athletic accomplishments and athletic prowess (Knight & Giuliano, 2003). Male athletes are perceived and assumed by the media to be heterosexual. Consequently, the media don't focus upon sexual orientation, but move on immediately to the athletic achievements of the male athletes. However, with female athletes, the media has a tendency to "heterosexualize" women by emphasizing their relationships with men. An emphasis on a woman's athletic prowess is secondary to an emphasis on her sexual orientation. This occurs because the media is anxious to overcome the image of homosexuality among women athletes. This research further showed that male and female athletes described as clearly heterosexual were perceived more favorably than athletes with an ambiguous sexual orientation.

Another concern related to sexual orientation is the rising number of male coaches who date, fall in love with, and sometimes marry the female athletes they train. This is a practice that has the potential of disrupting careers, interfering with performance, and leaving teammates angry and disillusioned (Wahl, Wertheim & Dohrmann, 2001). Relative to this practice, Mary Jo Jane, Director of the Tucker Center for Research on Girls and Women in Sport at the University of Minnesota, made the following observation: "But because of homophobia in and around women's sports, if it is a lesbian relationship, the negative perception is exacerbated—it quietly moves from the arena of bad judgment to the arena of deviance and immorality" (quoted in Wahl et al., 2001, p. 63).

Finally, we conclude this section with information derived from a qualitative investigation reported by Krane and Barber (2005). The daily identity tension of 13 lesbian college coaches was investigated. Results revealed that lesbian coaches are constantly negotiating with themselves about their social identities associated with being coaches of young women and being lesbians. They are confronted on the one hand, with the need to fight against homophobia; on the other hand with the need to protect their professional careers (i.e., remain silent). Results also show that these lesbian coaches did not passively accept their fate, but rather they fought against the prevailing heterosexist atmosphere and worked to create positive social change.

Summary

Sport and exercise psychology is the study of the effect of psychological and emotional factors on sport and exercise performance, and the effect of sport and exercise involvement on psychological and emotional factors.

Norman Triplett (1897) is cited as the first individual to conduct sport psychology research. Triplett analyzed the performance of cyclists under conditions of social facilitation. Coleman Griffith established the first sport psychology laboratory at the University of Illinois in 1925. In recent years, numerous scholarly societies have emerged to represent the discipline and application of sport psychology. In the United States, the most prominent are the North American Society for the Psychology of Sport and Physical Activity (NASPSPA) and the Association for the Advancement of Applied Sport Psychology (AAASP).

The issue of who is qualified to provide sport psychology services has been addressed by numerous professional organizations. The United States Olympic Committee developed the Sport Psychology Registry to identify individuals qualified to work with Olympic athletes. The AAASP developed procedures whereby qualified individuals could earn the title "Certified Consultant, AAASP." The roles and functions of the sport psychologist fall into the categories of clinical/counseling services, education, and research.

Concern is emerging over ethics associated with providing applied sport psychology services. In this regard the APA and AAASP have published ethical guidelines for providing services to clients. The AAASP guidelines will be discussed in a later chapter on psychological skills training.

As sport psychologists deal with the issue of certification and ethics, some have called for AAASP to spearhead a movement to accredit university sport psychology programs. Pros and cons of this proposed initiative were discussed.

Multiculturalism as it relates to both race and gender was discussed. Multiculturalism includes the concepts of diversity and inclusiveness relative to being accepting of people of different race, gender, and sexual orientation. The distinction between race thinking and racist thinking was made. Individuals are encultured merely by being born and raised in a particular group or culture. Acculturation, however, implies learning to look at the world through a multicultural lens.

An accreditation issue that must be addressed, either formally or informally, is multicultural training. Students preparing for careers as applied sport psychologists should receive training in multicultural counseling. Two models for addressing multicultural issues in practice include the universalistic model and the cultural compatibility model.

In the context of multiculturalism, both feminism and sexual orientation were discussed. Feminism is a movement to end sexism, sexist exploitation, and oppression. Heterosexual individuals are attracted to members of the opposite sex, while homosexual individuals are attracted to members of the same sex. Homophobic behavior was described as harmful behavior directed at individuals or groups who are believed to be gay or lesbian. Heterosexist behavior is behavior that implies that everyone in a group or team is heterosexual.

18   Part One   Understanding Sport Psychology

Critical Thought Questions

1. Considering the roles that physical education (kinesiology) and psychology have played in the development of sport psychology, what roles do you feel these two groups should play in defining sport psychology for the future?

2. Do you think that an individual trained in the exercise and sport sciences (physical education) should be able to use the word "psychologist" to describe what he does in sport? How do you think this issue is addressed within AAASP?

3. Do you think AAASP should champion a move to accredit university sport psychology

programs? If so, how do you think it should proceed?

4. Do you think multicultural training can help members of diverse teams be more accepting of one another? In your opinion, what must be done to accomplish this goal?

5. What is your opinion of the two approaches for providing multicultural training to minority athletes (universal versus cultural compatibility)?

6. What is the root cause of homophobia on sport teams? What steps must be taken to overcome homophobia and heterosexism?

Glossary

accreditation A process in which a professional organization establishes guidelines and then determines whether programs seeking accreditation meet the guidelines.

acculturation Learning to look at the world through a multicultural lens.

clinical/counseling sport psychologist The type of sport psychologist that is required to be licensed and have specialized training in clinical and/or counseling psychology.

cultural compatibility model A consulting model in which the racial/ethnic identity of the athlete is matched with the racial/ethnic identity of the sport psychology consultant.

cultural competence An individual is understanding of her own racial identity, other people's racial identities, and the role that race and cultural ethnicity play in a relationship.

diversity The representation in a group of people from diverse cultural backgrounds.

educational sport psychologist The type of sport psychologist that uses education as a medium for teaching athletes and coaches correct principles associated with sport psychology.

enculturation Values and attitudes one receives by being born into a specific culture.

feminism A movement to end sexism, sexist exploitation, and oppression.

gay A male who embraces a homosexual sexual orientation.

Griffith, Coleman The father of sport psychology in North America. In 1925, while at the University of Illinois, he established the first sport psychology laboratory in North America.

heterosexist behavior Behavior that implies that everyone in a group is heterosexual, or that everyone lives in a traditional family or is attracted to individuals of the opposite sex.

heterosexual Sexually attracted to members of the opposite sex.

homophobia Irrational fear and intolerance of homosexual individuals or groups.

homophobic behavior Harmful behavior directed at individuals who are believed to be gay or lesbian, or at groups that support such individuals.

homosexual Sexually attracted to members of the same sex.

inclusiveness Individuals are not excluded from a group because of their race, ethnic background, gender, sexual orientation, or religion.

lesbian A female who embraces a homosexual sexual orientation.

Martens, Rainer A former professor of sport psychology at the University of Illinois, identified in this book as the "father of modern sport psychology."

multicultural training Training that prepares sport psychologists to counsel athletes from different cultural/racial backgrounds.

Ogilvie, Bruce The father of applied sport psychology in North America.

race thinking Thinking about race issues in a nonracist way.

racist thinking Thinking in ways that discriminate against people of other races or cultures.

research sport psychologist The type of sport psychologist who is mainly interested in research

and in expanding the knowledge base in sport psychology.

sexism Intentionally or unintentionally overlooking or minimizing the contributions of the opposite sex, and/or saying or implying derogatory things about the opposite sex.

sexual orientation The ways individuals come to feel about their own sexuality, whether heterosexual, homosexual, or transsexual in nature.

Sport Psychology Registry A list of individuals in the area of psychology of sport who are qualified to work with Olympic athletes. The registry was initiated by the USOC.

Triplett, Norman The person who conducted and published what appears to be the first clear example of sport psychology research in North America.

universalistic model A consulting model in which athlete and sport psychologist are not matched according to cultural background; rather, the sport psychologist is trained in multicultural sensitivity issues.

USOC United States Olympic Committee.

white privilege The condition of being privileged simply by being white, compared to those who are not white.

CHAPTER 11

CHAPTER OUTLINE

1   Psychodynamic Perspectives

2   Humanistic Perspectives

3   Trait Perspectives

4   Personological and Life Story Perspectives

5   Social Cognitive Perspectives

6   Personality Assessment

7   Personality and Health and Wellness

PERSONALITY

Experiencing Psychology

WHAT MAKES YOU YOU?

You probably had a parent or grade-school teacher tell you that people are like snow-flakes, with no two exactly alike. They might have said something like, "You're special just because you are you." What makes you a snowflake and not a boring ice cube? How are you unique?

Fans of procedural crime dramas such as *CSI* and *Law & Order* know that one thing that can unmistakably identify a person is fingerprints. Left at a crime scene, a fingerprint (if it is in the law enforcement database) can catch the criminal every time, because fingerprints are unique. In the 100 years that fingerprints have been collected and with nearly 100 million fingers printed, no two people have had the same fingerprints. Still, you may be surprised that identical twins, who are genetically identical, do not have the same fingerprints. The reason they do not is that fingerprints are determined not simply by genes but also by prenatal environmental factors, so that even individuals with the same DNA do not have identical fingerprints.

The irises of our eyes are another physical characteristic that distinguishes us from all other people. Unlike fingerprints, irises cannot be worn down (or filed off, if you are thinking like a hit man)—they are stable and unique throughout a person's life. And irises have six times the number of distinguishing characteristics that fingerprints have.

Of course, the person who told you that you are unique was not talking about your fingerprints or irises but rather about the person that you are, with all of your personal characteristics—traits, abilities, beliefs, goals, and experiences. And that is what personality psychology, the topic of this chapter, is all about. To paraphrase Henry Murray, a personality psychologist, "All of us are in some ways like all other people, in some ways like some other people, and in some ways like no other person." By that, Murray meant that although we share certain attributes with all other human beings (such as our physical anatomy), and we share certain attributes with some others (for example, our family members and people who are the same age as we are), in other ways we are truly unique. Personality psychology explores the psychological attributes that make us who we are—the unified and enduring core characteristics that account for our existence as the same person throughout our lives. In short, personality psychology is the scientific study of what makes you you.

Personality psychologists can be found in nearly every subdiscipline of psychology, including clinical, developmental, social, and cognitive. Because the main topic of personality psychology is the person, its concerns intersect with many of the key concerns for *all* of psychology, including human development; characteristics that are likely to remain stable or change over the life span; effects of the social context, including culture; differences from individual to individual with respect to coping; and mental and physical illness.

Preview

In this chapter, we survey the classic theories of personality as well as more contemporary research in the field. We examine the nature of the person–situation debate, briefly consider how personality is assessed, and finally take stock of the central role of personality in health and wellness.

1 Psychodynamic Perspectives

Define personality and summarize the psychodynamic perspectives.

personality A pattern of enduring, distinctive thoughts, emotions, and behaviors that characterize the way an individual adapts to the world.

psychodynamic perspectives Views of personality as primarily unconscious (that is, beyond awareness) and as developing in stages. Most psychoanalytic perspectives emphasize that early experiences with parents play a role in sculpting personality.

Personality is a concept that is familiar to everyone but difficult to define. In this chapter, we define **personality** as a pattern of enduring, distinctive thoughts, emotions, and behaviors that characterize the way an individual adapts to the world.

Have you ever had a friend rave about a movie to you—and then, while sitting in the theater, you thought, "Am I seeing the *same* film?" Personality theorists and researchers ask why individuals react to the same situation in different ways, and they come up with different answers. Just as you and your friend might have differing takes on a movie, personality psychologists answer the question of what personality is in differing ways. Some emphasize traits, others highlight motivation, and still others focus on patterns of beliefs and thoughts. One common question that is often addressed in personality research is when and if personality characteristics cause behavior.

Psychodynamic perspectives view personality as being primarily unconscious (that is, beyond awareness) and as developing in stages. Most psychodynamic perspectives emphasize that early experiences with parents play an important role in sculpting the individual's personality. Psychodynamic theorists believe that behavior is merely a surface characteristic and that to truly understand someone's personality we have to explore the symbolic meanings of behavior and the deep inner workings of the mind (Hergenhahn & Olson, 2007). These characteristics were sketched by the architect of psychoanalytic theory, Sigmund Freud. As you learned in Chapter 1, some psychodynamic theorists who followed Freud have diverged from his theory but still embrace his core ideas.

Freud's Psychoanalytic Theory

Sigmund Freud (1917), one of the most influential thinkers of the twentieth century, was born in Austria in 1856 and died in London at the age of 83. Freud spent most of his life in Vienna, but he left the city near the end of his career to escape the Holocaust. A medical doctor who specialized in neurology, Freud developed his ideas about personality from his work with psychiatric patients.

Freud was extremely ambitious and wanted to change the world. And we can see that he largely succeeded in that goal by imagining ourselves in the following situation. In a romantic moment when you are kissing your significant other, imagine hearing your partner say, "I love you so much, Chris." But there is a problem: Chris is not your name; it is the name of your partner's previous love interest. How might you respond? Despite your loved one's protestations that it was an honest mistake, a complete accident, you know it must "mean

Sigmund Freud (1856–1939) *Freud's theories have strongly influenced how people in Western cultures view themselves and their world.*

something." *Freudian slips* are misstatements that Freud believed reveal unconscious thoughts. Freud is the only psychologist whose name has become a common part of our everyday language.

Freud has had such a phenomenal impact that just about everyone has an opinion about him, even those who have never studied his work. Most people assume that Freud thought everything was about sex. And that is true, except by *sex* Freud did not mean sexual activity in the usual sense. Freud defined sex as organ pleasure. Anything that was pleasurable was sex, according to Freud. So, if you have ever heard someone describe the joys of a double chocolate fudge cake as "better than sex," you might keep in mind that in Freud's view, eating that double chocolate fudge cake *is* sex.

Freud developed *psychoanalysis*, his approach to personality, out of his work with patients who were suffering from hysteria. *Hysteria* refers to physical symptoms that have no physical cause. For instance, a person might be unable to see, even with perfectly healthy eyes, or unable to walk, despite having no physical injury. During Freud's time, many young women suffered from physical problems that could not be explained through actual physical illness. Freud came to understand that hysterical symptoms were caused by unconscious psychological conflicts. These conflicts were generally centered on experiences in which the person wanted to do one thing but was forced to do another through the social pressures of Victorian society. One of Freud's patients, Fraulein Elisabeth Von R., suffered from horrible pains in her legs that prevented her from walking. Through analysis, Freud discovered that Fraulein Elisabeth had had a number of experiences in which she wanted nothing more than to take a walk, but she was prevented from doing so by her duty to her ill father.

TV and movie portrayals of hysterical symptoms typically culminate with a psychologist's unlocking the unconscious secret of the person's problem. On a soap opera, a young heroine's problems may be solved in one climactic episode: It turns out that she was hysterically blind because she saw her father cheating on her mother with another woman. Importantly, Freud believed that hysterical symptoms were *overdetermined*—that is, they had a multitude of causes in the unconscious. Unlocking one unconscious traumatic memory might work for Hollywood, but it does not represent Freud very well. Eventually, Freud came to use hysterical symptoms as his metaphor for understanding dreams, slips of the tongue, and ultimately all human behavior. Everything we do, according to Freud, has a multitude of unconscious causes.

On the basis of his work analyzing patients (as well as himself), Freud developed his model of the human personality. He described personality as being like an iceberg, existing mostly below the level of awareness, just as the massive part of an iceberg lies beneath the surface of the water. Figure 11.1 illustrates this analogy and how extensive the unconscious part of our mind is, in Freud's view.

Personality's Structures   Notice that Figure 11.1 shows the iceberg divided into three segments. The reason is that Freud (1917) believed that personality has three structures, which he called the id, the ego, and the superego. These Latin labels may not capture Freud's true meaning in naming the structures. The id is literally the "it," the ego is the "I," and the superego is the "above-I."

The **id,** that part of you that Freud called an "it," consists of unconscious drives and is the individual's reservoir of psychic energy. In Freud's view, the id has no contact with reality. The id works according to the *pleasure principle,* the Freudian concept that the id always seeks pleasure and avoids pain.

It would be a dangerous and scary world, however, if our personalities were all id. As young children mature, they learn they cannot slug other

"Good morning beheaded—uh, I mean beloved."
© The New Yorker Collection 1979 Dana Fradon from cartoonbank.com. All Rights Reserved.

id The Freudian structure of personality that consists of unconscious drives and is the individual's reservoir of psychic energy.

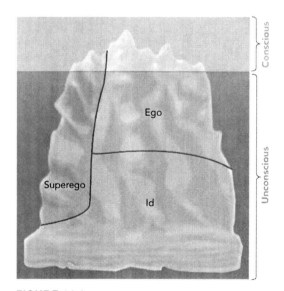

FIGURE 11.1

The Conscious and Unconscious Mind: The Iceberg Analogy The analogy of the conscious and unconscious mind to an iceberg is often used to illustrate how much of the mind is unconscious in Freud's theory. The conscious mind is the part of the iceberg above water; the unconscious mind, the part below water. Notice that the id is totally unconscious, whereas the ego and superego can operate at either the conscious or the unconscious level.

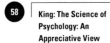
ego The Freudian structure of personality that deals with the demands of reality.

superego The Freudian structure of personality that harshly judges the morality of our behavior.

defense mechanisms The ego's protective methods for reducing anxiety by unconsciously distorting reality.

children in the face. They also learn that they have to use the toilet instead of their diaper. As children experience the demands and constraints of reality, a new structure of personality is formed—the **ego,** the Freudian structure of personality that deals with the demands of reality. According to Freud, the ego abides by the *reality principle.* It tries to bring the individual pleasure within the norms of society. Most of us accept the obstacles to satisfaction that exist in our world. We recognize that our sexual and aggressive impulses cannot go unrestrained. Few of us are voracious gluttons, sexual wantons, or cold-blooded killers. The ego helps us to test reality, to see how far we can go without getting into trouble and hurting ourselves. Whereas the id is completely unconscious, the ego is partly conscious. It houses our higher mental functions—reasoning, problem solving, and decision making, for example. For this reason, the ego is referred to as the executive branch of the personality; like an executive in a company, it makes the rational decisions that help the company succeed.

The id and ego do not consider whether something is right or wrong. The **superego** is the harsh internal judge of our behavior. The superego is reflected in what we often call "conscience" and evaluates the morality of our behavior. Like the id, the superego does not consider reality; it considers only whether the id's impulses can be satisfied in acceptable moral terms.

Both the id and the superego make life rough for the ego. Your ego might say, "I will have sex only occasionally and be sure to use an effective form of birth control." But your id says, "I want to be satisfied; sex feels so good." And your superego says, "I feel guilty about having sex at all."

Defense Mechanisms The ego calls on a number of strategies to resolve the conflict among its demands for reality, the wishes of the id, and the constraints of the superego. These **defense mechanisms** reduce anxiety by unconsciously distorting reality. For example, when the ego blocks the pleasurable pursuits of the id, a person feels anxiety, which the ego resolves by means of defense mechanisms. Figure 11.2 describes several defense

FIGURE 11.2

Defense Mechanisms Defense mechanisms reduce anxiety in various ways, in all instances by distorting reality.

Defense Mechanism	How It Works	Example
Repression	The master defense mechanism; the ego pushes unacceptable impulses out of awareness, back into the unconscious mind.	A young girl was sexually abused by her uncle. As an adult, she can't remember anything about the traumatic experience.
Rationalization	The ego replaces a less acceptable motive with a more acceptable one.	A college student does not get into the fraternity of his choice. He says that if he had tried harder he could have gotten in.
Displacement	The ego shifts feelings toward an unacceptable object to another, more acceptable object.	A woman can't take her anger out on her boss so she goes home and takes it out on her husband.
Sublimation	The ego replaces an unacceptable impulse with a socially acceptable one.	A man with strong sexual urges becomes an artist who paints nudes.
Projection	The ego attributes personal shortcomings, problems, and faults to others.	A man who has a strong desire to have an extramarital affair accuses his wife of flirting with other men.
Reaction Formation	The ego transforms an unacceptable motive into its opposite.	A woman who fears her sexual urges becomes a religious zealot.
Denial	The ego refuses to acknowledge anxiety-producing realities.	A man won't acknowledge that he has cancer even though a team of doctors has diagnosed his cancer.
Regression	The ego seeks the security of an earlier developmental period in the face of stress.	A woman returns home to mother every time she and her husband have a big argument.

mechanisms, many of which were introduced and developed by Freud's daughter Anna. All of them work to protect the ego and reduce anxiety.

Repression is the most powerful and pervasive defense mechanism, according to Freud; it pushes unacceptable id impulses out of awareness and back into the unconscious mind. Repression is the foundation for all of the psychological defense mechanisms, the goal of which is to push, or *repress,* threatening impulses out of awareness. Freud said that our early childhood experiences, many of which he believed were sexually laden, are too threatening and stressful for us to deal with consciously, so we reduce the anxiety of childhood conflict through repression.

Two final points about defense mechanisms need to be understood. First, they are unconscious; we are not aware that we are calling on them. Second, when used in moderation or on a temporary basis, defense mechanisms are not necessarily unhealthy. For example, the defense mechanism of *denial* can help a person cope with impending death, and the defense mechanism of *sublimation* means transforming our unconscious impulses into activities that benefit society. From Freud's perspective, defense mechanisms are a vital way for the ego to survive in a stressful world.

Psychosexual Stages of Personality Development   As Freud listened to his patients, he became convinced that their personalities were the result of experiences early in life. Freud believed that we go through universal stages of personality development and that at each stage of development we experience sex or pleasure in one part of the body more than in others. *Erogenous zones,* according to Freud, are parts of the body that have especially strong pleasure-giving qualities at particular stages of development. Freud thought that our adult personality is determined by the way we resolve conflicts between these early sources of pleasure—the mouth, the anus, and then the genitals—and the demands of reality.

- *Oral stage (first 18 months):* The infant's pleasure centers on the mouth. Chewing, sucking, and biting are chief sources of pleasure that reduce tension in the infant.
- *Anal stage (18 to 36 months):* During a time when most children are experiencing toilet training, the child's greatest pleasure involves the anus and urethra and the eliminative functions associated with them. Freud recognized that there is pleasure in "going" and "holding it" as well as in the experience of control over one's parents in deciding when to do either.
- *Phallic stage (3 to 6 years):* The name of Freud's third stage comes from the Latin word *phallus,* which means "penis." Pleasure focuses on the genitals as the child discovers that self-stimulation is enjoyable. In Freud's view, the phallic stage has a special importance in personality development because it triggers the Oedipus complex. This name comes from the Greek tragedy in which Oedipus unwittingly killed his father and married his mother. The **Oedipus complex** is the boy's intense desire to replace his father and enjoy the affections of his mother. Eventually, the boy recognizes that his father might punish him for these incestuous wishes, specifically by cutting off the boy's penis. *Castration anxiety* refers to the boy's intense fear of being mutilated by his father. To reduce this conflict, the boy identifies with his father, striving to be like him. The intense castration anxiety is repressed and serves as the foundation for the superego.

In the phallic stage, Freud recognized that there were differences between boys and girls. Freud believed that the lack of castration anxiety in girls explains why women never truly develop a superego in the same sense that men do. This physical fact explained why (in Freud's view) women are morally inferior to men and why women were "second-class citizens" in Victorian society. Freud's view of the phallic stage is where the notion that "anatomy is destiny" originates.

Freud believed that girls experience "castration completed," resulting in penis envy—the intense desire to obtain a penis by eventually marrying and bearing a son.

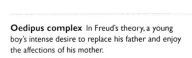

Oedipus complex In Freud's theory, a young boy's intense desire to replace his father and enjoy the affections of his mother.

Stage	Adult Extensions (Fixations)	Sublimations	Reaction Formations
Oral	Smoking, eating, kissing, oral hygiene, drinking, chewing gum	Seeking knowledge, humor, wit, sarcasm, being a food or wine expert	Speech purist, food faddist, prohibitionist, dislike of milk
Anal	Notable interest in one's bowel movements, love of bathroom humor, extreme messiness	Interest in painting or sculpture, being overly giving, great interest in statistics	Extreme disgust with feces, fear of dirt, prudishness, irritability
Phallic	Heavy reliance on masturbation, flirtatiousness, expressions of virility	Interest in poetry, love of love, interest in acting, striving for success	Puritanical attitude toward sex, excessive modesty

FIGURE 11.3

Defense Mechanisms and Freudian Stages If a person is fixated at a psychosexual stage, the fixation can color his or her personality in many ways, including the defense mechanisms the person might use to cope with anxiety.

Freud felt that women were somewhat childlike in their development and that it was good that fathers and eventually husbands would guide them throughout their lives. He asserted that the only hope for the moral development of women was education. Notably, Freud was never satisfied with his own approach to the development of girls and women. He always allowed women to pursue careers in psychoanalysis, and many of his earliest followers were women.

- *Latency period (6 years to puberty):* This phase is not a developmental stage but rather a kind of psychic time-out or intermission. After the drama of the phallic stage, the child represses all interest in sexuality. Although we now consider these years extremely important to development, Freud felt that this was a time in which no real development occurred.

- *Genital stage (adolescence and adulthood):* The genital stage is the time of sexual reawakening; the source of sexual pleasure now becomes someone outside of the family. Freud believed that unresolved conflicts with parents reemerge during adolescence. But once these conflicts are resolved, the individual becomes capable of developing a mature love relationship and functioning independently as an adult. Even in the best case, however, Freud felt that human beings were inevitably subject to intense conflict. Everyone, he believed, no matter how healthy or well adjusted, still has an id pressing for expression.

Freud argued that the individual may become fixated at any of these stages of development if he or she is underindulged or overindulged at a stage. For example, a parent might wean a child too early, be too strict in toilet training, punish the child for masturbation, or "smother" the child with too much attention. *Fixation* is the psychoanalytic defense mechanism that occurs when the individual remains locked in an earlier developmental stage. The issues from the psychosexual stage can color all aspects of the person's adult personality. The construct of fixation thus explains how, according to Freud's view, childhood experiences can have an enormous impact on adult personality. Figure 11.3 illustrates possible links between adult personality characteristics and fixation at the oral, anal, and phallic stages.

Psychodynamic Critics and Revisionists

Because Freud was among the first theorists to explore personality, over time some of his ideas have needed updating and revision, and some have been tossed out altogether. In particular, Freud's critics have said that his ideas about sexuality, early experience, social factors, and the unconscious mind were misguided (Adler, 1927; Erikson, 1968; Fromm, 1947; Horney, 1945; Jung, 1917; Kohut, 1977; Rapaport, 1967; Sullivan, 1953). His critics stress the following points:

- Sexuality is not the pervasive force behind personality that Freud believed it to be. Nor is the Oedipus complex as universal as Freud believed. Freud's concepts were heavily influenced by the setting in which he lived and worked—turn-of-the-century Vienna, a society that was, compared with contemporary society, sexually repressed and paternalistic.

collective unconscious Jung's term for the impersonal, deepest layer of the unconscious mind, shared by all human beings because of their common ancestral past.

archetypes The name Jung gave to the emotionally laden ideas and images that have rich and symbolic meaning for all people.

King: The Science of
Psychology: An
Appreciative View

11. Personality

Text

© The McGraw–Hill
Companies, 2008

61

- The first 5 years of life are not as powerful in shaping adult personality as Freud thought; later experiences deserve more attention.

- The ego and conscious thought processes play more dominant roles in our personality than Freud gave them credit for; he claimed that we are forever captive to the instinctual, unconscious clutches of the id. Also, the ego has a separate line of development from the id, so achievement, thinking, and reasoning are not always tied to sexual impulses.

- Sociocultural factors are much more important than Freud believed. In stressing the id's dominance, Freud placed more emphasis on the biological basis of personality. More contemporary psychodynamic scholars have especially emphasized the interpersonal setting of the family and the role of early social relationships in personality development.

The theories of three dissenters and revisionists—Horney, Jung, and Adler—have been particularly influential in the development of psychodynamic theories, the successors to Freud's psychoanalytic theory.

Horney's Sociocultural Approach   Karen Horney (1885–1952) rejected the classical psychoanalytic concept that anatomy is destiny and cautioned that some of Freud's most popular ideas were only hypotheses. She insisted that these hypotheses be supported with observable data before being accepted as fact. She also argued that sociocultural influences on personality development should be considered.

Karen Horney (1885–1952) *Horney developed the first feminist criticism of Freud's theory. Horney's view emphasizes women's positive qualities and self-evaluation.*

Consider Freud's concept of penis envy, which attributed some of the behavior of his female patients to their repressed desire to have a penis. Horney pointed out that women might envy the penis not because of some neurotic tendencies, but because of the status in society that is bestowed on those who have one. Further, she suggested that both sexes envy the attributes of the other, with men coveting women's reproductive capacities (Gilman, 2001).

Horney also believed that the need for security, not for sex, is the prime motive in human existence. Horney reasoned that an individual whose needs for security are met should be able to develop his or her capacities to the fullest extent. She viewed psychological health as allowing the person to freely and spontaneously express his or her talents and abilities.

Jung's Analytical Theory   Freud's contemporary Carl Jung (1875–1961) had a different complaint about psychoanalytic theory. Jung shared Freud's interest in the unconscious, but he believed that Freud underplayed the unconscious mind's role in personality. In fact, Jung believed that the roots of personality go back to the dawn of human existence. The **collective unconscious** is the impersonal, deepest layer of the unconscious mind, shared by all human beings because of their common ancestral past. In Jung's theory, the experiences of a common past have made a deep, permanent impression on the human mind.

The collective unconscious is expressed through what Jung called **archetypes,** emotionally laden ideas and images that have rich and symbolic meaning for all people. Jung believed that these archetypes emerge in art, literature, religion, and dreams (Merchant, 2006; Roesler, 2006). He used archetypes to help people understand themselves (Urban, 2005).

Two common archetypes are the anima (woman) and animus (man). Jung believed each of us has a passive "feminine" side and an assertive "masculine" side. Another archetype, the mandala, a figure within a circle, has been used so often in art that Jung took it to represent the self (Figure 11.4). The persona is still another archetype; Jung thought that the persona represented the public mask that we all wear during social

Carl Jung (1875–1961) *Swiss psychoanalytic theorist Carl Jung developed the concepts of the collective unconscious and archetypes.*

FIGURE 11.4

The Mandala as an Archetype of the Self In his exploration of mythology, Carl Jung found that the self is often symbolized by a mandala, from the Sanskrit word for "circle." Jung believed that the mandala represents the self's unity.

414   CHAPTER 11   Personality

interactions. Jung believed that the persona was an essential archetype because it allows us always to keep some secret part of ourselves hidden from others.

Adler's Individual Psychology   Alfred Adler (1870–1937) was another of Freud's contemporaries. In Adler's **individual psychology,** people are motivated by purposes and goals—perfection, not pleasure, is the key motivator in human life. Unlike Freud, who believed in the overwhelming power of the unconscious mind, Adler argued that people have the ability to consciously monitor their lives. He also considered social factors more important than sexual motivation in shaping personality (Silverman & Corsini, 1984).

Adler thought that everyone strives for superiority by seeking to adapt, improve, and master the environment. Striving for superiority is our response to the uncomfortable feelings of inferiority we experience as infants and young children when we interact with bigger and more powerful people. *Compensation* is Adler's term for the individual's attempt to overcome imagined or real inferiorities or weaknesses by developing one's own abilities. Adler believed that compensation is normal, and he said that we often make up for a weakness in one ability by excelling in a different ability. For example, a mediocre student might compensate by excelling in athletics.

Evaluating the Pychodynamic Perspectives

Although psychodynamic theories have diverged from Freud's original psychoanalytic version, they do share some core principles:

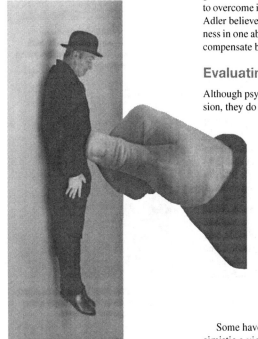

- Personality is determined both by current experiences and, as the original psychoanalytic theory proposed, by early life experiences.
- Personality can be better understood by examining it developmentally—as a series of stages that unfold with the individual's physical, cognitive, and socioemotional development.
- We mentally transform our experiences, giving them meaning that shapes our personality.
- The mind is not all consciousness; unconscious motives lie behind some of our puzzling behavior.
- The individual's inner world often conflicts with the outer demands of reality, creating anxiety that is not easy to resolve.
- Personality and adjustment—not just the experimental laboratory topics of sensation, perception, and learning—are rightful and important topics of psychological inquiry.

Some have criticized psychodynamic perspectives for presenting too negative and pessimistic a view of the person. For example, critics say, these perspectives place too much weight on early experiences within the family and their influence on personality and do not acknowledge that we retain the capacity for change and adaptation throughout our lives. Some psychologists believe moreover that Freud and Jung put too much faith in the unconscious mind's ability to control behavior. Others object that Freud overemphasized the importance of sexuality in understanding personality; we are not born into the world with only a bundle of sexual and aggressive instincts.

Some have argued, too, that psychoanalysis is not a theory that can be tested through empirical research. But in fact numerous empirical studies on concepts such as defense mechanisms and the unconscious have proved this criticism to be unfounded (Cramer, 2000; Jorgensen & Zachariae, 2006). Another version of this argument may be accurate, however. Although it is certainly possible to test hypotheses derived from psychoanalytic theory through research, the question remains whether psychoanalytically oriented individuals who believe strongly in Freud's ideas would be open to research results that call for serious changes in the theory.

In light of these criticisms, it may be hard to appreciate why Freud had and continues to have an impact on the field of personality and on psychology in general. It is useful to

individual psychology The term for Adler's approach, which views people as motivated by purposes and goals and as striving for perfection over pleasure.

keep in mind that Freud made a number of important contributions to psychology, including being the first to propose that childhood is important to later functioning, that development might be understood in terms of stages, and that unconscious processes might play a significant role in human life.

REVIEW AND SHARPEN YOUR THINKING

1 **Define personality and summarize the psychodynamic perspectives.**

- Define the concept of personality, describe the essence of the psychodynamic perspectives, and explain the key ideas in Freud's psychoanalytic theory.
- Discuss how the ideas of three psychodynamic critics and revisionists differed from Freud's.
- Identify the pros and cons of the psychodynamic perspectives.

What psychodynamic ideas may apply to all human beings? Which ones may not apply to everyone?

2 Humanistic Perspectives

Describe the humanistic perspectives.

Humanistic perspectives stress a person's capacity for personal growth, freedom to choose one's own destiny, and positive human qualities. Humanistic psychologists believe that each of us has the ability to cope with stress, to control our lives, and to achieve what we desire (Cain, 2001; Smith, 2001). Each of us has the capacity to break through and understand ourselves and our world; we can burst the cocoon and become a butterfly, say the humanists.

The humanistic perspectives provide clear contrasts to the psychodynamic perspectives, which often seem to be based on conflict, destructive drives, and a pessimistic view of human nature. The humanistic perspectives also contrast with behaviorism, discussed in Chapter 7, which at its extreme reduces human beings to puppets on the strings of rewards and punishments. Indeed, one of the motivational forces behind the development of humanistic psychology was to move beyond Freudian psychoanalysis and behaviorism to something that might capture the rich and potentially positive aspects of human nature.

Maslow's Approach

A leading architect of the humanistic movement was Abraham Maslow (1908–1970). Maslow referred to humanistic psychology as "third force" psychology because it stressed neither Freudian drives nor the stimulus–response principles of behaviorism.

In Chapter 10 we looked at Maslow's approach to motivation, which conceived of motivation as a hierarchy of needs. You may recall that at the top of Maslow's (1954, 1971) hierarchy was the need for self-actualization. Self-actualization is the motivation to develop one's full potential as a human being. Maslow described self-actualizers as spontaneous, creative, and possessing a childlike capacity for awe. According to Maslow, a person at this optimal level of existence would be tolerant of others, have a gentle sense of humor, and be likely to pursue the greater good. Self-actualizers also maintain a capacity for "peak experiences," or breathtaking moments of spiritual insight. As examples of self-actualized individuals, Maslow included Pablo Casals (cellist), Albert Einstein (physicist), Ralph Waldo Emerson (writer), William James (psychologist), Thomas Jefferson (politician), Eleanor Roosevelt (humanitarian, diplomat), and Albert Schweitzer (humanitarian).

humanistic perspectives Views of personality that stress the person's capacity for personal growth, freedom to choose a destiny, and positive qualities.

416 CHAPTER 11 Personality

Created nearly 40 years ago, Maslow's list of self-actualized individuals is clearly biased in some ways. Maslow was most interested in focusing on highly successful individuals who, in his mind, represented the best of the human species. Because Maslow concentrated on people who were successful in a particular historical context, his self-actualizers were limited to those who had opportunities for success in that context. Maslow thus named considerably more men than women, and most of the individuals were from Western cultures and of European ancestry. Today, we might add to Maslow's list individuals such as the Dalai Lama (Tenzin Gyatso), Tibetan spiritual and political leader; Wangari Maathai, a Kenyan woman acclaimed for her work on behalf of democracy and the environment; and Muhammad Yunus, a Bangladeshi banker and crusader against poverty. All are recipients of the Nobel Peace Prize in recent years.

Rogers's Approach

The other key figure in the development of humanistic psychology, Carl Rogers (1902–1987), began his career as a psychotherapist struggling to understand the unhappiness of the individuals he encountered in therapy. Rogers's groundbreaking work provided the foundation for more contemporary studies of self-esteem, personal growth, and self-determination.

Like Freud, Rogers began his inquiry about human nature with people who were troubled. In the knotted, anxious, defensive verbal stream of his clients, Rogers (1961) noted the things that seemed to be keeping them from having positive self-concepts and reaching their full potential as human beings.

Rogers believed that most people have considerable difficulty accepting their own true, innately positive feelings. He emphasized that we are all born with an innate tendency toward growth and a gut instinct that will lead us to make good choices. In a sense, we are born with the seeds of a wonderful person inside us. However, as we grow up, people who are central to our lives condition us to move away from our genuine feelings. Too often, we hear our parents, siblings, teachers, and peers say things like "Don't do that," "You didn't do that right," and "How can you be so stupid?" When we do something wrong, we often get punished. Parents may even threaten to withhold their love unless we conform to their standards, which Rogers called conditions of worth. He felt that through exposure to such conditions, we become alienated from our genuine feelings in order to be the person we are expected to be. We might come to despise who we really are in favor of an idealized image of who we are "supposed" to be. The conditions of worth placed on us by others eventually become the standards by which we judge ourselves. Though very different in many ways, both Freud and Rogers recognized that the conflict between the self and one's duty was a key problem for their patients.

The Self Through the individual's experiences with the world, a self emerges—the "I" or "me" of our existence. Rogers did not believe that all aspects of the self are conscious, but he did believe they are all accessible to consciousness. The self is a whole, consisting of one's self-perceptions (how attractive I am, how well I get along with others, how good an athlete I am) and the values we attach to these perceptions (good/bad, worthy/unworthy).

Self-concept, a central theme in the views of Rogers and other humanists, is an individual's overall perceptions and assessments of his or her abilities, behavior, and personality. In Rogers's view, a person who has an inaccurate self-concept is likely to be maladjusted.

In discussing self-concept, Rogers distinguished between the real self, which is the self resulting from our experiences, and the ideal self, which is the self we would like to be. The greater the discrepancy between the real self and the ideal self, a condition Rogers called incongruence, the more maladjusted we will be. To improve our adjustment and become "congruent," we can develop more positive perceptions of our real self, worry less about what others want, and increase our positive experiences in the world.

Carl Rogers (1902–1987) *Carl Rogers was a pioneer in the development of the humanistic perspective.*

self-concept A central theme in Rogers's and other humanists' views; self-concept refers to individuals' overall perceptions and assessments of their abilities, behavior, and personalities.

Unconditional Positive Regard, Empathy, and Genuineness   Rogers proposed three methods to help a person develop a more positive self-concept: unconditional positive regard, empathy, and genuineness.

Rogers said that because people, regardless of what they do, need to be accepted by others, we must accept them without strings attached. **Unconditional positive regard** is Rogers's term for accepting, valuing, and being positive toward another person regardless of the person's behavior. When a person's behavior is inappropriate, obnoxious, or unacceptable, the person still needs the respect, comfort, and love of others (Assor, Roth, & Deci, 2004). Rogers strongly believed that unconditional positive regard elevates the person's self-worth. However, Rogers (1974) distinguished between unconditional positive regard directed at the individual as a person of worth and dignity, and directed at the individual's behavior. For example, a therapist who adopts Rogers's view might say, "I don't like your behavior, but I accept you, value you, and care about you as a person."

Rogers also said that we can help others develop a more positive self-concept if we are *empathic* and *genuine.* Being empathic means being a sensitive listener and understanding another's true feelings. Being genuine means being open with our feelings and dropping our pretenses and facades. The importance Rogers placed on the therapist's being a genuine person in the therapeutic relationship demonstrates his strong belief in the positive character of human nature. For Rogers, we can help others simply by being present for them as the authentic persons we are.

According to Rogers, unconditional positive regard, empathy, and genuineness are three essential ingredients of healthy human relations. We can use these techniques to help other people feel good about themselves and to help us get along better with others (Bozarth, Zimring, & Tausch, 2001).

Evaluating the Humanistic Perspectives

The humanistic perspectives made psychologists aware that the way we perceive ourselves and the world around us is a key element of personality. Humanistic psychologists also reminded us that we need to consider the whole person and the positive bent of human nature (Bohart & Greening, 2001). Their emphasis on conscious experience has given us the view that personality contains a well of potential that can be developed to its fullest (Hill, 2000).

Some critics believe that humanistic psychologists are too optimistic about human nature and overestimate the freedom and rationality of humans. And some say the humanists may promote excessive self-love and narcissism by encouraging people to think so positively about themselves. Self-determination theory, which we considered in Chapter 10, demonstrates the way that psychologists have tested humanistic ideas that might appear abstract and difficult to test.

unconditional positive regard Rogers's term for accepting, valuing, and being positive toward another person regardless of the person's behavior.

2 Describe the humanistic perspectives.
- Define the main themes of the humanistic perspectives and explain the main elements of Rogers's theory.
- Evaluate the humanistic perspectives.

Is it possible both to be genuine and to provide unconditional positive regard? How would a humanistic psychologist approach the treatment of someone who has committed a truly despicable act (rape or murder)? How would you feel if you were counseling someone who admitted to doing something you find morally wrong?

trait An enduring personality characteristic that tends to lead to certain behaviors.

trait theories Theories stating that personality consists of broad, enduring dispositions (traits) that tend to lead to characteristic responses.

3 Trait Perspectives

Discuss the trait perspectives.

Through the ages, people have described themselves and others in terms of basic traits. A **trait** is an enduring personality characteristic that tends to lead to certain behaviors. Around 400 B.C.E., Hippocrates, the "father of medicine," described human beings as having one of four basic personalities, determined by their physical makeup: choleric (quick-tempered), phlegmatic (placid), sanguine (optimistic), or melancholic (pessimistic). Others have proposed different sets of traits, but some descriptions of personality have remained remarkably constant. More than 2,000 years ago, for example, Theophrastus described the basic traits of the "stingy man," the "liar," and the "flatterer." If you are setting up a friend on a blind date, you are likely to describe the person in terms of traits rather than as having a "good personality." The trait perspectives on personality have been the dominant approach for the past two decades.

Trait Theories

Trait theories state that personality consists of broad, enduring dispositions (traits) that tend to lead to characteristic responses. In other words, people can be described in terms of the basic ways they behave, such as whether they are outgoing and friendly or dominant and assertive. People who have a strong tendency to behave in certain ways are described as high on the traits; those who have a weak tendency to behave in these ways are described as low on the traits. Although trait theorists differ about which traits make up personality, they agree that traits are the fundamental building blocks of personality (Friedman & Schustack, 2006).

Gordon Allport (1897–1967), who is sometimes referred to as the father of American personality psychology, was particularly bothered by the negative view of humanity that psychoanalysis portrayed. He rejected the notion that the unconscious was central to an understanding of personality. He further believed that to understand healthy people, we must focus on their lives in the present, not on their childhood experiences. Allport, who took a pragmatic approach to understanding the person, asserted that if you want to know something about someone, you should "just ask him" (or her). Allport believed that personality psychology should focus on understanding healthy, well-adjusted individuals, whom he described as showing a positive but objective sense of self and others, interest in issues beyond their own experience, a sense of humor, common sense, and a unifying philosophy of life—typically but not always provided by religious faith (Allport, 1961). Allport was dedicated to the idea that psychology should have relevance to social issues facing modern society, and his scholarship has influenced not only personality psychology but also the psychology of religion and prejudice.

In defining personality, Allport (1961) stressed the uniqueness of each person and his or her capacity to adapt to the environment. For Allport, the unit we should use to understand personality is the trait. He defined traits as mental structures that make different situations the same for the person. For instance, if Gabi is sociable, she is likely to behave in an outgoing, happy fashion whether she is at a party or in a group study session. Allport's definition implies that behavior should be consistent across different situations.

We get a sense of the down-to-earth quality of Allport's approach to studying personality by looking at his study of traits. In the late 1930s, Allport and his colleague H. S. Odbert (1936) sat down with two big unabridged dictionaries and

Mother Goose & Grimm: © Grimmy, Inc. King Features Syndicate.

pulled out all the words that could be used to describe a person—a method called the *lexical approach.* This approach is based on the idea that if a trait is important to people in real life, it ought to be represented in the natural language people use to talk about one another. Furthermore, the more important a trait is, the more likely it is that it should be represented by a single word. Allport and Odbert started with 18,000 words and then pared down that list to 4,500.

As you can appreciate, 4,500 traits would be a rather difficult inventory by which to define a personality. Imagine that you are asked to rate a person, Ignacio, on some traits. You use a scale from 1 to 5, with 1 meaning "not at all" and 5 meaning "very much." If you give Ignacio a 5 on "outgoing," what do you think you might give him on "shy"? Clearly, we may not need 4,500 traits to summarize the way we describe personality. But how might we whittle down these descriptors further, without losing something important?

With advances in statistical methods and the advent of computers, the lexical approach became considerably less unwieldy, as researchers began to analyze these many words to look for underlying structures that might account for their overlap. In 1946, Raymond Cattell applied the relatively new statistical procedure of *factor analysis* to the Allport and Odbert traits. Cattell concluded that 16 underlying factors would summarize the data well, and this work led to the development of the 16PF, a personality scale that is still used today.

Factor analysis essentially tells us what items on a scale people are responding to as if they mean the same thing. For example, if Ignacio got a 5 on "outgoing," he probably would get a 5 on "talkative" and a 1 or 2 on "shy." One important characteristic of factor analysis is that it relies on the scientist to interpret the meaning of the factors, and the researcher must make some decisions about how many factors are enough to explain the data (Goldberg & Digman, 1994). In 1963, W. T. Norman reanalyzed the data Cattell used and concluded that only five factors were needed to summarize these traits. Norman's research set the stage for the dominant approach in personality psychology today: the five-factor model (Digman, 1990).

big five factors of personality The "supertraits" that are thought to describe the main dimensions of personality—specifically, neuroticism (emotional instability), extraversion, openness to experience, agreeableness, and conscientiousness.

The Five-Factor Model of Personality

Pick a friend and jot down 10 of that person's most notable personality traits. Did you perhaps list "reserved" or "a good leader"? "Responsible" or "unreliable"? "Sweet," "kind," or "friendly"? Maybe even "creative"? Researchers in personality psychology have found that there are essentially five broad personality dimensions that are represented in the natural language and that also summarize the various ways psychologists have studied traits (Costa & McCrae, 1998, 2006; Digman, 1990, 1996, 2002; Hogan, 1987, 2006; McCrae & Costa, 2006). The **big five factors of personality,** the "supertraits" that are thought to describe the main dimensions of personality, are neuroticism (emotional instability), extraversion, openness to experience, agreeableness, and conscientiousness. Although personality psychologists typically refer to the traits as N, E, O, A, and C on the basis of the order in which they emerged in a factor analysis, if you create an anagram from these first letters of the trait names, you get the word *OCEAN.* The traits are more fully defined in Figure 11.5.

FIGURE 11.5
The Big Five Factors of Personality
Each of the broad supertraits encompasses more narrow traits and characteristics. Use the acronym *OCEAN* to remember the big five personality factors (*openness, conscientiousness,* and so on).

O penness	**C** onscientiousness	**E** xtraversion	**A** greeableness	**N** euroticism (emotional stability)
• Imaginative or practical	• Organized or disorganized	• Sociable or retiring	• Softhearted or ruthless	• Calm or anxious
• Interested in variety or routine	• Careful or careless	• Fun-loving or somber	• Trusting or suspicious	• Secure or insecure
• Independent or conforming	• Disciplined or impulsive	• Affectionate or reserved	• Helpful or uncooperative	• Self-satisfied or self-pitying

; The Science of
chology: An
preciative View
    11. Personality   Text
© The McGraw–Hill
Companies, 2008

Critical Controversy   Can Personality Change?

As you talk on the phone with a friend, she tells you for what seems like the hundredth time about her boyfriend troubles. He never calls when he says he will. He always seems to have "forgotten" his wallet when they go out, and now she thinks he might be cheating on her *again*. As you count silently to 10, you are tempted to blurt it out: "Dump him already! He's never going to change!"

Of course, your friend might be banking on the notion that he *will* change. Can people really change? The answer to this question has implications for a variety of important life domains. For example, can criminals be rehabilitated? Can addicts truly recover from addictions? Do major life experiences such as marriage and parenthood cause personality changes? Can adults make changes to lead happier, healthier lives? Will all those self-help books ever help you to stop worrying and just enjoy life? And, of course, will that lousy boyfriend turn out to be suitable husband material after all?

Whether personality can change has been a topic of controversy throughout the history of the field of personality. Freud believed that personality was essentially fixed by the age of 6, with little development occurring over the rest of life. Jung split with Freud on this issue, believing that the most important development occurred during the middle years of life. One of psychology's most famous early thinkers, William James, once wrote that "it is well for the world that in most of us, by the age of thirty, the character has set like plaster, and will never soften again." Trait psychologists Paul Costa and Robert McCrae concluded that, based on their work, James was on target: They suggested that most traits are indeed "essentially fixed" by age 30, with little meaningful change occurring throughout the rest of adulthood (Costa & McCrae, 1992, 2006; McCrae & Costa, 2006).

However, other research has provided evidence that meaningful personality change continues over time (Roberts, Wood, & Caspi, 2007). Sanjay Srivastava and his colleagues (2003) examined evidence from a sample of 132,515 respondents to a website, who completed measures of the big five personality traits. Participants ranged in age from 21 to 60. Comparing trait scores for those at different ages, the researchers found evidence suggesting change over the life course. Conscientiousness increased, especially in the 20s. Agreeableness increased dramatically in the 30s. Neuroticism declined for women, but not for men, over the life course. Young women were higher on neuroticism to start with, suggesting that men and women become more similar on this dimension of personality over time. The results of this large-scale study point to the possibility that with age, people may be increasingly better adapted to meet the challenges of life.

The study by Srivastava and his colleagues suggesting that personality traits may change was a cross-sectional study in which different individuals were assessed at the same time. However, this type of study is susceptible to what are called *cohort effects*—the possibility that people in the same generation (for instance, everyone born in the 1950s) share some common characteristics because of their similar history and differ systematically from other generations (such as people born in the 1990s) (Schaie, 2007). Individuals who lived through the Great Depression, for example, might have some things in common that set them apart from others.

Even stronger evidence is provided by longitudinal studies that follow the same individuals over a long period of time. Recently, Brent Roberts and his colleagues (Roberts, Walton, & Viechtbauer, 2006) analyzed 92 different longitudinal studies that included thousands of participants ranging from 12 to over 80 years old and that measured aspects of the big five across the life course. They concluded that there is indeed strong, consistent evidence for trait changes throughout life, even into adulthood. Social dominance (a facet of extraversion), conscientiousness, and emotional stability (the opposite of neuroticism) were found to increase especially between the ages of 20 and 40. Social vitality, another facet of extraversion, and openness to experience increased most during adolescence but then declined in old age. Agreeableness showed a steady increase over the life course. Over time, people were not just getting older—they were getting more responsible, kinder, and less worried.

Keep in mind that by definition, traits are considered to be stable. They might be the least likely aspect of personality to change, as compared, for example, to beliefs or goals. To find change in even these relatively stable dimensions is extraordinary and speaks to the important possibility that people can grow and change, especially in positive ways, over the life span. Other aspects of personality such as resilience, wisdom, complexity, and insight have also been shown to increase through life experience (Helson & Soto, 2005; Helson, Soto, & Cate, 2006).

What does this mean for your friend and her loser boyfriend? He just might shape up, but she might have to wait a very long time—and aren't there other, more agreeable and conscientious fish in the sea?

What Do You Think?

- Do you think personality can change throughout a person's life? Explain.
- Think about what you were like 5 years ago. Which aspects of your personality have changed? Which have stayed the same?
- If you have a friend who wants to be more outgoing, what would your advice be?

Each of the five traits has been the topic of extensive research. Genetic factors have been shown to explain a substantial amount of variation in each of the big five traits. We consider a sampling of research findings on each trait here to give you a sense of the interesting work that has been inspired by the five-factor model:

"Henderson's got to go. His magnetic personality's not only disrupting the office, it's erasing all our software."

© CartoonStock.com.

- Neuroticism is related to feeling negative emotion more often than positive emotion in one's daily life and to experiencing more lingering negative states (Lucas & Fujita, 2000). Neuroticism has been shown to relate to more health complaints, although this association may not necessarily mean that neurotic individuals are actually more likely to be physically sick (Goodwin, Cox, & Clara, 2006).
- Extraverts are more likely than others to engage in social activities (Emmons & Diener, 1986).
- Openness is related to higher IQ, liberal values, open-mindedness, and tolerance. Openness to experience is related to creativity and creative accomplishments (King, McKee-Walker, & Broyles, 1996).
- Agreeableness is related to generosity, and when asked to make a wish for anything at all, agreeable people are more likely to make altruistic wishes such as "for world peace" (King & Broyles, 1997).
- Conscientiousness is linked to better-quality friendships (Jensen-Campbell & Malcolm, 2007) and has been shown to relate to healthy behaviors and longevity, an issue we return to at the end of this chapter (Mroczek, Spiro, & Griffin, 2006).

Keep in mind that because the five factors are theoretically independent of one another, a person can be any combination of them. Do you know a neurotic extravert or an agreeable introvert? Whether or not the big five traits are stable or can change has been an enduring debate in personality psychology. See the Critical Controversy to read about this debate.

Some research on the big five factors addresses the extent to which the factors appear in personality profiles in different cultures (Lingjaerde, Foreland, & Engvik, 2001; Miacic & Goldberg, 2007; Pukrop, Sass, & Steinmeyer, 2000). Do the five factors show up in the assessment of personality in cultures around the world? There is increasing evidence that they do (McCrae & Costa 2006; Ozer & Riese, 1994). Researchers have found that some version of the five factors appears in people in countries as diverse as Canada, Finland, Poland, China, and Japan (Paunonen & others, 1992). Research has generally supported the concept of the big five traits. Researchers have even begun to find evidence for the big five personality traits in animals, including domestic dogs (Gosling, Kwan, & John, 2003) and hyenas (Gosling & John, 1999). Despite this strong evidence, some personality researchers believe the big five might not end up being the final list of broad supertraits and that more specific traits are better predictors of behavior (Fung & Ng, 2006; Saucier, 2001; Simms, 2007).

In addition to studying change and stability in personality traits, psychologists also are interested in how such traits are linked to emotion. To read about this link, see the Intersection, which examines whether one of the big five traits—extraversion—might be involved in how happy individuals are.

Evaluating the Trait Perspectives

Studying people in terms of their personality traits has practical value. Identifying a person's traits allows us to know the person better. Also, the traits that we have influence our health, the way we think, our career success, and our relations with others (Levenson & Aldwin, 2006; Mroczek & Little, 2006; Roberts & others, 2007). Still, the trait approach has been critiqued for missing the importance of the situation in personality and behavior. Some have criticized the trait perspective for painting an individual's personality with very broad strokes. Dan McAdams (2001) has referred to the five-factor model as "the psychology of the stranger" because although it tells us much about what we might want to know about someone we have never met, it does not tell us very much about the nuances of each individual's personality. Personality psychologists who are interested in those nuances sometimes adopt the life story approach to personality, our next topic.

Personality and Emotion: Are Some People Happier Than Others?

Some people seem to go through life having fun, while others appear to be prone to feeling distress at even the slightest problem. You might think that most of our daily emotional experience can be explained by the events that happen to us—of course, you reason, a person is going to be happy if she is doing well in school and has a loving romantic partner, but unhappy if she is doing poorly and has just experienced a romantic breakup. But interestingly, research has shown that life events explain relatively little about our daily mood. Rather, there is considerable stability in a person's mood over time (Watson & Walker, 1996). That means that someone who says she is pretty happy today is likely to say she is pretty happy on another day, even years later. On average, some people appear to be happier than others.

If we want to explain this stability, we might try to think of aspects of the person that are themselves relatively stable, such as personality traits. Indeed, one of the most consistent findings in personality research is the strong relationship between personality traits and emotional experience. Extraverts, who are outgoing and sociable, report higher levels of positive mood than do introverts. David Watson, a personality and clinical psychologist who specializes in the study of mood, has suggested that positive emotion is the "affective core" of the trait of extraversion (Watson & Clark, 1997).

Why are extraverts so happy? Two types of explanations aim to account for this strong link. So-called *instrumental explanations* state that personality has an *indirect* effect on emotional experience— that is, personality might influence the lifestyle choices a person makes, and those choices influence mood. Perhaps extraverts are more likely to favor activities that are themselves related to higher positive mood. For example, social activities are strongly related to positive mood. Maybe extraverts are happier because they choose to spend more time with others. However, this explanation, though logically sensible, does not appear to be the case. Research has shown that extraverts are happier than introverts even when they are alone (Argyle & Lu, 1990; Lucas, 2007).

Happy activities and happy thoughts are available for everyone.

Alternative explanations for the strong relation between extraversion and positive affect are called *temperamental explanations*. These explanations state that personality has a *direct* effect on emotional experience, so that extraversion can be thought of as a predisposition to experiencing positive mood (Larsen & Ketelaar, 1991). Such explanations take two forms. First, it may be that extraverts are more responsive to positive situations, so that when they encounter a pleasant situation they are more reactive to it. This explanation would predict that extraverts should be happier than introverts only when they are in a pleasant situation. For instance, an extravert at a great party would feel happier than an introvert at the same party, but these two people would not differ in happiness while sitting in a class listening to a lecture. A second temperamental explanation suggests that extraversion and positive affect are strongly linked even in neutral situations. This explanation asserts that extraverts just carry a hefty bundle of positive mood with them wherever they go and whatever they do (Lucas, 2007).

Richard Lucas and Brendan Baird (2004) conducted a series of studies to address these differing temperamental predictions. In six studies, they exposed students who differed on extraversion to a variety of positive or neutral stimuli. The positive mood conditions included writing about a dream vacation or winning the lottery, viewing pleasant film clips about gardening or a Bill Cosby comedy routine, or reading jokes and cartoons. The neutral mood conditions included writing about taking a drive or going grocery shopping or watching a financial news report from PBS. In all of the studies, the strong relation between extraversion and positive affect was found even in the neutral conditions. Extraverts were happier than introverts regardless of whether the researchers had tried to put them in a pleasant mood. Even when they had just read a financial news report, the extraverts were happier. Finally, Lucas and Baird examined a variety of studies that used daily diary methods (described in Chapter 2) in which individuals were "beeped" at various times during the day and asked to rate how they were feeling at the moment. Examining the connection between extraversion and mood at any given moment, Lucas and Baird found that regardless of the situation, when beeped at random times, extraverts reported higher levels of positive affect.

If you are an introvert, you may be feeling your mood deflating right about now. But it is important to keep a few things in mind. First, introverts were *not* found to be *unhappy* in these studies. Introverts and extraverts alike responded with positive emotion toward the funny film clips. Second, introversion is not the same thing as shyness (Briggs, 1988). Introverts are not necessarily socially anxious or distressed. The introvert may be someone whose positive moods are more akin to contentment and quiet satisfaction than those of the outgoing extravert.

Indeed, for the introvert (and anyone else) who is interested in enhancing positive mood, research provides hints for effective strategies. First, introverts might take a lesson from extraverts and spend more time with the people they love. Second, extraverts have been found to be more likely than others to augment their positive moods so that happy moods persist longer and negative ones fade more rapidly (Hemenover, 2003). One way to capitalize on our positive moments in life is through savoring (Bryant & Veroff, 2007). Savoring—which means attending to our positive experiences and appreciating them— enhances our sense of well-being. Extraverts may have a shortcut to pleasurable experience, afforded to them by their basic personality. But even without the benefit of this disposition to happiness, happy activities and happy thoughts are available for everyone.

REVIEW AND SHARPEN YOUR THINKING

3 Discuss the trait perspectives.

- Define traits and describe the views of Allport.
- Identify the big five factors in personality.
- Evaluate the trait perspectives.

To what extent do you believe the big five factors capture your personality? Look at the characteristics of the five factors listed in Figure 11.5 and decide how you line up on each one. Then choose one of the factors, such as extraversion or openness, and give an example of how situation might influence the expression of this trait in your life.

4 Personological and Life Story Perspectives

Discuss the personological and life story perspectives.

Imagine giving a group of 1,000 people a questionnaire measuring them on each of the big five traits. In looking at their scores, you might conclude that people are *not* like snowflakes after all, but rather like Chips Ahoy cookies: They differ in small ways, but there are plenty that share very similar traits.

If two people have the same levels of the big five traits, do they essentially have the same personality? Researchers who approach personality from the personological and life story perspectives do not think so. Recall that we opened this chapter with the notion that each of us is unique and in some ways like no other human being on earth. **Personological and life story perspectives** stress that the way to understand the person is to focus on his or her life history and life story—aspects that distinguish that individual from all the other "snowflakes."

personological and life story perspectives Approaches to personality emphasizing that the way to understand the person is to focus on his or her life history and life story—aspects that distinguish that individual from all others.

Murray's Personological Approach

Henry Murray (1893–1988) was a young biochemistry graduate student when he became interested in the psychology of personality after meeting Carl Jung and reading his work. Murray went on to become the director of the Psychological Clinic at Harvard at the same time that Gordon Allport was on the faculty there. Murray and Allport saw personality very differently. While Allport was most comfortable focusing on conscious experience and traits, Murray embraced the psychodynamic notion of unconscious motivation.

Murray coined the word *personology* to refer to the study of the whole person. He famously stated that "the history of the organism is the organism," meaning that in order to understand a person, we have to understand that person's history, including all aspects of the person's life. At the Harvard clinic, Murray assembled specialists of all sorts—including medical professionals, anthropologists, psychologists, and sociologists—who would analyze individuals from every possible perspective and seek to understand each person. The findings of this exercise were published in *Explorations in Personality* in 1938.

Murray applied his insights into personality during World War II, when he was called upon by the Office of Strategic Services (a precursor to the CIA) to develop a psychological profile of Adolf Hitler. That document, produced in 1943, accurately predicted that Hitler would commit suicide rather than be taken alive by the Allies. Murray's analysis of Hitler was the first "offender profile," and it has served as a model for modern criminal profiling. Upon returning to Harvard after the war, Murray continued to do research in the field of personality. By chance, one of the participants in his studies was Theodore Kaczynski, who would later become infamous as the Unabomber, a mysterious terrorist who sent bomb-containing packages (which injured 29 people and killed 3 of them) to universities and airlines from the 1970s through the 1990s.

Henry Murray's psychological profile of Adolf Hitler, developed in 1943 during World War II, continues to serve as a model for criminal profiling today.

King: The Science of
Psychology: An
Appreciative View

11. Personality

Text

© The McGraw–Hill
Companies, 2008

*Research by David Winter (2004) has analyzed
presidential motives in inaugural addresses such as
those delivered by Richard M. Nixon (left) and
John F. Kennedy (right). Winter found that certain
needs revealed in these speeches corresponded to
later events during these individuals' terms in office.*

The aspect of Murray's research that has had the most impact on contemporary personality psychology is his approach to motivation. Murray believed that our motives are largely unknown to us, so that measures of motivation must be developed that do not just ask people to say what it is they want. Thus, along with Christiana Morgan, Murray developed the Thematic Apperception Test (or TAT), which we return to later in this chapter (Morgan & Murray, 1935). Moreover, a variety of scoring procedures have been developed for analyzing the unconscious motives that are revealed in imaginative stories (Smith, 1992).

Murray's approach to personality is reflected in current research on achievement, affiliation, and power motivation, as well as the intimacy motive, which we considered in Chapter 10. For example, David Winter (2005) analyzed the motives revealed in presidential inaugural addresses. He found that certain needs revealed in these speeches corresponded to later events during the person's tenure as president. For instance, presidents who scored high on need for achievement (such as Jimmy Carter) were less successful during their terms. Presidents who scored high on need for power tended to be judged as more successful (John F. Kennedy, Ronald Reagan), and presidents whose addresses included a great deal of warm, interpersonal imagery (suggesting high need for affiliation) tended to experience scandal during their presidencies (Richard M. Nixon).

The Life Story Approach and Identity

Following in the Murray tradition, Dan McAdams (2001, 2006) developed the *life story approach* to identity. Each of us has a unique life story, full of ups and downs. These stories represent our memories of what makes us who we are. McAdams found that the life story is a constantly changing narrative that serves to provide our lives with a sense of coherence. Just as Murray said that the history of the organism is the organism, McAdams suggested that our life stories are our identities.

McAdams has conducted research using large samples of individuals who have undergone "life story interviews." These interview responses are then coded for themes that are relevant to differing life stages and transitions. For example, McAdams and his colleagues found that kindergarten teachers (who are assumed to be high in generativity, which we considered in Chapter 4) are more likely to tell life stories characterized by a redemption pattern, with things going from bad to good. Other personality psychologists have relied on narrative accounts of life experiences as a means of understanding how individuals create meaning in life events (King & others, 2000). By using narratives, personal documents (such as diaries), and even letters and speeches, personality psychologists continue to look for the "deeper meaning" that cannot be addressed through self-report measures.

Finally, some personality psychologists take very seriously Murray's commitment to understanding the whole person, by focusing on just one case. *Psychobiography* is a means of inquiry in which the personality psychologist attempts to apply a personality theory to a single person's life (Runyon, 2007; Schultz, 2005). Freud himself wrote the first psychobiography in his analysis of Michelangelo. Some of the problems with his interpretations of Michelangelo's life have caused his work to become a road map for what a psychobiographer ought not to do (Elms, 2005).

Evaluating the Life Story Approach and Similar Perspectives

Studying individuals through narratives and personal interviews provides an extraordinarily rich opportunity for the researcher. Imagine having the choice of reading someone's diary versus seeing that person's scores on a questionnaire measuring traits. Not many would pass up the chance to read the diary. However, life story studies are difficult and time-consuming; personologist Robert W. White (1992) referred to the study of narratives as exploring personality "the long way."

Collecting interviews and narratives is often just the first step. In order for these personal stories to become scientific data, they must be transformed into numbers, a process involving extensive coding and content analysis. Further, for narrative studies to be worthwhile, they must tell us something we could not have found out in a much easier way (King, 2003). Psychobiographical inquiries moreover are prone to the biases of the scholars who conduct them and may not serve the scientific goal of generalizability.

REVIEW AND SHARPEN YOUR THINKING

4 Discuss the personological and life story perspectives.
- Summarize the personological approach of Murray.
- Explain how the life story approach is involved in understanding identity.
- Describe the advantages and disadvantages of using narratives in research.

What might the work of Winter on presidents likely say about the motives of President George W. Bush?

5 Social Cognitive Perspectives

Explain the social cognitive perspectives.

Social cognitive perspectives on personality emphasize conscious awareness, beliefs, expectations, and goals. While incorporating principles from behaviorism (see Chapter 7), social cognitive psychologists explore the person's ability to reason; to think about the past, present, and future; and to reflect on the self. They emphasize the person's individual interpretation of situations and thus focus on the uniqueness of each person by examining how behavior is tailored to the diversity of situations in which people find themselves. Social cognitive theorists are not interested in broad traits, but rather they investigate how more specific factors, such as beliefs, relate to behavior and performance. In this section we consider the two major social cognitive approaches, developed respectively by Albert Bandura and Walter Mischel.

Bandura's Social Cognitive Theory

B. F. Skinner, whose work we examined in Chapter 7, believed that there is no such thing as "personality"; rather, he emphasized behavior and felt that internal mental states were irrelevant to psychology. Albert Bandura (1986, 2001, 2006, 2007a, 2007b) found Skinner's approach to be far too simplistic for understanding human functioning. He took the basic tenets of behaviorism and added a recognition of the role of mental processes in determining behavior. While Skinner saw behavior as caused by the situation, Bandura pointed out that the person can cause situations, and sometimes the very definition of the situation itself depends on the person's beliefs about it. For example, is that upcoming exam an opportunity to show your stuff or a threat to your ability to achieve your goals? The test is the same either way, but a person's unique take on the test can influence a host of behaviors (studying, worrying, and so on).

Bandura's social cognitive theory states that behavior, environment, and person/cognitive factors are *all* important in understanding personality. Bandura coined the term *reciprocal determinism* to describe the way behavior, environment, and person/cognitive factors

Albert Bandura (1925–) *Bandura's practical, problem-solving–oriented social cognitive approach has made a lasting mark on personality theory and therapy.*

social cognitive perspectives Approaches to personality emphasizing conscious awareness, beliefs, expectations, and goals. Social cognitive psychologists explore the person's ability to reason; to think about the past, present, and future; and to reflect on the self.

426 CHAPTER 11 Personality

FIGURE 11.6
Bandura's Social Cognitive Theory
Bandura's social cognitive theory emphasizes reciprocal influences of behavior, environment, and person/cognitive factors.

self-efficacy The belief that one can master a situation and produce positive outcomes.

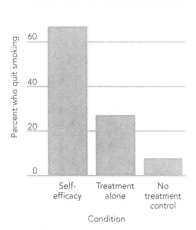

FIGURE 11.7
Self-Efficacy and Smoking Cessation In one study, smokers were randomly assigned to one of three conditions. In the self-efficacy condition, individuals were told they had been chosen for the study because they had great potential to quit smoking (Warnecke & others, 2001). Then, they participated in a 14-week program on smoking cessation. In the treatment-alone condition, individuals participated in the 14-week smoking cessation program but were told that they had been randomly selected for it. In the no-treatment control condition, individuals did not participate in the smoking cessation program. At the conclusion of the 14-week program, individuals in the self-efficacy condition were likelier to have quit smoking than their counterparts in the other two conditions.

interact to create personality (Figure 11.6). The environment can determine a person's behavior, and the person can act to change the environment. Similarly, person/cognitive factors can both influence behavior and be influenced by behavior. From Bandura's perspective, then, behavior is a product of a variety of forces, some of which come from the situation and some of which the person brings to the situation. We now review the important processes and variables Bandura used to understand personality.

Observational Learning Remember from Chapter 7 that Bandura believes that observational learning is a key aspect of how we learn. Through observational learning, we form ideas about the behavior of others and then possibly adopt this behavior ourselves. For example, a young boy might observe his father's aggressive outbursts and hostile exchanges with people; when the boy is with his peers, he interacts in a highly aggressive way, showing the same characteristics that his father's behavior does. Social cognitive theorists believe that we acquire a wide range of behaviors, thoughts, and feelings through observing others' behavior; these observations form an important part of our personalities.

Personal Control Social cognitive theorists emphasize that we can regulate and control our own behavior, despite our changing environment (Bandura, 2006; Mischel, 2004). For example, another young executive who observes her boss behave in a dominant and sarcastic manner may find the behavior distasteful and go out of her way to be encouraging and supportive of her subordinates. Or imagine that someone tries to persuade you to join a particular social club on campus and makes you an enticing offer. You reflect on the offer, consider your interests and beliefs, and decide not to join. Your *cognition* (your thoughts) leads you to control your behavior and resist environmental influence in this instance. One important aspect of the experience of control is the belief that one has the ability to produce change in one's world, or self-efficacy.

Self-Efficacy **Self-efficacy** is the belief that one can master a situation and produce positive outcomes. Bandura and others have shown that self-efficacy is related to a number of positive developments in people's lives, including solving problems, becoming more sociable, initiating a diet or an exercise program and maintaining it, and quitting smoking (Figure 11.7) (Bandura, 2001, 2006, 2007a, 2007b; Schunk, 2008; Schunk & Zimmerman, 2006). Self-efficacy influences whether people even try to develop healthy habits, as well as how much effort they expend in coping with stress, how long they persist in the face of obstacles, and how much stress and pain they experience (Brister & others, 2006; Clark & Dodge, 1999; Sarkar, Fisher, & Schillinger, 2006). Self-efficacy is related, too, to whether people initiate psychotherapy to deal with their problems and whether it succeeds (Longo, Lent, & Brown, 1992). Researchers also have found that self-efficacy is linked with successful job interviewing and job performance (Judge & Bono, 2001; Tay, Ang, & Van Dyne, 2006).

Self-efficacy helps people in unsatisfactory situations by encouraging them to believe that they can succeed. In Chapter 16, we consider the role of self-efficacy in important life changes such as weight loss and smoking cessation. How can you increase your self-efficacy? The following strategies can help (Watson & Tharp, 2007):

- Select something you expect to be able to do, not something you expect to fail at accomplishing. As you develop self-efficacy, you can tackle more daunting projects.
- Distinguish between past performance and your present project. You might come to expect from past failures that you cannot do certain things. However, remind yourself that your past failures are in the past and that you now have a new sense of confidence and accomplishment.
- Pay close attention to your successes. Some individuals have a tendency to remember their failures but not their successes.
- Keep written records so that you will be concretely aware of your successes. A student who sticks to a study schedule for 4 days and then fails to stick to it on the 5th day should not think, "I'm a failure. I can't do this." This statement ignores the fact that the student was successful 80 percent of the time (keeping to the schedule 4 out of 5 days).

- Make a list of the specific kinds of situations in which you expect to have the most difficulty and the least difficulty. Begin with the easier tasks and cope with the harder ones after you have experienced some success.

Bandura's (2001, 2006) social cognitive approach to personality has been especially influential in shaping researchers' understanding of achievement behavior and has laid the groundwork for various approaches to clinical practice, as we will see in Chapter 15.

Mischel's Contributions

Like Bandura, Walter Mischel is a social cognitive psychologist who has been interested in exploring how personality influences behavior. Mischel has left his mark on the field of personality in two notable ways. First, his critique of the idea of consistency in behavior ignited a flurry of controversy that has become known as the person–situation debate. Second, he has proposed the CAPS model, a new way of thinking about personality. We discuss each of these contributions in turn.

Consistency and the Person–Situation Debate Whether we are talking about unconscious sexual conflicts, traits, or motives, all of the approaches we have considered so far maintain that these various personality characteristics are enduring and influence behavior. These shared assumptions were attacked in 1968 with the publication of Walter Mischel's *Personality and Assessment,* a book that nearly ended the psychological study of personality.

To understand Mischel's argument, recall Gordon Allport's definition of a trait as a characteristic that ought to make different situations equivalent for a given person. This quality of traits suggests that a person should behave consistently in different situations—in other words, the individual should exhibit *cross-situational consistency.* For example, an outgoing person should act highly sociably whether she is at a party or in the library. However, Mischel looked at the research compiled on trait prediction of behavior and found it to be lacking. He concluded that there was no evidence for cross-situational consistency in behavior—and thus no evidence for the existence of personality as it had been previously assumed to exist.

Rather than understanding personality as consisting of broad, internal traits that make for consistent behavior across situations and time, Mischel said that personality often changes according to a given situation. Mischel asserted that behavior is discriminative—that is, a person looks at each situation and responds accordingly. Mischel's view is called *situationism,* the idea that personality and behavior often vary considerably from one context to another.

Personality psychologists responded to Mischel's situationist attack in a variety of ways, sparking what has become known as the *person–situation debate.* Researchers were able to show that it is not a matter of whether personality predicts behavior, but when and how it does so, often in combination with situational factors. The research findings were that (1) the narrower and more limited a trait is, the likelier it will predict behavior; (2) some people are consistent on some traits, and other people are consistent on other traits; and (3) personality traits exert a stronger influence on an individual's behavior when situational influences are less powerful. A very powerful situation is one that contains many clear cues about how a person is supposed to behave. For example, even a very talkative person typically sits quietly during a class lecture. But in weaker situations, such as during his or her leisure time, the person may spend most of the time talking. Moreover, individuals select the situations they are in, so that even if situations determine behavior, traits play a role in determining which situations they choose (such as going to a party or staying home to study) (Emmons & Diener, 1986).

Let's pause and consider what it means to be consistent. You might believe that being consistent is part of being a genuine, honest person and that tailoring behavior to different situations means being fake. On the other hand, consider that someone who never changes his or her behavior to fit a situation might be unpleasant—"a drag"—to have around. For example, think about someone who cannot put aside his competitive drive even when playing checkers with a 4-year-old. Clearly, adaptive behavior might involve sometimes being consistent and sometimes tailoring behavior to the situation.

428 CHAPTER 11 Personality

"Yes I'm a dog but I've got a great personality."
© CartoonStock.com.

Over time, Mischel (2004) has developed an approach to personality that he feels is better suited to capturing the nuances of the relationship between the individual and situations in producing behavior. Imagine trying to study personality without using traits or broad motives. What would you focus on? Mischel's answer to this dilemma is his CAPS theory.

CAPS Theory Although his 1968 book nearly ended interest in the influence of personality on behavior, Mischel has continued to conduct research in the field. Indeed, Mischel's (2004) work on delay of gratification, discussed in Chapter 10, has demonstrated remarkable stability in behavior over time. Recall that in that work, children who had been able to delay eating a cookie in an experimental session were also able to perform better in academic work in college. Mischel's revised approach to personality is concerned with stability or coherence in the pattern of behavior *over time,* not with consistency across differing situations. That is, Mischel and his colleagues have studied how behaviors in very different situations have a coherent pattern, such as a child's waiting to eat the cookie versus that same individual's (as a grown college student) deciding to stay home and study instead of going out to party.

In keeping with the social cognitive emphasis on the person's cognitive abilities and mental states, Mischel conceptualizes personality as a set of interconnected **cognitive affective processing systems (CAPS)** (Mischel, 2004; Mischel & Shoda, 1999). This approach means that our thoughts and emotions about ourselves and the world affect our interactions with the environment and become linked in ways that matter to behavior. Personal control and self-efficacy can be thought of as connections that a person has made among situations, beliefs, and behaviors. For instance, someone who is excited by the challenge of a new assignment given by a boss may think about all the possible strategies to reach his or her goal and get to work immediately. Yet this go-getter may respond to other challenges differently, depending on who gives the assignment.

CAPS is called a "bottom-up" approach to personality. That means it is concerned with how personality works, not with what it is (Shoda & Mischel, 2006). From the CAPS perspective, it makes no sense to ask a person "How extraverted are you?" because the answer is always, "It depends." A person may be outgoing in one situation (on the first day of class) and not another (right before an exam), and that unique pattern of flexibility is what personality is all about.

Not surprisingly, the CAPS approach focuses on the way people behave in different situations and how they uniquely interpret situational features. From this perspective, knowing that Sasha is an extravert tells us little about how she will behave in a group discussion in her psychology class. We need to know about Sasha's beliefs and goals in the discussion (for example, does she want to impress the instructor? is she a psychology major? are the members of the class good friends of hers?), as well as her personal understanding of the situation itself (is this an opportunity to shine, or is she thinking about her test for the next class?). Research using this approach generally involves observing individuals behaving in a variety of contexts in order to identify the patterns of associations that exist among beliefs, emotions, and behavior for each individual person across different situations.

Evaluating the Social Cognitive Perspectives

Social cognitive theory focuses on the influence of environment on personality. The social cognitive approach has fostered a scientific climate for understanding personality that highlights the observation of behavior. Social cognitive theory emphasizes the influence of cognitive processes in explaining personality and suggests that people have the ability to control their environment.

Critics of the social cognitive perspective on personality take issue with one or more aspects of the approach, charging that:

- The social cognitive approach is too concerned with change and situational influences on personality and does not pay adequate tribute to the enduring qualities of personality.
- Social cognitive approaches ignore the role biology plays in personality.
- In its attempt to incorporate both the situation and the person into its view of personality, social cognitive psychology tends to lead to very specific predictions for each person in any given situation, making generalizations impossible.

cognitive affective processing systems (CAPS) According to Mischel, a set of interconnected cognitive systems through which an individual's thoughts and emotions about self and the world become linked in ways that matter to behavior.

REVIEW AND SHARPEN YOUR THINKING

5 Explain the social cognitive perspectives.

- Define the social cognitive perspectives and describe Bandura's social cognitive theory.
- Describe two of Mischel's contributions to personality psychology.
- Evaluate the social cognitive perspectives.

How much does your personality depend on the situation? Give a specific example of how you are consistent or inconsistent from one situation to the next.

6 Personality Assessment

Characterize the main methods of personality assessment.

One of the great contributions of personality psychology to the science of psychology is its development of rigorous methods for measuring mental processes. Psychologists use a number of scientifically developed methods to evaluate personality (Gregory, 2007). They assess personality for different reasons, from clinical evaluation to career counseling and job selection (Hogan, 2006). Because personality psychology is primarily interested in the characteristics of the person, most personality tests are designed to assess stable, enduring characteristics, free of situational influence. The researcher's theoretical interest typically determines the method used to measure a particular psychological dimension. For example, a researcher interested in unconscious processes usually assesses personality by using a measure that does not rely on conscious knowledge.

Self-Report Tests

The most commonly used method of measuring personality characteristics is self-report. A **self-report test,** also called an *objective test* or *inventory,* directly asks people whether specific items describe their personality traits. For example, self-report personality tests include items such as:

- I am easily embarrassed.
- I love to go to parties.
- I like to watch cartoons on TV.

Self-report tests include many statements or questions such as these. Respondents choose from a limited number of answers (yes or no, true or false, agree or disagree). To get a sense of what a self-report personality test is like, see the Psychology and Life box.

Assessments of the Big Five Factors Paul Costa and Robert McCrae (1992) constructed the Neuroticism Extraversion Openness Personality Inventory—Revised (or NEO-PI-R, for short), a self-report test geared to assessing the five-factor model: openness, conscientiousness, extraversion, agreeableness, and neuroticism (emotional instability). The test also evaluates six subdimensions that make up the five main factors. Other measures of the big five traits have relied on the lexical approach and offer the advantage of being available without a fee. Measures of the big five generally contain items that are quite straightforward; for instance, the trait "talkative" might show up on an extraversion scale. These items have what psychologists call **face validity,** meaning the extent to which a test item appears to be valid to those who are completing it. In other words, a test item has face validity if it seems on the surface to fit the trait in question.

self-report test Also called an objective test or inventory, a type of test that directly asks people whether specific items (usually true/false or agree/disagree) describe their personality traits.

face validity The extent to which a test item appears to be valid to those who are completing it.

PSYCHOLOGY AND LIFE

Are You a Nice Person?

In personality psychology, the term *agreeableness* describes someone who is kind and sympathetic to others. Agreeable people tend to trust others and assume that others are trustworthy. They are gentle, altruistic, and generous. In short, agreeable people are nice. How nice are you? Take the questionnaire below to find out.

These items were taken from the agreeableness scale on Lewis Goldberg's International Personality Item Pool website that allows you to test yourself on any number of personality characteristics (Goldberg & others, 2006). This site (http://ipip.ori.org/ipip/) is accessible to all and allows free access to the scale for research purposes.

© CartoonStock.com.

1 = very inaccurate (does not describe you at all)

2 = moderately inaccurate

3 = neither accurate nor inaccurate

4 = moderately accurate

5 = very accurate (describes you very well)

1. _____ I am interested in people.
2. _____ I sympathize with others' feelings.
3. _____ I feel little concern for others.
4. _____ I insult people.
5. _____ I make people feel at ease.
6. _____ I feel others' emotions.
7. _____ I am not interested in other people's problems.
8. _____ I have a soft heart.
9. _____ I take time out for others.
10. _____ I am not really interested in others.

To find out how you did on this assessment, first recode your responses to items 3, 4, 7, and 10—that is, give each rating its opposite. So, for a 5 you get a 1, for a 4 you get a 2, and so on. Add these scores to your answers for items 1, 2, 5, 6, 8, and 9 and divide by 10. Although there are no norms for this particular scale, you can get a sense of how nice you are by comparing your score to the midpoint of the 1 to 5 scale. If your score is higher than 3, you are probably pretty nice. If your score falls below 3, you might think about doing some volunteer work—or at least do something nice for someone in your life!

Adherents of the trait perspectives such as the big five have strong faith in self-report tests, while acknowledging certain limitations. One problem with self-report tests centers on *social desirability*. To grasp the idea of social desirability, imagine answering the item "I am lazy at times." This statement is probably true for everyone, but would you feel comfortable admitting it? When motivated by social desirability, individuals say what they think the researcher wants to hear or what they think will make them look better. One way to measure the influence of social desirability is to give individuals a questionnaire designed to tap into this tendency. Such a scale typically contains many universally true but threatening items ("I like to gossip at times," "I have never said anything intentionally to hurt someone's feelings"). If scores on a trait measure correlate with this measure of social desirability, we know that the test takers were probably not being straightforward on the trait measure.

Another technique for getting around social desirability issues is to design scales so that it is virtually impossible for the respondent to know what the researcher is actually trying to measure. One means of accomplishing this goal is to use an **empirically keyed test,** a type of test that presents a host of questionnaire items to groups of people who are already known to differ in some central way (such as individuals with psychological disorders versus mentally healthy individuals). On the basis of the responses, the researcher can then select the items that best discriminate between the members of the differing groups (Segal & Coolidge, 2004). Items on an empirically keyed test rarely show a great deal of face validity.

MMPI   The **Minnesota Multiphasic Personality Inventory (MMPI)** is the most widely used and researched empirically keyed self-report personality test. The MMPI was initially constructed in the 1940s to assess "abnormal" personality tendencies and to improve the diagnosis of individuals with psychological disorders. The most recent version of the inventory, the MMPI-2, is still widely used around the world to assess personality and predict outcomes (Butcher, 2004; Butcher & others, 2006; Exterkate, Bakker-Brehm, & de Jong, 2007; Sellbom & others, 2006). The scale features 550 items and provides information on a variety of personality characteristics.

The MMPI is not only used by clinical psychologists to assess a person's mental health; it is also used to predict which individuals will make the best job candidates and which career an individual should pursue. With computers now widely employed to score the MMPI-2 (Forbey & Ben-Porath, 2007), some critics warn that the availability of computer scoring has tempted some untrained individuals to use the test in ways for which it has not been validated.

An important consideration with respect to empirically keyed tests is that we do not always know why a given test item distinguishes between two groups. Imagine, for example, that an empirically keyed test of achievement motivation includes an item such as "I prefer to watch sports on TV instead of romantic movies," or an item to distinguish between higher-paid versus lower-paid managers in a work setting. Do these items measure achievement motivation or, instead, simply the respondents' gender? Although it might seem like a good idea for test constructors to hide what they are ultimately trying to measure from test takers, having the participants know what they are being asked about may help them to give their best, most honest responses. If the test takers know that a questionnaire is about extraversion, for example, they might have a better understanding of what each item means. In sum, self-report test items can be rather transparent (for example, as in the NEO-PI-R) or relatively vague and difficult (as in the MMPI).

It is likely that you would be able to give a reasonably good assessment of your own levels of traits such as neuroticism and extraversion. But what about the more mysterious aspects of yourself and others? If you are like most people, you think of psychological assessments as tools to find out things you do not already know about yourself. For that objective, psychologists might turn to projective tests.

Projective Tests

A **projective test** presents individuals with an ambiguous stimulus and then asks them to describe it or tell a story about it—in other words, to *project* their own meaning onto the stimulus. Projective tests are based on the assumption that the ambiguity of the stimulus allows individuals to invest it with their feelings, desires, needs, and attitudes. The test is especially designed to elicit the individual's unconscious feelings and conflicts, providing an assessment that goes deeper than the surface of personality (Aiken & Groth-Marnat, 2006; Leichtman, 2004). Projective tests attempt to get inside the mind to discover how the test taker really feels and thinks, going beyond the way the individual overtly presents

empirically keyed test A type of test that presents a host of questionnaire items to groups of people who are already known to differ in some central way (such as individuals with a psychological disorder versus mentally healthy individuals).

Minnesota Multiphasic Personality Inventory (MMPI) The most widely used and researched empirically keyed self-report personality test.

projective test Personality assessment tool that presents individuals with an ambiguous stimulus and then asks them to describe it or tell a story about it—in other words, to *project* their own meaning onto it.

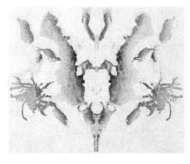

FIGURE 11.8

Type of Stimulus Used in the Rorschach Inkblot Test What do you see in this figure? Do you see two green seahorses? Or a pair of blue spiders? A psychologist who relies on the Rorschach test would examine your responses to find out who you really are.

FIGURE 11.9

Picture from the Thematic Apperception Test (TAT) What are these two women thinking and feeling? How did they come to this situation, and what will happen next? A psychologist who uses the TAT would analyze your story to find out your unconscious motives.

himself or herself. Projective tests are theoretically aligned with the psychodynamic perspectives on personality, which give more weight than the other perspectives to the unconscious.

Perhaps the most famous projective test is the **Rorschach inkblot test,** developed in 1921 by the Swiss psychiatrist Hermann Rorschach. This test uses an individual's perception of the inkblots to determine his or her personality. The test consists of 10 cards, half in black and white and half in color, which the individual views one at a time (Figure 11.8). The person taking the Rorschach test is asked to describe what he or she sees in each of the inkblots. For example, an individual may say, "I see two fairies having a tea party" or "This is the rabbit's face from the movie *Donnie Darko.*" These responses are scored for indicating various underlying psychological characteristics (Exner, 2003).

The Rorschach's usefulness in research is controversial. From a scientific perspective, researchers are skeptical about the Rorschach (Feshbach & Weiner, 1996; Garb & others, 2001; Hunsley & Bailey, 2001; Weiner, 2004). The test's reliability and validity have both been criticized. If the Rorschach were reliable, two different scorers would agree on the personality characteristics of the individual being tested. If the Rorschach were valid, it would predict behavior outside of the testing situation; that is, it would predict whether an individual will attempt suicide, become severely depressed, cope successfully with stress, or get along well with others. Conclusions based on research evidence suggest that the Rorschach does not meet these criteria of reliability and validity (Lilienfeld, Wood, & Garb, 2000). Thus, many psychologists have serious reservations about the Rorschach's use in diagnosis and clinical practice.

Although still administered in clinical circles, the Rorschach is not commonly used in personality research. However, the projective method itself remains a tool for studying personality, particularly the Thematic Apperception Test (TAT).

The **Thematic Apperception Test (TAT),** which, as we earlier saw, was developed by Henry Murray and Christiana Morgan in the 1930s, is designed to elicit stories that reveal something about an individual's personality. The TAT consists of a series of pictures like the one in Figure 11.9, each on an individual card or shown to the person in a slide. The TAT test taker is asked to tell a story about each of the pictures, including events leading up to the situation described, the characters' thoughts and feelings, and the way the situation turns out. The tester assumes that the person projects his or her own unconscious feelings and thoughts into the story (Herzberg, 2000; Moretti & Rossini, 2004). In addition to being administered as a projective test in clinical practice, the TAT is used in research on people's need for achievement, affiliation, power, intimacy, and a variety of other needs (Brunstein & Maier, 2005; Schultheiss & Brunstein, 2005; Smith, 1992); unconscious defense mechanisms (Cramer, 2007; Cramer & Jones, 2007); and cognitive styles (Woike & Matic, 2004; Woike, Mcleod, & Goggin, 2003).

Other Assessment Methods

Unlike either projective tests or self-report tests, behavioral assessment of personality is based on observing the individual's behavior directly (Cooper, Heron, & Heward, 2007). Instead of removing situational influences, as projective tests and self-report measures do, behavioral assessment assumes that personality cannot be evaluated apart from the environment (Heiby & Haynes, 2004).

Behavioral assessment of personality emerged from the tradition of behavior modification, which we considered in Chapter 7 (Martin & Pear, 2007). Recall that often the first step in the process of changing an individual's maladaptive behavior is to make baseline observations of its frequency. The therapist then modifies some aspect of the environment, such as getting the parents and the child's teacher to stop giving the child attention when he or she engages in aggressive behavior. After a specified period of time, the therapist will observe the child again

Type of Behavior	Item
Shared activities	We sat and read together. We took a walk.
Pleasing interactive events	My spouse asked how my day was. We talked about personal feelings. My spouse showed interest in what I said by agreeing or asking relevant questions.
Displeasing interactive events	My spouse commanded me to do something. My spouse complained about something I did. My spouse interrupted me.
Pleasing affectionate behavior	We held each other. My spouse hugged and kissed me.
Displeasing affectionate behavior	My spouse rushed into intercourse without taking time for foreplay. My spouse rejected my sexual advances.
Pleasing events	My spouse did the dishes. My spouse picked up around the house.
Displeasing events	My spouse talked too much about work. My spouse yelled at the children.

FIGURE 11.10

Items from the Spouse Observation Checklist Couples are instructed to complete an extensive checklist for 15 consecutive evenings. Spouses record their partner's behavior and make daily ratings of their overall satisfaction with the spouse's behavior. The Spouse Observation Checklist is a behavioral assessment instrument. Reprinted by permission of the publishers from Thematic Apperception Test by Henry A. Murray, Card 12F, Cambridge, Mass.: Harvard University Press, Copyright © 1943 by the President and Fellows of Harvard College, Copyright © 1971 by Henry A. Murray.

to determine if the changes in the environment were effective in reducing the child's maladaptive behavior.

What does a psychologist with a behavioral orientation do to assess personality? Direct observation may be desirable, but it is not always possible (Hartmann, Barrios, & Wood, 2004). When it is not, the psychologist might ask individuals to make their own assessments of behavior, encouraging them to be sensitive to the circumstances that produced the behavior and the outcomes or consequences of the behavior. For example, a therapist might want to know the course of marital conflict in the everyday experiences of a couple. Figure 11.10 shows a Spouse Observation Checklist that couples can use to record their partners' behavior.

Owing to the influence of social cognitive theory, the use of cognitive assessment in personality evaluation has increased. The strategy is to discover what thoughts underlie the individual's behavior—that is, how individuals think about their problems (Watson & Tharp, 2007). What kinds of thoughts precede maladaptive behavior, occur during its manifestation, and follow it? Cognitive processes such as expectations, planning, and memory are assessed, possibly by interviewing the individual or asking him or her to complete a questionnaire. An interview might include questions that address whether the individual exaggerates his faults and condemns himself more than is warranted. A questionnaire might ask a person what her thoughts are after an upsetting event, or it might assess the way she thinks during tension-filled moments. Many personality psychologists incorporate friend or peer ratings of individuals' traits or other characteristics. Personality psychologists also employ a host of psychophysiological measures, such as heart rate and skin conductance.

Whether personality assessments are being used by clinical psychologists, psychological researchers, or other practitioners, the choice of assessment instrument depends greatly on the researcher's theoretical perspective. Figure 11.11 summarizes which methods are associated with each of the theoretical perspectives. The figure also summarizes each approach, including its major assumptions, and gives a sample research question addressed by each. Personality psychology is a diverse field, unified by a shared interest in understanding the person—that is, you.

Rorschach inkblot test A widely used projective test that uses an individual's perception of inkblots to determine his or her personality.

Thematic Apperception Test (TAT) A projective test designed to elicit stories that reveal something about an individual's personality.

434 CHAPTER 11 Personality

Approach	Summary	Assumptions	Typical Methods	Sample Research Question
Psychodynamic	Personality is characterized by unconscious processes. Personality develops over stages, and childhood experiences are of great importance to adult personality.	The most important aspects of personality are unconscious.	Case studies, projective techniques.	How do unconscious conflicts lead to dysfunctional behavior?
Humanistic	Personality evolves out of the person's innate, organismic motives to grow and actualize the self. These healthy tendencies can be undermined by social pressure.	Human nature is basically good. By getting in touch with who we really are and what we really want, we can lead happier and healthier lives.	Questionnaires, interviews, observation.	Can situations be changed to support individuals' organismic values and enhance their well-being?
Social Cognitive	Personality is the pattern of coherence that characterizes a person's interactions with the situations he or she encounters in life. The individual's beliefs and expectations, rather than global traits, are the central variables of interest.	Behavior is best understood as changing across situations. To understand personality, we must understand what each situation means for a given person.	Multiple observations over different situations; videotaped behaviors rated by coders; questionnaires.	When and why do individuals respond to challenging tasks with fear vs. excitement?
Trait	Personality is characterized by a set of five general traits that are represented in the natural language that everyday people use to describe themselves and others.	Traits are relatively stable over time. Traits predict behavior.	Questionnaires, observer reports.	Are the five factors universal across cultures?
Personology and Life Story	To understand personality we must understand the whole person. Each person has a unique set of life experiences, and the stories we tell about those experiences make up our identities.	The life story provides a unique opportunity to examine the personality processes associated with behavior, development, and well-being.	Written narratives, TAT stories, autobiographical memories, interviews, and psychobiography.	How do narrative accounts of life experiences relate to happiness?

FIGURE 11.11

Approaches to Personality Psychology This figure summarizes the broad approaches to personality described in this chapter. Many researchers in personality do not stick with just one approach but apply the various theories and methods that are most relevant to their research questions.

REVIEW AND SHARPEN YOUR THINKING

6 **Characterize the main methods of personality assessment.**

- Explain self-report tests.
- Discuss projective techniques.
- Describe some other methods of personality assessment in addition to self-report and projective measures.

Think of a personality characteristic that you find interesting. How might you assess it?

7 Personality and Health and Wellness

Summarize how personality relates to health and wellness.

We regularly see headlines cautioning us that our personalities might be putting us at risk for heart disease, cancer, or some other illness. How exactly does personality relate to health and well-being?

King: The Science of
Psychology: An
Appreciative View

11. Personality

Text

© The McGraw–Hill
Companies, 2008

83

Conscientiousness and Personal Control

Personality can matter to health directly and indirectly. Personality might affect health indirectly by leading to behaviors that are either good or bad for you. An example is the trait of conscientiousness. Recall that conscientious individuals are responsible and reliable; they like structure and seeing a task to its completion.

Conscientiousness is not the sexiest trait, but it might well be the most important trait of the big five when it comes to health. Brent Roberts and his colleagues (Roberts, Walton, & Bogg, 2005) have suggested that conscientiousness plays a significant role in health and longevity. Conscientious people tend to do all those things that they are told are good for their health, such as getting regular exercise, avoiding drinking and smoking, wearing seatbelts, and checking smoke detectors. This capacity to follow a sensible plan may be just what it takes to do the mundane tasks required to live a long, healthy life. Indeed, in one study, individuals who were low in conscientiousness were more likely to die earlier than their high-conscientious counterparts (Wilson & others, 2004).

Another personality characteristic associated with taking the right steps to lead a long, healthy life is a sense of personal control (Wrosch, Heckhausen, & Lachman, 2006). Feeling in control can reduce the experience of stress during difficult times (Taylor, 2006; Thompson, 2001). Feeling in control can lead to the development of problem-solving strategies to cope with the stress. An individual with a good sense of personal control might say, "If I stop smoking now, I will not develop lung cancer" or "If I exercise regularly, I won't develop cardiovascular disease." A recent study revealed that a sense of personal control was linked to a lower risk for common chronic diseases such as cancer and cardiovascular disease (Sturmer, Hasselbach, & Amelang, 2006).

Like conscientiousness, a sense of personal control might also help people avoid a risky lifestyle that involves health-compromising behaviors. Consider a study of East German migrants to West Germany who found themselves unemployed (Mittag & Schwarzer, 1993). They often turned to heavy drinking for solace unless they had a sense of personal control (as measured by such survey items as "When I'm in trouble, I can rely on my ability to deal with the problem effectively"). Across a wide range of studies, a sense of personal control over the stressful events that go on around people has been related to emotional well-being, successful coping with a stressful event, behavior change that can promote good health, and good health (Little, Snyder, & Wehmeyer, 2006; Stanton, Revenson, & Tennen, 2007; Taylor, 2006; Taylor & Stanton, 2007).

Other personality characteristics appear to relate to health through more direct routes. These traits may exacerbate stress so that the person's very personality leads him or her to stress out more than someone else would. Still other traits may help to buffer a person against the effects of stress (Ozer & Benet-Martinez, 2006).

Type A/Type B Behavior Patterns

In the late 1950s, a secretary for two California cardiologists, Meyer Friedman and Ray Rosenman, observed that the chairs in their waiting rooms were tattered and worn, but only on the front edges. The cardiologists had also noticed the impatience of their cardiac patients, who often arrived exactly on time and were in a great hurry to leave. Intrigued by this consistency, they conducted a study of 3,000 healthy men between the ages of 35 and 59 over 8 years to find out whether people with certain behavioral characteristics might be prone to heart problems (Friedman & Rosenman, 1974). During the 8 years, one group of men had twice as many heart attacks or other forms of heart disease as the other men. Further, autopsies of the men who died revealed that this same group had coronary arteries that were more obstructed than those of the other men.

Friedman and Rosenman described the common personality characteristics of the men who developed coronary disease as the **Type A behavior pattern.** They theorized that a cluster of characteristics—being excessively competitive, hard-driven, impatient, and hostile—is related to the incidence of heart disease. Rosenman and Friedman labeled the behavior of the healthier group, who were commonly relaxed and easygoing, the **Type B behavior pattern.**

Type A behavior pattern A cluster of characteristics—such as being excessively competitive, hard-driven, impatient, and hostile—related to the incidence of heart disease.

Type B behavior pattern A cluster of characteristics—such as being relaxed and easygoing—related to good health.

Further research on the link between Type A behavior and coronary disease indicates that the association is not as strong as Friedman and Rosenman believed (Suls & Swain, 1998; R. Williams, 2001, 2002). However, researchers have found that certain components of Type A behavior are more precisely linked with coronary risk (Spielberger, 2004).

The Type A behavior component most consistently associated with coronary problems is hostility (Julkunen & Ahlstrom, 2006). People who are hostile outwardly or who turn anger inward are more likely to develop heart disease than their less angry counterparts (Eng & others, 2003; Matthews & others, 2004). Such people have been called "hot reactors" because of their intense physiological reactions to stress: Their hearts race, their breathing quickens, and their muscles tense up. One study found that hostility was a better predictor of coronary heart disease in older men than smoking, drinking, high caloric intake, or high levels of LDL cholesterol (Niaura & others, 2002).

A hostile personality may also affect the course of such diseases as AIDS. One study of 140 HIV-positive individuals found that the immune systems of those with hostile personalities who confronted distressing events weakened more than the immune systems of their counterparts who did not have hostile personalities (Ironson, 2001).

Optimism and Hardiness

One factor that is often related to positive functioning and adjustment is being optimistic (Peterson, 2006; Peterson & Seligman, 2003; Seligman & Pawelski, 2003; Smith & MacKenzie, 2006). Psychologists' interest in the concept of optimism has especially been fueled by Martin Seligman's (1990) theory and research on optimism. Seligman views optimism as a matter of how a person explains the causes of bad events. Optimists explain the causes of bad events as due to external, unstable, and specific causes. Pessimists explain bad events as due to internal, stable, and global causes.

Seligman's interest in optimism stemmed from his work on *learned helplessness,* which initially focused on animals who learned to become helpless (passive and unresponsive) after they experienced uncontrollable negative events (1975). In his view, pessimism is much like learned helplessness and the belief in an external source of control. Optimism is much like belief in self-efficacy and an internal source of control.

Martin Seligman (1942–) *Seligman went from pessimist to optimist and believes that others can, too. Seligman (1990) provided the details in his book* Learned Optimism. *Recall Seligman's interest in changing psychology from a discipline that focuses mainly on the negative aspects of life to one that spends more time charting the positive aspects of life.*

Other researchers have defined optimism as the expectancy that good things are more likely, and bad things less likely, to occur in the future (Carver & Scheier, 2004; Scheier & Carver, 1992; Srivastava & others, 2006). This view focuses on how people pursue their goals and values. In the face of adversity, optimists still believe that their goals and values can be attained. Their optimism keeps them working to reach their goals, whereas pessimism makes people give up.

Numerous research studies reveal that optimists generally function more effectively and are physically and mentally healthier than pessimists:

- *Physical health:* In one remarkable finding, people who were classified as optimistic at age 25 were healthier at ages 45 to 60 than those who had been classified as pessimistic (Peterson, Seligman, & Vaillant, 1988). In other studies, optimism has been linked to more effective immune system functioning and better health (Nes & Segerstrom, 2006; Segerstrom, 2003, 2005). Optimists also have been found to have lower blood pressure than pessimists (Räikkönen & others, 1999).
- *Mental health:* In one study, optimism was a better predictor than self-efficacy of the person's ability to avoid depression over time (Shnek & others, 2001). In another study, optimism was related to better mental health in cancer patients (Cohen, De Moor, & Amato, 2001). In a recent study, optimism was linked to decreased thoughts of suicide in college students (Hirsch, Conner, & Duberstein, 2007).

Another personality attribute that appears to allow a person to thrive during difficult times is **hardiness,** a trait characterized by a sense of commitment (rather than alienation) and of control (rather than powerlessness) and a perception of problems as challenges (rather than threats) (Maddi & others, 2006). The links among hardiness, stress, and illness were the focus of the Chicago Stress Project, which studied male business managers 32

hardiness A trait characterized by a sense of commitment and control and a perception of problems as challenges rather than threats.

to 65 years of age over a 5-year period (Kobasa, Maddi, & Kahn, 1982; Maddi, 1998). During the 5 years, most of the managers experienced stressful events such as divorce, job transfers, the death of a close friend, inferior performance evaluations at work, and work with an unpleasant boss.

In one aspect of the Chicago study, managers who developed an illness (ranging from the flu to a heart attack) were compared with those who did not (Kobasa, Maddi, & Kahn, 1982). Those who did not were likelier to have hardy personalities. Another aspect of the study investigated whether hardiness, along with exercise and social support, buffered stress and reduced illness in executives' lives (Kobasa & others, 1986). When all three factors were present in an executive's life, the level of illness dropped dramatically (Figure 11.12).

Other researchers also have found support for the role of hardiness in illness and health (Heckman & Clay, 2005; Matthews & Servaty-Seib, 2007). The results of hardiness research suggest the power of multiple factors, rather than any single factor, in buffering stress and maintaining health (Maddi, 1998; Maddi & others, 2006).

Traits and States

Thinking about the role of personality in health can sometimes be stressful itself. What if you know you are a touch on the hostile side? Or a pessimist? If personality is a stable aspect of a person, what good does it do you to find out that your personality is bad for physical health? Furthermore, does your discovery that you have traits that predispose you to illness mean that it is your own fault if you become ill?

One way to think about these issues is to focus on the difference between traits and states (Gupta & others, 2006; Marine & others, 2006). Traits are relatively enduring characteristics—the way a person generally is. States are more acute, time-limited experiences. A person's having a trait (such as hostility) that predisposes him or her to feelings of anger toward others does not mean that the individual is wired for a heart attack. We have to assume that the pathway from personality trait to disease goes through the state of anger. Thus, even someone who possesses the trait of hostility can take steps to avoid the state of anger—for example, by enrolling in an anger management class or seeking counseling. Knowing that one is prone to be pessimistic might be the first step toward learning to be more optimistic. After all, Seligman's best-seller was titled *Learned Optimism,* meaning that an optimistic style can be learned.

So, finding out that you have a personality style associated with stress or illness should not lead you to conclude that you are doomed. Rather, this information can allow you to take steps to improve your life, to foster good habits, and to make the most of your unique qualities.

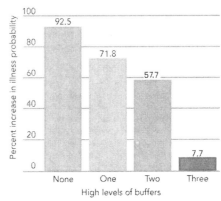

FIGURE 11.12

Illness in High-Stress Business Executives
In one study of high-stress business executives (all of whom were selected for this analysis because they were above the stress mean for the entire year of the study), a low level of all three buffers (hardiness, exercise, and social support) involved a high probability of at least one serious illness in that year. High levels of one, two, and all three buffers decreased the likelihood of at least one serious illness occurring in the year of the study.

REVIEW AND SHARPEN YOUR THINKING

7 Summarize how personality relates to health and wellness.
- Describe how conscientiousness and personal control relate to physical health.
- Define the Type A behavior pattern and describe its relation to coronary heart disease.
- Identify two personality characteristics related to successful coping with stress.
- Explain how the distinction between traits and states relates to the role of personality in health and illness.

Think of someone you know who seems to be especially good at handling life's challenges. What particular challenges has he or she faced? Would you describe this person as hardy? Optimistic? Hostile? Why?

SUMMARY

1 PSYCHODYNAMIC PERSPECTIVES

Define personality and summarize the psychodynamic perspectives.

Freud's Psychoanalytic Theory

Freud developed psychoanalysis through his work with hysterical patients. Hysterical symptoms are physical symptoms with no physical cause. Freud viewed these symptoms as representing conflicts between a person's desires and duty. Freud believed that most of the mind is unconscious, and he described the personality as having three structures: id, ego, and superego. The conflicting demands of these personality structures produce anxiety. Defense mechanisms protect the ego and reduce this anxiety. Freud was convinced that problems develop because of early childhood experiences. He said that we go through five psychosexual stages: oral, anal, phallic, latency, and genital. During the phallic stage, which occurs in early childhood, the Oedipus complex is a major source of conflict.

Psychodynamic Critics and Revisionists

A number of psychodynamic theorists criticized Freud for overemphasizing sexuality and the first 5 years of life. They argued that Freud gave too little credit to the ego, conscious thought, and sociocultural factors. Horney said that the need for security, not sex or aggression, is our most important need. Jung thought Freud underplayed the unconscious mind's role. He developed the concept of the collective unconscious and placed special emphasis on archetypes. Adler's theory, called individual psychology, stresses that people are striving toward perfection, not pleasure. Adler placed more emphasis on social motivation than Freud did.

Evaluating the Psychodynamic Perspectives

Weaknesses of the psychodynamic perspectives include overreliance on reports from the past, overemphasis of sexuality and the unconscious mind, a negative view of human nature, too much attention to early experience, and a male, Western bias. Strengths of the psychodynamic perspectives include recognizing the importance of childhood, conceptualizing development through stages, and calling attention to the potential role of unconscious processes in behavior. Psychodynamic perspectives have had a substantial influence on psychology as a discipline.

2 HUMANISTIC PERSPECTIVES

Describe the humanistic perspectives.

Maslow's Approach

Maslow called the humanistic movement the "third force" in psychology. Maslow developed the concept of a hierarchy of needs, with self-actualization being the highest human need.

Rogers's Approach

In Rogers's approach, each of us has a need for unconditional positive regard. As a result, the real self is not valued unless it meets the standards of other people. The self is the core of personality; it includes both the real and ideal selves. Rogers said that we can help others develop a more positive self-concept by treating them with unconditional positive regard, empathy, and genuineness. Rogers also stressed that each of us has the innate inner capacity to become a fully functioning person.

Evaluating the Humanistic Perspectives

The humanistic perspectives sensitize us to the importance of subjective experience, of consciousness, of self-conception, of consideration of the whole person, and of our innate positive nature. Humanistic psychology calls attention to the positive capacities of human beings. Its weaknesses are a tendency to be too optimistic and an inclination to encourage excessive self-love.

3 TRAIT PERSPECTIVES

Discuss the trait perspectives.

Trait Theories

A trait is an enduring personality characteristic that tends to produce certain behaviors. Trait theories emphasize that personality consists of broad, enduring dispositions that lead to characteristic responses. Trait theorists also are interested in how traits are organized within the individual. Traits are assumed to be essentially stable over time and across situations. Allport stated that traits render different situations functionally equivalent for the person. Allport used the lexical approach to personality traits, which involves using all the words in the natural language that could describe a person as a basis for understanding the underlying traits of personality.

The Five-Factor Model of Personality

The current dominant perspective in personality psychology is the five-factor model. The "big five" traits in this model include neuroticism, extraversion, openness to experience, agreeableness, and conscientiousness.

Evaluating the Trait Perspectives

Studying people in terms of their traits has practical value. Identifying a person's traits allows us better to predict the person's health, thinking, job success, and interpersonal skills. However, trait approaches have been criticized for focusing on broad dimensions and not attending to each person's uniqueness.

4 PERSONOLOGICAL AND LIFE STORY PERSPECTIVES

Discuss the personological and life story perspectives.

Murray's Personological Approach

Murray described personology as the study of the whole person, including all aspects of the person's life. Murray was interested in unconscious motivation and, with Morgan, developed the TAT, a projective measure of unconscious needs.

The Life Story Approach and Identity

Contemporary followers of Murray study personality through narrative accounts and interviews. McAdams introduced the life story approach to identity, which views identity as a constantly changing story with a beginning, a middle, and an end. Psychobiography is a form of personological inquiry that involves applying personality theory to one person's life.

Evaluating the Life Story Approach and Similar Perspectives

Life story approaches to personality reveal the richness of each person's unique life story. However, this work can be very difficult to carry out. Furthermore, psychobiography can be too subjective and may not be generalizable.

5 SOCIAL COGNITIVE PERSPECTIVES

Explain the social cognitive perspectives.

Bandura's Social Cognitive Theory

Social cognitive theory, created by Bandura and Mischel, states that behavior, environment, and person/cognitive factors are important in understanding personality. In Bandura's view, these factors reciprocally interact. Two important concepts in social cognitive theory are self-efficacy and personal control. Self-efficacy is the belief that one can master a situation and produce positive outcomes. Personal control refers to individuals' beliefs about whether the outcomes of their actions depend on their own acts (internal) or on events outside of their control (external). Numerous research studies reveal that individuals characterized by self-efficacy and high levels of control generally show positive functioning and adjustment.

Mischel's Contributions

Mischel's (1968) *Personality and Assessment,* arguing that personality varies across situations, attacked some key ideas of personality psychology. Mischel's situationist attack stressed that people do not behave consistently across different situations but rather tailor their behavior to suit particular situations. Personality psychologists countered that personality does predict behavior for some people some of the time. Very specific personality characteristics predict behavior better than very general ones, and personality characteristics are more likely to predict behavior in weak versus strong situations. Mischel and his colleagues have developed an approach to personality emphasizing a cognitive affective processing system (CAPS). Mischel has suggested that personality is best understood as a person's habitual emotional and cognitive reactions to specific situations.

Evaluating the Social Cognitive Perspectives

A strength of social cognitive theory is its focus on cognitive processes and self-control. However, social cognitive approaches have not given adequate attention to enduring individual differences, to biological factors, and to personality as a whole.

6 PERSONALITY ASSESSMENT

Characterize the main methods of personality assessment.

Self-Report Tests

Self-report tests assess personality traits by asking test takers questions about their preferences and behaviors. The most popular test for measuring the big five is the NEO-PI-R, which uses self-report items to measure each of the big five traits. Even though a self-report test may have face validity, it may elicit invalid responses, as when people try to answer in a socially desirable way. Empirically keyed tests, which rely on items that are indirect questions about some criterion, were developed to overcome the problem of face validity. The Minnesota Multiphasic Personality Inventory (MMPI) is the most widely used and researched self-report personality test; its 10 clinical scales assist therapists in diagnosing psychological problems.

Projective Tests

Projective tests, designed to assess the unconscious aspects of personality, present individuals with an ambiguous stimulus and then ask them to describe it or to tell a story about it. Projective tests are based on the assumption that the ambiguity of the stimuli allows individuals to project their personalities onto them. The Rorschach inkblot test is a widely used projective test, although its effectiveness is controversial. The Thematic Apperception Test (TAT) is another projective test that has been used in personality research.

Other Assessment Methods

Behavioral assessment seeks to obtain objective information about personality through observation of behavior and its environmental ties. Cognitive assessment seeks to discover individual differences in processing and acting on information through interviews and questionnaires. Other assessment tools include obtaining peer reports and psychophysiological measures.

7 PERSONALITY AND HEALTH AND WELLNESS

Summarize how personality relates to health and wellness.

Conscientiousness and Personal Control

Conscientiousness and personal control relate to health and longevity through their association with healthy lifestyle choices.

Type A/Type B Behavior Patterns

The Type A behavior pattern is a set of characteristics that may put an individual at risk for the development of heart disease. Type A behavior includes hostility, time urgency, and competitiveness. Type B behavior, in contrast, refers to a more easygoing style.

Optimism and Hardiness

Optimism and hardiness are traits that are related to enhanced psychological and physical wellness and particularly to thriving during difficult times.

Traits and States

Personality traits that are related to health and wellness can also be thought of as states. Thus, even if a person is low on these traits, he or she can still benefit by seeking out states that foster positive attributes.

Key Terms

personality, p. 408
psychodynamic perspectives, p. 408
id, p. 409
ego, p. 410
superego, p. 410
defense mechanisms, p. 410
Oedipus complex, p. 411
collective unconscious, p. 413

archetypes, p. 413
individual psychology, p. 414
humanistic perspectives, p. 415
self-concept, p. 416
unconditional positive regard, p. 417
trait, p. 418
trait theories, p. 418
big five factors of personality, p. 419

personological and life story perspectives, p. 423
social cognitive perspectives, p. 425
self-efficacy, p. 426
cognitive affective processing systems (CAPS), p. 428
self-report test, p. 429
face validity, p. 429
empirically keyed test, p. 431

Minnesota Multiphasic Personality Inventory (MMPI), p. 431
projective test, p. 431
Rorschach inkblot test, p. 432
Thematic Apperception Test (TAT), p. 432
Type A behavior pattern, p. 435
Type B behavior pattern, p. 435
hardiness, p. 436

440 CHAPTER 11   Personality

Apply Your Knowledge

1. Consider a facet of your personality that you might want to change. From the perspective of Freud's psychoanalytic theory, could you change this aspect of your personality? If so, how? From the perspective of the psychodynamic revisionists, would it be possible to make the desired change? If so, how?

2. How important has your childhood been to your adult personality? Choose an experience or series of experiences in childhood and describe how those experiences are represented in your current personality.

3. Mischel has argued that personality and behavior are discriminative across situations. Do the following speculative experiment to see just how easy (or difficult) it might be to change your personality. Choose some situation that you frequently encounter and think about how you would change your behavior from your typical routine. What specifically would you change? What do you imagine the experience would be like?

4. Type "personality test" into an Internet search engine, and take two or more of the tests available online. Based on the results, which of the perspectives on personality that you studied in this chapter do the results seem to reflect most? How might the structure of the test have affected the outcome?

5. Now ask a friend to take the same tests as if he or she were you. How much did your friend's results reflect your own views of your personality?

MODULE 41

Trait, Learning, Biological and Evolutionary, and Humanistic Approaches to Personality

"Tell me about Nelson," said Johnetta.

"Oh, he's just terrific. He's the friendliest guy I know—goes out of his way to be nice to everyone. He hardly ever gets mad. He's just so even-tempered, no matter what's happening. And he's really smart, too. About the only thing I don't like is that he's always in such a hurry to get things done. He seems to have boundless energy, much more than I have."

"He sounds great to me, especially in comparison to Rico," replied Johnetta. "He is so self-centered and arrogant that it drives me crazy. I sometimes wonder why I ever started going out with him."

Friendly. Even-tempered. Smart. Energetic. Self-centered. Arrogant.

The above exchange is made up of a series of trait characterizations of speakers' friends. In fact, much of our own understanding of others' behavior is based on the premise that people possess certain traits that are consistent across different situations. For example, we generally assume that if someone is outgoing and sociable in one situation, he or she is outgoing and sociable in other situations (Gilbert et al., 1992; Gilbert, Miller, & Ross, 1998; Mischel, 2004).

Dissatisfaction with the emphasis in psychoanalytic theory on unconscious—and difficult to demonstrate—processes in explaining a person's behavior led to the development of alternative approaches to personality, including a number of trait-based approaches. Other theories reflect established psychological perspectives, such as learning theory, biological and evolutionary approaches, and the humanistic approach.

Trait Approaches: Placing Labels on Personality

If someone asked you to characterize another person, it is probable that—like Johnetta and her friend—you would come up with a list of that individual's personal qualities, as you see them. But how would you know which of those qualities are most important to an understanding of that person's behavior?

Personality psychologists have asked similar questions. To answer them, they have developed a model of personality known as trait theory. **Trait theory** seeks to explain, in a straightforward way, the consistencies in individuals' behavior. **Traits** are consistent personality characteristics and behaviors displayed in different situations.

Trait theorists do not assume that some people have a trait and others do not; rather, they propose that all people possess certain traits, but that the degree to which a particular trait applies to a specific person varies and can be quantified. For instance, you may be relatively friendly, whereas I may be relatively unfriendly. But we both have a "friendliness" trait, although your degree of "friendliness" is higher than mine. The major challenge for trait theorists taking this approach has been to identify the

Key Concept

What are the major aspects of trait, learning, biological and evolutionary, and humanistic approaches to personality?

Trait theory: A model of personality that seeks to identify the basic traits necessary to describe personality.
Traits: Consistent personality characteristics and behaviors displayed in different situations.

458   Chapter 13 Personality

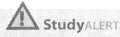

StudyALERT

All trait theories explain personality in terms of traits (consistent personality characteristics and behaviors), but they differ in terms of which and how many traits are seen as fundamental.

Extraversion
• Sociable
• Lively
• Active
• Assertive
• Sensation-seeking

Neuroticism
• Anxious
• Depressed
• Guilt feelings
• Low self-esteem
• Tense

Psychoticism
• Aggressive
• Cold
• Egocentric
• Impersonal
• Impulsive

FIGURE 1 According to Eysenck, personality could best be described in terms of just three major dimensions: extraversion, neuroticism, and psychoticism. Eysenck was able to predict behavior accurately in a variety of types of situations by evaluating people along these three dimensions (Eysenck, 1990). How do you think an airline pilot would score on Eysenck's scale?

specific primary traits necessary to describe personality. As we shall see, different theorists have come up with surprisingly different sets of traits.

ALLPORT'S TRAIT THEORY: IDENTIFYING BASIC CHARACTERISTICS

When personality psychologist Gordon Allport systematically pored over an unabridged dictionary in the 1930s, he came up with some 18,000 separate terms that could be used to describe personality. Although he was able to pare down the list to a mere 4,500 descriptors after eliminating words with the same meaning, he was left with a problem crucial to all trait approaches: Which of those traits were the most basic?

Allport eventually answered this question by suggesting that there are three fundamental categories of traits: cardinal, central, and secondary (Allport, 1961, 1966). A *cardinal trait* is a single characteristic that directs most of a person's activities. For example, a totally selfless woman may direct all her energy toward humanitarian activities; an intensely power-hungry person may be driven by an all-consuming need for control.

Most people, however, do not develop a single, comprehensive cardinal trait. Instead, they possess a handful of central traits that make up the core of personality. *Central traits*, such as honesty and sociability, are the major characteristics of an individual; they usually number from five to ten in any one person. Finally, *secondary traits* are characteristics that affect behavior in fewer situations and are less influential than central or cardinal traits. For instance, a reluctance to eat meat and a love of modern art would be considered secondary traits (Nicholson, 2003; Glicksohn & Nahari, 2007).

CATTELL AND EYSENCK: FACTORING OUT PERSONALITY

Later attempts to identify primary personality traits have centered on a statistical technique known as factor analysis. *Factor analysis* is a statistical method of identifying associations among a large number of variables to reveal more general patterns. For example, a personality researcher might administer a questionnaire to many participants, asking them to describe themselves by referring to an extensive list of traits. By statistically combining responses and computing which traits are associated with one another in the same person, a researcher can identify the most fundamental patterns or combinations of traits—called *factors*—that underlie participants' responses.

Using factor analysis, personality psychologist Raymond Cattell (1965) suggested that 16 pairs of *source traits* represent the basic dimensions of personality. Using those source traits, he developed the Sixteen Personality Factor Questionnaire, or 16 PF, a measure that provides scores for each of the source traits (Cattell, Cattell, & Cattell, 1993; 2000).

Another trait theorist, psychologist Hans Eysenck (1995), also used factor analysis to identify patterns of traits, but he came to a very different conclusion about the nature of personality. He found that personality could best be described in terms of just three major dimensions: *extraversion, neuroticism,* and *psychoticism.* The extraversion dimension relates to the degree of sociability, whereas the neurotic dimension encompasses emotional stability. Finally, psychoticism refers to the degree to which reality is distorted. By evaluating people along these three dimensions, Eysenck was able to predict behavior accurately in a variety of situations. Figure 1 lists specific traits associated with each of the dimensions.

THE BIG FIVE PERSONALITY TRAITS

For the last two decades, the most influential trait approach contends that five traits or factors—called the "Big Five"—lie at the core of personality. Using modern factor analytic statistical techniques, a host of researchers have identified a similar set of five factors that underlie personality. The five factors, described in

The Big Five Personality Factors and Dimensions of Sample Traits

Openness to experience

Independent—Conforming

Imaginative—Practical

Preference for variety—Preference for routine

Conscientiousness

Careful—Careless

Disciplined—Impulsive

Organized—Disorganized

Extraversion

Talkative—Quiet

Fun-loving—Sober

Sociable—Retiring

Agreeableness

Sympathetic—Fault-finding

Kind—Cold

Appreciative—Unfriendly

Neuroticism (Emotional Stability)

Stable—Tense

Calm—Anxious

Secure—Insecure

FIGURE 2 Five broad trait factors, referred to as the "Big Five," are considered to be the core of personality. You can memorize these traits by using the mnemonic OCEAN, representing the first letter of each trait. (Source: Adapted from Pervin, 1990, Chapter 3, and McCrae & Costa, 1986, p. 1002.)

Figure 2, are *openness to experience, conscientiousness, extraversion, agreeableness,* and *neuroticism* (emotional stability).

The Big Five emerge consistently across a number of domains. For example, factor analyses of major personality inventories, self-report measures made by observers of others' personality traits, and checklists of self-descriptions yield similar factors. In addition, the Big Five emerge consistently in different populations of individuals, including children, college students, older adults, and speakers of different languages. Cross-cultural research conducted in areas ranging from Europe to the Middle East to Africa also has been supportive. Finally, studies of brain functioning show that Big Five personality traits are related to the way the brain processes information (see Neuroscience in Your Life Figure 3; Rossier, Dahourou, & McCrae, 2005; McCrae et al., 2005; Schmitt et al., 2007).

In short, a growing consensus exists that the Big Five represent the best description of personality traits we have today. Still, the debate over the specific number and kinds of traits—and even the usefulness of trait approaches in general—remains a lively one.

StudyALERT

You can remember the "Big Five" set of personality traits by using the acronym OCEAN (*o*penness to experience, *c*onscientiousness, *e*xtraversion, *a*greeableness, and *n*euroticism).

EVALUATING TRAIT APPROACHES TO PERSONALITY

Trait approaches have several virtues. They provide a clear, straightforward explanation of people's behavioral consistencies. Furthermore, traits allow us to readily compare one person with another. Because of these advantages, trait approaches to personality have had an important influence on the development of several useful personality measures (Funder, 1991; Wiggins, 2003; Larsen & Buss, 2006).

460   Chapter 13 Personality

FIGURE 3 In a study examining participants' Big 5 trait scores, areas of the left orbitofrontal cortex (A) and right orbitofrontal cortex (B) were found to be related to extraversion scores. (Source: Deckersbach et al., 2006, Figure 2)

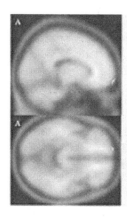
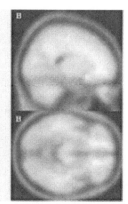

However, trait approaches also have some drawbacks. For example, we have seen that various trait theories describing personality come to very different conclusions about which traits are the most fundamental and descriptive. The difficulty in determining which of the theories is the most accurate has led some personality psychologists to question the validity of trait conceptions of personality in general.

Actually, there is an even more fundamental difficulty with trait approaches. Even if we are able to identify a set of primary traits, we are left with little more than a label or description of personality—rather than an explanation of behavior. If we say that someone who donates money to charity has the trait of generosity, we still do not know *why* that person became generous in the first place or the reasons for displaying generosity in a specific situation. In the view of some critics, then, traits do not provide explanations for behavior; they merely describe it.

Learning Approaches: We Are What We've Learned

The psychodynamic and trait approaches we've discussed concentrate on the "inner" person—the fury of an unobservable but powerful id or a hypothetical but critical set of traits. In contrast, learning approaches to personality focus on the "outer" person. To a strict learning theorist, personality is simply the sum of learned responses to the external environment. Internal events such as thoughts, feelings, and motivations are ignored. Although the existence of personality is not denied, learning theorists say that it is best understood by looking at features of a person's environment.

SKINNER'S BEHAVIORIST APPROACH

According to the most influential learning theorist, B. F. Skinner (who carried out pioneering work on operant conditioning), personality is a collection of learned behavior patterns (Skinner, 1975). Similarities in responses across different situations are caused by similar patterns of reinforcement that have been received in such situations in the past. If I am sociable both at parties and at meetings, it is because I have been reinforced for displaying social behaviors—not because I am fulfilling an unconscious wish based on experiences during my childhood or because I have an internal trait of sociability.

Strict learning theorists such as Skinner are less interested in the consistencies in behavior across situations than in ways of modifying behavior. Their view is that humans are infinitely changeable through the process of learning new behavior patterns. If we are able to control and modify the patterns of reinforcers in a situation, behavior that other theorists would view as stable and unyielding can be changed and ultimately improved. Learning theorists are optimistic in their attitudes about the potential for resolving personal and societal problems through treatment strategies based on learning theory.

SOCIAL COGNITIVE APPROACHES TO PERSONALITY

Not all learning theories of personality take such a strict view in rejecting the importance of what is "inside" a person by focusing solely on the "outside." Unlike other learning approaches to personality, **social cognitive approaches** emphasize the influence of cognition—thoughts, feelings, expectations, and values—as well as observation of other's behavior, on personality. According to Albert Bandura, one of the main proponents of this point of view, people can foresee the possible outcomes of certain behaviors in a specific setting without actually having to carry them out. This understanding comes primarily through *observational learning*—viewing the actions of others and observing the consequences (Bandura, 1986, 1999).

For instance, children who view a model behaving in, say, an aggressive manner tend to copy the behavior if the consequences of the model's behavior are seen to be positive. If, in contrast, the model's aggressive behavior has resulted in no consequences or negative consequences, children are considerably less likely to act aggressively. According to social cognitive approaches, then, personality develops through repeated observation of the behavior of others.

SELF-EFFICACY

Bandura places particular emphasis on the role played by **self-efficacy**, belief in one's personal capabilities. Self-efficacy underlies people's faith in their ability to carry out a specific task or produce a desired outcome. People with high self-efficacy have higher aspirations and greater persistence in working to attain goals and ultimately achieve greater success than do those with lower self-efficacy (Bandura, 2001; Bandura & Locke, 2003; Glickler, 2006).

How do we develop self-efficacy? One way is by paying close attention to our prior successes and failures. If we try snowboarding and experience little success, we'll be less likely to try it again. However, if our initial efforts appear promising, we'll be more likely to attempt it again. Direct reinforcement and encouragement from others also play a role in developing self-efficacy (Devonport & Lane, 2006).

Compared with other learning theories of personality, social cognitive approaches are distinctive in their emphasis on the reciprocity between individuals and their environment. Not only is the environment assumed to affect personality, but people's behavior and personalities are also assumed to "feed back" and modify the environment (Bandura, 1999, 2000).

SELF-ESTEEM

Our behavior also reflects the view we have of ourselves and the way we value the various parts of our personalities. **Self-esteem** is the component of personality that encompasses our positive and negative self-evaluations. Unlike self-efficacy, which focuses on our views of whether we are able to carry out a task, self-esteem relates to how we feel about ourselves.

Social cognitive approaches to personality: Theories that emphasize the influence of a person's cognitions—thoughts, feelings, expectations, and values—as well as observation of others' behavior, in determining personality.

Self-efficacy: Belief in one's personal capabilities. Self-efficacy underlies people's faith in their ability to carry out a particular behavior or produce a desired outcome.

Self-esteem: The component of personality that encompasses our positive and negative self-evaluations.

Self-efficacy, the belief in one's own capabilities, leads to higher aspirations and greater persistence.

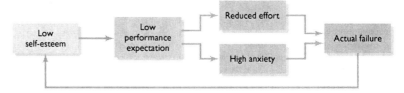

FIGURE 4 The cycle of low self-esteem begins with an individual's already having low self-esteem. As a consequence, the person will have low performance expectations and expect to fail a test, thereby producing anxiety and reduced effort. As a result, the person will actually fail, and failure in turn reinforces low self-esteem.

Although people have a general level of self-esteem, it is not unidimensional. We may see ourselves positively in one domain but negatively in others. For example, a good student may have high self-esteem in academic domains but lower self-esteem in sports (Crocker & Park, 2004; Swann, Chang-Schneider, & Larsen McClarty, 2007; Salmela-Aro & Nurmi, 2007).

Self-esteem has strong cultural components. For example, having high *relationship harmony*—a sense of success in forming close bonds with other people—is more important to self-esteem in Asian cultures than it is in more individualistic Western societies (Spencer-Rodgers et al., 2004; Lun & Bond, 2006).

Although almost everyone goes through periods of low self-esteem (after, for instance, an undeniable failure), some people are chronically low in self-esteem. For them, failure seems to be an inevitable part of life. In fact, low self-esteem may lead to a cycle of failure in which past failure breeds future failure.

Consider, for example, students with low self-esteem who are studying for a test. Because of their low self-esteem, they expect to do poorly on the test. In turn, this belief raises their anxiety level, making it increasingly difficult to study and perhaps even leading them not to work as hard. Because of these attitudes, the ultimate outcome is that they do, in fact, perform badly on the test. Ultimately, the failure reinforces their low self-esteem, and the cycle is perpetuated, as illustrated in Figure 4. In short, low self-esteem can lead to a cycle of failure that is self-destructive.

EVALUATING LEARNING APPROACHES TO PERSONALITY

Because they ignore the internal processes that are uniquely human, traditional learning theorists such as Skinner have been accused of oversimplifying personality to such an extent that the concept becomes meaningless. In the eyes of their critics, reducing behavior to a series of stimuli and responses, and excluding thoughts and feelings from the realm of personality, leaves behaviorists practicing an unrealistic and inadequate form of science.

Of course, some of these criticisms are blunted by social cognitive approaches, which explicitly consider the role of cognitive processes in personality. Still, learning approaches tend to share a highly *deterministic* view of human behavior, maintaining that behavior is shaped primarily by forces beyond the control of the individual. As in psychoanalytic theory (which suggests that personality is determined by the unconscious forces) and trait approaches (which views personality in part as a mixture of genetically determined traits), learning theory's reliance on deterministic principles deemphasizes the ability of people to pilot their own course through life.

Nonetheless, learning approaches have had a major impact on the study of personality. For one thing, they have helped make personality psychology an objective, scientific venture by focusing on observable behavior and their environment. In addition, they have produced important, successful means of treating a variety of psychological disorders. The degree of success of these treatments is a testimony to the merits of learning theory approaches to personality.

Biological and Evolutionary Approaches: Are We Born with Personality?

Approaching the question of what determines personality from a different direction, **biological and evolutionary approaches** to personality suggest that important components of personality are inherited. Building on the work of behavioral geneticists, researchers using biological and evolutionary approaches argue that personality is determined at least in part by our genes, in much the same way that our height is largely a result of genetic contributions from our ancestors. The evolutionary perspective assumes that personality traits that led to survival and reproductive success of our ancestors are more likely to be preserved and passed on to subsequent generations (Buss, 2001).

The importance of genetic factors in personality is illustrated by studies of twins. For instance, personality psychologists Auke Tellegen and colleagues at the University of Minnesota examined the personality traits of pairs of twins who were genetically identical but were raised apart from each other (Tellegen et al., 1988, 2004). In the study, each twin was given a battery of personality tests, including one that measured 11 key personality characteristics.

The results of the personality tests indicated that in major respects the twins were quite similar in personality, despite having separated at an early age. Moreover, certain traits were more heavily influenced by heredity than were others. For example, social potency (the degree to which a person assumes mastery and leadership roles in social situations) and traditionalism (the tendency to follow authority) had particularly strong genetic components, whereas achievement and social closeness had relatively weak genetic components (see Figure 5).

Biological and evolutionary approaches to personality: Theories that suggest that important components of personality are inherited.

 **Study**ALERT

Remember that biological and evolutionary approaches focus on the way in which people's genetic heritage affects personality.

Biological and evolutionary approaches to personality seek to explain the consistencies in personality that are found in some families.

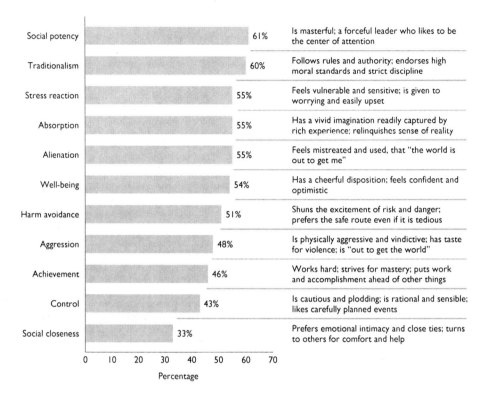

Social potency	61%	Is masterful; a forceful leader who likes to be the center of attention
Traditionalism	60%	Follows rules and authority; endorses high moral standards and strict discipline
Stress reaction	55%	Feels vulnerable and sensitive; is given to worrying and easily upset
Absorption	55%	Has a vivid imagination readily captured by rich experience; relinquishes sense of reality
Alienation	55%	Feels mistreated and used, that "the world is out to get me"
Well-being	54%	Has a cheerful disposition; feels confident and optimistic
Harm avoidance	51%	Shuns the excitement of risk and danger; prefers the safe route even if it is tedious
Aggression	48%	Is physically aggressive and vindictive; has taste for violence; is "out to get the world"
Achievement	46%	Works hard; strives for mastery; puts work and accomplishment ahead of other things
Control	43%	Is cautious and plodding; is rational and sensible; likes carefully planned events
Social closeness	33%	Prefers emotional intimacy and close ties; turns to others for comfort and help

Percentage

FIGURE 5 The inherited roots of personality. The percentages indicate the degree to which 11 personality characteristics reflect the influence of heredity. (Source: Tellegen et al., 1988.)

Temperament: The innate disposition that emerges early in life.

Furthermore, it is increasingly clear that the roots of adult personality emerge in the earliest periods of life. Infants are born with a specific **temperament,** an innate disposition. Temperament encompasses several dimensions, including general activity level and mood. For instance, some individuals are quite active, while others are relatively calm. Similarly, some are relatively easygoing, while others are irritable, easily upset, and difficult to soothe. Temperament is quite consistent, with significant stability from infancy well into adolescence (Caspi et al., 2003; Wachs et al., 2004; Evans & Rothbart, 2007).

Some researchers contend that specific genes are related to personality. For example, people with a longer dopamine-4 receptor gene are more likely to be thrill seekers than are those without such a gene. These thrill seekers tend to be extroverted, impulsive, quick-tempered, and always in search of excitement and novel situations (Zuckerman & Kuhlman, 2000; Robins, 2005; Golimbet et al., 2007).

Does the identification of specific genes linked to personality, coupled with the existence of temperaments from the time of birth, mean that we are destined to have certain types of personalities? Hardly. First, it is unlikely that any single gene is linked to a specific trait. For instance, the dopamine-4 receptor accounts for only around 10 percent of the variation in novelty seeking between different individuals. The rest of the variation is attributable to other genes and environmental factors (Keltikangas-Järvinen et al., 2004; Lahti et al., 2005).

More importantly, genes interact with the environment. As we see in discussions of the heritability of intelligence and the nature–nurture issue, it is impossible to completely divorce genetic factors from environmental factors. Although studies

Feldman: Understanding
Psychology, Ninth Edition

XIII. Personality

41. Trait, Learning,
Biological and
Evolutionary, and
Humanistic Approaches to
Personality

© The McGraw–Hill
Companies, 2009

of identical twins raised in different environments are helpful, they are not definitive, because it is impossible to assess and control environmental factors fully. Furthermore, estimates of the influence of genetics are just that—estimates—and apply to groups, not individuals. Consequently, findings such as those shown in Figure 5 must be regarded as approximations.

Finally, even if more genes are found to be linked to specific personality characteristics, genes still cannot be viewed as the sole cause of personality. For one thing, genetically determined characteristics may not be expressed if they are not "turned on" by particular environmental experiences. Furthermore, behaviors produced by genes may help to create a specific environment. For instance, a cheerful, smiley baby may lead her parents to smile more and be more responsive, thereby creating an environment that is supportive and pleasant. In contrast, the parents of a cranky, fussy baby may be less inclined to smile at the child; in turn, the environment in which that child is raised will be a less supportive and pleasant one. In a sense, then, genes not only influence a person's behavior—they also help produce the environment in which a person develops (Scarr, 1993, 1998; Plomin & Caspi, 1999; Kim-Cohen et al., 2003, 2005).

Although an increasing number of personality theorists are taking biological and evolutionary factors into account, no comprehensive, unified theory that considers biological and evolutionary factors is widely accepted. Still, it is clear that certain personality traits have substantial genetic components, and that heredity and environment interact to determine personality (Plomin et al., 2003; Ebstein, Benjamin, & Belmaker, 2003; Bouchard, 2004).

Infants are born with particular temperaments, dispositions that are consistent throughout childhood.

Humanistic Approaches: The Uniqueness of You

Where, in all the approaches to personality that we have discussed, is an explanation for the saintliness of a Mother Teresa, the creativity of a Michelangelo, and the brilliance and perseverance of an Einstein? An understanding of such unique individuals—as well as more ordinary sorts of people who have some of the same attributes—comes from humanistic theory.

According to humanistic theorists, all the approaches to personality we have discussed share a fundamental misperception in their views of human nature. Instead of seeing people as controlled by unconscious, unseen forces (as do psychodynamic approaches), a set of stable traits (trait approaches), situational reinforcements and punishments (learning theory), or inherited factors (biological and evolutionary approaches), **humanistic approaches** emphasize people's inherent goodness and their tendency to move toward higher levels of functioning. It is this conscious, self-motivated ability to change and improve, along with people's unique creative impulses, that humanistic theorists argue make up the core of personality.

Humanistic approaches to personality: Theories that emphasize people's innate goodness and desire to achieve higher levels of functioning.

ROGERS AND THE NEED FOR SELF-ACTUALIZATION

The major proponent of the humanistic point of view is Carl Rogers (1971). Along with other humanistic theorists, such as Abraham Maslow, Rogers maintains that all people have a fundamental need for **self-actualization**, a state of self-fulfillment in which people realize their highest potential, each in a unique way. He further suggests that people develop a need for positive regard that reflects the desire to be loved and respected. Because others provide this positive regard, we grow dependent on them. We begin to see and judge ourselves through the eyes of other people, relying on their values and being preoccupied with what they think of us.

According to Rogers, one outgrowth of placing importance on the opinions of others is that a conflict may grow between people's experiences and their *self-concepts*, the set of beliefs they hold about what they are like as individuals. If the

Self-actualization: A state of self-fulfillment in which people realize their highest potential, each in a unique way.

"So, while extortion, racketeering, and murder may be bad acts, they don't make you a bad person."

Unconditional positive regard:
An attitude of acceptance and respect on the part of an observer, no matter what a person says or does.

discrepancies are minor, so are the consequences. But if the discrepancies are great, they will lead to psychological disturbances in daily functioning, such as the experience of frequent anxiety.

Rogers suggests that one way of overcoming the discrepancy between experience and self-concept is through the receipt of unconditional positive regard from another person—a friend, a spouse, or a therapist. **Unconditional positive regard** refers to an attitude of acceptance and respect on the part of an observer, no matter what a person says or does. This acceptance, says Rogers, gives people the opportunity to evolve and grow both cognitively and emotionally and to develop more realistic self-concepts. You may have experienced the power of unconditional positive regard when you confided in someone, revealing embarrassing secrets because you knew the listener would still love and respect you, even after hearing the worst about you (Snyder, 2002; Marshall, 2007).

In contrast, *conditional positive regard* depends on your behavior. In such cases, others withdraw their love and acceptance if you do something of which they don't approve. The result is a discrepancy between your true self and what others wish you would be, leading to anxiety and frustration (see Figure 6).

EVALUATING HUMANISTIC APPROACHES

Although humanistic theories suggest the value of providing unconditional positive regard toward people, unconditional positive regard toward humanistic theories has been less forthcoming. The criticisms have centered on the difficulty of verifying the basic assumptions of the approach, as well as on the question of whether unconditional positive regard does, in fact, lead to greater personality adjustment.

Humanistic approaches have also been criticized for making the assumption that people are basically "good"—a notion that is unverifiable—and, equally important, for using nonscientific values to build supposedly scientific theories. Still, humanistic theories have been important in highlighting the uniqueness of human beings and guiding the development of a significant form of therapy designed to alleviate psychological difficulties (Cain, 2002; Bauman & Kopp, 2006).

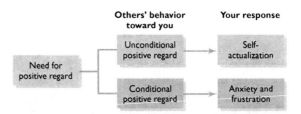

FIGURE 6 According to the humanistic view of Carl Rogers, people have a basic need to be loved and respected. If you receive unconditional positive regard from others, you will develop a more realistic self-concept; but if the response is conditional, it may lead to anxiety and frustration.

Comparing Approaches to Personality

In light of the multiple approaches we have discussed, you may be wondering which of the theories provides the most accurate description of personality. That is a question that cannot be answered precisely. Each theory is built on different assumptions and focuses on somewhat different aspects of personality (see Figure 7). Furthermore, there is no clear way to scientifically test the various approaches and their assumptions against one another. Given the complexity of every individual, it seems reasonable that personality can be viewed from a number of perspectives simultaneously (Pervin, 2003).

Theoretical Approach and Major Theorists	Conscious Versus Unconscious Determinants of Personality	Nature (Hereditary Factors) Versus Nurture (Environmental Factors)	Free Will Versus Determinism	Stability Versus Modifiability
Psychodynamic (Freud, Jung, Horney, Adler)	Emphasizes the unconscious	Stresses innate, inherited structure of personality while emphasizing importance of childhood experience	Stresses determinism, the view that behavior is directed and caused by factors outside one's control	Emphasizes the stability of characteristics throughout a person's life
Trait (Allport, Cattell, Eysenck)	Disregards both conscious and unconscious	Approaches vary	Stresses determinism, the view that behavior is directed and caused by factors outside one's control	Emphasizes the stability of characteristics throughout a person's life
Learning (Skinner, Bandura)	Disregards both conscious and unconscious	Focuses on the environment	Stresses determinism, the view that behavior is directed and caused by factors outside one's control	Stresses that personality remains flexible and resilient throughout one's life
Biological and Evolutionary (Tellegen)	Disregards both conscious and unconscious	Stresses the innate, inherited determinants of personality	Stresses determinism, the view that behavior is directed and caused by factors outside one's control	Emphasizes the stability of characteristics throughout a person's life
Humanistic (Rogers, Maslow)	Stresses the conscious more than unconscious	Stresses the interaction between both nature and nurture	Stresses the freedom of individuals to make their own choices	Stresses that personality remains flexible and resilient throughout one's life

FIGURE 7 The multiple perspectives of personality.

RECAP/EVALUATE/RETHINK

RECAP

What are the major aspects of trait, learning, biological and evolutionary, and humanistic approaches to personality?

- Trait approaches have been used to identify relatively enduring dimensions along which people differ from one another—dimensions known as traits. (p. 457)

- Learning approaches to personality concentrate on observable behavior. To a strict learning theorist, personality is the sum of learned responses to the external environment. (p. 458)

- Social cognitive approaches concentrate on the role of cognition in determining personality. Those approaches pay particular attention to self-efficacy and self-esteem in determining behavior. (p. 461)

- Biological and evolutionary approaches to personality focus on the way in which personality characteristics are inherited. (p. 463)

- Humanistic approaches emphasize the inherent goodness of people. They consider the core of personality in terms of a person's ability to change and improve. (p. 465)

468   Chapter 13 Personality

- The major personality approaches differ substantially from one another; the differences may reflect both their focus on different aspects of personality and the overall complexity of personality. (p. 467)

EVALUATE

1. Carl's determination to succeed is the dominant force in all his activities and relationships. According to Gordon Allport's theory, this is an example of a _____ trait. In contrast, Cindy's fondness for old western movies is an example of a _____ trait.
2. A person who enjoys activities such as parties and hang gliding might be described by Eysenck as high on what trait?
3. Proponents of which approach to personality would be most likely to agree with the statement "Personality can be thought of as learned responses to a person's upbringing and environment"?
   a. Humanistic
   b. Biological and evolutionary
   c. Learning
   d. Trait

4. A person who would make the statement "I know I can't do it" would be rated by Bandura as low on _____ - _____.
5. Which approach to personality emphasizes the innate goodness of people and their desire to grow?
   a. Humanistic
   b. Psychodynamic
   c. Learning
   d. Biological and evolutionary

RETHINK

1. If personality traits are merely descriptive and not explanatory, of what use are they? Can assigning a trait to a person be harmful—or helpful? Why or why not?
2. *From the perspective of an educator:* How might you encourage your students' development of self-esteem and self-efficacy? What steps would you take to ensure that their self-esteem did not become over-inflated?

Answers to Evaluate Questions

1. cardinal, secondary; 2. extraversion; 3. c; 4. self-efficacy; 5. a

KEY TERMS

trait theory p. 457
traits p. 457
social cognitive approaches to personality p. 461
self-efficacy p. 461

self-esteem p. 461
biological and evolutionary approaches to personality p. 463
temperament p. 464

humanistic approaches to personality p. 465
self-actualization p. 465
unconditional positive regard p. 466

Cox: Sport Psychology: | II. Motivation in Sport and | 6. Goal Perspective Theory
Concepts and Applications, | Exercise
Sixth Edition

© The McGraw–Hill
Companies, 2007

103

6 CHAPTER

Goal Perspective Theory

KEY TERMS

Achievement motivation
Adaptive motivational pattern
Cognitive restructuring
Competitive climate
Competitive orientation
Differentiated goal perspective
Ego involvement
Ego goal orientation
Goal involvement
Goal orientation
Maladaptive motivational
   pattern
Mastery climate
Mastery orientation
Matching hypothesis
Motivational climate
Perceived ability
Social approval goal orientation
Sportspersonship
Task involvement
Task goal orientation
Undifferentiated goal
   perspective

I n this chapter we will introduce a theory of
motivation that focuses upon the different ways
children and adults think about their own competence and about the different ways they conceptualize ability. The phrase *goal perspective theory* was
introduced by researchers to describe this approach

to theorizing about motivation. The word "goal" in
the phrase is a little confusing because goal perspective theory is not about setting goals; it is about
the different ways that athletes approach and think
about achievement situations. By way of example,
consider the goal perspective orientations of two

hypothetical athletes. Joe is 16 years old and has been playing tennis competitively for four years. His friends describe him as being a highly competitive person because he becomes very distraught if he loses a match. Winning seems to mean everything to him. For example, he once commented to a friend that he didn't care how he played the game, just as long as he was victorious. Contrast this orientation with that of Mary, a 16-year-old gymnast who has been competing for eight years but approaches every tournament from the perspective of having fun and doing her very best. Because of her work ethic and desire to excel, she puts in many hours of practice, but never seems to get overly upset when she does not win a competition. Her friends describe her as a person who strives for perfection but does not seem to be caught up in defeating her opponent. Her focus always seems to be on self-improvement and working hard. With this lay introduction to goal perspective theory, let us now turn our attention to a more theoretical discussion of goal perspective theory.

Nicholls' (1984, 1989) theory of motivation provides a framework for considering individuals' motivational perspectives across the lifespan. Nicholls' developmentally based theory of **achievement motivation** is a logical extension of both Bandura's theory of self-efficacy and Harter's theory of competence motivation. According to Nicholls (1984) and Duda (1989), the defining feature of achievement motivation is the way children come to view their own **perceived ability.** In goal perspective theory, the nature of perceived ability changes initially as a function of developmental level of the child, and later as a function of learning and **cognitive restructuring.** The sections of this chapter are logically developed to assure a systematic and clear understanding of the important concepts that make up Nicholls' goal perspective theory. Important concepts to be discussed in this chapter include (a) achievement goal orientations, (b) the developmental nature of goal orientation, (c) measuring goal orientation, (d) goal involvement, (e) goal orientation and moral reasoning, and (f) characteristics of task and ego goal orientation.

Athletes exhibiting a mature goal orientation understand the difference between ability, effort, and luck. Courtesy University of Missouri–Columbia Sports Information.

Achievement Goal Orientation

There are two **goal orientations** mentioned by Nicholls. They are task orientation and ego orientation. These two orientations are referred to as goal orientations because they differ as a function of the individual's achievement goal. In the case of **task goal orientation,** the goal is mastery of a particular skill. Perceived ability for the task-oriented individual is a function of perceived improvement from one point in time to the next. The task-oriented athlete perceives herself to be of high ability if she can perform a task better today than she could one week ago. The task-oriented individual continues to work for mastery of the skill she is working on, and enjoys feelings of self-efficacy and confidence in so doing.

At this point, you are probably thinking that everyone must be task oriented, because everyone enjoys mastering a task. Not necessarily. At some point in our lives we become aware of the consequences of social comparison. When we start to make social comparisons, we adopt a different sort of goal orientation. It is no longer enough simply to gain mastery over a skill and make personal improvements. We must also demonstrate that we can outperform another individual or other individuals. For the person with an **ego goal orientation,** perceived ability is measured as a function of outperforming others, as opposed to self-improvement. In some ways, this is a sorry state of affairs, as the ego-oriented individual's perceived ability and self-confidence is tied to how he compares with others as opposed to objective improvement in skill.

> Life used to be so simple. When I was a child I thought I was doing pretty good if I could skip a rock across a small stream. Now things are different. Not only do I have to skip the rock across the stream, but I have to do it better than the guy next to me (Anonymous).

Traditionalists such as Treasure, Duda, Hall, Roberts, Ames, and Maehr (2001) argue persuasively that there are only two basic goal orientations (task and ego goal orientation), while researchers such as Harwood, Hardy, and Swain (2000) have argued that a third or even fourth goal orientation might exist. For example, Gernigon, d'Arripe-Longueville, Delignieres, and Ninot (2004) conducted a qualitative study on judo competitors who they claimed revealed a third perspective for conceptualizing goal orientation. They described this third goal orientation to be ego involved in nature, but with a focus on avoiding embarrassment or defeat, as opposed to wanting to outperform the opponent. Two other groups of researchers identified **social approval goal orientation** to be a third goal perspective (Schilling & Hayashi, 2001; Stuntz & Weiss, 2003). Social goal orientation emphasizes the desire for social

acceptance through conformity to norms while displaying maximum effort.

Developmental Nature of Goal Orientation

According to Nicholls (1984, 1989), a child two to six years old views perceived ability in terms of how well she performed the task the last time. If the child notices an improvement in performance from time one to time two, she naturally assumes that ability has increased and that she is competent at performing the task. High amounts of effort in mastering the task are perceived by the child as evidence of high ability and competence. Competence is perceived by the child as a function of hard work and absolute capacity. At this early age, the child is said to be task oriented, as opposed to ego oriented.

At the age of six or seven, the child begins to view perceived ability in terms of how other children perform. The child becomes ego oriented, as opposed to task oriented. No longer is it enough to perform the task better than she performed it the last time; the child must now perform the task better than other children do. Perceived ability is now a function of one's own capacity as it is relative to that of others, as opposed to being a function of absolute ability. High ability and competence are only perceived as such if they are better than the performance of others.

After age 11 or 12, the child may exhibit either a task- or an ego-involved disposition, depending upon the situation at hand. Environmental factors causing a person to focus upon social comparisons will result in an ego-oriented disposition, while situations causing a person to focus upon personal mastery and improved performance will foster a task-oriented disposition.

From a developmental perspective, children mature with respect to how well they are able to differentiate between the concepts of effort, ability, and outcome. According to Nicholls, children pass developmentally through four levels as they

CONCEPT & APPLICATION

6.1

CONCEPT Children pass through four developmental levels in terms of their understanding of the concepts of effort, ability, and outcome. In Level 1 they cannot differentiate among concepts of effort, ability, and outcome; by Level 4, they can.

APPLICATION Knowing where a child is in the developmental hierarchy will help the adult leader

to plan activities for children. Keeping score with children in Level 1 makes no theoretical sense. If all the children try equally hard, they should exhibit the same ability and have the same score. That is how children in the first level see things, and forcing them to think in terms of winning and losing is only confusing.

come to fully understand these three concepts, as well as the concepts of luck and task difficulty.

Level 1 At this early level, the child views effort, ability, and outcome as the same thing. At this level of development, the child is said to have an **undifferentiated goal perspective.** To the child at this age level, effort, or trying hard, is the same as ability or having a successful outcome. Furthermore, the child has no concept of how luck differs from ability or how one task can be more difficult than another.

Level 2 At Level 2, the child is beginning to recognize that there is a difference between effort and ability, but the child believes that effort is the major determinant of achieving success. If you try hard and expend lots of effort, you will find success.

Level 3 The third level is transitional, in the sense that the child is beginning to differentiate between ability and effort. Sometimes the child will recognize that effort is not the same as ability, but at other times he will revert back to an undifferentiated conceptualization of the two.

Level 4 Children and adults in Level 4 have a **differentiated goal perspective.** At around age 12, the child can clearly distinguish among the concepts of ability, effort, luck, and outcome. She also

clearly understands the ramifications of task difficulty and recognizes that some tasks (opponents) will be more difficult than others. For example, the child understands that effort enhances performance of tasks requiring high ability (skill), but not that of tasks requiring luck. Furthermore, the child understands that low effort coupled with strong performance is probably indicative of high ability.

Research by Fry (2000) and Fry and Duda (1997) shows support for Nicholls' developmental theory of achievement motivation in the physical or sport and exercise domain. Children do in fact pass through these four developmental levels. Children in Level 1 exhibit a task goal orientation, but this is not by choice. The child simply cannot differentiate between effort and ability, so he thinks only in terms of mastery and trying hard. Children and adults in Level 4 have a mature concept of the meaning of effort and ability, and can therefore learn to exhibit either a task or an ego orientation toward achievement or competitive situations.

As a child matures, he will go from being task goal oriented to being more ego goal oriented. After the age of around 12, however, goal orientations fluctuate as a function of life's experiences as well as personality characteristics. Of interest is the effect that significant others may have on goal orientation in children. Carr and Weigand (2002) studied the relationship between the goal orientation of students ages 11 to 15 with their perception of their

148   Part Two   Motivation in Sport and Exercise

teachers, coaches, peers and sport heroes' goal orientations. Results showed that task-oriented children perceive significant others and sport heroes to favor a task-oriented learning environment.

Young children cannot differentiate between ability and effort, perceiving that trying hard is the same as ability. Conversely, older children can differentiate between effort and ability, recognizing that great effort may not mean success if ability is lacking. In a study reported by Chase (2001), measures of effort and persistence, future self-efficacy, and attributions for failure were obtained on 289 children of different sexes and ages (grades 3, 5, and 8) following a failure scenario. Dividing participants as a function of current self-efficacy, it was observed that (a) younger children score higher on effort than older children, and (b) low self-efficacy children attributed perceived failure to lack of ability more than high self-efficacy children did.

Measuring Goal Orientation

In order to determine whether individuals exhibit task and/or ego goal orientations, a number of inventories have been developed. These are the Task and Ego Orientation in Sport Questionnaire (TEOSQ), the Perceptions of Success Questionnaire (POSQ), and the Sports Orientation Questionnaire (SOQ). The TEOSQ (Duda, 1989; White & Duda, 1994) is composed of 15 items that measure task and ego orientation. The POSQ (Roberts, 1993; Roberts & Treasure, 1995) is composed of 12 items that measure competitiveness (ego orientation) and mastery (task orientation). The SOQ (Gill, 1993; Gill & Deeter, 1988) is composed of 25 items and purports to measure competitiveness, win orientation, and goal orientation. It is unclear, however, exactly how each of these factors compares with basic task and ego orientations (Marsh, 1994). Similar to the TEOSQ, a new 10-item inventory called the Goal Orientation in Exercise Scale (GOES; Kilpatrick, Bartholomew, & Reimer, 2003) was developed to measure task and goal orientation in the exercise as opposed to the sport environment.

The TEOSQ and the POSQ result in separate scores representing an athlete's level of task orientation and ego orientation. Somewhat confusing is the fact that in the POSQ, task orientation is named **mastery orientation** and ego orientation is named **competitive orientation.** It would appear, however, that the mastery and competitive orientation labels are more descriptive of the concepts being measured. While somewhat controversial (Harwood, Hardy, & Swain, 2000; Pierce & Burton, 1998), the two goal orientations are conceptualized as being independent of each other. An individual can be high on both orientations, low on both, or some combination of high and low on both.

The notion that task and ego goal orientations are independent, or orthogonal to each other, is supported in the sport psychology literature (Gernigon et al., 2004; Harwood & Hardy, 2001; Harwood & Swain, 2001). This means that an athlete can be task and ego goal oriented at the same time. In other words, being high on task orientation does not necessarily mean that that you have to be low on ego goal orientation. The two goal orientations are not at opposite ends of the same continuum. This concept is illustrated clearly in figure 6.1.

FIGURE 6.1 | Task and goal orientation are independent or orthogonal to each other.

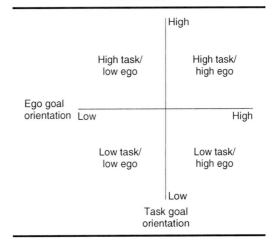

Goal Involvement

Related to the measurement issue is the observation by Nicholls (1989) and L. Williams (1998) that there are really two types of goal perspective. One is referred to as goal orientation as described above, and the other is called goal involvement. Instruments such as the TEOSQ and POSQ measure goal orientation (i.e., task and ego orientation) and represent dispositional or personality traits relative to the two orientations. Conversely, **goal involvement** is a situation-specific state measure of how an individual relates to an achievement situation at a specific point in time.

According to Nicholls (1989), situations that heighten awareness of social evaluation induce a state of **ego involvement,** accompanied by feelings of increased anxiety. Conversely, situations that do not heighten an awareness of social evaluation evoke a state of **task involvement,** accompanied by feelings of low anxiety. To be ego involved is to display characteristics of an ego-oriented person in a specific situation. To be task involved is to display characteristics of a task-oriented person in a specific situation. As might be surmised, goal involvement is greatly influenced by the motivational climate or environment, a topic we will discuss in the next section.

L. Williams (1998) reported an investigation in which the concept of goal involvement was measured and studied in a sport-related environment. In this investigation, goal involvement was measured using the Goal Involvement in Sport Questionnaire (GISQ), which is nothing more than the TEOSQ with situation-specific instructions. Instead of asking an athlete how she generally felt relative to an item on the TEOSQ, Williams asked the athlete to indicate how she felt "right now" on the same item relative to a current situation. In the Williams study, the "current situation" was either a team practice or a team competition. The results of the investigation confirmed that athletes exhibit higher levels of task involvement and lower levels of anxiety prior to a practice than prior to an actual game.

Motivational Climate

We don't really look at 8–0, we look at each match. We try to prepare for each match that we are going to play, and our focus is what we're doing out on the court. Regardless of the opponent we've got to prepare to play and we've got to take care of business. And if we work hard hopefully good things will happen (Susan Kreklow, Volleyball Coach, University of Missouri–Columbia, Hopp, 2000).

Perhaps of greater import than whether an individual is task or ego oriented is the **motivational climate** that the individual is placed in. Just as individuals can be task or ego oriented, learning environments can also be task or ego oriented. An ego-oriented environment, with its emphasis upon social comparison, can be particularly harmful to low-ability youth. Conversely, high-ability children seem to thrive in either environment. The effects of a mastery-, or task-oriented, learning environment can reverse the negative effects of an ego orientation (Amos, 1992).

The Perceived Motivational Climate on Sport Questionnaire (PMCSQ; Seifriz, Duda, & Chi, 1992) and the PMCSQ–2 (Newton, 1994; Newton, Duda, & Yin, 2000) were developed to assess an athlete's perception of whether a motivational climate emphasized mastery-based (task orientation) or competitive-based (ego orientation) goals. A **mastery climate** is one in which athletes receive positive reinforcement from the coach when they (a) work hard, (b) demonstrate improvement, (c) help others learn through cooperation, and (d) believe that each player's contribution is important. A **competitive climate** is one in which athletes perceive that (a) poor performance and mistakes will be punished, (b) high-ability athletes will receive the most attention and recognition, and (c) competition between team members is encouraged by the coach. For purposes of clarification, it should be noted that in the literature "competitive climate" is often referred to as "performance climate."

As one reflects upon the differences between the two climates, it is instructive to reflect back once again on Bill Walton's contrast of the coaching styles of his own college coach, John Wooden, and Bobby Knight. In light of what is written above about the two contrasting motivational climates, consider Bill Walton's poignant statement:

> We all need motivation. It's a particularly important aspect of sports because the tiniest of margins often separates the winners from the losers. Yet with Knight, we're not talking about a constructive approach to making people perform by challenging them on their positions or on their failures in life. Knight does it to denigrate. Doesn't Indiana know that universities are supposed to be about how you teach? Teaching is about building confidence, about making people feel better about what they do and who they are (Walton, 2000, p. 96).

In explaining goal perspective theory, we have introduced and explained two different kinds of goal orientation, two different kinds of goal involvement, and two different kinds of motivational climate. These several concepts are summarized in table 6.1.

Epstein (1989) and Treasure and Roberts (1995) have proposed that a mastery-oriented climate can be created by the coach or teacher that will be instrumental in developing and fostering self-confidence and intrinsic motivation in youth sport participants. As originally coined by Epstein,

the acronym TARGET has come to represent the manipulation of environmental conditions that will lead to a mastery climate conducive to the development of intrinsic motivation. It is proposed that coaches address each of these conditions in order to create a mastery environment. The conditions are as follows:

1. *Tasks*—Tasks involving variety and diversity facilitate an interest in learning and task involvement.
2. *Authority*—Students should be given opportunities to participate actively in the learning process by being involved in decision making and monitoring their own personal progress.
3. *Reward*—Rewards for participation should focus upon individual gains and improvement, and away from social comparisons.
4. *Grouping*—Students should be placed in groups so that they can work on individual skills in a cooperative learning climate.
5. *Evaluation*—Evaluation should involve numerous self-tests that focus upon effort and personal improvement.
6. *Timing*—Timing is critical to the interaction of all of these conditions.

Motivational climate is important because it can influence both goal orientation (disposition) and goal involvement (state). Over time, an emphasis on a mastery or task goal climate can cause an athlete to have more of a mastery goal

TABLE 6.1 | Characteristics of Different Types of Goal Orientation, Goal Involvement, and Motivational Climate

Goal Orientation (Personality Trait)	Goal Involvement (Psychological State)	Motivational Climate (Environment)

1. Task or Mastery Orientation
  a. Effort important
  b. Mastery important
2. Ego or Competitive Orientation
  a. Social comparisons important
  b. Winning important
	1. Task or Mastery Involvement
	  a. Athlete works hard
	  b. Athlete strives for mastery
	2. Ego or Competitive Involvement
	  a. Athlete defines ability as winning
	  b. Athlete strives to win
		1. Mastery Climate
		  a. Effort rewarded
		  b. Cooperation emphasized
		2. Competitive Climate
		  a. Mistakes punished
		  b. Competition encouraged

CONCEPT & APPLICATION

6.2

CONCEPT   The climate and environment created by the coach or teacher can be a powerful determinant as to whether a young athlete will increase in intrinsic motivation and self-confidence.

APPLICATION   TARGET structures provide specific suggestions as to how the coach can create an atmosphere conducive to the development of self-confidence and the motive to achieve success.

Factors such as making practices interesting, involving athletes in decision making, basing rewards on individual gains, and creating an atmosphere of cooperation are all important TARGET structures. Other strategies used by coaches to enhance self-confidence include (a) instruction/drilling, (b) encouraging positive self-talk, (c) acting self-confident, (d) liberal use of praise, and (e) physical conditioning sessions.

CONCEPT & APPLICATION

6.3

CONCEPT   Perceived ability moderates the effect that a high competition motivational climate will have on self-esteem. Those most vulnerable to a loss of self-esteem associated with an ego-involved competitive environment are the low-ability athletes.

APPLICATION   Coaches must be mindful that a planned competitive environment affects each member of a team differently. High-ability athletes will probably not be negatively affected by

an ego-involved climate, but they can benefit from a mastery climate. Because a mastery climate promises beneficial outcomes for all athletes, the focus of practice situations should be upon teamwork, skill mastery, and cooperative behavior that will be beneficial to the whole team. Competitive game-like situations can be beneficial to all athletes if they are organized in a way that does not always result in the low-ability athletes' losing or coming up second best.

orientation (Gano-Overway & Ewing, 2004; Harwood & Swain, 2002; Weigand & Burton, 2002). With this in mind, it is useful to examine the positive benefits of creating a mastery-focused motivational climate for athletes. Some of the benefits associated with a mastery motivational climate include enhanced perception of competence, increased satisfaction, reduced boredom, perceived ability, reduced rough play, heightened effort, greater enjoyment, and increased self-esteem (Boixados, Cruz, Torregrosa, & Valiente, 2004; Halliburton & Weiss, 2002; Weigand & Burton, 2002). An investigation reported by

Reinboth and Duda (2004) is of particular interest, as it shows how motivational climate can interact with perceived ability to affect self-esteem. A motivational climate that is highly ego involved (competitive environment) can have a deleterious effect upon self-esteem, but only when associated with perceived low ability. This means that in the presence of an ego-involved environment, self-esteem is protected if the athlete enjoys the perception of high personal ability. As illustrated in figure 6.2, this also means that the low-ability athlete is particularly vulnerable to a decline in self-esteem in the presence of a competitive environment.

151

FIGURE 6.2 | The deleterious effects of an ego-involved competitive climate on a perceived low-ability athlete's self-esteem.

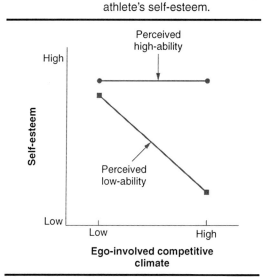

Source: Reinboth & Duda, 2004.

Goal Orientation and Moral Functioning

In this section we relate the concept of moral functioning with the concept of good or bad **sportspersonship.** Athletes who perform with a high level of moral functioning are said to exhibit good sportspersonship, while those exhibiting a low level of moral functioning are said to exhibit unsportspersonlike behavior. Low moral functioning is linked to goal orientation; because "the ego-oriented athlete's perceptions of competence are dependent on outdoing others, he or she may be more likely to break the rules and behave in an unsportspersonlike fashion when winning is at stake" (Kavussanu & Ntoumanis, 2003, p. 503). Conversely, task goal orientation is linked to sportspersonlike behavior because the athlete's focus is upon the task at hand and whether or not she performs up to her potential. With these basic

concepts in place, let's look at some of the recent literature on the subject.

Research by Kavussanu and Ntoumanis (2003) showed that participation in contact sports is predictive of an ego goal orientation, which in turn is predictive of lower levels of moral functioning in terms of judgments, intentions, and actual behaviors (more willingness to break rules, risk injury, and deliberately hurt opponents). This research showed a strong relationship between an ego goal orientation and reported low levels of moral functioning, while task orientation had the opposite effect. After reviewing the related literature, Kavussanu, Roberts, and Ntoumanis (2002) observed that unbridled competition reduces prosocial behavior, whereas cooperation enhances prosocial behavior. Observing the frequency of unsportspersonlike behaviors in competitive sport, they conclude with the following statement:

> The roots of unsportspersonlike conduct encountered in the sport context may reside within one's own athletic team. Many of the inappropriate actions we observe in the sport realm might be the result of certain social norms that become predominant in each team over time thereby reinforcing unsportspersonlike behaviors (Kavussanu et al., 2002, p. 362).

Lemyre, Roberts and Ommundsen (2002) measured dispositional goal orientation, perceived ability, and moral functioning in 511 male youth soccer players. Moral functioning was measured as a function of respect for social conventions, respect for rules and officials, respect for one's full commitment toward sport, and true respect and concern for the opponent. Results showed that (a) ego goal orientation has a negative effect on all four measures of sportspersonship, (b) perceived ability has a positive significant effect on all four measures of moral reasoning, and (c) perceived ability moderates (determines) the relationship between ego goal orientation and respect for rules and officials. The highest respect for rules and officials occurs with low ego goal orientation and

112

Cox: Sport Psychology:
Concepts and Applications,
Sixth Edition

II. Motivation in Sport and
Exercise

6. Goal Perspective Theory

© The McGraw–Hill
Companies, 2007

CONCEPT & APPLICATION

6.4

CONCEPT An ego goal orientation and focus upon a competitive environment are related to low moral functioning and low sportspersonship. This relationship is due to the focus upon outperforming or defeating the opposition that is present in ego goal oriented/involved achievement situations.

APPLICATION If as a coach or teacher you are concerned about the unsportspersonlike behavior of your athletes you must turn your attention to

the kind of social environment that is fostered during practices and games. If the social norm is to win at all costs, then the seeds of unsportspersonship are embedded within the fabric of the team. This can only be reversed by changing the motivational climate of the team from being focused on competition and winning at all costs to one of cooperation and a focus upon effort, teamwork, and skill improvement.

high perceived ability, whereas the lowest respect occurs with high ego goal orientation and low perceived ability.

Similarly, Stuntz and Weiss (2003) studied the relationship between goal orientation (including social approval goal orientation) and moral functioning as measured by an instrument designed to measure legitimacy of and intention to use unsportspersonlike play during competition. Results showed that goal orientation predicts unsportspersonlike behavior, with an ego orientation being positively related to bad intentions, and task orientation being negatively related to bad intentions. For boys, but not girls, social approval goal orientation was predictive of bad intentions. If coach, friends, or peers approve, boys indicate a willingness to engage in unsportspersonlike behavior. Kavussanu and Roberts (2001) noted a sex difference relative to how male and female collegiate basketball players think about moral functioning. The female basketball players in this sample were more task goal oriented than the males and had higher levels of moral functioning. Utilizing a sample of young urban tennis players (50 percent African American), Fry and Newton (2003) reported that perceiving the tennis environment to be task involving is associated with liking the instructor and having a sense of sportspersonship. Conversely, perceiving the environment as ego involving was associated with not liking the instructor and poor sportspersonship.

Characteristics of Task and Ego Goal Orientations

A task or mastery goal orientation is associated with the belief that success is a function of effort and mastery. Mastery-oriented individuals feel most successful when they experience personal improvement that they believe is due to their hard work and effort. They gain a sense of accomplishment through learning and mastering a difficult task. Task-oriented individuals, regardless of their perception of personal ability, tend to exhibit **adaptive motivational patterns.** This means that they choose to participate in challenging tasks that allow them to demonstrate persistence and sustained effort. As a general rule, a mastery goal orientation is associated with positive perceptions and behaviors. Mastery-oriented persons focus on developing skill, exerting effort, and self-improvement (Carpenter & Yates, 1997; Fry & Duda, 1997; Williams, 1998).

An ego or competitive goal orientation is associated with the belief that success is a function of how well a person performs relative to other people. Ability is independent of effort. If a person performs well against other competitors, yet does not expend much effort, this is evidence of great ability. Thus, for the ego-oriented athlete, success is outperforming an opponent using superior ability as opposed to high effort or personal improvement.

| 6.5 | CONCEPT & APPLICATION |

CONCEPT In terms of satisfaction, enjoyment, and performance, it is desirable for an athlete to exhibit a high as opposed to a low task orientation. This is true regardless of the athlete's perception of ability.

APPLICATION Regardless of perceived ability, highly task-oriented individuals believe that

success, satisfaction, and enjoyment are a function of the effort that they expend striving for mastery. Because task and ego goal orientations are believed to be independent of each other, it is desirable to encourage an athlete to exhibit mastery behaviors and beliefs regardless of her ego orientation. This can be accomplished through cognitive restructuring or by exposing the athlete to a mastery climate.

An ego-oriented individual who has high perception of ability should exhibit adaptive motivational patterns (engage willingly in challenging tasks). However, an ego-oriented individual who has low perception of ability should exhibit a **maladaptive motivational pattern.** Because his motivation is to win and he does not believe he can win, he will not likely take part in a challenging activity. The obvious disadvantage of an ego orientation is that it discourages participation simply for the fun of it unless one is certain of experiencing success. In summary, ego-oriented individuals focus on beating others with minimal effort in order to enhance their social status (Carpenter & Yates, 1997; Fry & Duda, 1997; Williams, 1998).

Research on goal orientation has revealed that individuals who are high in task orientation can also be high in ego orientation; other combinations of the two orientations are also possible. In other words, the two orientations are independent of each other. The best combination is for a young athlete to be high in both orientations (Dunn, Dunn, Syrotuik, 2002). Individuals with high task and ego orientations exhibit the highest levels of motivation and perceived competence. The worst combination in terms of motivation and perceived competence is to be low in both task and ego orientations. Individuals in this category tend to be primarily young women. Children dominated by a task orientation tend to be more motivated than children dominated by an ego

orientation (Fox, Goudas, Biddle, Duda, & Armstrong, 1994).

Several studies point to the superiority of a task orientation over an ego orientation in athletes. King and Williams (1997), utilizing martial arts students as participants, demonstrated that task but not ego orientation was related to martial arts performance. Furthermore, they observed that task orientation but not ego orientation was related to students' perceptions of satisfaction and enjoyment. Similarly, Vlachopoulos and Biddle (1999) reported a large-scale study in which goal orientation was measured in over one thousand British physical education students. The results of the investigation led investigators to conclude that a task orientation should be promoted for physical education students and athletes. Their data indicated that task and not ego orientation has the potential to promote success and positive affect in young athletes, independent of perceived ability.

While it sometimes appears from the literature that an ego goal orientation is usually undesirable, this conclusion is oversimplified and could be misleading. An ego goal orientation in the presence of a very low task goal orientation is undesirable, but in combination with a high level of task orientation, this is not necessarily the case. Using a statistical procedure called cluster analysis, Hodge and Petlichkoff (2000) grouped 257 rugby players into distinct goal orientation group combinations.

CONCEPT & APPLICATION

6.6

CONCEPT   It is not desirable for an athlete to be highly ego oriented if he harbors feelings of low ability. However, if an athlete perceives that he is highly skilled, then to be ego oriented is not entirely undesirable, especially if the athlete is also highly mastery oriented.

APPLICATION   It is always important to remember that the two types of goal orientation are independent of each other. Research has shown that in

terms of performance, satisfaction, and enjoyment, it is best to be high in both task and ego orientation. The athlete's perception of his own ability is of critical importance. An athlete who is ego oriented and has low perception of ability is at risk of avoiding competitive challenges for fear of failing. For this reason, it is important for the coach or sport psychologist to be aware of an athlete's goal orientation and perception of ability.

(*Cluster analysis* magnifies differences between athletes in different groups while at the same time minimizing differences between athletes that are within the same cluster.)

The results showed that high levels of perceived rugby ability are associated with a high degree of ego orientation when coupled with high or moderately high levels of task orientation. Thus, in terms of perceived ability and competence, high levels of ego orientation are not necessarily bad. Cluster analysis further showed that level of ego orientation, and not level of task orientation, may be the critical factor in predicting perceived ability in rugby players. A moderate level of task orientation and high level of ego orientation yielded the highest level of perceived ability in the cluster analysis.

The observation that an ego goal orientation is not always bad was further clarified in a study reported by Wang and Biddle (2001). The focus of this investigation was upon goal orientation in combination with conceptions of ability and self-determination theory. In this study, 2,969 British students (ages 11–15) completed inventories measuring goal orientation, conceptions of ability, self-determination, and perceived competence. Using cluster analysis procedures, the researchers were able to differentiate five distinct cluster profiles ranging from highly motivated to amotivated. The two highest motivational clusters were

characterized as being high in task goal orientation, able to view ability as changeable, high in self-determination, and high in perceived competence. The next-to-highest motivational cluster, however, was also high in ego goal orientation, making it clear that an ego goal orientation in combination with a high task orientation is associated with high levels of motivation.

Interaction between Goal Orientation and Motivational Climate

Based upon theory, it may be hypothesized that the best combination of goal orientation and motivational climate is to be task and ego oriented in conjunction with a mastery climate. This combination should yield the highest levels of actual performance, personal satisfaction, and enjoyment. Following this, in terms of desirability, would be the combination of high task orientation, low ego orientation, and a mastery climate. The least desirable combination would be to be low in both task and ego orientation and be placed in a competitive climate. The interaction between goal orientation and motivational climate is illustrated in figure 6.3 along with predictions of best performance, satisfaction, and enjoyment. As can be observed in this figure, best performance,

FIGURE 6.3 | In terms of a goal orientation by motivational climate interaction, best outcomes in terms of performance, satisfaction, and enjoyment are expected at cell 3 and 4, while the worst are expected at cell 5.

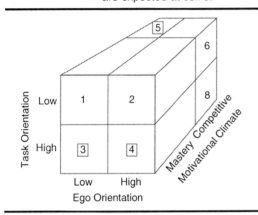

satisfaction, and enjoyment are predicted to occur in cells 3 and 4, with worst in cell 5. Research to confirm or modify these theoretical predictions in the physical domain has just recently begun to emerge.

Treasure (1997) measured elementary-age children's perceptions of motivational climate and related these perceptions to the children's perceptions of ability, satisfaction, attitudes, and boredom. A perceived climate that was high in competition but low in mastery yielded feelings of low effort, high ability, and high boredom. A perceived climate that was moderately high in competition and high in mastery yielded feelings associated with high satisfaction, belief that both ability and effort were important for success, and belief that the participant was high in ability. Treasure concluded that a mastery climate should be promoted and that a competitive climate should be deemphasized in order to increase motivation and self-confidence in children.

Treasure and Roberts (1998) measured perceived motivational climate and goal orientations of adolescent females. It was observed that a strong mastery climate was associated with feelings that effort was important for success, and a strong competitive environment was associated with feelings that ability and deception were important. Additionally, they were able to identify two interactions that support the hypothesis that an interactive relationship exists between goal orientation and motivational climate. In terms of predicting the belief that ability was important for success, it was observed that motivational climate interacts with goal orientation. Specifically, ego orientation moderates the relationship between a competitive climate and the belief that ability is important. If ego orientation was low, a competitive climate did not predict the importance of ability; if ego orientation was high, a competitive climate did predict the importance of ability. Furthermore, in terms of predicting the belief that mastery experiences were important for success, it was again observed that motivational climate interacts with goal orientation. Specifically, task orientation moderates the relationship between a mastery climate and the belief that mastery experiences were important. The perception that mastery experiences were important increased as the perception of mastery climate increased for both high and low task-oriented females, but at a faster rate for high task-oriented individuals.

Bar-Eli et al. (1997b) categorized male high school participants as being low task and low ego oriented, low task and high ego oriented, high task and low ego oriented, and high task and high ego oriented. They then had the participants from each goal orientation category participate in four separate 1600-meter races in which competitive and mastery climate conditions were manipulated. Best running times were recorded for the competitive conditions compared to the mastery conditions, with no evidence of an interaction with goal orientation. These results were counter to the expected results shown in figure 6.3.

CONCEPT & APPLICATION

6.7

CONCEPT   It is hypothesized that an interactive relationship exists between goal orientation and motivational climate in predicting such things as satisfaction, beliefs about success, performance, and enjoyment. The exact nature of this relationship, however, is not known at this time.

APPLICATION   It is important for the coach or sport psychologist to be aware of the goal orientation of the athletes, but also to be aware of the motivational climate that is being created for the athletes. The coach must recognize and be sensitive to issues raised by the athletes relative to a disparity between goal orientation and the motivational climate. Knowing why an ego-oriented athlete might object to a mastery-oriented climate should be of great use to the coach.

In an investigation reported by Newton and Duda (1999), the interaction between motivational climate and goal orientation was studied using junior female volleyball players. They investigated the hypothesis that best results in terms of predicting intrinsic motivation and expectations of success would occur in situations in which the motivational climate was matched with the goal orientation. In this model, best results should occur under conditions of high task orientation in a mastery climate and conditions of high ego orientation in a competitive environment. Looking at figure 6.3, best outcome would be expected in cells 3 and 4 when high task orientation and high mastery climate are matched; and in cells 6 and 8 when high ego orientation and high competitive climate are matched. The **matching hypothesis** was not supported in this research, but the investigators did observe that greater intrinsic motivation was observed in conditions of task orientation and mastery climate than in conditions of ego orientation and competitive climate. A significant interaction was observed between task orientation and task climate in predicting the belief that effort leads to success. Specifically, task orientation moderates the relationship between mastery climate and the belief that effort is important in determining success. As a perception of mastery climate increases, so does the perception that effort is important. But the strength of this relationship increases as task orientation increases from low to high. A high level of mastery environment in combination with a high level of task orientation yields the highest level of effort belief.

Related to the matching hypothesis, introduced above, is an important study underscoring the importance of goal orientation, perceived ability, and task difficulty to exerted effort and wall-climbing performance. In this investigation, the dispositional goal orientations and perceived ability of 500 French school boys ages 12 to 16 were measured (Sarrazin, Roberts, Cury, Biddle, & Famose, 2002). Based on these results, 78 boys with extreme scores in goal orientation and perceived rock climbing ability were assigned to one of four groups: (a) High Task (low ego) and High Perceived Ability (HPA); (b) High Task (low ego) and Low Perceived Ability (LPA); (c) High Ego (low task) and High Perceived Ability (HPA); and (d) High Ego (low task) and Low Perceived Ability (LPA). Following this, all 78 participants completed five 8-meter-high rock wall climbing courses (random), with their exerted effort (percentage of heart rate reserve) and performance recorded. During these five climbs, a motivational climate was created to match the group that they were assigned to (e.g., a mastery climate was created for boys high in task goal orientation). Results of the experiment were similar for both performance and exerted effort, with the results for effort illustrated in figure 6.4. Differences in exerted

FIGURE 6.4 | Effects of task difficulty, goal orientation, and perceived ability on exerted effort.

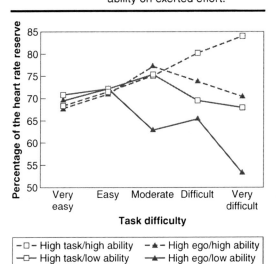

Source: Adapted with permission from Sarrazin, P., Roberts, G., Cury, F., Biddle, S., & Famose, J.P. (2002). Exerted effort and performance in climbing among boys: The influence of achievement goals, perceived ability, and task difficulty. *Research Quarterly for Exercise and Sport, 73* (4), 425–36.

effort (HR reserve) do not become evident until the moderately difficult rock climbing courses are attempted. As the course becomes more difficult, the superiority of the group high in task goal orientation in combination with high perceived ability becomes more evident. Similarly, the inferiority of the group high in ego orientation and low in perceived ability becomes more evident as the task becomes more difficult. Perceived ability moderates (determines) the relationship between task difficulty and goal orientation on exerted effort and performance. Children who suffer from perceived low ability simply do not do well or try hard when confronted with a difficult climbing task. This is further exacerbated by having a disposition toward an ego goal orientation. In terms of goal orientation, it is important to note that this study does not address the situation that would occur if children were categorized as being high in both task and ego goal orientation at the same time (or vice versa). As indicated earlier, we would expect children high in perceived ability, task orientation, and ego orientation to perform well and to exert effort in challenging situations.

Summary

Goal perspective theory is a developmentally based theory of achievement motivation. Children pass through four developmental levels as they move from not being able to differentiate between ability and effort to being able to differentiate between the two at about 12 years of age. Three psychological constructs are important in understanding goal perspective theory. These three constructs are goal orientation, goal involvement, and motivational climate.

There are two dispositional goal orientations mentioned by Nicholls. These two are task orientation and ego orientation. The goal orientation that an athlete has determines how she will evaluate

her own ability. Task-oriented children perceive ability as being a function of effort and mastery. Ego-oriented children perceive ability as being a function of social comparison. The terms *task* and *ego orientation* are used interchangeably with the terms *mastery* and *competitive orientation*. Additional goal orientations are suggested by some researchers.

Goal orientation is a personality disposition, whereas goal involvement is a situation-specific state, or way of responding to an achievement situation at a specific point in time. There are two kinds of goal orientations. They are task or mastery goal orientation and ego or competitive goal orientation.

Just as individuals can be task or ego oriented, motivational climates can be task or ego oriented. A task-oriented environment is referred to as a mastery climate, while an ego-oriented environment is referred to as a competitive climate. A mastery climate is one in which effort, mastery, and cooperation are emphasized. A competitive or performance climate is one in which social comparison and competition are emphasized. Research supports the efficacy of providing a mastery climate for enhancing learning, self-confidence, and perceived ability.

New research relating the concept of moral functioning to sportspersonship was discussed.

Research suggests a link between sportspersonship and task and ego goal orientation. Contact sports are linked to an ego goal orientation, which is predictive of lower levels of moral functioning in terms of judgments, intentions, and actual behaviors.

An important area of needed research is to study the interaction between goal orientation and motivational climate. Theory suggests that certain goal orientation dispositions should do best in certain motivational climates relative to success, satisfaction, and enjoyment. Sustained research in this area will be important in identifying the best strategies to help young athletes to become confident and motivated.

Critical Thought Questions

1. Goal orientations are described as being relatively stable personality dispositions. Yet, research suggests that a person's disposition to be ego involved can be changed over time to be more mastery oriented through long-term exposure to a mastery climate. Critically discuss this paradoxical issue.

2. It seems as though a child moves developmentally from having a task orientation relative to perceived ability to having an ego orientation at about age 12. Yet, a task orientation is often described as being more desirable than an ego orientation in terms of developing self-confidence and experiencing satisfaction and enjoyment in sport. Are we saying that moving backwards developmentally is desirable? Explain.

3. What do you think is the most desirable motivational climate for developing self-confidence and motivation in children and young athletes? Explain why you think this is so. Provide a detailed description of your ideal motivational climate.

4. Why would an ego goal orientation or competitive orientation be more associated with poor sportspersonship than a mastery goal orientation? What is there about the ego orientation that causes an athlete to be more willing to break rules and perhaps inflict harm on another athlete?

5. Bill Walton's discussion of the differences between the legendary John Wooden and Indiana's Bobby Knight seems to parallel the distinction between the two motivational climates described in this chapter. How do you feel about this comparison? How do you feel about Bill Walton's assessment of the two coaches? Incidentally, approximately three months after Walton wrote his article in *Time* magazine, Bobby Knight was fired as the men's basketball coach at Indiana. As we mentioned in an earlier chapter, he was later hired as head men's coach at Texas Tech University.

6. Develop and discuss your own theory as to how goal orientation and motivational climate should interact relative to success, satisfaction, and enjoyment.

160   Part Two   Motivation in Sport and Exercise

Glossary

achievement motivation An athlete's predisposition to approach or avoid a competitive situation.

adaptive motivational pattern Motivation to participate in challenging activities.

cognitive restructuring The use of cognitive or mental skills to restructure or change the way one views certain situations.

competitive climate An environment in which athletes perceive that mistakes will be punished and competition between teammates will be encouraged.

competitive orientation Goal disposition that perceives ability as a function of outperforming others as opposed to self-improvement (see ego orientation).

differentiated goal perspective Ability of a child to clearly distinguish or differentiate among the concepts of ability, effort, luck, and outcome.

ego involvement A situation-specific manifestation of being ego- or competition-oriented. Similar to ego orientation.

ego goal orientation Goal disposition that perceives ability as being a function of outperforming others as opposed to self-improvement (see competitive orientation).

goal involvement A situation-specific state measure of how an individual relates to an achievement situation at a specific point in time.

goal orientation A person's disposition to be task goal oriented and/or ego goal oriented.

maladaptive motivational pattern Lack of motivation to participate in challenging activities.

mastery climate Environment in which athletes receive positive reinforcement from the coach when they work hard, cooperate, and demonstrate improvement.

mastery orientation Goal disposition to view perceived ability as a function of effort and improvement (see task orientation).

matching hypothesis As used in this chapter, the term relates to matching a person's goal orientation with a person's motivational climate to bring about maximum achievement benefits.

motivational climate The motivational environment a person is placed in relative to factors that relate to mastery or competition.

perceived ability A conceptualization of ability that is based upon how a person views the relationships between ability, effort, mastery, and social comparison.

social approval goal orientation The desire for social acceptance through conformity to norms while displaying maximum effort.

sportspersonship Performance of athletic tasks with a high level of moral functioning. Those exhibiting a low level of moral functioning are said to exhibit unsportspersonlike behavior.

task involvement A situation-specific manifestation of being task- or mastery-oriented; similar to task orientation.

task goal orientation Goal disposition to view perceived ability as a function of effort and improvement (see mastery orientation).

undifferentiated goal perspective Point of view in which a child cannot distinguish or differentiate among the concepts of ability, effort, luck, and outcome.

Motivation and Emotion

▶ OUTLINE

Prologue: Leap of Faith

Looking Ahead

Explaining Motivation
Instinct Approaches: Born to Be Motivated
Drive-Reduction Approaches: Satisfying Our Needs
Incentive Approaches: Motivation's Pull
Cognitive Approaches: The Thoughts Behind Motivation
Maslow's Hierarchy: Ordering Motivational Needs
Reconciling the Different Approaches to Motivation

Looking Back

Key Terms and Concepts

Ask Yourself

► PROLOGUE: LEAP OF FAITH

Kerri Strug following her injury during the Olympic Games.

Forget the searing pain that followed a hard landing at the end of her vault: Just the sound of her ankle snapping was enough to signal to Kerri Strug that she had injured herself badly, and that ordinarily the next step would be to abandon the meet. But it took more than a badly twisted ankle to stop the 18-year-old Strug, a little-known member of the U.S. women's gymnastic team in the 1996 Olympics. With the team holding a slim lead over the Russian gymnast team, Strug knew that the gold medal was in her hands—or, more accurately, in her ankle.

Knowing full well that continuing might worsen her injury so much that her career would be finished, Kerri limped to the start of the runway. Putting aside the pain, she dashed to the horse, and performed nearly flawlessly. As she raised her arms in victory, though, she fell to the mat in agony, her eyes filled with tears. She had to be carried away to await her score, which was an unusually high 9.712. Although her injury prevented her own individual participation in further events, it led the gymnastics team to a gold medal.

In her eyes, there was no question that her selfless act was worthwhile. "I knew if I didn't make it, we wouldn't win the Gold," said Strug. "So I said a quick prayer and asked God to help me out. I don't know how I did the vault, but I knew I had to do it" ("Leap of Faith," 1996, p. 118).

► LOOKING AHEAD

What was the motivation behind Strug's act of courage? Was it the anticipation of the gold medal? The potential rewards that would follow if she succeeded? The mere thrill of participating? The fear of letting her teammates down? The satisfaction of finally achieving a long-sought goal?

Motivation:
The factors that direct and energize the behavior of humans and other organisms.

In this module we consider the issues that can help to answer such questions as we address the topic of motivation and the related area of emotion. **Motivation** concerns the factors that direct and energize the behavior of humans and other organisms.

Psychologists who study motivation seek to discover the particular desired goals—the *motives*—that underlie behavior. Motives are exemplified in behavior as basic as drinking to satisfy thirst or as inconsequential as taking a stroll to get exercise. To the psychologist specializing in the study of motivation, underlying motives are assumed to steer one's choice of activities.

The study of motivation, then, consists of identifying why people seek to do the things they do. Psychologists studying motivation ask questions such as these: "Why do people choose particular goals for which to strive?" "What specific motives direct behavior?" "What individual differences in motivation account for the variability in people's behavior?" "How can we motivate people to behave in particular ways, such as eating certain foods, quitting smoking, or engaging in safer sexual practices?"

In this module we consider motivation and emotion. We begin by focusing on the major conceptions of motivation, discussing how the different motives and needs people experience jointly affect behavior. We consider the various explanations for motivation, moving from theories that favor instincts to ones that focus on cognitive and social factors. As we will see, all seek to explain the energy that guides people's behavior in particular directions.

After reading this module you will be able to answer the following questions:

- *What does the concept of motivation seek to explain?*
- *How does motivation direct and energize behavior?*

▶ EXPLAINING MOTIVATION

In just an instant, John Thompson's life changed. That's all it took for an auger, an oversized, drill-like piece of farm equipment powered by a tractor, to rip off both of his arms when he slipped, falling against the rotating machinery.

Yet it was in the moments following the accident that Thompson demonstrated incredible bravery. Despite his pain and shock, he ran 400 feet to his house. Using the bone hanging from his left shoulder to open the door, he ran inside and dialed for help with a pen gripped in his teeth. When emergency crews arrived 30 minutes later, he told them where to find ice and plastic bags so that his severed arms could be packed for possible surgical reattachment. Thompson's rescuers came none too soon: By the time surgery could start, he had lost half his blood. (Nelson, 1992)

What explains John Thompson's enormous motivation to stay alive? Like many questions involving motivation, this one has no single answer. Clearly, biological aspects of motivation were at work: He obviously experienced a powerful drive to keep himself alive, spurring him to act quickly before he lost so much blood that his life would drain away. But cognitive and social factors, such as his desire to see family and friends, also helped fuel his will to survive.

The complexity of motivation has led to the development of a variety of conceptual approaches to its understanding. Although they vary in the degree to which they focus on biological, cognitive, and social factors, all seek to explain the energy that guides people's behavior in particular directions.

Instinct Approaches: Born to Be Motivated

Instincts:
Inborn patterns of behavior that are biologically determined rather than learned.

When psychologists first sought to explain motivation, they turned to **instincts,** inborn patterns of behavior that are biologically determined rather than learned. According to instinct approaches to motivation, people and animals are born with preprogrammed sets of behaviors essential to their survival. These instincts provide the energy that channels behavior in appropriate directions. Hence, sex might be explained as a response to an instinct for reproduction, and exploratory behavior might be viewed as motivated by an instinct to examine one's territory.

There are several difficulties with such a conception, however. For one thing, psychologists have been unable to agree on what the primary instincts are. One early psychologist, William McDougall (1908), suggested that there are eighteen instincts, including pugnacity and gregariousness. Others found even more, with one sociologist claiming that there are exactly 5,759 (Bernard, 1924). Clearly, such an extensive enumeration provides little more than labels for behavior.

No explanation based on the concept of instincts goes very far in explaining *why* a specific pattern of behavior, and not some other, has appeared in a given species. Furthermore, the variety and complexity of human behavior, much of which is clearly learned, are difficult to explain if instincts are the primary motivational force. Therefore, conceptions of motivation based on instincts have been supplanted by newer explanations, although instinct approaches still play a role in certain theories. For example, Freud's work suggests that instinctual drives of sex and aggression motivate behavior. Moreover, many animal behaviors clearly have an instinctual basis.

Drive-reduction approaches to motivation:
A theory suggesting that when people lack some basic biological requirement such as water, a drive to obtain that requirement (in this case, the thirst drive) is produced.

Drive:
Motivational tension, or arousal, that energizes behavior in order to fulfill some need.

Drive-Reduction Approaches: Satisfying Our Needs

In rejecting instinct theory psychologists first proposed simple drive-reduction theories of motivation in its place (Hull, 1943). **Drive-reduction approaches to motivation** suggest that when people lack some basic biological requirement such as water, a drive to obtain that requirement (in this case, the thirst drive) is produced.

To understand this approach we need to begin with the concept of drive. A **drive** is motivational tension, or arousal, that energizes behavior in order to fulfill some need. Many basic kinds of drives, such as hunger, thirst, sleepiness, and sex, are related to biological needs of the body or of the species as a whole. These are called *primary drives*. Primary drives contrast with *secondary drives*, in which no obvious biological need is being fulfilled. In secondary drives, needs are brought about by prior experience and learning. As we will discuss later, some people have strong needs to achieve academically and in their careers. We can say that their achievement need is reflected in a secondary drive that motivates their behavior.

We usually try to satisfy a primary drive by reducing the need underlying it. For example, we become hungry after not eating for a few hours and may raid the refrigerator, especially if our next scheduled meal is not imminent. If the weather turns cold, we put on extra clothing or raise the setting on the thermostat in order to keep warm. If our body needs liquids in order to function properly, we experience thirst and seek out water.

Homeostasis:
The process by which an organism strives to maintain some optimal level of internal biological functioning by compensating for deviations from its usual, balanced internal state.

Homeostasis The reason for such behavior is homeostasis, a basic motivational phenomenon underlying primary drives (see Figure 1). **Homeostasis** is the process by which an organism strives to maintain some optimal level of internal biological functioning by compensating for deviations from its usual, balanced internal state. Although not all basic biological behaviors related to motivation fit a homeostatic model—sexual behavior is an example of one that does not—most of the fundamental needs of life, including the need for food, water, stable body temperature, and sleep, can be explained reasonably well by such an approach.

Unfortunately, although drive-reduction theories provide a good explanation of how primary drives motivate behavior, they are inadequate when

Homeostasis

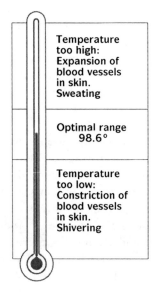

Figure 1
Homeostasis keeps body temperature within an optimum range. When temperature becomes either too high or too low, the body reacts in ways that help it to revert to the desired temperature range.

it comes to explaining behaviors in which the goal is not to reduce a drive but rather to maintain or even to increase a particular level of excitement or arousal. For instance, some behaviors seem to be motivated by nothing more than curiosity. Anyone who has rushed to pick up newly delivered mail, who avidly follows gossip columns in the newspaper, or who yearns to travel to exotic places, knows the importance of curiosity in directing behavior. And it is not just human beings who display behavior indicative of curiosity: Monkeys will learn to press a bar just to be able to peer into another room, especially if they can glimpse something interesting (such as a toy train moving along a track). Monkeys will also expend considerable energy solving simple mechanical puzzles, even though their behavior produces no obvious reward (Harlow, Harlow, & Meyer, 1950; Mineka & Hendersen, 1985; Loewenstein, 1994).

Similarly, many of us go out of our way to seek thrills through such activities as riding a roller coaster and steering a raft down the rapids of a river. Such behaviors certainly don't suggest that people act only to reduce drives, as drive-reduction approaches would indicate.

Both curiosity and thrill-seeking behavior, then, shed doubt on drive-reduction approaches as a complete explanation for motivation. In both cases, rather than seeking to reduce an underlying drive, people and animals appear to be motivated to *increase* their overall level of stimulation and activity. In order to explain this phenomenon, psychologists have devised an alternative: arousal approaches to motivation.

Arousal Approaches: Beyond Drive Reduction Arousal approaches seek to explain behavior in which the goal is to maintain or increase excitement (Berlyne, 1967; Brehm & Self, 1989). According to **arousal approaches to motivation,** each of us tries to maintain a certain level of stimulation and activity. As with the drive-reduction model, if our stimulation and activity levels become too high, we try to reduce them. But in contrast to the drive-reduction model, the arousal model also suggests that if the levels of stimulation and activity are too low, we will try to *increase* them by seeking stimulation.

People vary widely as to the optimal level of arousal they seek out, with some people needing especially high levels of arousal (Babbitt, Rowland, & Franken, 1990; Stacy, Newcomb, & Bentler, 1991; Cocco, Sharpe, & Blaszczynski, 1995). For example, psychologists have hypothesized that individuals such as comic John Belushi, DNA researcher Sir Francis Crick, daredevil Evel Knievel, and bank robbers Bonnie and Clyde exhibited a particularly high need for arousal (Farley, 1986). Such people may attempt to avoid boredom by seeking out challenging situations (Zuckerman, 1991, 1994).

It is not just the celebrated who pursue arousal; many of us characteristically seek out relatively high levels of stimulation. You can get a sense of your own characteristic level of stimulation by completing the questionnaire in Table 1.

Arousal approaches to motivation: The belief that we try to maintain a certain level of stimulation and activity, increasing or reducing them as necessary.

TABLE 1
Do You Seek Out Sensation?

How much stimulation do you crave in your everyday life? You will have an idea after you complete the following questionnaire, which lists some items from a scale designed to assess your sensation-seeking tendencies. Circle either *A* or *B* in each pair of statements.

1. *A* I would like a job that requires a lot of traveling.
    B I would prefer a job in one location.
2. *A* I am invigorated by a brisk, cold day.
    B I can't wait to get indoors on a cold day.
3. *A* I get bored seeing the same old faces.
    B I like the comfortable familiarity of everyday friends.
4. *A* I would prefer living in an ideal society in which everyone was safe, secure, and happy.
    B I would have preferred living in the unsettled days of our history.
5. *A* I sometimes like to do things that are a little frightening.
    B A sensible person avoids activities that are dangerous.
6. *A* I would not like to be hypnotized.
    B I would like to have the experience of being hypnotized.
7. *A* The most important goal of life is to live it to the fullest and to experience as much as possible.
    B The most important goal of life is to find peace and happiness.
8. *A* I would like to try parachuting.
    B I would never want to try jumping out of a plane, with or without a parachute.
9. *A* I enter cold water gradually, giving myself time to get used to it.
    B I like to dive or jump right into the ocean or a cold pool.
10. *A* When I go on a vacation, I prefer the comfort of a good room and bed.
    B When I go on a vacation, I prefer the change of camping out.
11. *A* I prefer people who are emotionally expressive, even if they are a bit unstable.
    B I prefer people who are calm and even-tempered.
12. *A* A good painting should shock or jolt the senses.
    B A good painting should give one a feeling of peace and security.
13. *A* People who ride motorcycles must have some kind of unconscious need to hurt themselves.
    B I would like to drive or ride a motorcycle.

Scoring Give yourself one point for each of the following responses: 1*A*, 2*A*, 3*A*, 4*B*, 5*A*, 6*B*, 7*A*, 8*A*, 9*B*, 10*B*, 11*A*, 12*A*, 13*B*. Find your total score by adding up the number of points and then use the following scoring key:

0–3 very low sensation seeking

4–5 low

6–9 average

10–11 high

12–13 very high

Keep in mind, of course, that this short questionnaire, for which the scoring is based on the results of college students who have taken it, provides only a rough estimate of your sensation-seeking tendencies. Moreover, as people get older, their sensation-seeking scores tend to decrease. Still, the questionnaire will at least give you an indication of how your sensation-seeking tendencies compare with those of others.

Source: From Zuckerman, M. (Feb. 1978). The search for high sensation. *Psychology Today*, pp. 30–46. Reprinted with permission from *Psychology Today Magazine*. Copyright © 1978 (Sussex Publishers, Inc.).

Feldman: Pathways to
Psychology

Feeling and Experiencing
the World

Motivation and Emotion

© The McGraw–Hill
Companies, 2000

127

Incentive Approaches: Motivation's Pull

When a luscious dessert is brought to the table after a filling meal, its appeal has little or nothing to do with internal drives or with the maintenance of arousal. Rather, if we choose to eat the dessert, such behavior is motivated by the external stimulus of the dessert itself, which acts as an anticipated reward. This reward, in motivational terms, is an *incentive*.

Incentive approaches to motivation:
The theory explaining motivation in terms of external stimuli.

Incentive approaches to motivation attempt to explain why behavior is not always motivated by an internal need, such as the desire to reduce drives or to maintain an optimum level of arousal. Instead of focusing on internal factors, incentive theory explains motivation in terms of the nature of the external stimuli, the incentives that direct and energize behavior. In this view, properties of external stimuli largely account for a person's motivation.

Although the theory explains why we may succumb to an incentive (like a mouth-watering dessert) even though internal cues (like hunger) are lacking, it does not provide a complete explanation of motivation, since organisms seek to fulfill needs even when incentives are not apparent. Consequently, many psychologists believe that the internal drives proposed by drive-reduction theory work in tandem with the external incentives of incentive theory to "push" and "pull" behavior, respectively. Thus, at the same time we seek to satisfy our underlying hunger needs (the push of drive-reduction theory), we are drawn to food that appears particularly appetizing (the pull of incentive theory). Rather than contradicting each other, then, drives and incentives may work together in motivating behavior (Petri, 1996).

Cognitive Approaches: The Thoughts Behind Motivation

Cognitive approaches to motivation:
The focus on the role of our thoughts, expectations, and understanding of the world.

Cognitive approaches to motivation focus on the role of our thoughts, expectations, and understanding of the world. For instance, according to one cognitive approach, *expectancy-value theory*, two kinds of cognitions underlie our behavior. The first is our expectation that a behavior will cause us to reach a particular goal, and the second is our understanding of the value of that goal to us. For example, the degree to which we are motivated to study for a test will be based jointly on our expectation of how well our studying will pay off (in terms of a good grade) and the value we place on getting a good grade. If both expectation and value are high, we will be motivated to study diligently; but if either one is low, our motivation to study will be relatively lower (Tolman, 1959; McInerney et al., 1997).

Intrinsic motivation:
Motivation by which people participate in an activity for their own enjoyment, not for the reward it will get them.

Cognitive theories of motivation draw a key distinction between intrinsic and extrinsic motivation. **Intrinsic motivation** causes us to participate in an activity for our own enjoyment, rather than for any tangible reward that it will bring us. In contrast, **extrinsic motivation** causes us to do something for a tangible reward.

Extrinsic motivation:
Motivation by which people participate in an activity for a tangible reward.

According to research on the two types of motivation, we are more apt to persevere, work harder, and produce work of higher quality when motivation for a task is intrinsic rather than extrinsic (Harackiewicz & Elliot, 1993; Ryan & Deci, 1996; Elliot & Harackiewicz, 1996). Some psychologists go further, suggesting that providing rewards for desirable behavior may cause intrinsic motivation to decline and extrinsic motivation to increase, although this conclusion is controversial (e.g., Cameron & Pierce, 1994, 1996; Eisenberger & Cameron, 1996; Kohn, 1996; Lepper, Keavney, & Drake, 1996). In one demonstration of this phenomenon, a group of nursery school students were promised a reward for drawing with magic markers (an activity for which they had previously shown high motivation). The reward served to reduce their enthusiasm for the task, for they later showed considerably less zeal for drawing (Lepper & Greene, 1978). It was as if the promise of reward undermined their intrinsic interest in drawing, turning what had been play into work.

Such research suggests the importance of promoting intrinsic motivation and indicates that providing extrinsic rewards (or even just calling attention to them) may actually undermine the effort and quality of performance. Parents might think twice, then, about offering their children monetary rewards for getting good report cards. Instead, the research on intrinsic motivation suggests that better results would come from reminding them of the pleasures that can come from learning and mastering a body of knowledge.

Maslow's Hierarchy: Ordering Motivational Needs

What do Eleanor Roosevelt, Abraham Lincoln, and Albert Einstein have in common? Quite a bit, according to a model of motivation devised by psychologist Abraham Maslow: Each of them reached and fulfilled the highest levels of motivational needs underlying human behavior.

Maslow's model considers different motivational needs to be ordered in a hierarchy, and it suggests that before more sophisticated, higher-order needs can be met, certain primary needs must be satisfied (Maslow, 1970; 1987). The model can be conceptualized as a pyramid (see Figure 2) in which the more basic needs are at the bottom and the higher-level needs are

Figure 2
Maslow's hierarchy shows how our motivation progresses up the pyramid from a basis in the broadest, most fundamental biological needs up to higher-order ones. (After Maslow, 1970.)

at the top. In order for a particular need to be activated and thereby guide a person's behavior, the more basic needs in the hierarchy must be met first.

The most basic needs are those described earlier as primary drives: needs for water, food, sleep, sex, and the like. In order to move up the hierarchy, a person must have these basic physiological needs met. Safety needs come next in the hierarchy; Maslow suggests that people need a safe, secure environment in order to function effectively. Physiological and safety needs compose the lower-order needs.

Only when the basic lower-order needs are met can a person consider fulfilling higher-order needs, such as the need for love and a sense of belonging, esteem, and self-actualization. Love and belongingness needs include the need to obtain and give affection and to be a contributing member of some group or society. After these needs are fulfilled, the person strives for esteem. In Maslow's thinking, esteem relates to the need to develop a sense of self-worth by knowing that others are aware of one's competence and value.

Self-actualization:
A state of self-fulfillment in which people realize their highest potential in their own unique way.

Once these four sets of needs are fulfilled—no easy task—the person is ready to strive for the highest-level need, self-actualization. **Self-actualization** is a state of self-fulfillment in which people realize their highest potential in their own unique way. When Maslow first proposed the concept, he used it to describe just a few well-known individuals such as Eleanor Roosevelt, Lincoln, and Einstein. But self-actualization is not limited to the famous. A parent with excellent nurturing skills who raises a family, a teacher who year after year creates an environment that maximizes students' opportunities for success, and an artist who realizes her creative potential might all be self-actualized. The important thing is that people feel at ease with themselves and satisfied that they are using their talents to the fullest. In a sense, achieving self-actualization produces a decline in the striving and yearning for greater fulfillment that marks most people's lives and instead provides a sense of satisfaction with the current state of affairs (Jones & Crandall, 1991).

Unfortunately, research has not been able to validate the specific ordering of the stages of Maslow's theory, and it has proven difficult to measure self-actualization objectively (Haymes, Green, & Quinto, 1984; Weiss, 1991; Neher, 1991). However, Maslow's model is important for two reasons: It highlights the complexity of human needs, and it emphasizes that until more basic biological needs are met, people will be relatively unconcerned with higher-order needs. If people are hungry, their first interest will be in obtaining food; they will not be concerned with such needs as love and self-esteem. The model helps explain why victims of disasters such as famine and war may suffer the breakdown of normal family ties and be unconcerned with the welfare of anyone other than themselves.

Reconciling the Different Approaches to Motivation

Now that we have examined several different approaches to motivation (summarized in Figure 3), it is reasonable to wonder which of them provides

Approach	Description
Instinct	People and animals are born with preprogrammed sets of behaviors essential to their survival.
Drive reduction	When some basic biological requirement is lacking, a drive is produced.
Arousal	People seek an optimal level of stimulation. If the level of stimulation is too high, they act to reduce it; if it is too low, they act to increase it.
Incentive	External stimuli direct and energize behavior.
Cognitive	Thoughts, expectations, and understanding of the world direct motivation.
Hierarchy of needs	Needs form a hierarchy; before higher-order needs are met, lower-order needs must be fulfilled.

Figure 3
Approaches
to motivation.

the fullest account of motivational phenomena. Actually, many of the conceptual approaches are complementary, rather than contradictory, and it is often useful to employ several theories simultaneously in order to understand a particular motivational system (Deci, 1992). When we consider people's specific motives, such as the needs for food, achievement, affiliation, and power, we can draw upon several of these theories to gain a better understanding of motivation.

▶ LOOKING BACK

- *How does motivation direct and energize behavior?*

    1. The topic of motivation considers the factors that direct and energize behavior. Drive is the motivational tension that energizes behavior in order to fulfill a need. Primary drives relate to basic biological needs. Secondary drives are those in which no obvious biological need is fulfilled.
    2. Motivational drives often operate under the principle of homeostasis, by which an organism tries to maintain an optimal level of internal biological functioning by making up for any deviations from its usual state.
    3. A number of broad approaches to motivation move beyond explanations that rely on instincts. Drive-reduction approaches, though useful for primary drives, are inadequate for explaining behavior in which the goal is not to reduce a drive but to maintain or even increase excitement or arousal. In contrast, arousal approaches suggest that we try to maintain a particular level of stimulation and activity.

4. Incentive approaches, an alternative explanation of motivation, focus on the positive aspects of the environment that direct and energize behavior. Finally, cognitive approaches to motivation focus on the role of thoughts, expectations, and an individual's understanding of the world. One cognitive theory—expectancy-value theory—suggests that expectations that a behavior will accomplish a particular goal and our understanding of the value of that goal underlie behavior.

5. Maslow's hierarchy of needs suggests that there are five needs: physiological, safety, love and belongingness, esteem, and self-actualization. Only after the more basic needs are fulfilled is a person able to move toward higher-order needs.

▶ KEY TERMS AND CONCEPTS

motivation

instincts

drive-reduction approaches
 to motivation

drive

homeostasis

arousal approaches to motivation

incentive approaches to motivation

cognitive approaches to motivation

intrinsic motivation

extrinsic motivation

self-actualization

▶ ASK YOURSELF

Which approaches to motivation are most commonly used in the workplace? How might each approach be used to design employment policies that can sustain or increase motivation?

How does Maslow's hierarchy of needs apply to situations in which workers are paid subsistence wages? How does it apply to situations in which workers receive adequate wages?

A writer who works all day composing copy for an advertising firm has a hard time keeping her mind on her work and continually watches the clock. After work she turns to a collection of stories she is creating and writes long into the night, completely forgetful of the clock. What ideas from your reading on motivation help to explain this phenomenon?

▶ REFERENCES

Babbitt, T., Rowland, G., & Franken, R. (1990). Sensation seeking and participation in aerobic exercise classes. *Personality and Individual Differences, 11,* 181–184.

Berlyne, D. (1967). Arousal and reinforcement. In D. Levine (Ed.), *Nebraska symposium on motivation.* Lincoln: University of Nebraska Press.

Bernard, L. L. (1924). *Instinct: A study in social psychology.* New York: Holt.

Brehm, J. W., & Self, E. A. (1989). The intensity of motivation. *Annual Review of Psychology, 40,* 109–131.

Cameron, J., & Pierce, W. D. (1994). Reinforcement, reward, and intrinsic motivation: A meta-analysis. *Review of Educational Research, 64,* 363–423.

Cameron, J., & Pierce, W. D. (1996). The debate about rewards and intrinsic motivation: Protests and accusations do not alter the results. *Review of Educational Research, 66,* 39–51.

Cocco, N., Sharpe, L., & Blaszczynski, A. P. (1995). Differences in preferred level of arousal in two subgroups of problem gamblers: A preliminary report. *Journal of Gambling Studies, 11,* 221–229.

Deci, E. L. (1992). On the nature and functions of motivation theories. *Psychological Science, 3,* 167–176.

Eisenberger, R., & Cameron, J. (1996). Detrimental effects of reward. *American Psychologist, 51,* 1153–1166.

Elliot, A. J., & Harackiewicz, J. M. (1996). Approach and avoidance achievement goals and intrinsic motivation: A mediational analysis. *Journal of Personality and Social Psychology, 70,* 461–475.

Farley, F. (1986, May). The big T in personality. *Psychology Today,* pp. 44–52.

Harackiewicz, J. M., & Elliot, A. J. (1993). Achievement goals and intrinsic motivation. *Journal of Personality and Social Psychology, 65,* 904–915.

Harlow, H. F., Harlow, M. K., & Meyer, D. R. (1950). Learning motivated by a manipulation drive. *Journal of Experimental Psychology, 40,* 228–234.

Haymes, M., Green, L., & Quinto, R. (1984). Maslow's hierarchy, moral development, and prosocial behavioral skills within a child psychiatric population. *Motivation and Emotion, 8,* 23–31.

Hull, C. L. (1943). *Principles of behavior.* New York: Appleton-Century-Crofts.

Jones, A., & Crandall, R. (Eds.). (1991). Handbook of self-actualization. *Journal of Social Behavior and Personality, 6,* 1–362.

Kohn, A. (1996). By all available means: Cameron and Pierce's defense of extrinsic motivators. *Review of Educational Research, 66,* 1–4.

Leap of faith. (1996, August 5). *People Magazine,* p. 118.

Lepper, M. R., & Greene, D. (Eds.). (1978). The hidden costs of reward. Hillsdale, NJ: Erlbaum.

Lepper, M. R., Keavney, M., & Drake, M. (1996). Intrinsic motivation and extrinsic rewards: A commentary on Cameron and Pierce's meta-analysis. *Review of Educational Research, 66,* 5–32.

Loewenstein, G. (1994). The psychology of curiosity: A review and reinterpretation. *Psychological Bulletin, 116,* 75–98.

Maslow, A. H. (1970). *Motivation and personality* (2nd ed.). New York: Harper & Row.

Maslow, A. H. (1987). *Motivation and personality* (3rd ed.). New York: Harper & Row.

McDougall, W. (1908). *Introduction to social psychology.* London: Methuen.

McInerney, D. M., Roche, L. A., McInerney, V., & Marsh, H. W. (1997). Cultural perspectives on school motivation: The relevance and application of goal theory. *American Educational Research Journal, 34,* 207–236.

Mineka, S., & Henderson, R. W. (1985). Controllability and predictability in acquired motivation. *Annual Review of Psychology, 36,* 495–529.

Neher, A. (1991). Maslow's theory of motivation: A critique. *Journal of Humanistic Psychology, 31,* 89–112.

Nelson, M. (1992, February 3). Too tough to die. *People Weekly,* pp. 30–33.

Petri, H. L. (1996). *Motivation: Theory, research, and applications* (4th ed.). Pacific Grove, CA: Brooks/Cole.

Ryan, R. M., & Deci, E. L. (1996). When paradigms clash: Comments on Cameron and Pierce's claim that rewards do not undermine intrinsic motivation. *Review of Educational Research, 66,* 33–38.

Stacy, A. W., Newcomb, M. D., & Bentler, P. M. (1991). Social psychological influences on sensation seeking from adolescence to adulthood. *Personality and Social Psychology Bulletin, 17(6),* 701–708.

Tolman, E. C. (1959). Principles of purposive behavior. In S. Koch (Ed.), *Psychology: A study of a science* (Vol. 2). New York: McGraw-Hill.

Weiss, A. S. (1991). The measurement of self-actualization: The quest for the test may be as challenging as the search for the self. *Journal of Social Behavior and Personality, 6,* 265–290.

Zuckerman, M. (1991). One person's stress is another person's pleasure. In C. D. Spielberger, I. G. Sarason, Z. Kulczar, & G. L. Van Heck (Eds.), *Stress and emotion: Anxiety, anger, and curiosity.* New York: Hemisphere.

Zuckerman, M. (1994). *Behavioral expressions and biosocial bases of sensation seeking.* New York: Cambridge University Press.

CHAPTER

12

Arousal–Performance Relationships

Daniel M. Landers, *Arizona State University, Emeritus*
Shawn M. Arent, *Rutgers University*

Most athletes at some time or another have experienced an unexpected breakdown in their performance. Consider, for a moment, the following illustrative examples. A U.S. Olympic weight lifter in international competition surprisingly deviates from his customary preparatory routine before a clean and jerk and totally forgets to chalk his hands. As might be expected, he misses the lift. A gymnast preparing for a high flyaway dismount from the still rings suddenly focuses on self-doubts concerning his ability to perform the stunt without the presence of a spotter. These doubts, coupled with an increased fatigue level brought about by a long routine, cause him to freeze and release the rings prematurely. Finally, a sprinter who appears lackadaisical and lethargic during precompetition warm-up records one of her worst 100m times.

These are just a few examples of what athletes and coaches usually refer to as lack of concentration, "choking" under pressure, or failure to get the athlete "up" for competition. Sport competition can generate much anxiety and worry, which in turn can affect physiological and thought processes so dramatically that performance often deteriorates. In your own athletic or coaching experience, you have probably perceived a racing heartbeat, a dry mouth, butterflies in your stomach, cold and clammy hands, trembling muscles, or an inability to clearly focus thoughts. In these situations you may have told yourself that you were "too tight" or tense or that you "couldn't think straight." Common expressions like these often prompt practical questions concerning whether the athlete should be fired up as much as possible or relaxed as much as possible before an important competition. Or perhaps there is some in-between state that should be sought.

These concerns are generally related to the topic of motivation and, more specifically, to the concept of arousal. Understanding arousal and its effects on athletic performance, finding ways to estimate the arousal demands of a particular sport, and assessing arousal levels of individual athletes form the focus of this chapter. In the first section we will describe arousal and its effects and then outline a model for understanding its influence on athletic performance. In the second section we will describe the major hypotheses and research evidence for the arousal–performance relationship. Finally, in the third section we will describe a method whereby the coach or sport psychologist can estimate the optimal arousal level for a specific sport skill and for specific athletes.

The Nature of Arousal

Before considering how arousal is related to performance, it is necessary to clarify the nature of the arousal construct. This will be done by first defining arousal, followed by a discussion of its origin and how it is generated. Finally, various techniques for measuring arousal will be presented.

Defining Arousal and Related Constructs

In the psychological literature behavior is viewed as varying on only two dimensions—intensity and direction. The term *arousal* is used synonymously with the term *activation,* and these terms both refer to the intensity level of behavior (Duffy, 1957). Both of these terms also refer to a nondirective generalized bodily activation or arousal dimension. According to Malmo (1959), **arousal** consists of neural excitation on a continuum ranging from a comatose state to a state of extreme excitement as might be manifested in a panic attack. Conceptually, Duffy (1962) argues that any given point on this continuum is determined by "the extent of release of potential energy, stored in the tissues of the organism, as shown in activity or response" (p. 17). For our purposes, arousal will be viewed as an energizing function that is responsible for harnessing the body's resources for intense and vigorous activity (Sage, 1984).

Using Martens's (1974) analogy, the energy produced by increases in arousal can be likened to the engine of an automobile, which, when the car is in neutral or park, can be varied along a revolutions per minute (rpm) continuum without affecting the direction (forward or reverse) of the car. The nondirectional term *arousal* has no more positive or negative connotations than the rpm continuum described here. However, like the human, when the car is in motion and the speed is too fast for the road conditions, inappropriate levels of energy in the automobile (rpm) can disrupt efficient driving performance. The ideal

rpm intensity should match the requirements for the desired task outcome (e.g., quick acceleration) to produce the greatest performance efficiency. Sometimes, however, this is not the case. The engine may be racing with the car in a forward gear but with the emergency brake on. This unnatural state is akin to what we will refer to later as a **performance disregulation,** in which extraneous influences (e.g., the brake or anxiety brought about by negative, self-defeating thought processes) interfere with the natural coordinative action of the skill being performed. The human engine refers to both the activation of the brain and the innervation of different physiological systems. Without the proper arousal athletes may simply be left "spinning their wheels."

Unlike the car engine, our human engine cannot be turned off—at least not while we are alive! Even as you sleep, there is electrical activity in your brain as well as small amounts in the muscles. Thus, arousal is a natural, ongoing state. However, when arousal levels become extremely high, you may experience unpleasant emotional reactions associated with the autonomic nervous system. This maladaptive condition is often referred to as *stress* or *state anxiety* or *distress* (Selye, 1950). Although anxiety, stress, and arousal are related concepts, they are not conceptually the same (Figure 12-1). There has been considerable confusion in the research literature resulting from these terms being used interchangeably. Recall that arousal is nondirective generalized bodily arousal-activation, and anxiety is an unpleasant emotional state.

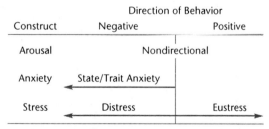

Figure 12-1 **Direction of behavior for arousal, anxiety, and stress**

According to Spielberger (1975), the condition of anxiety is an emotional state or reaction characterized by (a) varying intensity; (b) variation over time; (c) the presence of recognizable unpleasant feelings of intensity, preoccupation, disturbance, and apprehension; and (d) a simultaneous pronounced activation of the vegetative (autonomic) nervous system. Like anxiety, stress also identifies the direction the behavior takes. Selye (1950) maintains that stress can be either positive (called *eustress*) or negative (called *distress*) in direction. In the psychological literature distress and anxiety both describe the kind of negative emotional state Spielberger (1975) is referring to in his definition. Thus, anxiety and distress can occur when arousal levels are high, but they do not have to occur at higher levels of arousal if athletes maintain control over all aspects of their performance. Thus, these terms are not conceptually and operationally the same as arousal.

Eustress is associated with one's ability to use stress in a constructive way that is beneficial to performance. Each of the theories presented here has something to say about the amount of arousal that may be conducive to producing eustress. Levels of anxiety and distress are influenced by perceptions of certainty or uncertainty and whether one can control the situation at hand. When there is total assurance of being successful, the competition is often taken for granted and the resulting underaroused state is maladaptive for effective performance. Basically, we know that some degree of uncertainty is necessary to increase arousal and motivation, but too much uncertainty can be anxiety producing. Thus, the anxiety response associated with higher states of arousal is typically related to an athlete's perceived inability to deal with the specific situation (e.g., task difficulty or demands). As we will see in a later section of this chapter, anxiety reactions to competition can result in ineffective performance, faulty decision making, and inappropriate perception. Helping athletes harness arousal so that it will not become an uncontrollable anxiety response is one of the major tasks performed by sport psychologists. It is important to bear in mind that sport psychologists do not seek to make people unemotional zombies but instead attempt to teach skills that will enable athletes to better control arousal and, thereby, more effectively cope with anxiety.

Origin of Arousal States

The structures for controlling arousal are located in the brain and primarily involve the cortex, reticular formation, the hypothalamus, and the limbic system. These centers interact with the adrenal medulla and the somatic and autonomic systems to determine overall arousal. We can demonstrate the integration of these different systems in an athletic situation by means of the following example.

A field hockey goalie sits in the dressing room minutes before an important match. She *begins to worry* about an upcoming game, which happens to be the biggest game of the season. These thoughts lead to anxiety about her performance. Her worrying may not be realistic, but to her body that does not matter. Technically speaking, as she worried, messages were being sent by a quick route to the amygdala, and another message by a longer route to the thalamus and then on to the cerebral cortex (Gorman, 2002). The amygdala, an almond-shaped cluster of cells in the midbrain, reacts quickly by activating physiological responses that are associated with fear, worry, and threat. Even before the source of the fear can be verified by higher brain centers (i.e., cerebral cortex), the amygdala activates the sympathetic nervous system causing the adrenal medulla to pump the catecholamines epinephrine and norepinephrine (also called adrenaline and noradrenaline) into the bloodstream (Gorman, 2002; Krahenbuhl, 1975). The rapid increase in these catecholamines and cortisol prepares her body and mind for an emergency "fight or flight" situation. Autonomic nervous system measures such as heart rate, blood pressure, and breathing begin to increase, and muscles in general begin to tighten. The blood supply begins to be shunted away from the digestive system and redirected to the larger muscles of the arms and legs through vasodilation. While all of these physiological reactions

224   Chapter 12   Arousal–Performance Relationships

are already underway, the cerebral cortex begins to receive information on the worry or fear that this athlete is experiencing. The cerebral cortex analyzes this information to determine whether or not a threat exists. If analysis determines that the situation the athlete is in is not perceived to be a threat, the prefrontal cortex sends out an "all-clear signal" to the amygdala and the physiological responses described above are terminated. By contrast, if the cerebral cortex perceives the situation the athlete currently faces as a threat, then a fear label is attached to it and this is sent to the amygdala. In this case, the amygdala continues to send out a "fear alarm" and the already initiated physiological responses continue or may even increase. Having conscious awareness, she may interpret these changes as further support for her lack of ability and readiness, leading to a debilitating cycle of worry and physiological disruption of homeostasis (i.e., disregulation). The hockey goalie is now in an overly aroused or anxious state. Needless to say, we would not expect her to perform well in this condition.

How Arousal Is Generated

From the foregoing example, we can see that the athlete's fleeting self-doubt was the starting point of a chain reaction that ultimately led to an overaroused state. This chain reaction along with the host of other factors involved in the arousal–performance relationship is outlined in Figure 12-2.

Our hockey goalie had a self-doubt that prompted physiological and subsequent cognitive appraisal that led her to conclude that her capabilities did not meet the demands of the upcoming game. This combination of an important meaningful event and doubts about her ability was responsible for generating anxiety and worry. Whether this process starts with an internal thought or an external stimulus, the amygdala triggers a physiological reaction in advance of full-fledged cognitive appraisal (Gorman, 2002). Once cognitive appraisal is initiated and the threat or doubt is confirmed, physiological reactions described in Figure 12-2 (see entries 1–4 under C) are heightened. When these physiological reactions are heightened, she begins to interpret the feelings as well (see entry 4 under D). Not knowing how to cope with the physiological reactions can create even more worry and apprehension (see entries 1–4 under D). Notice also that, once performance begins, aspects of the athlete's behavior (see entries 1–4 under E) are fed back for cognitive appraisal (see entries 1–4 under D) that may further intensify anxiety. As we will see later, this process can be influenced

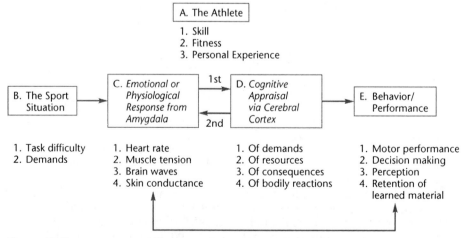

Figure 12-2 **Factors that affect the arousal–performance relationship**

by individual difference variables such as skill level, personality, physical and psychological fitness, and competitive experience.

Measurement of Arousal

Because arousal affects so many bodily functions, it appears to be an easy construct to measure. Unfortunately, this is not the case. We will discuss three types of arousal measurement and two types of anxiety measurement and highlight the advantages and disadvantages of each (Table 12-1).

Physiological measures. In sport psychology research much frustration has resulted from the lack of consistent agreement among different physiological variables and questionnaire measures. However, this poor correspondence has occurred because many investigators believed similar results would be found with a physiological arousal-activation measure and an anxiety questionnaire measure. It would not be expected that nondirective physiological measures of generalized bodily activation or arousal state would necessarily be consistent with questionnaire measures of negative emotional states like anxiety.

A more important concern is the low correlation found among physiological measures explained by Lacey, Bateman, and Van Lehn's (1953) principle of "autonomic response stereotypy." For example, in the same stressful situation, athlete A might display an elevated heart rate, and athlete B might show an increase in blood pressure. This principle suggests that averaging one physiological variable (e.g., heart rate) across the group may conceal individual arousal reactions.

To overcome this problem, Duffy (1962) has recommended the use of multiple physiological measures as an index of the arousal response. From these multiple measures, if athlete A is found to be a heart rate responder when exposed to stressors like competition, this measure would be singled out for comparison of athlete A in conditions varying in levels of perceived stress. By using each person's most responsive autonomic measure, greater differentiation can be

achieved and thus more meaningful information can be gleaned.

The current view concerning physiological measures is that they are far more complex than first thought. However, with increased understanding of physiological processes and the continuing trend of cheaper, more sophisticated equipment, physiological measures have considerable potential as reliable indicators of the arousal response.

Biochemical measures. The adrenal gland is responsible for the release of epinephrine and norepinephrine into the bloodstream in times of stress. Also, a variety of corticosteroids enter the blood during high arousal. Increases in amines or cortisol have been examined primarily by analyzing either the blood or urine. Blood analysis usually involves drawing blood from the athlete by syringe or catheter. The analysis is complex and requires sophisticated equipment. Another disadvantage is that drawing blood can be traumatic or stressful to some athletes, thus confounding the results of the study. Urine analysis is less invasive but suffers from the same cost and time disadvantages as blood analysis. Furthermore, the usefulness of the analyses differs due to the speed at which the hormones of interest show up in the blood or urine. At this point it is also unclear how accurately serum measures reflect the brain's overall hormonal levels.

Questionnaires. Many questionnaires have been used to measure arousal, but unfortunately most of these are anxiety measures and not arousal measures. Only two questionnaires are specifically designed to assess nondirective generalized bodily activation, or arousal. These are the Activation-Deactivation Adjective Checklist (AD-ACL, Thayer, 1986) and the Somatic Perception Questionnaire (SPQ, Landy & Stern, 1971). The AD-ACL has been used in the exercise and sport literature. Unlike the SPQ, it contains two bipolar activation dimensions. Within the broader dimension of energetic arousal, which is generalized, nondirective bodily activation, the AD-ACL has two subscales of Energy (General Activation) and Tiredness (Deactivation-Sleep).

226 Chapter 12 **Arousal–Performance Relationships**

Table 12-1 **Some Common Physiological, Biochemical, and Questionnaire Measures of Arousal and Anxiety**

Measure and Description

I. Arousal Measures

  A. Physiological

    1. Central

      Electroencephalography (EEG). Changes occur in brain wave patterns from an alpha or relaxed state (8–14 Hz) to beta or a more aroused state (14–30 Hz).

    2. Automatic

      Electrical properties of the skin. This measure assesses either the amount of skin conductance or resistance to an electric current. Elevations in arousal cause increased perspiration, which increases the flow of the current.

      Heart rate. Increases in heart rate, the pattern of beats, and heart rate variability can all be indexes of arousal.

      Blood pressure. Increases in blood pressure are also associated with increased arousal levels and can be measured by cannulation or by the stethoscope and pressure-cuff method.

      Muscle activity. Muscle tension can be measured by electromyography (EMG), which measures the firing rate of motor units by means of surface electrodes attached to the muscle.

  B. Biochemical

    1. Epinephrine. Epinephrine is released from the adrenal medulla during times of stress. This can be measured in the urine and blood.

    2. Norepinephrine. Also elevated during stressful activities, this catecholamine can be measured by the same techniques used to analyze epinephrine.

    3. Cortisol. This steroid hormone is released from the adrenal cortex when the organism is confronted with either physical/emotional stressors or declining blood glucose levels.

  C. Questionnaires

    1. Somatic Perception Questionnaire (Landy & Stern, 1971)

    2. Activation Deactivation Adjective Checklist (Thayer, 1967)

II. Anxiety Measures

  A. Unidimensional Questionnaires

    1. State-Trait Anxiety Inventory (Spielberger, Gorsuch, & Lushene, 1970)

    2. Sport Competition Anxiety Test (Martens, 1977)

  B. Multidimensional Questionnaires

    1. Cognitive-Somatic Anxiety Questionnaire (Schwartz, Davidson, & Goleman, 1978)

    2. Competitive State Anxiety Inventory-2 (CSAI-2); (Martens, Burton, Vealey, Smith, & Bump, 1983; Martens, Burton, Vealey, Bump, & Smith, 1990)

    3. Sport Anxiety Scale (SAS; Smith, Smoll, & Schutz, 1990)

The other dimension, which is a directional measure of one's mood state, consists of the subscales of Tension (High Activation) and Calmness (General Deactivation). There is some evidence that the AD-ACL yields a better assessment of global arousal-activation than do individual physiological measures (Thayer, 1967, 1970). These questionnaire measures have broader use in a variety of sport settings. They are quick and easy to administer and are less cumbersome and intrusive than most physiological measures. However, the physiological measures are less dependent on athletes' linguistic and cultural background and are also less susceptible to behavioral artifacts (e.g., halo effects, demand characteristics, social desirability).

Anxiety Measures

The majority of sport studies published on the topic of arousal contain information derived from anxiety questionnaires. As has been pointed out earlier, it is a mistake to use the terms *arousal* and *anxiety* interchangeably. Recall that arousal is considered a nondirectional energizing function, whereas anxiety is negative in direction in that it is an emotional state or reaction characterized by unpleasant feelings of intensity, preoccupation, disturbance, and apprehension. Although the constructs of arousal and anxiety may at times be highly related, arousal is conceptually and operationally not the same as anxiety, and therefore, theories based on the construct of arousal should not be replaced by anxiety-based theories (Anderson, 1990; Neiss, 1988).

Even though anxiety measures are not appropriate for examining the arousal-performance relationship, the fact that they are so prevalent in this literature warrants some discussion of these measures. Most of these *anxiety* questionnaires focus on cognitive and physiological manifestations associated with an anxiety response. Some measure cognitive and physiological responses by differentiating between them (CSAI-2, SAS), whereas others (STAI) contain cognitively and physiologically related items, but no differentiation is made between them (see Table 12-1).

Many questionnaires are designed to assess both trait and state forms of anxiety. **Trait anxiety** is a *general* predisposition to respond across many situations with high levels of anxiety. To assess trait anxiety, individuals are asked to rate how they generally feel. **State anxiety** is much more specific, referring to an individual's anxiety at a particular moment. People who are high in trait anxiety are expected to respond with

higher levels of state anxiety, or situationally specific anxiety. The State-Trait Anxiety Inventory (Spielberger, Gorsuch, & Lushene, 1970) is a popular example of a well-researched questionnaire that assesses both dimensions of anxiety.

A more recent development in the construction of anxiety questionnaires is the trend toward multidimensional instruments. Three questionnaires, one non–sport specific (Schwartz, Davidson, & Goleman, 1978) and the others sport specific (Martens et al., 1983, 1990; Smith, Smoll, & Schutz, 1990), have subdivided anxiety into the components of somatic and cognitive aspects. The CSAI-2 (Martens et al., 1983, 1990) has somatic and cognitive state anxiety subscales plus a self-confidence scale. The SAS (Smith et al., 1990) has a somatic trait anxiety scale and two cognitive trait anxiety scales—one for worry and one for concentration disruption. Somatic or bodily anxiety is assessed by questions such as "How tense are the muscles in your body?" Cognitive anxiety would be indicated by affirmative responses to questions such as "Do you worry a lot?" By subdividing anxiety into its component parts, more will be understood about its nature and more effective therapies can thus be designed.

The Relationship between Arousal and Motor Performance

In the motor behavior literature two hypotheses have been advanced to explain the relationship between arousal and performance. We will first consider the drive theory hypothesis and then the inverted-*U* hypothesis.

Drive Theory

Although this is not a view held by all psychologists, for our purposes we will equate the term *drive* with *arousal*. In other words, drive and arousal convey what we referred to earlier as the intensity dimension of behavior.

Drive theory, as modified by Spence and Spence (1966), predicts that performance (P) is a multiplicative function of habit (H) and

228   Chapter 12   Arousal–Performance Relationships

drive (D): $P = H \times D$. The construct of habit in this formulation refers to the hierarchical order or dominance of correct or incorrect responses. According to this hypothesis, increases in arousal should enhance the probability of making the dominant responses. When performance errors are frequently made, as in the early stages of skill acquisition, the dominant responses are likely to be incorrect responses. Conversely, when performance errors are infrequent, the dominant response is said to be a correct response. Increases in arousal during initial skill acquisition impair performance, but as the skill becomes well learned, increases in arousal facilitate performance. This latter situation would be likened to a eustress state.

For example, a novice basketball player shooting free throws only sinks 3 shots out of 10; therefore, the incorrect response (a miss) is dominant. The drive theory hypothesis would predict that given greater pressure the novice player is likely to miss more than 7 shots out of 10. By contrast, the all-star basketball player may average 8 successful shots for every 10 attempted. In this case, because the dominant response is a correct response, an increase in arousal should enhance the player's chance of sinking more than 8 shots out of 10.

It is questionable whether a linear relationship between arousal and performance can be found for accuracy tasks such as free throw shooting. However, Oxendine (1984) argues that linear relationships, as depicted in Figure 12-3, do exist for gross motor activities involving strength and speed. These types of activities are typically overlearned, with strongly formed habit patterns. It seems likely, therefore, that a very high level of arousal is desirable for optimal performance in these types of gross motor skills. Support for this view comes from anecdotal evidence regarding superhuman feats performed in emergency situations in which unexpected physical strength and speed were required (e.g., a mother lifting a station wagon off her trapped child).

At first glance these examples seem to provide ample evidence to support a drive theory explanation for sport skills involving strength and speed. Contrary to Oxendine's analysis, however, we

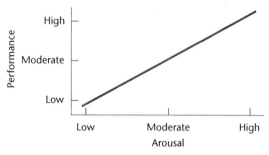

Figure 12-3 **The linear relationship between arousal and performance as suggested by drive theory**

would like to argue on conceptual grounds that the "fight or flight" arousal responses produced in these emergency situations are not appropriate comparisons to the sport situation. The sport setting is highly structured, often involving complex decision making and perceptual strategies in addition to the performance of a motor skill. The surge of adrenaline resulting from an emergency situation may enhance strength and speed in an uncontrolled manner, which may actually be detrimental to actual sport performances. For example, there are many instances of overaroused sprinters recording false starts in intense competition. Similarly, many superenergized weight lifters have forgotten to chalk up or have lifted the barbell in a biomechanically inefficient way in major competitions. Thus, on experiential grounds it appears that even among weight lifters and sprinters there are limits to the amount of arousal the athlete can tolerate without suffering performance decrements.

The drive theory has not fared much better when the experimental evidence from the motor behavior literature has been examined. For example, Freeman (1940) has shown that, with high levels of arousal, reaction times are slower than when arousal levels are in the moderate range. Furthermore, in other arousal-producing situations (e.g., audience effects) where the drive theory has received extensive support, it is now known that these effects were so small as to be of trivial practical significance (Bond & Titus, 1983;

Daniel M. Landers and Shawn M. Arent   229

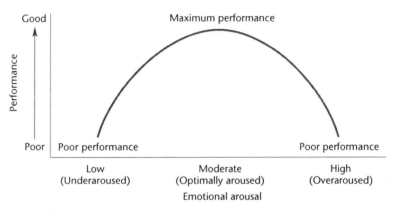

Figure 12-4 The inverted-*U* relationship between arousal and performance

Landers, Snyder-Bauer, & Feltz, 1978). Thus, it appears that other hypotheses, such as the inverted-*U*, need to be considered to explain the highly complex network of skills characteristic of sport performance.

Inverted-*U* Hypothesis

The inverted-*U* relationship between arousal and performance is shown in Figure 12-4. The **inverted-*U* hypothesis** predicts that as arousal increases from drowsiness to alertness there is a progressive increase in performance efficiency. However, once arousal continues to increase beyond alertness to a state of high excitement, there is a progressive decrease in task performance. Thus, the inverted-*U* hypothesis suggests that behavior is aroused and directed toward some kind of balanced or optimal state. In Selye's (1950) terms, this balanced state could also be termed *eustress*.

The idealized curve shown in Figure 12-4 is not usually seen with actual data that is based on relatively small sample sizes and only a few levels of manipulated arousal. As presented in statistics classes, most things in nature will resemble symmetrical bell-shaped curves, provided there are hundreds of cases and numerous (more than 30) levels of the independent variable. With

nearly all of the tests of the inverted-*U* hypothesis having fewer than 20 subjects and only three to five levels of arousal, it is unrealistic to expect perfectly symmetrical bell-shaped curves (i.e., idealized inverted-*U*); instead, the curve usually resembles an unsymmetrical inverted *V*. The key point is that the relationship between arousal and performance is curvilinear, with best performance occurring at an intermediate point within the range of arousal being examined.

The curvilinear relationship between arousal and performance is observed across studies with considerable regularity. This can be seen in Figure 12-5, where the curve for the difficult task looks more like an inverted *V*. This curve may have more closely resembled an inverted-*U* if 1-second increments in seconds of delay had been used. Other motor behavior laboratory studies (Martens & Landers, 1970; Wood & Hokanson, 1965) have shown support for the curvilinear relationship predicted by the inverted-*U* hypothesis. Other experiments do not show inverted-*U* curves (Murphy, 1966; Pinneo, 1961). In these studies investigators have manipulated incentive or threat to produce changes in arousal. Therefore, most of the research on this topic is limited because in most studies arousal has been examined as a dependent rather than independent variable. Anderson (1990) and Neiss (1988)

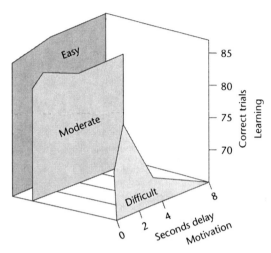

Figure 12-5 **A three-dimensional model illustrating the Yerkes-Dodson Law. Rats were held underwater and deprived of air for varying numbers of seconds, after which they were allowed to escape by selecting the correct door. The optimal level of motivation for learning depended on task difficulty**
Source: Broadhurst, 1957.

both argued that, if one wished to examine the effects of arousal on performance, data cannot be derived from anxiety or incentive manipulations. Furthermore, these arousal manipulations should be relative to arousal levels of each participant. In other words, arousal should be standardized as a percentage of a person's maximum arousal to control for baseline differences because of factors such as fitness, experience, and genetics.

Fortunately the few studies (Babin, 1966; Levitt & Gutin, 1971; Arent & Landers, 2003) that have manipulated arousal by increasing levels of physical activity have found support for the inverted-*U* hypothesis. For example, in the Arent and Landers study, participants were randomly assigned to one of eight arousal groups and they were all told they were competing for a cash prize. The eight arousal groups were 20, 30, 40, 50, 60, 70, 80, or 90% of relative heart

rate reserve (HRR). The use of HRR, which is highly correlated to maximal oxygen uptake, allowed for standardization of arousal relative to each participant. While participants rode a bicycle ergometer at their assigned percentage of HRR they responded to 12 stimulus presentations, and measures of reaction time, movement time, and overall response time were assessed. The results showed a statistically significant curvilinear relationship between arousal and reaction- and response-time performance (see Figure 12-6), accounting for 13.2% and 14.8% of the variance in performance, respectively. For movement time, the results showed a significant linear relationship between arousal and performance, accounting for 9.7% of the performance variance. Arent and Landers attributed the differences in measures of movement time to task characteristics and complexity issues that will be examined next.

Task characteristics. From an arousal perspective, the characteristics of a skill or activity are essential determinants of performance. In the early 1900s it was known that the optimal level of arousal varied among different tasks. Using laboratory animals, Yerkes and Dodson (1908) found that, on more complex tasks, the decrement in performance under increasing arousal conditions occurred earlier than it did for less complex tasks. The interaction of task complexity with arousal level is clearly illustrated in Broadhurst's (1957) experiment (see Figure 12-5). In this study arousal was created by holding rats underwater for zero, 2, 4, or 8 seconds prior to allowing them to swim underwater to complete a two-choice maze. In one condition the choice was made easier by making the correct escape door more obvious (brightly painted lines), whereas in the more difficult condition the doors were nearly the same. As shown in Figure 12-5, decrements in time to negotiate the maze occurred much earlier (after 2 seconds of submergence) in the more complex decision-making situation. Thus, higher levels of arousal can be tolerated on simpler tasks before performance is curtailed.

What does all of this mean for the performance of sport skills? Basically, the complexity

Williams: Applied Sport
Psychology: Personal
Growth to Peak
Performance, Sixth Edition

II. Mental Training for
Performance Enhancement

12. Arousal–Performance
Relationships

© The McGraw–Hill
Companies, 2010

145

Daniel M. Landers and Shawn M. Arent   231

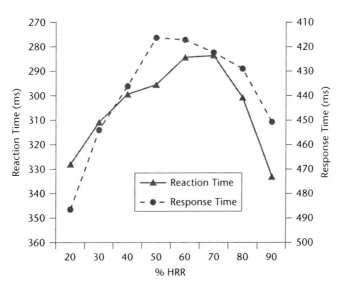

Figure 12-6 **Reaction and response time as a function
of percent of maximum heart rates reserve**
Source: Arent & Landers, 2003

characteristics of the motor skill need to be analyzed to determine how much arousal is optimal.
A number of factors that must be considered
appear in Table 12-2. Take, for example, the pre-
cision and steadiness characteristics required for
successful execution of a skill (Figure 12-7). For
very precise fine motor skills that involve steadiness or control of unwanted muscle activity

(e.g., putting a golf ball), very little arousal can
be tolerated without accompanying performance
decrements. However, for tasks such as weight
lifting that involve gross motor skills, a much
higher level of arousal can be achieved before
performance is impaired.

In addition to considering factors associated with the motor act itself, it is important to

Table 12-2 **The Complexity of Motor Performance**

Decision	Perception	Motor Act
Number of decisions necessary	Number of stimuli needed	Number of muscles
Number of alternatives per decision	Number of stimuli present	Amount of coordinative actions
Speed of decisions	Duration of stimuli	Precision and steadiness required
Sequence of decisions	Intensity of stimuli Conflicting stimuli	Fine motor skills required

Source: Based on Billing, 1980.

232   Chapter 12   Arousal–Performance Relationships

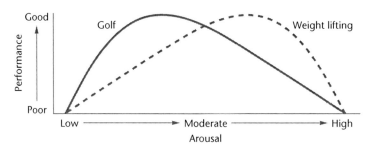

Figure 12-7 Sport-specific optimal levels of arousal

consider the decisional and perceptual characteristics of the task. The underwater swimming of the rats in Broadhurst's (1957) experiment was an example of varying the complexity of alternative *decisions*. Generally speaking, tasks with higher decisional demands require lower arousal levels for optimal performance compared to tasks with lower decisional demands.

The relationship of *perception* to the inverted-*U* hypothesis has been studied primarily in situations where individuals are attending to potentially conflicting stimuli. A number of studies (see Landers, 1978, 1980, for reviews) have shown that when dual tasks are performed individuals will generally allocate more attention to one of them to maintain or better their performance. This strategy is typically chosen because it is believed humans have very limited spare attentional capacity for focusing attention on task-irrelevant cues when they are performing complex motor skills.

There are many examples of attention being shifted away from secondary tasks to enhance the concentration necessary to perform the primary task. The experimental situation called the *dual-task paradigm* involves creating differing levels of arousal while subjects are performing a primary task and, at the same time, periodically reacting to a tone or a visual stimulus (Landers, Wang, & Courtet, 1985; Weltman & Egstrom, 1966).

From similar studies in which the dual-task paradigm has been used, Bacon (1974) offers the generalization that arousal effects depend on the degree of attention the stimuli attract, with "sensitivity loss systematically occurring to those cues which initially attract less attention" (p. 86). Other investigators (e.g., Easterbrook, 1959) suggest that arousal acts to narrow the range of cue utilization, which results in the inverted-*U* function previously described. The underaroused performer, for example, has a broad perceptual range and, therefore, either through lack of effort or poor selectivity accepts irrelevant cues uncritically. Performance in this case is understandably poor. When arousal increases to a moderate or optimal level, perceptual selectivity increases correspondingly and performance improves, presumably because the performer tries harder or is more likely to eliminate task-irrelevant cues. Arousal increases beyond this optimal point result in further perceptual narrowing, and performance deteriorates in accord with the inverted-*U* hypothesis. For instance, a highly anxious football quarterback may focus attention too narrowly and therefore not be able to perceive task-relevant cues such as a cheating safety or his third receiver open downfield. The ideas of both Bacon (1974) and Easterbrook (1959) suggest that the effects of arousal impair performance through a loss of perceptual sensitivity by interfering with athletes' capacity to process information.

Individual differences. The optimal level of arousal for a particular task is also dependent on factors that are unique to the individual. Coaches who routinely give pep talks to all athletes on their team before competitions may not

Daniel M. Landers and Shawn M. Arent   233

be aware that these arousing talks may not be beneficial for all athletes. Because of inherent personality differences and strength of dominant habits associated with the sport skill, some athletes can perform effectively at much higher levels of arousal than other athletes. People differ in the amount of prior experience with a task as well as the amount of practice they have had. As we discussed earlier, the strength of the correct habit response varies from one person to the next. The person who has greater skill—that is, has a stronger habit hierarchy—may be better able to offset the detrimental effects of increased arousal more effectively than the individual who is less skillful and possesses a weaker habit strength.

Of course, habit patterns may not always be appropriate. Landers (1985) has indicated that subtle changes in habit patterns may lead to **disregulation**, which is defined as a physiological measure of arousal that either negatively correlates with performance or creates some degree of discomfiture for the performer. For example, in our work with a world champion archer, we found that he had developed a habit of tightly squinting his nonsighting eye following the release of the arrow. At the end of several hours of shooting, this resulted in a tension headache. With the archer having to concentrate so much on the act of shooting, it was difficult for him to focus on the source of his problem. To correct this, it was necessary for us to bring the disregulation to his conscious awareness by providing an electromyographic signal of the electrical activity around his non-sighting eye. After several shots

with this type of biofeedback, the squinting, which lasted for several seconds, was reduced to a blink and the headaches disappeared.

Perhaps the greatest individual difference factor is personality. The most relevant personality variables affecting optimal arousal levels are anxiety and extroversion/introversion. For instance, in the aforementioned study by Arent and Landers (2003), somatic anxiety as measured by Sport Anxiety Scale (SAS) (Smith, Smoll & Schutz, 1990), significantly contributed to the amount of reaction- and response-time variance over and above the amount of variance explained by physiological arousal alone. Neither cognitive (as measured by either the Cognitive-Somatic Anxiety Questionnaire 2 [CSAI-2] or the SAS) nor somatic anxiety (as measured by the CSAI-2) accounted for a significant amount of performance variance. Arent and Landers suggested that the failure of the CSAI-2 somatic measure to predict performance is probably related to the better psychometric characteristics of the SAS. These findings suggest that if an athlete is high-strung and intolerant of stressful situations (i.e., high perceived somatic anxiety or introverted), even a small amount of arousal can put him or her over the top an the inverted-U curve (Figure 12-8). By contrast, if the athlete is calm, cool, and collected (i.e., low perceived somatic anxiety or extroverted), he or she will be able to tolerate much higher levels of arousal without suffering a performance impairment.

Another factor emphasized by Mahoney (1979) is the ability of the individual to cope

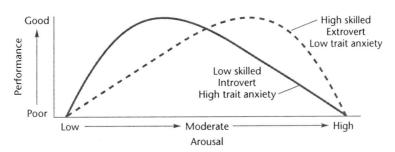

Figure 12-8 **Athlete-specific optimal levels of arousal**

with relatively high levels of arousal. This coping model emphasizes the individual's reaction to and ability to deal with arousal, since this may be "a significant determinant of its course and its effects on performance" (p. 436). For instance, if two athletes have a high absolute heart rate of 120 bpm, one athlete may be able to cope with this level of sympathetic disturbance and the other may not. With this view, there is less concern with physiological departures from normal levels and more emphasis on teaching athletes psychological skills (e.g., relaxation, imagery, self-talk). This view recognizes that a certain amount of energy (arousal) is needed for sporting activities, and a greater amount of arousal is not necessarily bad as long as the athlete can cope with it.

This point was recognized several years ago in research on rifle and pistol shooters (Landers et al., 1980). At that time some sport psychologists (Coleman, 1977; Nideffer, 1978) believed that better shooters actually decreased their heart rates below preshooting, resting levels while performing. However, research results (Landers et al., 1980; Tretilova & Rodmiki, 1979) showed that elite shooters invariably increased their heart rate above resting levels when they fired. In fact, if they did not increase heart rate at least 5 bpm above preshooting levels, they displayed poor performance (Tretilova & Rodmiki, 1979). Some elite gold medalist shooters had heart rates in excess of 50 bpm above preshooting levels and performed quite well. According to Mahoney (1979), when considering the inverted-U notion, the important factor is determining what level of arousal (usually a range) an individual athlete can cope with and still perform optimally.

Given individual differences in personality, habit patterns associated with the skills, and ability to cope with arousal and stress, it is clear that the relationship between arousal and performance is best assessed on an individual basis. Somewhere between the very diverse extremes of comatose state and panic attack, each athlete will have a "zone of optimal functioning" (Hanin, 1978). This is referred to as the Individualized Zone of Optimal Functioning (IZOF; Hanin, 2000). For some this arousal zone will be much

higher than is evident for other athletes (Landers, 1981). The trick is to know where this zone is for each athlete and then to help the athlete reproduce this arousal state more consistently from one competition to the next.

Unfortunately, in the sport psychology literature the IZOF model has only been operationalized with measures of anxiety. The questionnaires employed do not measure arousal per se, and, thus, the results of these studies should not be used to make direct inferences to the inverted-U hypothesis (Anderson, 1990; Neiss, 1988). In addition, the study by Arent and Landers (2003) shows that physiological measures of arousal explain double the amount of performance variance than measures of somatic anxiety. If performance enhancement is the desired goal, then investigators need to use either physiological measures or questionnaires that can directly measure arousal. However, the techniques presented for determining the IZOF are instructive and can be used in future research employing physiological measures or the AD-ACL. One technique, presented by Hanin (1978), had divers and gymnasts recollect and evaluate, with the aid of a retrospective anxiety scale, "how they felt before or at the time of a definite competition in the past" (Hanin 1978, p. 240). Furthermore, they were asked to recollect that state "in which they found themselves to act most effectively and achieve the highest result" (p. 242). This retrospectively determined "health anxiety" was then used to help determine an IZOF for each individual athlete. This was done by having an athlete recollect and rate his or her precompetitive anxiety prior to four favorable past competitions. If these ratings yielded values varying by only four points, the IZOF for this athlete would range, for example, between the extremes of these values, with the athlete's optimal level being the midpoint between these extremes.

Hanin (1978) believes these ratings of typical past behavior "allow one, with some credibility, to predict his emotional and behavioral manifestations and actions in situations of competitive stress" (p. 240). These retrospective ratings could then be used to estimate the level of anxiety in forthcoming competitions. If the

Daniel M. Landers and Shawn M. Arent   235

athlete is outside his or her individually determined IZOF, the anxiety level needs to be raised or lowered by (a) altering the subjective significance of the upcoming activity; (b) increasing the athlete's confidence in his or her ability to cope with the upcoming competition; (c) limiting the number of people giving input to the athlete; and (d) creating a less stressful social environment (Hanin, 1978).

A similar approach has been used by Sonstroem and Bernardo (1982) without reliance on retrospective ratings of precompetition state anxiety. Using the State-Trait Anxiety Scale (Spielberger et al., 1970), they had athletes give ratings before each game. Over time, a pattern of ratings began to appear for each athlete, and these were then used to predict *optimal* anxiety levels from which individual IZOFs could be computed. Using a variety of different sports, Hanin (1978) and Sonstroem and Bernardo (1982) have shown that if athletes are outside their IZOFs, the outcome is typically poorer performance.

Suggested Modifications and Alternatives to the Inverted-*U* Hypothesis

The inverted-*U* hypothesis does not provide a theoretical explanation for the arousal–performance relationship; it merely posits that this relationship is curvilinear without explaining what internal state or process produces it. There are explanations for this hypothesis, but only a few have been tested in a sport context. Three of these theories/models have been presented within the confines of the inverted-*U* hypothesis— Easterbrook's cue utilization theory as a description of the interaction of task characteristics and perception, Mahoney's coping model as an explanation of individual differences in coping ability, and Hanin's IZOF model as a technique for operationally defining individual anxiety differences at the level of the individual athlete. Other theories go beyond simply clarifying certain aspects of the arousal–performance relationship predicted by the inverted-*U* hypothesis. These more recent theories have been motivated by discontent with the ability of the inverted-*U* hypothesis as a way of predicting exactly where in the expansive

range between panic attack and comatose states performance is at an optimal level. In this case, investigators have provided conceptual distinctions that, like the IZOF model, mistakenly equate anxiety with arousal and view anxiety as multidimensional. Thus, these models and theories differ dramatically from the concepts in the inverted-*U* hypothesis and were proposed as alternatives in an attempt to better explain the relationship between arousal and performance. Two of these alternative explanations, the multidimensional anxiety theory and the catastrophe cusp model, will be discussed next.

Multidimensional anxiety theory related to performance.   This theory, developed by Burton (1988) and Martens et al. (1990), posits that anxiety has two different components: a cognitive component associated with fear about the consequences of failure and a somatic component reflecting perceptions of the physiological response to psychological stress. Although this theory assumes a sort of Cartesian dualism between mind and body, the authors maintain that mind and body are intertwined, but not completely. Martens et al. (1990) predicted that cognitive anxiety remains high and essentially stable prior to competition, whereas somatic anxiety peaks later (i.e., immediately prior to arrival at the site of the competition). This hypothesis has been tested in a "time to competition" paradigm and has generally been confirmed (Barnes, Sime, Dienstbier, & Plake, 1986; Burton, 1988; Gould, Petlichkoff, Simons, & Vevera, 1987; Gould, Petlichkoff, & Weinberg, 1984; Jones & Cale, 1989; Martens et al., 1990; Parfitt, 1988; Parfitt & Hardy, 1987; Speigler, Morris, & Liebert, 1968). However, this hypothesis does not deal directly with how these anxiety components influence arousal levels or the inverted-*U* relationship between arousal and performance.

To link this theory to performance, another prediction from multidimensional theory (Martens et al., 1990, pp. 123–124) is that somatic anxiety dissipates once performance begins, whereas cognitive anxiety can vary throughout performance because the subjective probability of success can change throughout performance.

Thus, Martens et al. (1990) predicted an inverted-U relationship between somatic anxiety and performance and a linear negative relationship between cognitive anxiety and performance. Despite the initial popularity that multidimensional theory has had in predicting performance, there are many problems with these performance predictions.

1. This theory has little relevance to the inverted-U relationship between arousal and performance since arousal measures have rarely been employed.

2. Multidimensional theorists have used the CSAI-2 questionnaire to measure cognitive and somatic anxiety. In an experimental study in which arousal was manipulated, Arent and Landers (2003) showed that CSAI-2 anxiety measures do not reliably predict performance. Other nonexperimental studies that have not manipulated arousal (Burton, 1988; Gould et al., 1984) have actually shown contradictory results that are not supportive of the theory. Likewise meta-analytic findings (Craft, Magyar, Becker, & Feltz, 2003) of 29 CSAI-2 studies (175 effect sizes and 2,905 participants) showed that the relationship between somatic/cognitive anxiety and performance was −.03 and .01, respectively, and these correlations were not significant from zero. Furthermore, cognitive anxiety consistently showed a positive rather than a negative performance relationship.

3. Among CSAI-2 nonexperimental studies that have tested for an inverted-U relationship between anxiety and performance (Burton, 1988; Gould et al., 1987; Randle & Weinberg, 1997; Woodman, Albinson, & Hardy, 1997), the only consistent relationship has been a curvilinear relationship between somatic anxiety and performance. However, an experimental arousal study (Arent & Landers, 2003) failed to find a significant CSAI-2 somatic anxiety-performance relationship, but did find a significant relationship with SAS somatic anxiety.

In summary, there is now mounting evidence that cognitive and somatic anxiety are not linearly related to sport performance. There is, however, consistent evidence that there is a curvilinear relationship between somatic anxiety and performance. In terms of the cognitive anxiety/performance relationship, research findings have not supported the hypothesized negative linear relationship derived from multidimensional anxiety theory.

Catastrophe cusp model. One problem with the multidimensional anxiety theory "is that it attempts to explain the three-dimensional relationship between cognitive anxiety, somatic anxiety and performance in terms of a series of two-dimensional relationships" (Hardy & Parfitt, 1991).

The three-dimensional model proposed by Hardy and Parfitt is derived from Zeeman's (1976) catastrophe cusp model, which was originally designed to describe ocean wave action. Hardy and Fazey (1987) suggest that the inverted-U relationship between physiological arousal and performance varies along another dimension defined as a *splitting factor,* which they arbitrarily identified as cognitive anxiety. They argued that this splitting factor determines whether the effects of physiological arousal (on performance) are smooth and small, large and catastrophic, or somewhere in between these extremes. According to Hardy and Fazey (1987), physiological arousal is not necessarily detrimental to performance, particularly if the skill is simple or well learned. However, when cognitive anxiety is high and dominant, "the curve is discontinuous and represents a catastrophic fall off in performance once the optimal peak is passed" (p. 29). Discontinuity, or sudden large jumps, occur along the normal factor (i.e., physiological arousal continuum) is referred to as *hysteresis.* A visual example of what this may look like can be found in Figure 12-5, where there is a sharp decline in performance under difficult conditions with relatively low levels of arousal. It is suggested that this may occur because cognitive anxiety distracts the athlete or creates doubt (consciously or unconsciously) about what is beneficial and what is detrimental physiological arousal.

Daniel M. Landers and Shawn M. Arent   237

A better way of addressing the catastrophe cusp theory is to experimentally examine the inverted-*U* relationship between arousal and performance and then determine if cognitive and somatic anxiety alter the shape of the curve or predict performance. Arent and Landers (2003) have done this and did not find support for the catastrophe cusp theory. When physiological arousal levels were from 70% to 90% of maximum heart rate reserve, the catastrophic fall-off in performance predicted by Hardy and Fazey was not at all evident (Figure 12-6). Analysis of the effects of anxiety on performance indicated that only SAS somatic anxiety predicted a curvilinear relationship with performance. The failure of the CSAI-2 cognitive measure to show any relationship to performance also supports the idea that Hardy and Fazey may have used an ineffectual splitting factor in their catastrophe cusp model. It may be that, for tasks of this type in which the cognitive load is relatively low, cognitive anxiety does not predict performance well.

The studies that have thus far been conducted have not supported the catastrophe cusp model. Many of these studies have had problems in the methodology employed (i.e., extremely small sample sizes and questionable statistical analyses). Furthermore, because of its complexity, Gill (1994) believes the model is of dubious value because it is difficult to test. The three-dimensional cusp catastrophe is only the second level of complexity, and Fazey and Hardy (1988) have suggested five additional higher dimensional catastrophes (i.e., swallowtail, butterfly, hyperbolic, elliptic, and parabolic). Hardy (1996) has responded to Gill's criticism with the argument that "complexity is an insufficient reason for rejecting any theory or model . . ." (p. 140). Actually, the philosophy of science offers adequate grounds for rejecting needlessly complex models and theories. The principle of parsimony maintains that given a simple and a complex description for the same phenomenon, each with empirical support, the simple description should prevail. Therefore, rather than viewing the simplicity of the inverted-*U* as a weakness (Gould & Krane, 1992), it is seen as a scientific advantage.

Estimating the Relationship between an Athlete's Optimal Arousal and Performance

As indicated previously, the optimal arousal level will depend on task characteristics as well as individual difference factors. To help athletes learn to regulate arousal during the competition, it is important that the coach or sport psychologist compare the arousal demands of the sport task to the athlete's typical competitive arousal state. We recommend the following guidelines. Select a specific task such as playing the quarterback position in football. Avoid global activities such as gymnastics, football, or basketball, and be as task specific as you can! Once you zero in on the task, answer the questions in Table 12-3. For example, high scores (3s and 4s) in the sport of archery on motor act characteristics (C1–4) would produce high total task scores. In short sprints, however, the decision/perceptual processes would in general receive low values (1s and 2s), and the gross motor nature of sprinting would keep the overall task score at a relatively low level. When using this table, bear in mind that it is only a rough guideline for estimating the complexity of your sport.

Total your scores and see where your chosen skill falls on the range in Table 12-4. If the skill has a low score, this indicates that the average athlete can be psyched up to a greater extent and still perform optimally. If an athlete performing this task is low trait anxious and typically responds to competition in a constantly laid-back way, you may need to supplement normal psych-up procedures by teaching the athlete some of the energizing techniques presented in Chapter 13. However, if the athlete scores over 32 in the specific skill you have selected, he or she will not usually be able to tolerate as much arousal. In this case it is important for the coach to extensively train the athlete in the basic skills so as to develop correct habits that are less susceptible to the debilitating effects of arousal. For those more complex skills coaches should particularly avoid implementing last-minute changes in technique; a weak habit strength for the skill

238   Chapter 12   Arousal–Performance Relationships

Table 12-3 **Estimating Complexity of Motor Performance**

A. Decision of Characteristics of Skill

1. Number of decisions necessary	0 None	1 Few	2 Some	3 Several	4 Many
2. Number of alternatives per decision	0 None	1 Few	2 Some	3 Several	4 Many
3. Speed of decisions	0 Not relevant	1 Very slow	2 Slow	3 Fast	4 Very fast
4. Sequence of decisions	0 Not relevant, only one decision	1 Sequence of 2	2 Sequence of 3	3 Sequence of 4	4 Sequence of 5 or more

B. Perception Characteristics of Skill

1. Number of stimuli needed	0 None	1 Few	2 Some	3 Several	4 Many
2. Number of stimuli present	0 Very few	1 Few	2 Some	3 Several	4 Many
3. Duration of stimuli	0 More than 20 sec	1 More than 10 sec	2 More than 5 sec	3 More than 2 sec	4 Less than 2 sec
4. Intensity of stimuli	0 Very intense	1 Intense	2 Moderately intense	3 Low intensity	4 Very low intensity
5. Clarity of correct stimulus among conflicting stimuli	0 Very obvious	1 Obvious	2 Moderately obvious	3 Subtle difference	4 Very subtle difference

C. Motor Act Characteristics of Skill

1. Number of muscle actions to execute skill	0 1–2	1 3–4	2 5–6	3 7–8	4 9 or more
2. Amount of coordination of actions	0 Minimal	1 A little	2 Some	3 Several coordinative actions	4 A great deal
3. Precision and steadiness required	0 None	1 Minimal	2 Some	3 Considerable	4 A great deal
4. Fine motor skill required	0 None, only gross motor skill	1 Minimal	2 Some	3 Considerable	4 A great deal

will make the athlete more susceptible to the disruptive effects of arousal.

In addition to reinforcing the strength of correct habits, it is also important (in complex skills) to pay greater heed to the relaxation, imagery, and cognitive coping strategies presented in Chapters 13, 14, and 15. Athletes who display consistent, high-level performance during practice

Daniel M. Landers and Shawn M. Arent   239

Table 12-4 Optimum Arousal Level and Complexity Scores for a Variety of Typical Sport Skills

Level of Arousal	Complexity Score Range	Sport Skills
5 (extremely excited)	0–10	Football blocking, running 200 meters to 400 meters
4 (psyched up)	11–16	Short sprints, long jump
3 (medium arousal)	17–21	Basketball, boxing, judo
2 (some arousal)	22–31	Baseball, pitching, fencing, tennis
1 (slight arousal)	32 +	Archery, golf, field goal kicking

Source: Based on Oxendine, 1984, and Billing, 1980.

or unimportant competition but then fail to perform effectively in major competitions will have an even greater need to practice these coping techniques regularly.

To determine an optimal level of arousal for a given skill, athletes should be examined individually. This is most easily done by administering one of the arousal questionnaires (preferably the AD-ACL) listed in Table 12-1. By using either retrospective arousal ratings (Hanin, 1978) or ratings before each competition and noting performance levels associated with the arousal scores, a coach or sport psychologist should eventually be able to determine the athlete's IZOF. Having this as a basis, the athlete's arousal in a given competition can be compared to the arousal score associated with a personal best performance. If these arousal scores are discrepant, the coach or sport psychologist should use energizing techniques (Chapter 13) or relaxation, imagery, or other psychological skills (Chapters 13, 14, 15) to bring the athlete's arousal levels in closer alignment with the predefined IZOF.

Armed with the information in this chapter and the techniques described in Chapter 11, the athletes with whom coaches work will be better equipped to select, develop, and use the arousal self-regulation skills presented in Chapter 13. Often, coaches and sport psychologists want to identify athletes with inappropriate arousal levels for the tasks they are performing. Figure 12-2

suggests some areas that will serve as a guide in the identification process. The situation (B) of greatest interest, of course, is competition. The cognitive (C), physiological (D), and behavioral (E) response of athletes in the competitive situation can be compared to responses in noncompetitive situations (i.e., practice conditions). Marked discrepancies in these responses, accompanied by a poor competitive performance, may provide clues that the athlete is overaroused or underaroused.

At the level of cognitive appraisal (C), the coach or sport psychologist should look for signs of distraction before competition. This is usually indicated by an athlete who is not paying attention to the coach's pregame instructions. The athlete may express more concern than is normal by making statements that indicate a certain degree of self-doubt about his or her ability to meet the competitive demands. This identification process is often simplified at a cognitive appraisal level when the athlete recognizes the excessive worry and comes to the coach or sport psychologist for help.

Even without this self-disclosure, many times it is possible to detect physiological or emotional responses (D) that relate to cognitive appraisal (C) as described in Figure 12-2. Where there is a consistent shift to poor performance from practice to competition, the coach or sport psychologist should look for obvious signs of emotional reactivity (e.g., flushed face, sweaty palms, dilated pupils). Another way of getting more direct verification of the arousal mismatch is to administer various measures of arousal (e.g., AD-ACL) throughout the competitive season. Some physiological measures are also quite easy for a coach or sport psychologist to use. For instance, Landers (1981) and Tretilova and Rodmiki (1979) tracked heart rates of top U.S. and Soviet rifle shooters and found an optimal heart rate increase above resting values where best performance scores were fired.

Finally, at a behavioral level (Figure 12-2E) much can be gained from careful observation of the athlete's motor activity, actions, and speech characteristics. Hyperactivity before a performance can be gleaned from erratic behaviors such as pacing, fidgeting, and yawning. An unusually high or low energy level before or during competition may also indicate an inappropriate level of arousal. Rapid speech that sounds abnormal for a particular athlete may provide a reason for the coach or sport psychologist to inquire further into an athlete's arousal state.

The above-mentioned cognitive, physiological, and behavioral manifestations of arousal should not be the last step of the identification process. These factors are only indicators or clues that can serve as a basis for discussions with the athlete. Don't mistake fidgeting because the athlete needs to go to the bathroom as a sign of overarousal. Check out these possible signs of arousal to see what meaning the athlete gives to them. This interpretation is essential in the final determination of over-arousal. As we will see in the next three chapters, interpretation is also important for designing interventions to help bring arousal levels under control.

Summary

In this chapter we have attempted to provide a basic understanding of arousal–performance relationships. The drive theory and inverted-U hypothesis were presented, the former theory emphasizing the development of correct habits to insulate the athlete against the effects of arousal and the latter hypothesis stressing the determination and maintenance of an optimal arousal level for the task to be performed. To determine optimal arousal levels, several task characteristics as well as individual differences in state anxiety and skill must be considered.

In addition, two recent theories/models, which have been advocated as possible replacements for the inverted-U, were addressed and found to have conceptual and methodological flaws in many of the studies examining them. Although some scientific problems with tests of the inverted-U have been reported, a recent study (Arent & Landers, 2003) that has been designed to overcome these problems has still found support for the inverted-U hypothesis. Thus, the weight of the scientific evidence continues to favor the inverted-U hypothesis as the best description for how arousal affects performance.

We have provided guidelines to help coaches and sport psychologists estimate the arousal demands in reference to the complexity of the task to be performed. Finally, we have made suggestions to help identify athletes who are over- or underaroused. We anticipate that, by increasing their understanding of arousal–performance relationships, coaches and sport psychologists will be able to better assess the task demands and more accurately determine appropriate arousal levels for their athletes.

Daniel M. Landers and Shawn M. Arent   241

Study Questions

1. Diagram the predictions of drive theory and the inverted-*U* theory under conditions of a well-learned skill and under conditions of a novice performer learning a new skill. After diagramming, explain in words exactly where the two theories predict different performance outcomes.

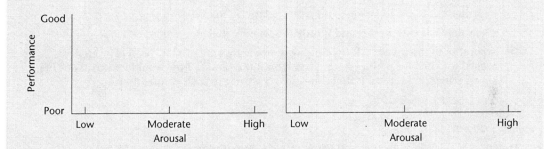

2. In 1965 Zajonc proposed a drive theory explanation for the effects of a passive audience on an individual's performance. Zajonc hypothesized that an audience produced an increase in an individual's arousal level. Assuming that Zajonc was correct and arousal is increased by an audience, how would such an increase affect the performance of a novice performer and an elite performer? According to drive theory, would you desire an audience for the novice or elite performer?

3. Describe Easterbrook's theory of cue utilization and how it provides an explanation for the inverted-*U* relationship between arousal and performance.

4. You are aware of two athletes at your school who display markedly different patterns of emotional excitement when practicing and competing. The 200-meter sprinter becomes much more emotional than the golfer. They both seem to perform well in their respective psychological states. Describe why these vastly different states may make sense in terms of the inverted-*U* hypothesis.

5. Describe what is meant by the term *arousal*. How does arousal relate to the term *anxiety?* Under what conditions might the arousal state of an individual trigger an anxiety response?

6. Describe the ways in which arousal has been measured. What do you consider to be the strengths and weaknesses of these measures?

7. What two factors are known to modify the shape of the inverted-*U* relationship?

8. How would you go about determining the complexity of motor skills such as free throw shooting in basketball versus maneuvering against three players to shoot a layup? According to the task complexity score, which task is more prone to the disruptive effects of arousal?

Williams: Applied Sport
Psychology: Personal
Growth to Peak
Performance, Sixth Edition

II. Mental Training for
Performance Enhancement

12. Arousal–Performance
Relationships

© The McGraw–Hill
Companies, 2010

156

9. Which of the following athletes would you be most concerned about in terms of holding up under the effects of stress in an upcoming competition? Explain your choice.

- Athlete A is an outgoing individual who is relatively unskilled.

- Athlete B is an introverted person but is one of your most skilled players.

- Athlete C tends to be highly anxious and has recently made some changes in her tennis serving technique.

- Athlete D is low in anxiety and is also relatively unskilled.

- Athlete E is extroverted and is only moderately skilled.

10. According to the inverted-U hypothesis, a moderate or "optimal" level of arousal is needed for effective performance. Throughout the season, how would you go about helping an athlete achieve an optimal arousal state prior to each competition?

References

Anderson, K. J. (1990). Arousal and the inverted-U hypothesis: A critique of Neiss's "Reconceptualizing arousal." *Psychological Bulletin, 107,* 96–100.

Arent, S. M., & Landers, D. M. (2003). Arousal, anxiety, and performance. A reexamination of the inverted-U hypothesis. *Research Quarterly for Exercise & Sport, 74,* 436–444.

Babin, W. (1966). *The effect of various work loads on simple reaction latency as related to selected physical parameters.* Unpublished doctoral dissertation, University of Southern Mississippi, Hattiesburg.

Bacon, S. J. (1974). Arousal and the range of cue utilization. *Journal of Experimental Psychology, 103,* 81–87.

Barnes, M. W., Sime, W., Dienstbier, R., & Plake, B. (1986). A test of construct validity of the CSAI-2 questionnaire in male elite college swimmers. *Journal of Sport Psychology, 17,* 364–374.

Billing, J. (1980). An overview of task complexity. *Motor Skills: Theory Into Practice, 4,* 18–23.

Bond, C. F., & Titus, L. J. (1983). Social facilitation: A meta-analysis of 241 studies. *Psychological Bulletin, 94,* 265–292.

Broadhurst, P. L. (1957). Emotionality and the Yerkes-Dodson Law. *Journal of Experimental Psychology, 54,* 345–352.

Burton, D. (1988). Do anxious swimmers swim slower?: Reexamining the elusive anxiety–performance relationship. *Journal of Sport and Exercise Psychology, 10,* 45–61.

Coleman, J. (1977, December). Normal stress reactions in shooting. *The Rifleman,* 19–20.

Cox, R. H. (1990). *Sport psychology: Concepts and applications.* Dubuque, IA: Brown.

Craft, L. L., Magyar, T. M., Becker, B. J., & Feltz, D. L. (2003). The relationship between the Competitive State Anxiety Inventory-2 and athletic performance: A meta-analysis. *Journal of Sport & Exercise Psychology, 25,* 44–65

Duffy, E. (1957). The psychological significance of the concept of "arousal" and "activation." *Psychological Review, 64,* 265–275.

Duffy, E. (1962). *Activation and behavior.* New York: Wiley.

Easterbrook, J. A. (1959). The effect of emotion on cue utilization and the organization of behavior. *Psychological Review, 66,* 183–201.

Fazey, J. & Hardy, L. (1988). The Inverted-*U* Hypothesis: Catastrophe for sport psychology. *British Association of Sports Sciences Monograph No. 1.* Leeds, UK: The National Coaching Foundation.

Freeman, G. L. (1940). The relationship between performance level and bodily activity level. *Journal of Experimental Psychology, 26,* 602–608.

Gill, D. L. (1994). A sport and exercise psychology perspective on stress. *Quest, 44,* 20–27.

Gorman, C. (2002, June 10). The science of anxiety. *Time,* 47–54.

Gould, D., & Krane, V. (1992). The arousal–performance relationship: Current status and future directions. In T. Horn (Ed.), *Advances in sport psychology* (pp. 119–141). Champaign, IL: Human Kinetics.

Gould, D., Petlichkoff, L., Simons, J., & Vevera, M. (1987). Relationship between competitive state anxiety inventory-2 subscale scores and pistol shooting performance. *Journal of Sport Psychology, 9,* 33–42.

Gould, D., Petlichkoff, L., & Weinberg, R. (1984). Antecedents of, temporal changes in, and relationships between CSAI-2 subcomponents. *Journal of Sport Psychology, 6,* 289–304.

Hanin, Y. L. (1978). A study of anxiety in sports. In W. F. Straub (Ed.), *Sport psychology: An analysis of athlete behavior* (pp. 236–256). Ithaca, NY: Mouvement Publications.

Hanin, Y. L. (2000). Successful and poor performance and emotions. In Y. L. Hanin (Ed.), *Emotions in sport* (pp. 157–187). Champaign, IL: Human Kinetics.

Hardy, L. (1996). Testing the predictions of the cusp catastrophe model of anxiety and performance. *The Sport Psychologist, 10,* 140–156.

Hardy, J. P. L., & Fazey, J. A. (1987). *The inverted-U hypothesis—a catastrophe for sports psychology and a statement of a new hypothesis.* Paper presented at a meeting of the North American Society for the Psychology of Sport and Physical Activity, Vancouver, Canada.

Jones, J. G., & Cale, A. (1989). Relationships between multidimensional competitive state anxiety and cognitive and motor subcomponents of performance. *Journal of Sport Sciences, 7,* 129–140.

Krahenbuhl, G. S. (1975). Adrenaline, arousal and sport. *Journal of Sports Medicine, 3,* 117–121.

Lacey, J. I., Bateman, D. E., & Van Lehn, R. (1953). Heart rate feedback-assisted reduction in cardiovascular reactivity to a videogame challenge. *The Psychological Record, 39,* 365–371.

Landers, D. M. (1978). Motivation and performance: The role of arousal and attentional factors. In W. Straub (Ed.), *Sport psychology: An analysis of athletic behavior.* Ithaca, NY: Mouvement Publications.

Landers, D. M. (1980). The arousal–performance relationship revisited. *Research Quarterly, 51,* 77–90.

Landers, D. M. (1981). Reflections of sport psychology and the Olympic athlete. In J. Segrave & D. Chu (Eds.), *Olympism* (pp. 189–200). Champaign, IL.: Human Kinetics.

244   Chapter 12   Arousal–Performance Relationships

Landers, D. M. (1985). Psychophysiological assessment and biofeedback: Applications for athletes in closed skill sports. In J. H. Sandweis & S. Wolf (Eds.), *Biofeedback and sport science* (pp. 63–105). New York: Plenum.

Landers, D. M., Christina, R. W., Hatfield, B. D., Daniels, F. S., Wilkinson, M., & Doyle, L. A. (1980, April). Research on the shooting sports: A preliminary report. *The American Rifleman, 128* (4), 36–37, 76–77.

Landers, D. M., Snyder-Bauer, R., & Feltz, D. L. (1978). Social facilitation during the initial stage of motor learning: A reexamination of Martens's audience study. *Journal of Motor Behavior, 10,* 325–337.

Landers, D. M., Wang, M. Q., & Courtet, P. (1985). Peripheral narrowing among experienced and inexperienced rifle shooters under low- and high-stress conditions. *Research Quarterly, 56,* 57–70.

Landy, F. J., & Stern, R. M. (1971). Factor analysis of a somatic perception questionnaire. *Journal of Psychosomatic Research, 15,* 179–181.

Levitt, S., & Gutin, B. (1971). Multiple choice reaction time and movement time during physical exertion. *Research Quarterly, 42,* 405–410, 423–443.

Mahoney, M. J. (1979). Cognitive skills and athletic performance. In P. C. Kendall & S. D. Hollon (Eds.), *Cognitive-behavioral interventions: Theory, research, and procedures.* New York: Academic Press.

Malmo, R. B. (1959). Activation: A neuropsychological dimension. *Psychological Review, 66,* 367–386.

Martens, R. (1974). Arousal and motor performance. In J. H. Wilmore (Ed.), *Exercise and sport science reviews* (pp. 155–188). New York: Academic Press.

Martens, R. (1977). *Sport competitive anxiety test.* Champaign, IL: Human Kinetics.

Martens, R., Burton, D., Vealey, R. S., Bump, L. A., & Smith, D. E. (1990). Development and validation of the competitive state anxiety inventory-2. In R. Martens, R. S. Vealey, & D. Burton, *Competitive anxiety in sport* (pp. 123–124, 160). Champaign, IL: Human Kinetics.

Martens, R., Burton, D., Vealey, R., Smith, D., & Bump, L. (1983). *The development of the competitive state anxiety inventory-2 (CSAI-2).* Unpublished manuscript.

Martens, R., & Landers, D. M. (1970). Motor performance under stress: A test of the inverted-U hypothesis. *Journal of Personality and Social Psychology, 16,* 29–37.

Murphy, L. E. (1966). Muscular effort, activation level and reaction time. *Proceedings of the 74th Annual Convention of the American Psychological Association* (p. 1). Washington, DC: APA.

Neiss, R. (1988). Reconceptualizing arousal: Psychobiological states in motor performance. *Psychological Bulletin, 103,* 345–366.

Nideffer, R. M. (1978). *Predicting human behavior: A theory and test of attentional and interpersonal style.* San Diego: Enhanced Performance Associates.

Oxendine, J. B. (1984). *Psychology of motor learning.* Englewood Cliffs, NJ: Prentice Hall.

Parfitt, C. G. (1988). *Interactions between models of stress and models of motor control.* Unpublished doctoral dissertation, University College of North Wales.

Parfitt, C. G., & Hardy, L. (1987). Further evidence for the differential effects of competitive anxiety upon a number of cognitive and motor subcomponents. *Journal of Sport Sciences, 5,* 62–63.

Pinneo, L. R. (1961). The effects of induced muscle tension during tracking on level of activation and on performance. *Journal of Experimental Psychology, 62,* 523–531.

Randle, S., & Weinberg, R. (1997). Multidimensional anxiety and performance: An exploratory examination of the zone of optimal functioning hypothesis. *The Sport Psychologist, 11,* 169–174.

Sage, G. (1984). *Motor learning and control.* Dubuque, IA: Brown.

Schwartz, G. E., Davidson, R. J., & Goleman, D. (1978). Patterning of cognitive and somatic processes in the self-regulation of anxiety: Effects of meditation versus exercise. *Psychosomatic Medicine, 40,* 321–328.

Selye, H. (1950). *Stress.* Montreal: Acta.

Smith, R. E., Smoll, F. L., & Schutz, R. W. (1990). Measurement and correlates of sport-specific cognitive and somatic trait anxiety: The sport anxiety scale. *Anxiety Research, 2,* 263–280.

Sonstroem, R. J., & Bernardo, P. (1982). Intraindividual pregame state anxiety and basketball performance: A reexamination of the inverted-*U* curve. *Journal of Sport Psychology, 4,* 235–245.

Speigler, M. D., Morris, L. W., & Liebert, R. M. (1968). Cognitive and emotional components of test anxiety: Temporal factors. *Psychological Reports, 22,* 451–456.

Spence, J. T., & Spence, K. W. (1966). The motivational components of manifest anxiety: Drive and drive stimuli. In C. D. Spielberger (Ed.), *Anxiety and behavior* (pp. 291–326). New York: Academic Press.

Spielberger, C. D. (1975). Anxiety: State-trait process. In C. D. Spielberger & I. G. Sarason (Eds.), *Stress and anxiety* (Vol. 1, pp. 115–143). New York: Hemisphere.

Spielberger, C. D., Gorsuch, R. L., & Lushene, R. E. (1970). *Manual for the State-Trait Anxiety Inventory (STAI).* Palo Alto, CA: Consulting Psychologists Press.

Thayer, R. E. (1967). Measurement of activation through self-report. *Psychological Reports, 20,* 663–679.

Thayer, R. E. (1970). Activation states as assessed by verbal report and four psychophysiological variables. *Psychophysiology, 7,* 86–94.

Thayer, R. E. (1986). Activation-deactivation adjective checklist: Current overview and structural analysis. *Psychological Reports, 58,* 607–614.

Tretilova, T. A., & Rodmiki, E. M. (1979). Investigation of emotional state of rifle shooters. *Theory and Practice of Physical Culture, 5,* 28.

Weltman, A. T., & Egstrom, G. H. (1966). Perceptual narrowing in novice divers. *Human Factors, 8,* 499–505.

246 Chapter 12 **Arousal–Performance Relationships**

Wood, C. G., & Hokanson, J. E. (1965). Effects of induced muscle tension on performance and the inverted-*U. Journal of Personality and Social Psychology, 1,* 506–510.

Woodman, T., Albinson, J. G., & Hardy, L. (1997). An investigation of the zones of optimal functioning hypothesis within a multidimensional framework. *Journal of Sport and Exercise Psychology, 19,* 131–141.

Yerkes, R. M., & Dodson, J. D. (1908). The relation of strength of stimulus to rapidity of habit formation. *Journal of Comparative Neurology of Psychology, 18,* 459–482.

Zeeman, E. C. (1976). Catastrophe theory. *Scientific American, 234,* 65–83.

CHAPTER 1

The Psychology of Physical Activity

The Journey of a Thousand Miles Starts in Front of Your Feet.

(Lao-Tzu)

CHAPTER OBJECTIVES

After completing this chapter you will be able to

- Outline the importance of physical activity from a physiological perspective.

- Estimate the numbers of people who are physically active.

- Describe the currently accepted guidelines for a physically active lifestyle.

- Differentiate among the key terms used in the area known as the psychology of physical activity.

Key terms

active living	intervention
body image	physical activity
cognition	prediction
description	psychology of physical
environment	activity
exercise	psychophysiological
exercise addiction	reactivity
explanation	self-esteem
health	tomato effect

From the perspective of personal fitness, consider the quote used to introduce this chapter. The road to physical fitness and a healthy lifestyle starts in front of our feet. However, there is evidence that remarkably few of us are on that journey. In fact, it would seem that participation in physical activity and exercise shows signs of a **tomato effect.** An interesting term—you may ask, "What's a tomato effect?" Moreover, because it sounds mysterious and a bit dangerous, you may also be tempted to ask, "And how can this so-called tomato effect be eradicated?"

The *tomato effect* is a term James and Jean Goodwin (1984) used to describe a phenomenon whereby highly efficacious therapies are ignored or rejected. Generally, the reason for this rejection is that the therapies do not seem to make sense in light of popular beliefs or common understandings. A tomato effect can also occur if people simply ignore the evidence available.

The term tomato effect is derived from the history of the fruit in North America. The tomato was originally discovered in Peru and transported to

> **tomato effect** A phenomenon whereby highly efficacious therapies are ignored or rejected because the therapies do not seem to make sense in light of popular beliefs or common understandings, or because the available evidence is simply ignored.

Spain from which it made its way to Italy, France, and most of Europe. By 1560, the tomato played a significant role in the diet of most Europeans. In North America, however, tomatoes were avoided because they were considered poisonous. The basis for this belief was that tomatoes belong to the nightshade family of fruits and that several nightshade plants can cause death if eaten in sufficient quantities. Thus, for more than 200 years, tomatoes were not grown commercially in North America. In fact, a significant turning point did not occur until 1820. Apparently, in a dramatic gesture, Robert Gibbon Johnson ate a tomato on the courthouse steps in Salem, New Jersey—and survived! Subsequently, tomatoes began to be accepted as a nutritious food source. It wasn't until the 20th century, however, that commercial marketing of the tomato began in earnest. Today it represents one of the largest commercial crops in North America (Goodwin & Goodwin, 1984).

EFFICACY OF PHYSICAL ACTIVITY

According to Goodwin and Goodwin (1984), the use of aspirin for the alleviation of pain, swelling, and stiffness of rheumatoid arthritis was also characterized by a tomato effect—"high doses of aspirin became an accepted treatment some 70 years after the initial studies demonstrating its efficacy" (p. 2389). What about physical activity? Is a tomato effect toward physical activity prevalent in society?

One part of the answer to that question, of course, pertains to whether physical activity is an efficacious activity. Scientists have spent a large portion of the previous century conducting research on the physiological, physical, and biological benefits of chronic physical activity. What their research has shown is that every system of the body benefits when a person engages in frequent physical activity (Haskell, 1994). In terms of the skeletal system, for example, frequent physical activity leads to increased bone density in youth and an increased likelihood that bone mineral density will be retained in older adults. What about the muscle system? Fre-

FIT FACTS

Is the message being sent?

Newspapers are said to provide information that reflects the public interest. If that is the case, a content analysis of newspapers shows only a minimal interest in fitness, exercise, and physical activity.

(Theberge, 1991)

quent physical activity brings hypertrophy, strength, and endurance as well as increased capillarization, maximal blood flow, and increased metabolic capacity. In the cardiovascular system, frequent physical activity contributes not only to increased cardiac mass but also to increased stroke volume and cardiac output at rest and during physical activity, and to lower heart rate and blood pressure at rest and during submaximal physical activity. The respiratory system experiences increased ventilatory-diffusion efficiency during physical activity as well as possible decreased work associated with breathing. What about the metabolic system? Being physically active is associated with decreased triglycerides, increased high-density cholesterol, increased insulin-mediated glucose uptake, and decreased adiposity (Haskell, 1994).

These substantial physiological benefits are no secret. Within the past 10 to 15 years, there has been an almost global endorsement of the value of physical activity. For example, Biddle (1995) noted that "physical activity is considered important in contemporary European society" (p. 3). As another example, Dr. Audrey Manley (1996), the former Surgeon General of the United States, in her preface to the report on the relationship of physical activity and health, pointed out:

> For more than a century, the Surgeon General of the Public Health Service has focused the nation's attention on important health issues . . . this new report . . . about the relationship between physical activity and health status, follows in this notable tradition. . . . We must get serious about improving

4 SECTION ONE   Introduction to the Psychology of Physical Activity and Exercise

the health of the nation by affirming our commitment to healthy physical activity on all levels: personal, family, community, organizational, and national. Because physical activity is so directly related to preventing disease and premature death and to maintaining a high quality of life, we must accord it the same level of attention that we give other important public health practices that affect the entire nation. Physical activity thus joins the front ranks of essential health objectives, such as sound nutrition, the use of seat belts, the prevention of adverse health effects of tobacco. (p. 5)

There is absolutely no doubt that physical activity can be described as efficacious.

PREVALENCE OF PHYSICAL ACTIVITY

A second part of the question, is a tomato effect toward physical activity prevalent in society, pertains to whether the society in general tends to avoid physical activity. Are people eating the tomatoes? Or stated another way, is physical activity being embraced by a large portion of the world's population? Unfortunately, the answer seems to be a qualified no. Data collected in the United States shows that almost 30% of the population is physically inactive. An additional 40% to 50% of the population is characterized as not having participated in the recommended amount of physical activity necessary to gain health benefits [USDHSS] (United States Department of Health & Human Services, 2000). Further, these statistics have remained relatively consistent for the past decade (USDHSS, 2000).

Another perspective is provided by the comprehensive analysis undertaken by Caspersen, Merritt, and Stephens (1994). They attempted to summarize international physical activity patterns and trends in four countries: Australia, Canada, Finland, and the United States. Table 1-1 provides an overview from their work. These four countries were chosen because large, generally representative samples had been tested in each. Also, survey administration, sampling procedures, and measures of physical activity were consistent over the time periods studied.

It is apparent from Table 1-1 that substantial differences are present among the four countries. The number of sedentary individuals varies markedly, from a low of 16.1% in Finland to a high of 43% in Canada. Over the length of time between surveys, there was a slight decline in the number of sedentary individuals, from 2.3% in the United States to 15% in Canada. Also, the length of time between surveys did differ markedly across the four countries. Thus, a useful way to compare trends is to compute average annual increases. Using that method, the largest annual increases in physical activity from the lowest to the highest intensity of physical activity occurred in Australia and Canada.

The evidence in Table 1-1 provides the basis for suggesting that people are apparently becoming somewhat more active. However, the recent CDC (2001) findings contribute to the suggestion that the increases highlighted by Caspersen and his associates (1994) may have reached a plateau. The point is that few individuals are physically active on a regular basis, and this situation seems to generalize across a number of industrialized nations.

GUIDELINES FOR PHYSICAL ACTIVITY

A possible reason for the high rate of sedentariness may be a misperception that exercise-mediated health benefits can only be achieved by *strenuous, sustained* aerobic activity. Such perceptions were fostered by the original exercise guidelines established by the American College of Sports Medicine in 1978 (see Table 1-2 for the 1978 exercise guidelines). These guidelines were based on the improvement of cardiovascular fitness; however, these guidelines were often applied to general health (Haskell, 1994). Recently, recommendations by leading authorities have significantly influenced the traditional beliefs about the amount, intensity, and frequency of exercise that is necessary to elicit physical and psychological benefits.

How much physical activity do we need to achieve the health-related benefits? The new guidelines established by the American College of Sports Medicine and the Centers for Disease Control state

■ **TABLE 1-1** Prevalence Estimates for Physical Activity in Selected Countries

	Physical Activity Level								
	Lowest			Moderate			Highest		
		Prevalence (%)			Prevalence (%)			Prevalence (%)	
COUNTRY	DESCRIPTION OF ACTIVITY DEFINITION	MOST RECENT	TOTAL CHANGE	DESCRIPTION OF ACTIVITY DEFINITION	MOST RECENT	TOTAL CHANGE	DESCRIPTION OF ACTIVITY DEFINITION	MOST RECENT	TOTAL CHANGE
Australia[a]	No aerobic activity reported over 2 weeks	26.5	−5	>0 to <1,600 kcal/wk over 2 weeks of aerobic activities	56%	+1.5	>1,600 kcal/wk over 2 weeks of aerobic activity	17.5	+3.5
Canada[b]	0 to 1.4 kcal/kg/day (<600 kcal/wk)	43	−15	1.5 to 2.9 kcal/kg/day of any intensity activity (>~600 to <~1,250 kcal/wk)	24	+7	3+ kcal/kg/day of any intense activity (>~1,250 kcal/wk)	33	+8
Finland[c]	A few times a year or less of physical activity to produce light sweating or cannot exercise	16.1	−6.6	1 time/wk or 2 to 3 times/month of physical activity to produce light sweating	33.3	−0.7	2+ times/wk and 30+ min/occasion of physical activity to produce light sweating	51.3	+7.3
United States[d]	No physical activity during the past month	30.5	−2.3	3+ times/wk & 20+ min/occasion of physical activity either not reaching 60% of age- and sex-specific max cardiorespiratory capacity or not involving rhythmic contractions of large muscles	31.9	+0.5	3+ times/wk & 20+ min/occasion of physical activity at 60%+ of age- and sex-specific max cardiorespiratory capacity involving rhythmic contractions of large muscles	9.1	+2.1

Note. From "International Physical Activity Patterns: A Methodological Perspective," by C. J. Caspersen, R. K. Merritt, and T. Stephens, 1994, in R. K. Dishman, Ed., *Advances in Exercise Adherence* (pp. 73–110), Champaign, IL: Human Kinetics. Used with permission.

[a]Dept. of Arts, Sport, Environment, Tourism, and Territories (1984–1987).
[b]Canada Fitness Survey (1981–1988).
[c]National Public Health Institute (1982–1991).
[d]Behavioral Risk Factor Surveillance System (26 states; 1986–1990).

6 SECTION ONE Introduction to the Psychology of Physical Activity and Exercise

■ **TABLE 1-2** A Comparison of the Past and Present Guidelines for Physical Activity

ACTIVITY CHARACTERISTIC	FORMER ACSM GUIDELINES[a]	PRESENT CDC/ACSM GUIDELINES[b]
Frequency	3–5 times/week	4–7 ("most, preferably all") days of the week
Intensity	Vigorous (60%–80% of max)	Moderate
Duration	At least 20 min	Accumulation of $\geq$ 30 min of daily activity in bouts of at least 10 min
Type	Aerobic activity	Any activity that can be performed at an intensity similar to that of brisk walking

[a]ACSM, 1978.
[b]Pate et al., 1995.

that adults should accumulate a minimum of 30 minutes of moderate intensity physical activity on most, if not all, days of the week (Pate et al., 1995; see Table 1-2). Moderate intensity physical activity, for example, would include brisk walking at a pace of three to four miles per hour, climbing stairs, or doing heavy housework. The accumulation of physical activity indicates that people can engage in shorter bouts of activity spread out over the course of the day. For example, a person could go for a 10-minute brisk walk in the morning, afternoon, and evening to cumulate the daily goal of 30 minutes. The suggestion that physical activity can be accumulated over the course of the day, rather than performed continuously in a single session, was motivated by the difficulties reported by numerous individuals in trying to find a block of 30 minutes per day for physical activity (Sallis & Owen, 1998).

The current guidelines emphasize moderate intensity levels for a duration of 30 minutes. Does this guideline mean that people can achieve the health-related benefits of exercise without engaging in physical activity at vigorous intensity levels or for durations greater than 30 minutes? The answer to this question is an emphatic *no!* The benefits of physical activity are related to the effort that one devotes. Thus, additional health and fitness advantages are gained from physical activities that are undertaken for longer durations or at more strenuous intensity levels or both ([USDHHS], 1996).

What are the physical activity guidelines for youth? It is recommended that youth engage in a minimum of 30 minutes of moderate intensity physical activity per day (Biddle, Sallis, & Cavill, 1998). Maintaining the 30-minute minimal standard keeps the recommendation for youth consis-

The misperception that exercise-related health benefits can only be achieved by strenuous sustained aerobic activity is a possible reason for the high rate of sedentariness.
©PhotoDisk/Volume 67/Fitness and Well-Being

tent with the adult guidelines. The ultimate goal, however, is for youth to be active for at least one hour daily. Two specific research findings have led to the view that one hour per day of physical activity is preferred (Sallis & Owen, 1998). The first is that most young people are already active 30 minutes per day. The second is that despite 30 minutes of daily physical activity, the prevalence of obesity in developed nations is increasing (Biddle et al.). Thus, experts feel that the guideline of one hour might help deter the increase in childhood obesity (Sallis & Owen).

KNOWLEDGE OF BENEFITS OF PHYSICAL ACTIVITY

Scientists, health care professionals, and politicians are aware of the physical, biological, and physiological benefits of physical activity and exercise. A third part of the question pertaining to whether a tomato effect toward physical activity exists in society is whether the portion of the population who are not physically active (i.e., the non–tomato eaters) have a full understanding of the benefits of a physically active lifestyle. Godin, Cox, and Shephard (1983) queried physically active and inactive individuals on their knowledge and beliefs about physical activity. An overview is provided in Table 1-3. In most instances, inactive individuals held similar beliefs to active individuals about the benefits of physical activity. That is, in agreement with active people, inactive people see physical activity as a means to control body weight, be more healthy, relieve tension, improve physical appearance, feel better, and meet people. Yet they don't participate—in large numbers at least.

So the answer to the question, does participation in physical activity show evidence of a tomato effect? seems to be a qualified yes. An efficacious activity is not being wholeheartedly endorsed by a relatively large proportion of the population. The question then becomes, how do we overcome the tomato effect toward physical activity? One useful approach is through science—science that focuses on the psychology of physical activity and exercise.

■ **TABLE 1-3**   Differences in Beliefs About Exercise Held by Physically Active and Inactive Individuals

BELIEF	PHYSICALLY ACTIVE VS. INACTIVE INDIVIDUALS
Helps me control my body weight	Both active and inactive agree
Helps me be healthier	Both active and inactive agree
Is physically damaging	Both active and inactive disagree
Relieves my tension	Both active and inactive agree
Improves my physical appearance	Both active and inactive agree
Helps me feel better	Both active and inactive agree
Is time consuming	Both active and inactive agree
Helps me meet people	Both active and inactive agree
Improves my mental performance	Active agree more than inactive
Helps me be physically fit	Active agree more than inactive
Helps me fill my free time	Active agree more than inactive

Note. Adapted from "The Impact of Physical Fitness Evaluation on Behavioral Intentions Toward Regular Exercise," by G. Godin, M. H. Cox, and R. J. Shepherd, 1984, *Canadian Journal of Applied Sport Sciences, 8,* 240-245.

THE PSYCHOLOGY OF PHYSICAL ACTIVITY

If physical activity is efficacious, one important challenge facing scientists, health professionals, and governments is to help a large segment of the population become more physically active. This achievement is not likely to come through additional research in physiology of exercise, although that discipline will undoubtedly provide answers to important questions such as how much activity is necessary to obtain physiological benefits. As a science, physiology of exercise does not concern itself with general issues associated with understanding and modifying behavior, influencing public opinion, motivating people, and/or changing people's attitudes. Nor is it a

8 SECTION ONE Introduction to the Psychology of Physical Activity and Exercise

concern of the biomechanics, history, or sociology of sport. Questions concerning human attitudes, cognitions, and behavior fall directly under the mandate of psychology.

Psychology is a science devoted to an understanding of human behavior. In turn, the area of science we refer to in this book as the **psychology of physical activity** is devoted to an understanding of (a) individual attitudes, cognitions, and behaviors in the context of physical activity and exercise and (b) the social factors that influence those attitudes, cognitions, and behaviors.

Historical Developments

Rejeski and Thompson (1993) noted that although interest has been directed toward the psychology of physical activity since 1897, the majority of research has appeared since the early 1970s. Several reasons were advanced by Rejeski and Thompson for the relatively slow development of the psychology of physical activity as a science. First, the popularity of sport preceded the popularity of general physical activity within the general population. Thus, scientists inevitably gravitated toward sport to ask and attempt to answer research questions. Second, the importance of physical activity for disease prevention and the maintenance of general health has long been suspected but not fully known until recently. Consequently, understanding the psychological dimensions of involvement in physical activity was not perceived to be a pressing priority. Finally, throughout history, the use of a biomedical model has been the traditional approach to understanding health and well-being; the dominant concern is with the treatment of disease as opposed to its prevention. Only recently has the importance of a biopsychological approach to disease prevention been acknowledged.

Topics of Interest

When research into the psychological aspects of involvement in physical activity increased in the 1970s, it tended to focus on an understanding of hu-

man attitudes, cognitions, and behaviors in the context of physical activity and exercise. Evidence of this focus is provided by the 10 most prevalent topics investigated to date (Rejeski and Thompson, 1993):

1. Mental health (examination of the influence of acute and chronic physical activity on mental health parameters such as anxiety and depression)
2. **Body image** and **self-esteem** (examination of the influence of acute and chronic physical activity on self-perceptions and self-esteem)
3. **Psychophysiological reactivity** (examination of the influence of acute and chronic physical activity on modulating psychological and physiological responses to social stressors)
4. Perceived exertion/fatigue/exercise symptoms (examining subjective perceptions of physical functioning during acute bouts of physical activity)
5. Adherence (identification of the determinants of involvement in chronic physical activity)
6. Performance and metabolic responses (identification of psychological correlates of physical performance and metabolic responses)
7. Sleep (examination of the impact of acute and chronic physical activity on quantity and quality of sleep)

psychology of physical activity The area of science devoted to an understanding of individual attitudes, cognitions, and behaviors in the context of physical activity and exercise and of the social factors that influence those attitudes, cognitions, and behaviors.

body image A subjective perception of one's external appearance.

self-esteem A global and relatively stable evaluative construct reflecting the degree to which an individual feels positive about himself or herself.

psychophysiological reactivity The influence of acute and chronic physical activity on modulating psychological and physiological responses to social stressors.

8. **Cognition** (examination of the influence of acute and chronic physical activity on mental acuity)
9. Corporate (examination of the influence of acute and chronic physical activity on outcomes in the workplace, e.g., absenteeism, stress)
10. **Exercise dependence** (examination of the nature and consequences of obsessive involvement in physical activity)

Because humans are by nature social creatures, later researchers have also focused on an understanding of the social factors that influence attitudes, cognitions, and behaviors associated with involvement in physical activity. The five main categories of social factors that have been examined in relation to involvement in physical activity are (Carron, Hausenblas, & Mack, 1996):

1. Family (examination of the role played by family members including siblings, spouses, children, and parents in sustaining involvement in physical activity programs)
2. Important others (examination of the role played by non–family members such as physicians and work colleagues in sustaining involvement in physical activity programs)
3. Other exercisers (comparison of being physically active alone or in the presence of others)
4. Cohesion (examination of an impact of a cohesive, unified group in sustaining involvement in physical activity programs)
5. Leadership (examination of the role played by the exercise leader in sustaining involvement in physical activity programs)

Related Terms

A variety of behaviors have been researched under the umbrella term *psychology of physical activity*. Researchers and practitioners, operating under the assumption that definitional clarity is essential for effective communication, have taken care to draw a distinction among these diverse behaviors (Gauvin, Wall, & Quinney, 1994). An overview of the various terms is presented in Table 1-4.

■ **TABLE 1-4**   Terms Used Within the Field of the Psychology of Physical Activity

TERM	DEFINITION
Physical activity[a]	Any body movement produced by skeletal muscles and resulting in a substantial increase over the resting energy expenditure
Exercise[a]	Form of physical activity undertaken with a specific objective such as the improvement of fitness, health, or physical performance
Health[a]	Human condition with physical, social, and psychological dimensions, each characterized by a continuum with positive and negative poles
Active living[b]	A way of life in which physical activity is valued and integrated into daily life

Note. Adapted from "Physical Activity, Fitness, and Health: Research and Practice," by L. Gauvin, A. E. T. Wall, and H. A. Quinney, 1994, in H. A. Quinney, L. Gauvin, and A. E. T. Wall, Eds., *Toward Active Living* (pp. 1–5), Champaign, IL: Human Kinetics.
[a]From Bouchard and Shephard (1991).
[b]From Fitness Canada (1991).

Physical activity is a term used to describe body movements produced by the skeletal muscles that require energy expenditures above what is typical at rest (Bouchard & Shephard, 1991, p. 3). Implicit within this definition is the fact that physical

cognition   Pertaining to the mental processes of comprehension, judgment, memory, and reasoning, as contrasted with emotional and volitional processes.

exercise dependence   Obsessive involvement in physical activity.

physical activity   Any body movement produced by skeletal muscles and resulting in a substantial increase over the resting energy expenditure.

activity includes exercise, sport, work, leisure time activity, and so on (Gauvin, Wall, & Quinney, 1994).

On the other hand, **exercise** is a specific form of physical activity in which the individual engages for the purpose of improving fitness, physical performance, or health (Bouchard & Shephard, 1991). According to Bouchard and Shephard, a characteristic that helps define exercise is that the individual must conform to a recommended frequency, intensity, and duration in order to achieve the specific purpose desired. If an individual does conform to recommended levels, the usual result is *fitness*, in other words, the ability to perform work satisfactorily.

Health may be viewed as a human condition with physical, social, and psychological dimensions, each characterized by a continuum varying from positive to negative poles (Bouchard & Shephard, 1991). Both physical activity and exercise, along with a number of other activities such as maintaining a proper diet and refraining from smoking, contribute to development and maintenance of health on the positive end of the continuum. Although every health behavior is important in its own right, our book concentrates on physical activity and exercise.

Finally, **active living** is a term introduced by Fitness Canada (1991) to represent a lifestyle in which physical activity plays a dominant role. Active living is intended to emphasize the importance of physical activity within the individual's total life experience.

Health Versus Physical Activity Versus Rehabilitation Psychology

Students interested in various activities associated with a healthy lifestyle are often uncertain about where various research issues might lie. For example, does the topic of how smoking cessation influences endurance performance fall within the domain of health psychology or the psychology of physical activity or rehabilitation psychology? Endurance performance seems relevant to the area of the psychology of physical activity, whereas cigarette smoking seems to relate to health psychology.

Rejeski and Brawley (1988) developed an organizational framework to answer questions pertaining to the classification of research findings. Essentially, they proposed that the dependent variable (i.e., outcome) should be used as the main classification factor. Thus, a research problem that deals with the influence of smoking cessation on endurance performance would fall within the domain of physical activity psychology because endurance performance is the outcome of interest. Conversely, a research problem that deals with the influence of endurance training on smoking cessation would fall within the domain of health psychology because smoking cessation is the outcome of interest. Also, according to Rejeski and Brawley, research in which physical activity is used as an intervention to offset disabled, impaired, or diseased states falls within the domain of rehabilitation psychology.

ORGANIZATION OF THE BOOK

This book is subdivided into five sections. Section 1 is devoted to introductory material and issues of definition (Chapter 1) as well as protocols used for the measurement of physical activity (Chapter 2).

The remaining sections of the book relate to the four general stages through which all areas of science proceed. The first stage is **description.** The descriptive stage is essential because it informs us about "what is." A large proportion of the research in exercise psychology has been descriptive in na-

---

exercise   A specific form of physical activity in which the individual engages for the specific purpose of improving fitness, physical performance, or health.

health   A human condition with physical, social, and psychological dimensions, each characterized by a continuum varying from positive to negative poles.

active living   A way of life in which physical activity is valued and integrated into daily life.

description   The first stage of science, which informs about "what is."

ture, and in Sections 2 and 3 of this book, we describe individual and situational correlates of physical activity. Section 2 is an overview of research that has centered on the individual. In Chapters 3, 4, 5, and 6, we discuss the cognitive, social, psychological, personality, and psychobiological benefits of a physically active lifestyle. In Chapter 7, we focus on the potential negative behaviors associated with physical activity—exercise dependence, steroid use, and eating disorders. In Chapter 8, we outline the individual correlates of physical activity.

An important characteristic that helps define the psychology of physical activity as a discipline is its focus on the social factors that influence individual behavior. Section 3 of the book is an overview of research that has centered on the individual participant's **environment.** In Chapter 9, we focus on the physical activity class. Social support from others has been linked to a number of positive outcomes including improved health and reduced morbidity, and in Chapter 10, we discuss the nature and consequences of social support. In Chapter 11, we outline the environmental correlates of physical activity.

The second and third stages of science, **explanation** and **prediction,** involve theory development and testing. In Section 4 of the book, we advance various theoretical models to explain and predict involvement in exercise and physical activity. In Chapter 12, we deal with one of the most extensively used theoretical models—self-efficacy theory. We introduce the health belief model and protection motivation theory—two somewhat similar theoretical approaches—in Chapter 13. The theories of rea-

soned action and planned behavior are outlined in Chapter 14. We present a currently popular approach to the study of involvement in physical activity, the transtheoretical model, in Chapter 15. In Chapter 16, the final chapter of Section 3, we discuss self-determination theory and personal investment theory.

The fourth stage of science is **intervention,** or control. The intervention stage involves the application of what has been learned from the other three stages. Because the benefits of physical activity are so important for the individual and for society in general, numerous attempts have been made to develop effective intervention strategies. Section 5 of the book is an overview of various interventions, including those that have focused on individual level strategies (Chapter 17), group level strategies (Chapter 18), and community level programs (Chapter 19). Finally, in Chapter 20, we focus on the efficacy and fidelity of intervention strategies.

> **environment**   All of the many factors, physical and psychological, that influence or affect the life and survival of a person.
>
> **explanation**   The second stage of science, which involves theory development.
>
> **prediction**   The third stage of science, which involves theory testing.
>
> **intervention**   The fourth stage of science (also called control), which involves application of what has been learned from the previous three stages.

Summary

Is there a tomato effect—a tendency for people to avoid physical activity? Many benefits are associated with involvement in physical activity and exercise. Further, large portions of the population consider physical activity to be healthy and beneficial. Nonetheless, throughout the world, the levels of inactivity are still unacceptably high. Behavior change and attitude change are necessary. Both

changes fall within the domain of psychology as a science. This book focuses on information from the area of science referred to as the psychology of physical activity.

We defined several terms related to the field of the psychology of physical activity. *Physical activity* is muscular movement that increases energy expenditure. *Exercise* refers to a specific type of physical

12 SECTION ONE   Introduction to the Psychology of Physical Activity and Exercise

activity that leads to improved fitness, physical performance, and/or health. *Health* is a combination of physical, social, and psychological dimensions that can vary from positive to negative. *Active living* represents a lifestyle that values physical activity and integrates it into daily life.

Topics in the area of the psychology of physical activity often seem to overlap with areas such as rehabilitation psychology or health psychology. In this book, we incorporate information from research in which physical activity was the dependent (outcome) variable.

CHAPTER **4**

Physical Activity and Mood

True Enjoyment Comes from Activity of the Mind and Exercise of the Body.
(Wilhelm von Humboldt)

CHAPTER OBJECTIVES

After completing this chapter you will be able to

- Differentiate among the various terms used to represent mood.

- Discuss the role that physical activity plays in the alleviation of anxiety.

- Discuss the role that physical activity plays in the alleviation of depression.

- Discuss the role that physical activity plays in other manifestations of mood.

- Understand the consequences of combining pharmacologic treatments with physical activity.

- Outline the explanations offered to account for the psychological benefits associated with being more physically active.

Key terms

clinical depression	positive affect
negative affect	state anxiety
nonclinical depression	trait anxiety
POMS	

Considerable anecdotal testimony supports the popular belief that physical activity and exercise contribute to a "feel good" state in the individual. The quote by Wilhelm von Humboldt used to introduce this chapter is consistent with this popular belief. He suggested that exercise of the body contributes to feelings of true enjoyment. Science seldom relies on popular beliefs, however. As a consequence, researchers over a number of years have concentrated their efforts on examining the impact of physical activity and exercise on the mood states of the individual.

What does that research indicate? Interestingly, despite hundreds of studies, a number of meta-analyses (e.g., Calfas & Taylor, 1994; Craft & Landers, 1998; Kugler, Seelback, & Krüskemper, 1994; Landers & Petruzzello, 1994; Long & van Stavel, 1995; D. G. McDonald & Hodgdon, 1991; North et al., 1990; Petruzzello, Landers, Hatfield, Kubitz, & Salazar, 1991; Schlicht, 1994), narrative reviews (e.g., Ekkekakis & Petruzzello, 1999; Landers & Arent, 2001; Salmon, 2001), and even reviews of reviews (e.g., Scully, Kremer, Meade, Graham, & Dudgeon, 1998), there is still some debate.

One reason for the debate is that *mood* is a complex construct to operationally define and different authors have used the term in different ways. For example, Landers and Arent (2001) pointed out that a number of constructs fall under the category of mood-like states. Feelings of anxiety, depression, fatigue, anger, and confusion are considered to be manifestations of **negative affect** or mood. Conversely, feelings of vigor, pleasantness, and euphoria are considered to be manifestations of **positive affect** or mood. The researchers also noted, however, that theoreticians (Lazarus, 1991) make a distinction between mood versus affect, claiming that these constructs represent psychological states along an *emotional continuum*. Mood is considered to be more transient and less stable, whereas affect is considered to be more enduring. Consequently, for example, anxiety is a type of affect whereas vigor is a type of mood.

A second reason for the debate is that physical activity—particularly its intensity—is difficult to operationally define. Even "maximal intensity," for example, is difficult to identify. This point was illustrated by Salmon (2000), who noted that "maximal exertion is not a purely physiological limit; even when exercising 'to exhaustion,' the offer of financial reward further increases its intensity" (p. 34). It has been even more difficult to equate workloads described as being at less than maximal intensity (see Ekkekakis & Petruzzello, 1999, for a full discussion on this issue).

A third reason for the debate is that differences exist between people, that the same individual is not completely consistent in his or her response from one physical activity bout to another, and that considerable differences exist in the demands imposed by different activities. In short, all people do not respond to the same workload in the same way or even consistently from time to time. As Ekkekakis and Petruzzello (1999) pointed out, "affective responses to exercise have been shown to be affected by biological and psychological individual difference variables, the physical and social environment, and the objective and perceived attributes of the exercise stimulus, as well as several psychological states" (p. 339).

Finally, adding to the debate, some theoreticians (e.g., Morgan, 1997; Raglin, 1997) have even suggested that evidence showing a physical activity–improved mood relationship could easily reflect a behavioral artifact. Fundamentally, the argument they advance is that people who like to exercise and expect to feel good following physical activity will report that they do. Conversely, people who do not like exercise either avoid physical activity or do not report the positive mood benefits espoused by advocates. So the physical activity–mood relationship might reflect nothing more than the testimonials of advocates.

As is the case in any debate, it's necessary to finally draw conclusions based on the evidence available. The positions endorsed here (i.e., the conclusions we draw) are the ones most strongly supported by research evidence garnered to date and highlighted through empirical summaries (i.e., meta-analyses).

Because the research literature in the physical activity sciences has not progressed to the point where strong distinctions have been made in research between mood and affect, the two types of psychological states are combined in this chapter and referred to as mood. In the first part of this chapter, we discuss the two affective states most frequently examined in the physical activity sciences—anxiety and depression. In the final section of this chapter, we address the relationship of physical activity to a variety of other positive and negative moods—vigor, anger, and so on.

PHYSICAL ACTIVITY AND ANXIETY

Anxiety is considered to be a negative emotional state characterized by feelings of nervousness, worry, and apprehension and by activation or arousal of the body. It arises "in the face of demands that tax or exceed the resources of the system [emphasis removed] or . . . demands to which there are no readily available or automatic adaptive responses" (Lazarus & Cohen, 1977, p. 109). In modern society, anxiety represents a serious health problem. For example, a report from the National Institute of Mental Health (Regier et al., 1984) indicated that anxiety neurosis is the largest mental health problem in the United States, affecting 8% (13.1 million) individuals.

---

negative affect   Feelings such as anxiety, depression, fatigue, anger, and confusion.

positive affect   Feelings such as vigor, pleasantness, and euphoria.

40 SECTION TWO The Individual and Physical Activity

Theorists consider it important to differentiate between **state anxiety** and **trait anxiety**. State anxiety is "an existing or current emotional state characterized by feelings of apprehension and tension and associated with activation of the organism" (Martens, Vealey, & Burton, 1990, p. 9). The critical phrase that serves to differentiate state from trait anxiety is *existing or current*. State anxiety refers to the level of anxiety that an individual experiences at any given point in time. Thus, for example, state anxiety is generally elevated for most individuals immediately prior to important events such as exams and piano recitals. The physical activity–state anxiety relationship is the focus of discussion in this chapter. The impact of physical activity on individual personality characteristics such as trait anxiety is discussed in Chapter 5.

General Effects

A number of meta-analyses have statistically summarized the research on physical activity and state anxiety (e.g., Calfas & Taylor, 1994; Kugler et al., 1994; Landers & Petruzzello, 1994; Long & van Stavel, 1995; D. G. McDonald & Hodgon, 1991; Petruzzello et al., 1991). The number (and types) of

state anxiety The level of anxiety that an individual experiences at any given point in time.

trait anxiety The predisposition to perceive certain environmental stimuli as threatening or nonthreatening and to respond to these stimuli with varying levels of state anxiety.

studies included in those different meta-analyses has varied widely. Nonetheless, the overriding conclusion reached was that physical activity is associated with a reduction in anxiety. The magnitude of the reduction reported has varied from small to moderate (i.e., ES = .15 to .56).

The beneficial effects that physical activity has on state anxiety seems to begin within 5 minutes of the cessation of acute exercise. Although there is some research that shows that this beneficial effect could last from 4 to 6 hours, it is generally accepted that the duration is substantially less—up to approximately 2 hours (Landers & Petruzzello, 1994).

Task Type. A question of interest for practitioners is whether the anxiety reduction found following physical activity is restricted to one particular type of task, such as those involving the aerobic system. In their meta-analysis, Petruzzello and his colleagues (1991) found that aerobic activities (e.g., walking, jogging, running, swimming, cycling) are all equally associated with a small reduction in state anxiety (ES = .26). Conversely, however, nonaerobic activities—activities such as weight training, for example—were not found to be associated with reductions in self-reported state anxiety (ES = −.05).

The Dose-Response Issue. A second question of interest for practitioners relates to the dose-response issue: what dosage of the treatment (physical activity in this case) is necessary to obtain the desired response (reduced state anxiety in this case). Ekkekakis and Petruzzello (1999) noted that two assumptions typically provide the foundation for any prescriptions pertaining to the amount of physical activity necessary to produce reductions in state anxiety. The first is that physical activity must reach some minimal threshold in terms of intensity and duration. They also noted that the threshold advocated varies slightly. For example, Dishman (1986) proposed that exercise should be carried out at an intensity of 70% of maximal oxygen uptake or 70% of maximal heart rate for at least 20 minutes. Similarly, Raglin and Morgan (1985) advocated an intensity of 60% of maximal oxygen uptake. The second assumption is that physical activity carried out at excessively high intensities (e.g., 80% to 90% of

Popular belief is that physical activity can have an affect on mood.

maximal heart rate) and/or duration (e.g., a marathon) will have a detrimental impact on state anxiety. In short, what is implicitly suggested here is a happy medium: Too little physical activity has no appreciable effect on anxiety and too much has a negative effect.

Ekkekakis and Petruzzello (1999) pointed out that research does not support either of these two assumptions. One way to consider the dose-response issue is from the perspective of the length of the physical activity session. In the meta-analysis carried out by Petruzzello and his colleagues (1991) the programs in the studies were categorized according to whether physical activity lasted 0 to 20 minutes, 21 to 30 minutes, 31 to 40 minutes, or greater than 40 minutes. The researchers found that anxiety reduction is present *following* physical activity regardless of the duration of the program.

Another way of looking at the dose-response issue is to consider the intensity of the physical activity stimulus rather than the time involved. Two possible measures of intensity are, of course, an individual's exercising heart rate and that person's exercising oxygen uptake as a percentage of his or her maximum. When Petruzzello and his colleagues (1991) carried out their analyses, they found that anxiety reduction is present *following* physical activity regardless of the intensity of the program.

A slightly different picture is present for anxiety responses *during* physical activity. Ekkekakis and Petruzzello (1999) noted that "affective responses during exercise appear to be sensitive to dose effects, with increasing intensity and progressing duration

being generally associated with reduced affective positivity" (p. 366).

Physical Activity Versus Other Treatment Modalities. Individuals who are suffering from anxiety may choose any of a number of possible treatments to alleviate their symptoms. Some of the more popular treatments include quiet rest, progressive relaxation, meditation, biofeedback, and hypnosis. In some of the studies Petruzzello et al. (1991) reviewed, different types of treatments—including physical activity—were compared against a control condition. These studies offer insight into the comparative benefits of physical activity versus other treatment modalities.

When Petruzzello et al. (1991) examined the reductions in state anxiety across the various strategies used, no differences were found. In short, practitioners providing counsel to individuals suffering from anxiety can be confident that physical activity is as effective as treatments such as hypnosis, meditation, and so on.

PHYSICAL ACTIVITY AND DEPRESSION

In the health sciences, a distinction is made between **clinical depression** and **nonclinical depression.** The latter is viewed as a mental state characterized by feelings of gloom and listlessness. Generally, it arises as a result of a loss of some type, such as a death, a family breakup, or negative changes in job status. However, depression can also arise in periods immediately following completion of some

---

clinical depression   A lowered mood or loss of interest/pleasure for a minimum of two weeks and accompanied by at least five of the following symptoms: loss of appetite, weight loss/gain, sleep disturbance, psychomotor agitation or retardation, energy decrease, sense of worthlessness, guilt, difficulty in concentrating, thoughts of suicide.

nonclinical depression   A mental state characterized by feelings of gloom and listlessness.

42 SECTION TWO   The Individual and Physical Activity

long-anticipated pleasurable event, such as a birth, a holiday period, or a major assignment.

There is less consensus on what constitutes clinical depression. The American Psychiatric Association (1987) considers it to be a lowered mood or loss of interest/pleasure for a minimum of at least two weeks. Furthermore, at least five of the following symptoms must be present: loss of appetite, weight loss or gain, sleep disturbance, psychomotor agitation or retardation, decrease in energy, sense of worthlessness, guilt, difficulty in concentrating, and thoughts of suicide.

There has been a long-standing interest in the potential benefits of physical activity and exercise as an intervention strategy for the treatment of depression (e.g., Franz & Hamilton, 1905). Numerous studies have been undertaken, but some of those studies suffer from poor research design, and others, from small or nonrepresentative samples. Therefore, it is difficult for readers unfamiliar with the area to make sense out of the body of research. Fortunately, meta-analyses have been carried out over the past 10 years. One, by North et al. (1990), focused on all forms of depression. Another, by Craft and Landers (1998), focused on clinical depression only. The two reviews provide an opportunity for researchers to examine the role of physical activity on depression for both nonclinical and clinical individuals.

Nonclinical Depression

The purpose of the North et al. (1990) meta-analysis was to summarize the total population of studies dealing with depression and physical activity, and some of the studies they reviewed included samples of individuals undergoing treatment for depression. Nonetheless, in one of their analyses, North and his colleagues subdivided their studies according to the nature of the participants. As Table 4-1 shows, physically active high school students (ES = .60), health club members (ES = .49), community citizens (ES = .49), and college students and faculty (ES = .16) all exhibited reductions in depression as a result of their involvement in physical activity.

■ **TABLE 4-1**   The Relationship Between Physical Activity and Nonclinical Depression

MEASURE	AVERAGE EFFECT SIZE[1]
Types of participants in the study	
High school students	.60
Health club members	.49
Community citizens	.49
College students/faculty	.16
Purpose underlying physical activity	
Academic experiment	.67
General health	.29

[1]An effect size of .20 is small, one of .50 is medium, and one of .80 is large. The effect sizes are all positive, indicating that reductions in depression are associated with involvement in physical activity.

In another set of analyses, North and his colleagues (1990) subdivided their studies on the basis of the stated purpose of the physical activity. They found that individuals involved in physical activity for general health (ES = .29) or as a result of an academic experiment (ES = .67) demonstrated reductions in depression. The results, taken as a whole, provide strong evidence that physical activity is beneficial for individuals experiencing nonclinical depression.

Clinical Depression

Eight years after the report by North and his colleagues (1990), Craft and Landers (1998) were able to include an additional 17 studies dealing with the influence of physical activity on individuals suffering from clinical depression or depression resulting from mental illness. The results from the North et al. and Craft and Landers meta-analyses were similar (see Table 4-2). North and his colleagues reported antidepressant effects from physical activity for indi-

■ **TABLE 4-2**   Physical Activity for Individuals Undergoing Treatment for Depression

MEASURE	AVERAGE EFFECT SIZE[1]
Individual's purpose for physical activity (North et al., 1990)	
Medical rehabilitation	.97
Psychological rehabilitation	.55
Individuals receiving treatment for depression (Craft & Landers, 1998)	.72

[1]An effect size of .20 is small, one of .50 is medium, and one of .80 is large. The effect sizes are all positive, indicating that reductions in depression are associated with involvement in physical activity.

viduals under medical treatment (i.e., for postmyocardial infarction, cardiovascular risk, pulmonary problems, or hemodialysis; ES = .97) as well as those undergoing psychological rehabilitation (ES = .55). Similarly, as Table 4-2 shows, Craft and Landers reported an overall moderate to large effect (ES = .72). Physical activity is therefore a useful treatment for individuals suffering from depression to such an extent that they must obtain professional help.

Factors Influencing the Impact of Physical Activity on Depression

The North et al. (1990) and Craft and Landers (1998) studies combined also provide some insight into how various conditions might moderate the impact of physical activity on depression. Keep in mind, however, that the North et al. search for moderators involved the total population of studies they analyzed (i.e., individuals of all levels of depression were included).

The Dose-Response Issue.   One conclusion that comes out consistently from both meta-analyses is that the duration of physical activity is important.

The longer the physical activity program goes on, the greater is the impact on depression. For example, Craft and Landers (1998) found that physical activity for 9 weeks or greater led to a large decrease in depression (ES = 1.18). Even physical activity periods of shorter duration are effective, however. Programs of 8 weeks or less were reported to produce a moderate change in depression (ES = .54). Although Craft and Landers found differences in effect sizes when they compared physical activity periods of different duration (i.e., minutes per session) as well as physical activity periods of different intensity, no statistically significant findings emerged.

Task Type.   All forms of exercise—weight training, aerobic activity, walking—are equally beneficial in terms of their impact on depression. Craft and Landers (1998) urged caution, however, in drawing conclusions about the role that type of physical activity might play in reducing depression in clinical populations. They noted that 83% of physical activity situations "alleging to be aerobic did not result in fitness gains over 5%. This makes a comparison between [aerobic and nonaerobic programs] difficult at best" (pp. 350–351).

Characteristics of the Individual.   Comparisons have been made of studies in which the characteristics of the individuals were different. No evidence has been found to suggest that the beneficial effects of physical activity are restricted to specific groups of individuals. Males and females, individuals across the age span, individuals varying markedly in health status, individuals undergoing psychological and medical treatment, and individuals initially depressed versus not depressed all showed reductions in depression as a result of involvement in physical activity. Craft and Landers (1998) did point out that the law of initial values is present in terms of physical activity and clinical depression in that individuals with moderate to severe depression benefited more than individuals with mild to moderate depression (i.e., ES = .88 versus ES = .34 respectively).

Physical Activity Versus Other Treatments.   A word of caution is necessary before too much emphasis is placed on physical activity as a treatment

44 SECTION TWO   The Individual and Physical Activity

for depression. Physical activity is effective. However, Craft and Landers (1998) found that it is no more effective than group or individual psychotherapy and behavioral interventions. North and his colleagues (1990) found that the combination of physical activity and psychotherapy produced the largest decrease in depression.

INTERACTION OF PHYSICAL ACTIVITY AND PSYCHOTHERAPEUTIC DRUGS

Psychotherapeutic medications such as the tricyclic antidepressants, neuroleptics, and benzodiazapines have been linked with numerous physical side effects. These side effects include dizziness, nausea, drowsiness, and dry mouth (Martinsen & Stanghelle, 1997). Although the physiological consequences of combining pharmacologic treatments with exercise has been thoroughly examined, knowledge of the synergistic effects of psychotropic medications and physical activity is limited. Because both exercise and psychotherapeutic drugs are routinely prescribed as part of the treatment strategy for psychological disturbance (Morgan & Goldston, 1987), knowledge of the effects that the interaction of these interventions may have on physical and psychological health is of great importance. To date, however, the relationship between exercise and psychotherapeutic medications has not been systematically investigated.

An obvious concern of combining exercise with drug therapy involves the potential health risks that may arise from the physical side effects of the medication and the physiological demands of exercise. Some studies indicate that tricyclic antidepressants may compromise cardiac output (Vohra, Burrows, & Sloma, 1975) and consequently impinge on a person's ability to exercise safely. In contrast to this assertion, other researchers have found that therapeutic doses of antidepressants have little impact on cardiac function and do not impair a person's ability to perform physical activity (Glassman & Bigger, 1981; Veith, Raskind, & Claswell, 1982). Thus, psy-

chotherapeutic drugs do not appear to make exercise an unsafe activity. Nevertheless, they are associated with numerous side effects that may make physical activity more difficult. For example, the use of psychotherapeutic drugs has been linked with drowsiness, decreased cardiac output, and reduced blood pressure responses both at rest and during exercise. It is possible that these physical changes may make exercise more difficult (Carlsson, Dencker, Grimby, & Heggendal, 1967) and subsequently decrease an individual's motivation to engage in regular physical activity. Nevertheless, due to the health benefits of physical activity, exercise is not contraindicated for individuals taking drugs (Martinsen & Stanghelle, 1997). Benzodiazapines may decrease psychomotor performance; however, findings do not indicate that they significantly impair exercise tolerance, duration, or cardiac function (Eimer, Cable, Gal, Rothenberg, & McCue, 1985; Stratton & Halter, 1985). Therefore, although psychotropic medications do impact physiological factors, exercising concomitantly with the use of psychotherapeutic drugs does not appear to increase the risk of adverse physical health complications.

Given that exercise has been consistently associated with reductions in depression and anxiety (Morgan, 1994; Raglin, 1997), it is plausible that physical activity would enhance the beneficial effect of medications. However, only two studies have investigated this relationship, and the findings are mixed. In one study, Martinsen (1987) examined the influence of exercise therapy and a combination of exercise therapy with tricyclic antidepressants in a sample of 43 patients with major depressive disorder. Although both treatments had a beneficial effect on depression, the addition of exercise failed to increase the antidepressant effect of the medication. In the second study (Martinsen, Hoffart, & Solberg, 1989), results favored the combination of medication and exercise over exercise alone for the reduction of depression in a sample of 99 patients diagnosed with unipolar depressive disorder. Finally, in a related area, case studies of three male runners with bipolar disorder (Martinsen & Stanghelle, 1997) revealed that attempts to taper their lithium intake and replace it with running were unsuccessful. Specifically, all three men experienced a relapse and resumed their previous lithium treatment within a year. In short, although results that address the synergistic effects of exercise and medication remain equivocal, the efficacy of combining exercise with medication in the treatment of mental illness warrants additional inquiry.

In summary, findings indicate that people do not assume additional health risk when they combine exercise with psychotherapeutic drug therapy (Martinsen & Morgan, 1997). It appears that when each are prescribed under appropriate medical supervision, exercise can be safely combined with pharmacologic medications. It is unclear if the combination of psychotherapeutic medications and exercise is more effective than the use of either treatment alone. However, relatively little research addressing this possibility has been conducted at the present time, and the synergistic effects of exercise and psychotherapeutic medications requires further exploration.

PHYSICAL ACTIVITY AND OTHER MEASURES OF MOOD

A commonly used measure to assess mood has been the Profile of Mood States, or **POMS** as it is more commonly called (McNair, Lorr, & Droppleman, 1971). The POMS assesses six moods: the five negative moods of anger, tension, fatigue, depression, and confusion, and the one positive mood of vigor.

In 1991, D. G. McDonald and Hodgdon undertook a meta-analysis of studies available at that time that had examined the impact of physical activity on mood. An overview of the findings of their meta-analysis are presented in Table 4-3. All six of the mood states examined in the POMS are influenced by physical activity. The five negative mood states (i.e., anger, tension, fatigue, depression, confusion) all show significant reductions, varying from an effect

....
POMS   Profile of Mood States.
....

■ **TABLE 4-3**   The Relationship Between Physical Activity and Various Indices of Mood Assessed in the Profile of Mood States Test

MEASURE	AVERAGE EFFECT SIZE[1]
Tension	.32
Anger	.18
Vigor	.40
Fatigue	.27
Confusion	.40

[1]An effect size of .20 is small, one of .50 is medium, and one of .80 is large. A positive effect size indicates improvements over control groups or baseline conditions.

size of .18 for anger to an effect size of .40 for confusion. Similarly, the one positive mood state, vigor, shows a moderate increase in magnitude following a bout of physical activity (ES = .40).

More recently, Arent, Landers, and Etnier (in press) undertook a meta-analysis of 32 studies that had examined the influence of physical activity on the mood states of older (> 65 years) participants. Their results were consistent with those reported for younger participants: Physical activity was associated with significantly enhanced positive and significantly reduced negative mood states. Moreover, positive changes in mood states were more likely to occur in either aerobic activities or resistive training activities than in either motivational control groups, no treatment control groups, or groups involved in yoga.

POSSIBLE REASONS FOR THE BENEFITS OF PHYSICAL ACTIVITY

In Chapter 1, we pointed out that science proceeds from description to explanation to prediction to control/intervention. Investigations of the link between acute and chronic bouts of physical activity and psychological states and traits have produced a substantial body of descriptive research. That research shows

46   SECTION TWO   The Individual and Physical Activity

that the link is positive—often small but nevertheless always positive. Acute and chronic physical activity are associated with positive psychological benefits, with the latter being more beneficial than the former. A question that now arises is, why is physical activity beneficial? What are the underlying reasons for these benefits? A number of explanations have been advanced.

Physiological Mechanisms

Some of the explanations offered for why exercise and physical activity have a beneficial impact on various psychological states have a biological basis. These include the thermogenic, monoamine, endorphin, opponent-process, and cerebral changes hypotheses.

Thermogenic Hypothesis. For thousands of years, humans have used techniques that raise body temperature (e.g., saunas, warm showers) as a form of therapy. The thermogenic hypothesis as an explanation for the psychological benefits of exercise was only advanced recently, however. DeVries, Beckman, Huber, and Dieckmeier (1968) found that the elevations that occur in core temperature during and after moderate to intense exercise are associated with concomitant decreases in muscle tension. This reduction in muscle tension, in turn, is associated with relaxation, enhanced mood states, and reduced anxiety.

The thermogenic hypothesis may help to account for the positive changes in state anxiety and stress reactivity following physical activity. However, there is no basis for suggesting that increased body temperature explains the positive changes in depression or cognitive functioning that are associated with acute or chronic physical activity.

Monoamine Hypothesis. The monoamine hypothesis has relevance for both the physical activity–depression and physical activity–cognitive functioning relationships. Fundamentally, it is based on a proposed facilitative effect from physical activity on neurotransmitters such as dopamine, norepinephrine, and serotonin. Specific neural pathways in the brain are associated with specific cognitive activities as well as specific mood states such as depression, pleasure, anxiety, and so on. The neuro-

transmitters serve as chemical messengers to help transmit neural impulses across the synapses between neurons. If the neurotransmitters are present in sufficient quantities to adhere to the receptor site, the neural impulse is transmitted; if not, neural impulses are not transmitted.

High levels of norepinephrine have been found to be associated with better memory (Zornetzer, 1985). Also, low levels have been associated with depression (J. M. Weiss, 1982). Furthermore, various medical treatments for depression, such as drugs and electroconvulsive therapy, have been found to produce an increase in dopamine, norepinephrine, and serotonin (e.g., Grahame-Smith, Green, & Costain, 1978).

Physical activity also has been identified as a stimulus that increases the quantity of neurotransmitters present in the brain—at least in laboratory rats (B. S. Brown, Payne, Kin, Moore, & Martin, 1979). However, the evidence from research on humans, while promising, is by necessity only indirect because monoamine levels can only be assessed in blood plasma, cerebrospinal fluid, and urine.

Endorphin Hypothesis. The endorphin hypothesis also has relevance to the relationship of physical activity to reduced depression. The beneficial psychological effects that accompany physical activity are attributed by many theorists to increased levels of endorphins—peptides similar in chemical structure to morphine. Endorphins (beta-endorphins, met-enkephalins, leu-enkephalins) act to reduce pain and can contribute to feelings of euphoria. The so-called runner's high is attributed to increased levels of endorphins. Also, endurance training is related to changes in levels of resting plasma beta-endorphins and reduced depression (e.g., Lobstein & Rasmussen, 1991). However, as Appenzeller, Standefer, Appenzeller, and Atkinson (1980) have cautioned, while endurance running may produce increases in beta-endorphins, "whether this increase persists after physical activity and is responsible for runner's high, the behavioral alterations of endurance trained individual's improved libido, heightened pain threshold, absence of depression, and other anecdotal effects of endurance training remains conjectural" (p. 419).

Research with animals has produced results that are promising to the endorphin hypothesis (e.g., Christie & Chesher, 1982). However, as with the monoamine hypothesis, research with humans, by necessity, has yielded indirect evidence only. Thus, in attempting to draw conclusions from that research, theorists have suggested that the interrelationships among increased physical activity, enhanced psychological states, and increased endorphin levels remains inconclusive (e.g., Morgan, 1985).

Opponent-Process Hypothesis. The opponent-process hypothesis, which was advanced by Solomon (1980), uses physiological mechanisms to account for psychological changes. According to Solomon, the brain is organized to oppose either pleasurable or aversive emotional processes—to bring the system back to homeostasis. Thus, the appearance of a stimulus (pleasurable or aversive) serves to activate the sympathetic nervous system. This activation is referred to as the *a process*. In an effort to return the body to homeostasis, a *b process* is also aroused—possibly through activation of the parasympathetic nervous system.

Moderate to high intensity physical activity can be considered the a process—a generally taxing, unpleasant stimulus. With acute or chronic bouts of physical activity, the strength of the a process remains constant (i.e., we continue to strive for a training effect by placing increasingly greater physical demands on our system). The opponent process activated by physical activity—or b process—could be enhanced psychological moods (or relaxation, or reduced state anxiety). Over time (i.e., with chronic physical activity), the a process remains constant while the b process increases in strength.

There is some support for the opponent-process hypothesis. Boutcher and Landers (1988) found that trained runners who had adapted to the demands of exercise showed reductions in anxiety; untrained runners did not. Also, Petruzzello and his colleagues (1991) proposed that Solomon's opponent-process hypothesis is "an attractive explanation for the exercise-induced anxiety reduction" (p. 160) they found in their meta-analysis.

FIT FACTS

Is the reduced anxiety that a person experiences after physical activity simply due to a sense of relief that the activity is over?

Not likely. There is no support for the view that just prior to physical activity, anxiety becomes elevated above normal (because of the anticipation of a potentially threatening event) and then merely returns to normal following the activity.

(Petruzzello, 1995)

Cerebral Changes Hypothesis. Two hypotheses pertaining to cerebral changes have been advanced to account for the relationship between chronic and acute physical activity and improved cognitive functioning (Etnier et al., 1997). One is related to the fact that exercise produces structural changes in the brain, including increased density of the vasculature of the cerebral cortex and shorter vascular diffusion distances (Issacs, Anderson, Alcantara, Black, & Greenough, 1992). A second is related to cerebral blood flow; moderate to high intensities of physical activity lead to large increases in cerebral blood flow (e.g., Heroltz et al., 1987). With this increased cerebral blood flow, there is an increase in essential nutrients such as glucose and oxygen available to the brain (Chodzko-Zajko, 1991). As a consequence, cognitive functioning is thought to be enhanced.

Etnier and her colleagues (1997) suggested that their meta-analysis on the relationship of physical activity to cognitive functioning (see Chapter 3) provided indirect evidence against both of the cerebral change hypotheses. They pointed out that none of the variables relating to the duration of the physical activity program—number of weeks of exercise, number of days of exercise per week—were related to the size of the effect for enhanced cognitive functioning. Furthermore, evidence of improved physical fitness was unrelated to enhanced cognitive functioning. Etnier et al. concluded that the mechanisms that might help to explain the improvements in cognitive

48 SECTION TWO The Individual and Physical Activity

functioning associated with physical activity "must be one of the following: (a) physiological mechanisms independent of aerobic fitness; (b) physiological mechanisms related to aerobic fitness, but occurring prior to changes in aerobic fitness; or, (c) psychological mechanisms independent of aerobic fitness and exercise" (p. 268).

Cognitive Mechanisms

Some of the explanations offered for why exercise and physical activity have a beneficial impact on various psychological states have a cognitive basis. These include the expectancy and distraction hypotheses.

Expectancy Hypothesis. Is it possible that physical activity is one giant placebo effect? That is, individuals expect to feel better psychologically when they are more physically active, so, not surprisingly, they do. The proliferation of information in the popular media and other sources has convinced many people of the benefits of physical activity. Thus, when they begin to be active (or cease to maintain activity), they expect to and do experience psychological changes.

Desharnais, Jobin, Cote, Levesque, & Godin (1993) did find some evidence for a placebo effect. Patients who were informed that the program in which they were engaged was sufficient to enhance psychological well-being showed self-esteem improvements similar to physically active patients. However, other research that has manipulated expectancies (i.e., tested for a placebo effect) has shown that there are benefits from physical activity beyond those resulting from expectancy alone (e.g., McCann & Holmes, 1984).

Distraction Hypothesis. The distraction or "time-out" hypothesis that was advanced by Bahrke and Morgan (1978) is based on the assumption that time away from the stress of day-to-day routines can serve as a distraction and contribute to the psychological benefits associated with physical activity. Thus, physical activity represents one activity from among a variety that can produce positive changes in mental health. Also, as Morgan (1988; Morgan & O'Connor, 1989) pointed out, the distraction hypothesis does not contradict other cognitive or physiological mechanisms. Distraction or time-out could simply be one reason for the positive psychological outcomes that come from being physically active.

The Bahrke and Morgan (1978) hypothesis has been tested in studies in which the effects of physical activity versus time-out (i.e., quiet rest periods) have been controlled. Physical activity was found to produce greater positive psychological changes than did time-out alone (Roth, 1989; Roth, Bachtler, & Fillingam, 1990). So, time-out may be useful and important, but the individual taking that time-out would be better advised to engage in physical activity.

Summary

Scientists have had a long-standing interest in the association between physical activity and improvements in both positive mood states such as vigor and pleasantness and negative mood states such as anxiety and depression. The results from that body of research are unequivocal. For males and females across the age spectrum, physical activity involvement is related to improvements in mood.

In some areas, because of the greater number of studies available, it has been possible to determine whether certain variables might serve to moderate the activity–mood change relationship. Insofar as anxiety is concerned, the type of activity is important. Aerobic activities such as jogging are associated with a reduction in state anxiety but nonaerobic activities such as weight training are not. The beneficial effects of physical activity are not dependent on either the duration of the activity or its intensity.

Within 5 minutes of the cessation of acute exercise, the individual begins to experience the reductions in state anxiety. Although some research shows that this beneficial effect could last from 4 to 6 hours, it is generally accepted that the duration is substantially less—up to approximately 2 hours. A variety of protocols have been used in an attempt to alleviate anxiety. Physical activity is as effective as other treatments such as hypnosis, meditation, relaxation, and so on.

Insofar as depression is concerned, both aerobic and nonaerobic activities are associated with reductions in depression. Also, the longer the physical activity program goes on, the greater impact it has on depression. All categories of individuals—males and females, individuals across the age span, individuals varying markedly in health status, individuals undergoing psychological and medical treatment, and individuals initially depressed versus not depressed—show reductions in depression as a result of involvement in physical activity. However, the law of initial values is present—individuals with moderate to severe depression benefit more than do individuals with mild to moderate depression.

Physical activity has proven to be effective as an intervention strategy to reduce depression. However, it is no more effective than group or individual psychotherapy and behavioral interventions. Finally, physical activity is associated with improvements in other positive and negative mood states such as vigor, confusion, anger, fatigue, and tension.

CHAPTER **15**

The Transtheoretical Model and Physical Activity

One Size Does Not *Fit All.*

CHAPTER OBJECTIVES

After completing this chapter you will be able to

- Describe the constructs of the transtheoretical model.

- Discuss the research that has applied the transtheoretical model.

- Discuss the advantages and limitations of the transtheoretical model.

Key terms

action	preparation
contemplation	processes of change
decisional balance	self-efficacy
maintenance	stages of change
precontemplation	temptation
precontemplation believers	termination
precontemplation nonbelievers	

For most people, changing unhealthy behaviors to healthy behaviors is often challenging. Change usually does not occur all at once; it is a lengthy process that involves progressing through several stages. At each stage, the cognitions and behaviors of the individual are different, so one approach to facilitating behavioral change is not appropriate. The concept of stages—or a "one size does not fit all" philosophy (Marcus et al., 2000)—forms the basis for the transtheoretical model of behavior change (also referred to as the stages of change model) developed by Prochaska and his colleagues at the University of Rhode Island. This model emerged from a comparative analysis of leading theories of psychotherapy and behavior change. In developing the model, the goal was to provide a systematic integration of a field that had fragmented into more than 300 theories of psychotherapy (Prochaska & Velicer, 1997). The transtheoretical model includes five constructs—stages of change, decisional balance, processes of change, self-efficacy, and temptation—that are important for an understanding of the process of volitional change. After applying it to their work on smoking cessation, the researchers extended the model in an attempt to better understand a broad range of health and mental health behaviors such as nutrition, weight control, alcohol abuse, eating disorders, unplanned pregnancy protection, mammography screening, sun exposure, substance abuse, and physical activity (Prochaska & Velicer). The latter, of course, represents the focus in this chapter.

CONSTRUCTS OF THE TRANSTHEORETICAL MODEL

Five main constructs make up the transtheoretical model: stages of change, decisional balance, processes of change, self-efficacy, and temptation. Each of these constructs is outlined in detail in the following sections.

Stages of Change

One of the major contributions of the transtheoretical model to the health field is the recognition that behavior change unfolds slowly over time through a series of stages. Benjamin Franklin recognized this fact more than 300 years ago when he noted:

> To get the bad customs of a country changed and new ones, thought better, introduced, it is necessary first to remove the prejudices of the people, enlighten their ignorance, and convince them that their interests will be promoted by the proposed changes: and this is not the work of a day. (cited in USDHHS, 1999, p. 73)

There are three main aspects to the stages of change construct. First, stages fall somewhere between traits and states. Traits are stable and not open to immediate change. States, on the other hand, are readily changeable and typically lack stability. Thus, for example, an individual who is chronically anxious would be known to have high trait anxiety. Conversely, an individual who has severe butterflies before a race would be known to possess high state anxiety.

Second, stages are both stable and dynamic. That is, although stages may last for a considerable period, they are susceptible to change. Prochaska and DiClemente (1986) have hypothesized that as individuals change from an unhealthy to a healthy behavior, they move through a number of stages at varying rates and in a cyclical fashion with periods of progression and relapse. For example, a sedentary man initially may begin to think about physical activity's benefits (e.g., have more energy) and costs (e.g., time away from watching television). Then, a few months later, he may buy a pair of walking shoes. Six months

later he may go walking three times a week. After a year of walking regularly, however, he may become overwhelmed with the stress of work and stop walking. The cessation of physical activity would represent a regression to an earlier stage. In short, individuals going through the process of behavioral change typically cycle (or progress and relapse) through a series of stages as they recognize the need to change, contemplate making a change, make the change, and finally, sustain the new behavior (Culos-Reed et al., 2001). Figure 15-1 provides a graphic illustration of the stages of change.

Third, there are six stages through which people pass in attempting any health behavior change: **precontemplation** (not intending to make changes), **contemplation** (intending to make changes within the foreseeable future, which is defined as the next

---

precontemplation The stage at which a person does not intend to make changes.

contemplation The stage at which a person intends to make changes within the foreseeable future, which is defined as the next 6 months.

preparation The stage at which a person intends to change in the immediate future, which is defined as within 1 month.

action The stage at which a person actively engages in a new behavior.

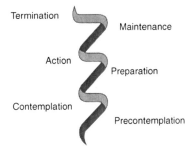

Figure 15-1 Stages of change. The spiral pattern represents the dynamic forward and backward movement through the stages.

6 months), **preparation** (intending to change in the immediate future, which is defined as within 1 month), **action** (actively engaging in the new behavior), **maintenance** (sustaining change over time), and **termination** (eliminating the probability of relapse; Cardinal, 1999; Cardinal, 2000; Reed et al., 1997). Operational definitions for the various stages are outlined in Table 15-1. Also, a more comprehensive description of each stage is provided in the following sections.

Precontemplation ("I won't or I can't"). People in the precontemplation stage are not considering or do not want to change their behavior. The so-called couch potato is an example of someone in the precontemplation stage. Precontemplators typically deny having a problem and have no intention of making a behavior change in the foreseeable future. As Table 15-1 shows, the foreseeable future is typically defined as within the next 6 months—the period of time most people might use if they are considering a behavior change (Prochaska & Marcus, 1994).

The hallmark of precontemplation is a lack of intention to take action regardless of the reason or excuse (Reed, 1999). An individual may be in precontemplation because he or she does not think

physical activity is valuable or thinks it's valuable but may be overwhelmed by barriers such as lack of time. Precontemplators are the most difficult people to stimulate into behavioral change. They often think that change is not even a possibility. Educating them about the problem behavior is critical in helping them to start thinking about becoming more healthy.

Reed and her colleagues (1999) reported the existence of two types of precontemplators, each of whom have different reasons for not planning to engage in physical activity. **Precontemplation non-believers** either do not believe in regular physical activity or do not see the value of engaging in it. **Precontemplation believers** do believe that physical activity is a worthwhile behavior but they cannot seem to start participating in it. The precontemplation nonbelievers need to become aware of and learn to appreciate the pros, or benefits, of physical activity, such as improving mood states and energy levels. In contrast, the precontemplation believers need help overcoming the cons of exercising, such as taking time away from other activities (Reed, 1999).

Contemplation ("I might").   Individuals in the contemplation stage acknowledge that they have a problem and are thinking about changing their behavior sometime within the next 6 months. They see a need for change because they are aware of the costs and benefits of changing their behavior. For example, they may realize that physical activity reduces their chance of having heart disease (a pro, or

■ **TABLE 15-1**   Operational Definitions of the Stages of Exercise Change

STAGE	OPERATIONAL DEFINITION
Precontemplation	I do not intend to begin exercising in the next 6 months.
Contemplation	I intend to begin exercising in the next 6 months.
Preparation	I intend to begin exercising regularly in the next 30 days.
Action	I have been exercising, but for less than 6 months.
Maintenance	I have been exercising for more than 6 months.

Note. Adapted from "What Makes a Good Algorithm: Examples from Regular Exercise," by G. R. Reed, W. F. Velicer, J. O. Prochaska, J. S. Rossi, and B. H. Marcus, 1997, *American Journal of Health Promotion, 12,* 57–66.

maintenance   The stage at which a person sustains change over time.

termination   The stage in which a person has 0% temptation to engage in old behavior and 100% self-efficacy in all previously tempting situations.

precontemplation nonbeliever   A person who either does not believe in regular physical activity or does not see the value of engaging in it.

precontemplation believer   A person who believes that physical activity is a worthwhile behavior but cannot seem to start participating in it.

benefit, of exercise). However, they also acknowledge that physical activity will take time away from doing other things such as working and spending time with family and friends (a con, or cost, of exercise). Contemplators are generally open to new information and interested in knowing more about the benefits of change. At this stage, however, people are not committed to the change because they are only contemplating or thinking about it. Therefore, they may become a chronic contemplator, never moving beyond the information-gathering phase (Prochaska & Marcus, 1994; Reed, 1999).

Preparation ("I will"). In the preparation stage, people are seriously considering or planning to change their activity level in the near future, usually within the next month. The preparation stage has both a behavioral and an intentional component. For example, preparers may have bought a pair of running shoes, joined a running club, and even gone for a half-hour walk once a week. They may also intend to increase the frequency of their walk from once to three times a week within the next month. These individuals often have strong incentives to change based on optimistic views about the beneficial outcomes. Preparation is a relatively unstable stage because people in this stage are more likely than precontemplators or contemplators to progress over the next six months (Prochaska & Marcus, 1994).

Action ("I am"). Individuals who have recently changed their behavior (i.e., within the last 6 months) are considered to be in the action stage. This stage requires the greatest commitment of time and energy. To be classified within the action stage insofar as physical activity is concerned, the individual must meet the minimal physical activity recommendations developed by the American College of Sports Medicine and Centers for Disease Control and Prevention (USDHHS, 1996). The recommendations state that adults should accumulate 30 minutes or more of moderate intensity physical activity (e.g., brisk walking) on most, preferably all, days of the week (Pate et al., 1995). Because the person in the action stage has only recently established the new habit, attentiveness is necessary because relapse is common (Reed, 1999).

Maintenance ("I have"). Once the individual has been regularly active for 6 consecutive months, he or she is deemed to have progressed into the maintenance stage. Although the new behavior has become better established, boredom and a loss of focus can become a real danger. The constant vigilance initially required to establish a new habit is exhausting and difficult to sustain. It is at this time that a person works to reinforce the gains made through the various stages of change and strives to prevent lapses and relapses (Reed, 1999).

Termination. Once a behavior has been maintained for more than 5 years, the individual is considered to have exited from the cycle of change, and a fear of relapse is eliminated. This stage is the ultimate goal for all people searching for a healthier lifestyle. Termination is the stage in which the person has 0% temptation to engage in the old behavior and 100% self-efficacy in all previously tempting situations. Research on the termination stage for physical activity is limited. For example, Cardinal (1999) examined whether a termination stage exists for physical activity. The criteria he used were the same as those just outlined—5 or more years of continuous involvement in physical activity and 100% self-efficacy in an ability to remain physically active for life. Of the 551 adults surveyed, 16.6% were classified within the termination stage. Cardinal concluded that individuals in the termination stage are resistant to relapse irrespective of common barriers given for not being physically active (e.g., lack of time, bad weather, no energy). The existence of a termination stage for exercise has also been found in research conducted by Fallon and Hausenblas (2001).

Decisional Balance

Decision making was first conceptualized by Janis and Mann (1977) as a decisional "balance sheet" that assesses the importance that an individual places on the potential advantages, or *pros*, and disadvantages, or *cons*, of a behavior. The **decisional balance** between

> **decisional balance** The balance between the potential advantages and disadvantages of a behavior.

the pros and cons varies depending on which stage of change the individual is in. When the cons of exercise (e.g., takes time away from other activities) are of greater importance than the pros of exercise (e.g., improves psychological well-being), motivation to change behavior (i.e., move from being sedentary to engaging in physical activity) is low. Thus, for example, in the precontemplation and contemplation stages, the cons are assumed to outweigh the pros. In the preparation stage, the pros and cons are believed to be relatively equal. In the action, maintenance, and termination stages, the pros are thought to outweigh the cons. DiClemente and his colleagues (1991) noted that an assessment of the pros and cons is relevant for researchers to understand and predict transitions among the first three stages of change (i.e., precontemplation, contemplation, and preparation). During the action and maintenance stages, however, these decisional balance measures are much less important predictors of progress.

Processes of Change

Ten **processes of change** represent the behaviors, cognitions, and emotions that people engage in during the course of changing a behavior. These processes are (a) *gathering information* (i.e., determining the pros and cons of the positive behavior); (b) *making substitutions* (substituting a positive behavior for a negative one); (c) *being moved emotionally* (experiencing and expressing feelings about the consequences of the positive behavior); (d) *being a role model* (considering how the negative behavior impacts on significant others); (e) *getting social support* (using significant others to effect change); (f) *developing a healthy self-image* (instilling the positive behaviors as an integral component of self-image); (g) *taking advantage of social mores* (taking advantage of social situations that encourage the positive behavior); (h) *being rewarded* (being rewarded by oneself or others for engaging in the positive behavior); (i) *using cues* (using cues as a catalyst for the positive behavior); and (j) *making a commitment* (becoming committed to the positive behavior). The 10 processes of change can be divided into 5 experiential or cogni-

tive processes (i.e., gathering information, being moved emotionally, being a role model, developing a healthy self-image, and taking advantage of social mores), and 5 behavioral or environmental processes (i.e., making substitutions, getting social support, making a commitment, being rewarded, and using cues).

Table 15-2 outlines the various processes of change and provides a description for each. The processes of change provide information on *how* shifts in behavior occur. As Culos-Reed and her colleagues (2001) noted, there is limited evidence about the processes that individuals experience as they move from being sedentary to engaging in regular physical activity.

Self-Efficacy

Self-efficacy is a judgment regarding a person's ability to perform a behavior required to achieve a certain outcome. Not surprisingly, self-efficacy is believed to be critical to behavior change (Bandura, 1997; see Chapter 12 for a detailed discussion of self-efficacy). Self-efficacy is proposed to change with each stage, presumably increasing as the individual gains confidence through, for example, successful attempts to increase physical activity. Conversely, self-efficacy may decrease if an individual falters and spirals back to an earlier stage.

Support for the role that self-efficacy plays in the transtheoretical model was provided by Gorely and Gordon (1995) in a study of Australian adults 50 to 65 years of age. The researchers found that self-efficacy to overcome barriers to exercise increased systematically from precontemplation to contemplation to preparation to action to maintenance. Further support for the effectiveness of self-efficacy was found by Sullum, Clark, and King

---

processes of change The behaviors, cognitions, and emotions that people engage in during behavior change.

self-efficacy Judgment regarding a person's ability to perform behavior.

■ **TABLE 15-2**   The Processes of Change

CLASSIC TERM	REVISED TERM	DESCRIPTION
Consciousness raising	Gathering information	Gathering information about regular physical activity (learning the pros and cons of exercising)
Counter-conditioning	Making substitutions	Substituting sedentary behavior with activity
Dramatic relief	Being moved emotionally	Experiencing and expressing feelings about the consequences of being active
Environmental reevaluation	Being a role model	Considering and assessing how inactivity affects friends, family, and citizens
Helping relationships	Getting social support	Getting support for one's intention to exercise
Self-reevaluation	Developing a healthy self-image	Appraising one's self-image as a healthy regular exerciser
Social-liberation	Taking advantage of social mores	Taking advantage of social policy, customs, and mores that enhance physical activity (e.g., New Year's resolutions)
Reinforcement management	Being rewarded	Rewarding oneself or being rewarded by others for making changes
Stimulus control	Using cues	Using cues to remember to engage in physical activity
Self-liberation	Making a commitment	Committing oneself to becoming or staying a regular exerciser

Note. Adopted from "Adherence to Exercise and the Transtheoretical Model of Behavior Change," by G. R. Reed, 1999, in S. Bull, Ed., *Adherence Issues in Sport and Exercise* (pp. 19–46), New York: Wiley.

(2000) in a study of 52 physically active college students. The researchers assessed the students' levels of self-efficacy at baseline and then tracked their physical activity behavior for approximately 8 weeks. They found that students who became inactive (i.e., relapsed) over the 8 weeks had lower self-efficacy at baseline than did those who maintained their exercise level.

Temptation

Temptation represents the intensity of the urges to engage in a specific behavior (or habit) when in the

---

temptation   Urge to engage in a behavior during difficult situations.

---

midst of difficult situations (Grimley, Prochaska, Velicer, Blais, & DiClemente, 1994). Temptation and self-efficacy function inversely across the stages of change, with temptation being a better predictor of relapses (Redding & Rossi, 1999). For example, in the maintenance stage, in which a smoker has successfully eliminated smoking behavior for at least six months, temptation is one of the best predictors of a relapse and the subsequent recycling to earlier stages of change (Redding & Rossi). Research examining the temptation construct for physical activity behavior is limited. In a recent study, Hausenblas and her colleagues (2001) found a negative relationship between temptations to *not* exercise and self-efficacy. That is, maintainers reported the lowest temptation to not exercise and the highest confidence in engaging in exercise behavior compared to individuals in the other stages.

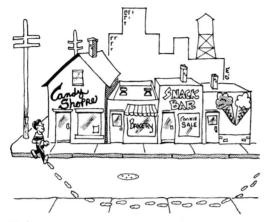

There are many ways to avoid temptations.

ADVANTAGES AND LIMITATIONS OF THE TRANSTHEORETICAL MODEL

Advantages

Reed (1999) noted at least three advantages to dividing a population into the stages of change. The first is that using a stages perspective provides researchers with the opportunity to match interventions to the different needs of individuals in each of the stages. As a consequence, researchers and health care professionals are able to target specific interventions for the total population (i.e., those who have not yet made a behavior change and are at risk as well as those who have changed but may be at risk of relapse). For example, limited success has been observed for traditional interventions in terms of promoting the adoption and maintenance of a physically active lifestyle. This lack of success may be attributed, in part, to the fact that an educational focus has been utilized rather than a behavioral and motivational focus. Many sedentary individuals are not ready to adopt regular exercise because they are unmotivated. Providing them with advice and a physical activity prescription is unlikely to lead to be-

FIT FACTS

At what age do people begin to receive the health-related benefits from engaging in regular physical activity?

All individuals older than 2 years of age benefit from incorporating at least 30 minutes of moderate- to vigorous-intensity physical activity into their daily lives.

(USDHHS, 1996)

havior change. Therefore, the traditional physical activity intervention may fail to recruit the vast majority of sedentary individuals because they have no intention of becoming active. This finding reflects an incongruity between what is typically offered (action-oriented programs) and population motivational readiness to change (inactive and not intending to become active). Consequently, it is important that health care professionals customize interventions to meet the specific motivational needs of the majority of individuals who are either inactive or underactive.

A second advantage is that adopting a stages of change approach provides researchers with the opportunity to subdivide the at-risk population into precontemplation, contemplation, and preparation stages. This identification of the three types of people at risk allows health care professionals to proactively try to recruit individuals who are most in need but the least likely to react to a physical activity program (i.e., precontemplators and contemplators). It is important to note that the distribution across these stages varies by age. For example, Nigg and his colleagues (1999) found that for people aged 75 and older, 39% were classified in the precontemplation stage, 5% in the contemplation stage, and 10% in the preparation stage. In comparison, for adults less than 55 years of age, 17% were classified in the precontemplation stage, 14% in the contemplation stage, and 18% in the preparation stage.

A third advantage is associated with recruitment and retention. An individual's readiness to change can predict the likelihood that that person

166   SECTION FOUR   Models for Involvement in Physical Activity

will successfully adopt and maintain a healthy lifestyle. Recruitment of people at an earlier stage can be successful if (a) health professionals proactively target them, and (b) an intervention is used that is matched to the specific stage of change. Proactive recruitment by either telephone or a personal letter coupled with stage-matched interventions have resulted in good participation rates (Reed, 1999). As Marcus and her colleagues (2000) stated, " 'One-size-fits-all' programs are rarely as effective as programs that tailor treatment to at least some aspects of the individual or group" (p. 39).

Research by Lichtenstein and Hollis (1992) serves to illustrate Marcus's point. Lichtenstein and Hollis had little success with an action-oriented approach to smoking cessation. That is, following intensive proactive recruitment, participants spent 5 minutes in a counseling session with the physician. If the participant could not be convinced to sign up for a smoking cessation clinic, the next 10 minutes were spent with a nurse. If the participant was still unwilling to sign up for the program, 12 minutes were spent with a health educator and watching a video. The final push was a follow-up telephone call from a counselor. All this labor produced only a 1% participation rate.

Limitations

Because of the advantages of the transtheoretical model, it is not surprising that the model's framework has been applied frequently to change people's health behaviors. Unfortunately, application has occurred without proper validation of the transtheoretical model. That is, as Culos-Reed and her colleagues (2001) noted, limited evidence exists on the theorizing, testing, and critiquing of the model. Thus, Culos-Reed et al. concluded that "there appears to have been a readiness to accept the TTM [transtheoretical model] for application beyond any reasonable amount of validation evidence that would be expected for theories in the behavioral sciences" (p. 713).

Furthermore, Joseph, Curtis, and Skinner (1997) stated five limitations of the transtheoretical model (see Culos-Reed et al., 2001). First, research

does not support the six stages of change as a robust construct. Second, support for the relationship between the processes of changes and the stages of change is equivocal. Third, the transtheoretical model is mostly descriptive as opposed to explanatory. For example, the characteristics within the stages are described, but causal processes are not tested (Culos-Reed et al.). Fourth, the transtheoretical model fails to include the influence of moderator variables (e.g., gender, age, ethnicity). Finally, the integrating of various theories (e.g., self-efficacy, decisional balance) to develop the transtheoretical model places these theories at odds with each other within the transtheoretical model. For example, Bandura (1997) stated that stages should reflect qualitative change and provide an invariant and nonreversible sequence. However, people's progression through the stages of change of the transtheoretical model is reversible (i.e., people can relapse), and advancement from one stage to the next does not reflect a qualitative change (Weinstein, Rothman, & Sutton, 1998).

PHYSICAL ACTIVITY RESEARCH EXAMINING THE TRANSTHEORETICAL MODEL

The transtheoretical model was first applied to physical activity in the late 1980s by Sonstroem (1987), and since then its popularity has grown. Over the last decade the model has been used to examine physical activity in cross-sectional studies and to a lesser extent in longitudinal and quasi-experimental intervention studies. In fact, a literature search found more than 50 studies from 1987 to 2000 that have validated, expanded, applied, and challenged the transtheoretical model for physical activity behavior. Culos-Reed and her colleagues (2001) noted that research on physical activity that also has used the transtheoretical model as a theoretical framework can be classified into one of the following three categories: (a) studies that combine the stages of change with the variables in other social-cognitive models, (b) cross-sectional studies that examine various transtheoretical model constructs, and (c) interventions to enhance a physically active lifestyle that are based on the constructs of the model. Studies in each of these three areas are highlighted in the following sections.

Stages of Change and Social-Cognitive Models

An important construct in both the health belief model (Rosenstock, 1990) and protection motivation theory (Maddux & Rogers, 1983) is perceived severity—an individual's feelings about the seriousness of a health condition if it is contracted or not treated. Courneya (1995b) noted that previous research has been unable to find that perceived severity is an important construct for motivation to engage in physical activity. People may agree that being physically inactive can contribute to coronary problems, but there is no link between people's perceptions of the severity of the problem and their tendency to adopt a physically active lifestyle.

Courneya (1995b) suggested that the absence of a relationship between perceptions of severity and motivation to change could be due in part to the tendency for researchers to implicitly adopt a two-stage model of exercise behavior change whereby the population is considered to be either inactive or active. Consequently, he compared perceptions of the severity of a sedentary lifestyle among 270 senior citizens who were classified within the various stages of the transtheoretical model. He found that the perceived severity of the consequences of an inactive lifestyle were less for individuals in the precontemplation stage than for those in the contemplation stage. However, the contemplation stage represented a plateau in that it did not differ from any of the active stages (i.e., preparation, action, maintenance). Courneya concluded that the main function of perceived severity of physical inactivity is to motivate people to seriously consider becoming physically active. This perception of severity is then maintained through the active stages.

In a 3-year longitudinal study, Courneya, Nigg, and Estabrooks (1998) examined the relationships among the theory of planned behavior (see

FIT FACTS

At what age do declines in physical activity levels begin?

Declines begin at age 6 and continue over the life cycle. Approximately 70% of adults over age 45 do not engage in regular exercise.

(Orleans, 2000)

Chapter 14 for a detailed discussion of the theory of planned behavior), stages of change, and physical activity behavior in 131 older adults (aged 60 years and over). Participants completed an initial questionnaire sent by mail that assessed the constructs contained in the theory of planned behavior (i.e., attitude, perceived control, subjective norm, and intention) and the stages of change. Three years later, the participants received a telephone call in which their current exercise stage and behavior were assessed. The researchers found that the theory of planned behavior constructs were significant predictors of exercise change and that exercise behavior was best predicted by intention rather than by stages of change. The authors concluded that their results provided "evidence for the long term predictive validity of the theory of planned behavior in the exercise domain and [question] . . . the necessity of combining both intention and stage in a single predictive model" (p. 355).

Finally, Courneya and Bobick (2000) examined, in a cross-sectional design with 427 college students, the processes and stages of change of the transtheoretical model with the theory of planned behavior constructs. They found that the theory of planned behavior constructs mediated 8 of the 10 relationships between the processes of change and stages of change. Also, perceived behavioral control was predicted by behavioral/environmental processes of changes. In contrast, attitude was predicted by both cognitive/experiential and behavioral processes. The authors concluded that the integrated model produced insights into how (i.e., processes of change) and why (i.e., theory of planned behavior constructs) individuals successfully change their exercise behavior.

168 SECTION FOUR   Models for Involvement in Physical Activity

Cross-Sectional Studies

Marcus and her colleagues were the first to develop self-report instruments to measure the constructs of the transtheoretical model. Through a series of studies they developed measures for the stages of change, self-efficacy, process of change, and decisional balance (Marcus, Selby, et al., 1992 [self-efficacy and stages of change]; Marcus, Rossi, Selby, Niaura, & Abrams, 1992 [pros and cons]; Marcus, Rakowski, & Rossi, 1992 [decisional balance]). Recently, Hausenblas and her colleagues (2001) developed a measure of temptation to not engage in physical activity. Numerous studies have examined various constructs of the transtheoretical model, particularly the stages of change; however, research examining the complete model for physical activity is limited.

One of the few studies to examine all the components of the transtheoretical model (excluding temptation) was undertaken by Nigg and Courneya (1998) with 819 high school students. The students completed measures of decisional balance, self-efficacy, processes of change, and stages of change. The distribution of the sample across the stages of change was 2.1% in precontemplation, 4.2% in contemplation, 28.7% in preparation, 15.7% in action, and 49.3% in maintenance. The study results generally supported the tenets of the transtheoretical model, with the constructs being significant discriminators of at least one stage of change.

Another comprehensive study examining all the constructs within the transtheoretical model was the Gorely and Gordon (1995) research with older Australian adults. Gorely and Gordon also found general support for the model in that the utility of the various processes of change was shown to fluctuate across the stages, that self-efficacy increased systematically from contemplation through maintenance, and that the balance in the importance of the pros and cons for physical activity changed from precontemplation to maintenance.

Important questions about the transtheoretical model revolve around the validity of the various stages. Do contemplators truly differ from precontemplators? Do the latter differ from preparers? If research shows that the answers to these questions are yes, it would provide support for the validity of the transtheoretical model. Measures that have been used to examine differences among individuals classified within the various stages have included objective physical indices (% body fat, VO_2 max) and self-reports of physical activity (e.g., Buxton, Wyse, Mercer, & Hale, 1995; Cardinal, 1997; Hausenblas et al., 1999; Reed et al., 1997). The literature applying the stages of change to exercise behavior does not appear to have achieved consensus on the pattern of stage differences in measures of exercise behavior. The failure to detect common patterns of stage differences may be due to the use of different measures and populations.

For example, in a validation study, Cardinal (1997) examined the validity of the stages of change with 135 adults (M age = 34.7). Participants were classified by stage of change and then compared by their scores on a bicycle submaximal aerobic fitness test, on the Leisure-Time Exercise Questionnaire (see Chapter 2 for a description), and on their body mass index. The results of the study revealed a decrease in body mass index across the stages of change. That is, participants in the precontemplation stage had the highest body mass index scores, and participants in the maintenance stage had the lowest body mass index scores. Also, a linear improvement in submaximal aerobic fitness and self-report of exercise was evidenced across the stages. That is, participants in the precontemplation stage were the least aerobically fit, whereas participants in the maintenance stage were the most aerobically fit. See Figure 15-2 for a graphic display of the results. Cardinal concluded that the study findings offered objective support for the stages of change for exercise behavior.

Intervention Research

Marcus and her colleagues (1992) conducted the first intervention study based on the transtheoretical model. The intervention was designed to increase the adoption of physical activity among 610 community volunteers. At baseline, 39% of the participants were in the contemplation stage, 37% were in the prepara-

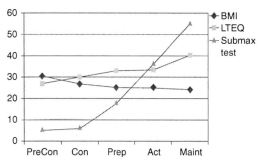

Figure 15-2   Relationship between the stages of change and measures of physical activity.
Note. BMI = body mass index; LTEQ = Leisure-Time Exercise Questionnaire; Submax test = submaximal bicycle test; PreCon = precontemplation; Con = contemplation; Prep = preparation; Act = action; Maint = maintenance. From "Construct Validity of Stages of Change for Exercise Behavior," by B. J. Cardinal, 1997, *American Journal of Health Promotion, 12,* 68–74.

tion stage, and 24% were in the action stage. A 6-week stage-matched intervention consisting of three different sets of self-help materials, a resource manual describing activity options, and weekly fun walks and activity nights were delivered. A subsample of 236 participants were telephoned poststudy to determine the efficacy of the intervention. The results showed that 17% of subjects were in contemplation, 24% were in preparation, and 59% were in action, thus demonstrating that subjects had become significantly more active during the intervention.

In a worksite intervention study, Marcus and her colleagues (1998) used the transtheoretical model constructs to design an intervention to increase the initiation, adoption, and maintenance of physical activity among 1,559 employees. The employees were randomized into either a stage-matched self-help intervention or a standard self-help intervention. Printed physical activity promotion materials were given to subjects at baseline and again 1 month later. The stage-matched group received a motivationally tailored intervention that consisted of five manuals. Each manual focused on one of the stages of change. In comparison, the standard self-help intervention consisted of five manuals on physical activity developed by the American Heart Association. These

manuals were used because they represent typical action-oriented material available to the public. Assessments of motivational readiness for physical activity and time spent in physical activity participation were conducted at the beginning of the program and 3 months later. At the 3-month follow-up, more individuals in the stage-matched group demonstrated positive changes than did individuals in the standard self-help group. Conversely, more individuals in the standard self-help group failed to progress to another stage or even showed regression to an earlier stage compared to the stage-matched group.

Physicians and other health care providers can be important avenues for reaching sedentary individuals and encouraging increases in physical activity levels. Health care providers have the potential to play a vital role in effecting change in the physical activity levels of their patients, with 70% of adults reporting at least one visit to a health care clinic each year (Logsdon, Lazaro, & Meier, 1989). A project called the Provider-Based Assessment and Counseling for Exercise (Calfas et al., 1996; Calfas, Sallis, Oldenburg, & Ffrench, 1997) is one example of a physical activity intervention employing physician counseling that was based on the transtheoretical model and social cognitive theory. In this intervention, 12 primary care physicians provided 3 to 5 minutes of physical activity counseling for their patients. Counseling was tailored to the patients' level of activity and readiness to become active. Evaluation of the Provider-Based Assessment and Counseling for Exercise program at the follow-up assessment of 4 to 6 weeks revealed that patients receiving the counseling increased their duration of walking and demonstrated a greater increase in readiness to become active than did patients not receiving the counseling.

Another physician-based intervention (called the Physically Active for Life intervention; Goldstein et al., 1999) based on the transtheoretical model and social cognitive theory involved 24 physicians who were randomly assigned to either an intervention or control condition. Physicians in the intervention condition provided 3 to 5 minutes of physical activity counseling to their patients. In comparison, physicians in the control condition did not give any physical activity counseling. Results showed that at a 6-week follow-up, individuals in the intervention condition were more likely to be in more advanced stages of motivational readiness for physical activity than were individuals in the control condition. This effect was not maintained at an 8-month follow-up, and the intervention did not produce significant changes in self-reported physical activity. These results suggest that more intensive interventions are needed to promote the adoption of physical activity among sedentary adults in primary care settings.

Summary

This chapter examined the transtheoretical model and its application to physical activity behavior. Over the last decade the transtheoretical model has been increasingly applied to examine physical activity behavior in cross-sectional studies and to a lesser extent in longitudinal and quasi-experimental intervention studies. The core constructs of the model are the stages of change, processes of change, decisional balance, self-efficacy, and temptation. The most frequently examined construct of the transtheoretical model in the exercise domain has been the stages of change construct. The stages of change assesses people's progression and regression through five main stages as they attempt to become physically active: precontemplation (not intending to make changes), contemplation (intending to make changes in the foreseeable future), preparation (immediate intention to change), action (actively engaging in the new behavior), and maintenance (sustaining change over time).

The processes of change are the overt and covert activities that individuals use to alter their experiences and environments to modify behavior change. Decisional balance focuses on the benefits (pros) and costs (cons) of a behavior and is thought to be important in the decision-making process. Self-efficacy is a judgment regarding a person's ability to perform a behavior required to achieve a certain outcome. Finally, temptation is the intensity of a person's urges to engage in a specific habit when in the midst of difficulty.

CHAPTER **16**

Motivational Theories of Exercise and Physical Activity

I Know Not the Course Others May Take; But As for Me, Give Me Liberty or Give Me Death.
(Patrick Henry)

CHAPTER OBJECTIVES

After completing this chapter you will be able to

- Define motivation and explain how it is manifested in behavior.

- Differentiate among the various manifestations of motivation that form the basis for self-determination theory.

- Identify the most commonly cited motives for involvement in physical activity.

- Understand how self-determination theory is used to account for involvement in physical activity.

- Explain the main tenets of personal investment theory.

- Understand how personal investment theory is used to account for involvement in physical activity.

Motivation, a derivative of the Latin word *movere* meaning "to move," is the psychological construct used to account for the *why* of behavior. Why do people select certain options over others?

For example, why do you choose to lift weights or run during your free time rather than watch television? Your *selection* of specific activities over others represents your underlying motivation. Motivation-as-reflected-in-selectivity is illustrated by Patrick Henry's famous quote. Henry's sentiments also illustrate the important role that autonomy/self-determination plays in behavior. A motivational theory that is grounded in the concept of self-determination is one of the theories discussed in this chapter.

Why do you expend effort to accomplish an activity? For example, why do you strain to complete that 10th repetition during a set of bench presses? The *effort* you expend on an activity reflects your underlying motivation. Why do you continue to persist in the face of daunting challenges? For example, you may run four to five times a week, week after week. The *persistence* you demonstrate in that activity also reflects your underlying motivation.

Historically, attempting to better understand motivation—the why of behavior—has been the foundation of psychology. The earliest work was characterized by an emphasis on *instincts* (e.g.,

Key terms	
amotivation	incentive congruency
autonomy	measure
competence	intrinsic motivation
external regulation	introjected regulation
identified regulation	relatedness

172 SECTION FOUR   Models for Involvement in Physical Activity

Freud, 1933) and *drives* (e.g., Hull, 1943). More recently, however, there has been a shift in perspective (or paradigm, as it is also called). Currently, the emphasis is on understanding individual cognitions, perceptions, and emotions. The various theories presented in previous chapters of this book—self-efficacy theory, the health belief model, protection motivation theory, the theories of reasoned action and planned behavior, and the transtheoretical model—all are illustrative of the modern paradigm. Each emphasizes the role that social cognitions, perceptions, and/or emotions play in human behavior. In this chapter, we outline self-determination theory and personal investment theory—two additional approaches that also emphasize social cognitions, perceptions, and emotions.

SELF-DETERMINATION THEORY

Self-determination theory had its origins in the search for understanding the relative influence of intrinsic interest and extrinsic rewards on human behavior. As a consequence, attention was directed toward understanding the function of rewards. A generalization that resulted from the earliest work was that extrinsic rewards can be perceived by a recipient in one of two ways. One way pertains to receiving information about *competence*. Thus, for example, a young child who receives a special treat for playing well in a competition likely would perceive that reward as an affirmation that he or she is competent. Another way pertains to receiving information about *control*. If that same young child is given the special treat as an inducement to participate in the competition, that reward could be perceived to be a bribe to have the child compete. Rewards that convey information to the individual that he or she is highly competent enhance intrinsic motivation. Conversely, however, rewards that convey information that the recipient is no longer fully in control of the reasons for behavior reduce intrinsic motivation.

An anecdote about an old man who lived on a quiet cul-de-sac clearly illustrates the impact of rewards perceived to play a controlling function (Casady, 1974). Unfortunately for the old man, a group of boys began playing games outside his

home. The noise became unbearable. So one day, he called them into his house and told them how much he enjoyed their activity. He also indicated that his hearing was failing and, therefore, offered to pay each of them a quarter if they would return the next day and make even more noise. The boys agreed, returned the next day, made a tremendous amount of noise, and were paid. The process was repeated on the second day. The boys returned, made the required amount of noise, and were paid the agreed-upon fee. The third day, however, the old man told the boys he would have to reduce the fee to 20 cents because he was running out of money. Finally, on the fourth day, he informed the boys that he would again have to reduce their fee—this time to 5 cents each. The boys became angry and informed the old man that it wasn't worth their time and effort to make noise for only 5 cents. So, they told him, they wouldn't return. And the cul-de-sac became quiet once again. As the story illustrates, the boys' motivation for an activity that had been highly enjoyable was reduced after rewards were introduced that were perceived to be controlling their behavior.

Sources of Motivation

Early research emphasized the independence of intrinsic and extrinsic motivation; if one was present, it was assumed that the other could not be. However, when research showed that this approach did not adequately explain human behavior, Deci and Ryan (Deci, 1992; Deci & Ryan, 1985, 1991; R. M. Ryan, 1993) developed self-determination theory. Vallerand and his colleagues (Vallerand, 1997; Vallerand, Blais, Brière, & Pelletier, 1989; Vallerand, Deci, & Ryan, 1987; Vallerand et al., 1992, 1993) have carried out a considerable amount of research in the sport sciences with self-determination theory. In self-determination theory, extrinsic and intrinsic motivation are assumed to fall along a continuum (see Figure 16-1). At one end of the continuum is **amotivation**—the absence of motivation toward an activity.

---

amotivation   The absence of motivation toward an activity.

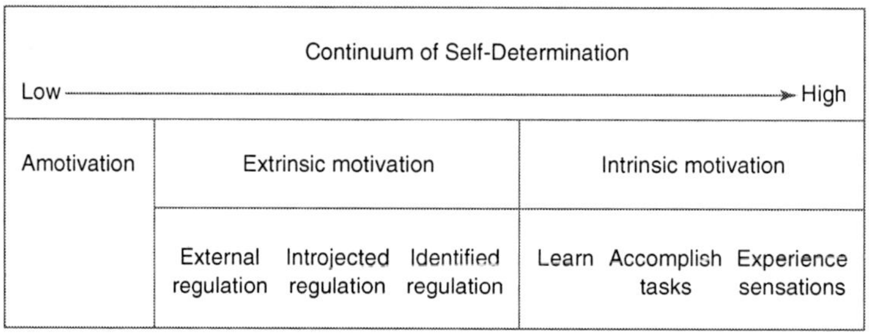

Figure 16-1   A proposed motivational sequence.
Note. Based on Li, 1999, and Vallerand & Losier, 1999.

In the middle of the continuum lies *extrinsic motivation.* According to self-determination theorists, extrinsic motivation is best viewed as multidimensional in nature. One dimension is **external regulation,** the "purest" form of extrinsic motivation. The individual engages in a behavior solely to receive a reward or to avoid punishment. Consider the case of a person who has been told by his or her physician that an immediate consequence of continued inactivity could be hospitalization. So, grudgingly, a program of physical activity is initiated. That person could be considered to be motivated through external regulation.

A dimension of extrinsic motivation that is slightly further along the continuum is **introjected regulation.** It represents the incomplete internalization of a regulation that was previously solely external. To continue our example, our reluctant exerciser might eventually progress to where he or she was no longer at high risk. However, if the person maintained a physical activity program because of a sense of "should" or "must," the source of motivation would be introjected regulation. The distinction between external regulation and introjected regulation lies in the fact that, in the latter case, the individual has begun to internalize the motivation for the behavior.

A third extrinsic motivation dimension that is slightly further along the continuum is **identified regulation.** Here the individual freely chooses to carry out an activity that is not considered to be enjoyable per se but is thought to be important to achieve a personal goal. The individual internalizes

the sentiment "I want to." Identified regulation can be illustrated by an individual who is regularly physically active but does not enjoy the activity in the least; he or she views it as essential for weight control.

At the other extreme on the continuum is **intrinsic motivation,** which is the motivation to do an activity for its own sake or for the pleasure it provides. Vallerand and his colleagues (1989, 1992, 1993) have proposed that intrinsic motivation is also multidimensional in nature. One form is reflected in intrinsic motivation toward *knowledge*—the pleasure of engaging in an activity to learn something new about the activity. An individual who chooses to run a marathon to learn how his or her body will respond under that stress provides an example of this form of intrinsic motivation. For exercise and physical activity contexts, Li (1999) has renamed this dimension of intrinsic motivation *to learn.*

---

external regulation   A type of extrinsic motivation in which an individual engages in a behavior solely to receive a reward or avoid punishment.

introjected regulation   The incomplete internalization of a regulation that was previously solely external.

identified regulation   A type of extrinsic motivation in which an individual freely chooses to carry out an activity that is not considered to be enjoyable but is thought to be important to achieve a personal goal.

intrinsic motivation   The motivation to do an activity for its own sake or for the pleasure it provides.

174 SECTION FOUR Models for Involvement in Physical Activity

A second type is intrinsic motivation toward *accomplishment*. Our would-be marathoner might also want the satisfaction of completing such a long distance. For physical activity and exercise contexts, Li (1999) refers to this dimension as intrinsic motivation *to accomplish tasks*.

Finally, the third type is reflected in intrinsic motivation toward *stimulation*. It represents motivation to experience the pleasant sensations derived from the activity itself. An individual who is physically active because of the bodily sensations accompanying physical activity—sweating, elevated heart rate, muscles responding to the increased load—exemplifies intrinsic motivation toward stimulation. For the context of exercise and physical activity, Li (1999) has renamed this type of intrinsic motivation *to experience sensations*.

The Antecedents of Intrinsic and Extrinsic Motivation

Motives for Physical Activity. Figure 16-2 provides an overview of self-determination theory. According to Deci and Ryan, the various goals or motives that individuals have for an activity are driven by psychological needs that have as their basis a striving toward growth and the actualization of personal potential. It is useful to examine the typical goals or motives for becoming involved in exercise and physical activity because they could have implications for self-determination. According to Willis and Campbell (1992), the following motives have been identified through research: improve or main-tain health and fitness including, for example, the prevention of coronary heart disease; improve physical appearance including, for example, losing body weight; experience a sense of enjoyment, including, for example, obtaining personal satisfaction and fun from an activity; have a social experience such as being in the company of others; and obtain the psychological benefits such as, for example, those documented in Chapters 3 through 6.

Carron and Estabrooks (1999), in their survey of 186 older adults (i.e., >65 years) who were participants at a center devoted to the study of activity and aging, identified four dominant motives. These motives included functional health (e.g., to improve arm strength); psychological well-being (e.g., to feel good); general health (e.g., to stay in shape); and social interactions (e.g., to meet and be with others).

On the basis of other research and a theoretical understanding of incentives for exercise and physical activity, Markland, Hardy, and Ingledew (Markland & Hardy, 1993; Markland & Ingledew, 1997) developed the *Exercise Motivation Inventory* to assess motives for exercise and physical activity. The 14 motives they identified were stress management, revitalization, enjoyment, challenge, social recognition, affiliation, competition, health pressures, ill-health avoidance, positive health, weight management, appearance, strength, and nimbleness.

How do these various motives relate to the self-determination continuum illustrated in Figure 16-1? On the basis of their research, Markland and Ingledew (1997) cautioned that "whilst some motives, such as enjoyment, challenge and appearance im-

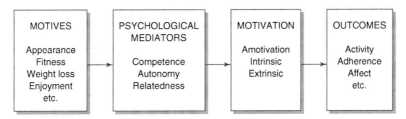

Figure 16-2 The relationships among motives; perceptions of autonomy, competence, and relatedness; intrinsic and extrinsic motivation; and various outcomes.
Note. Based on Li, 1999, and Vallerand & Losier, 1999.

Carron–Hausenblas–Estabrooks:
The Psychology of Physical
Activity

IV. Models for Involvement
in Physical Activity

16. Motivational Theories
of Exercise and Physical
Activity

© The McGraw–Hill
Companies, 2003

200

provement conform reasonably well to conventional definitions of either intrinsic or extrinsic motivation, for others the position is not so obvious" (p. 374). Thus, drawing on self-determination theory, they argued that motives for physical activity "may be better represented by a behavioural regulation continuum ranging from completely non-self-determined to completely self-determined forms of regulation" (p. 374). The relationship between where a motive lies on the behavioral regulation continuum and its implications for affect associated with physical activity as well as adherence is discussed in the following section.

Perceptions of Self-Determination. As Figure 16-2 shows, the motives and goals that an individual has for physical activity are interpreted by the individual in terms of the degree to which they satisfy three psychological needs: autonomy, competence, and relatedness. The need for **autonomy** refers to the desire to be self-initiating in the regulation of personal behavior. If a sense of autonomy is present, intrinsic motivation is facilitated. Both the anecdote about the old man who lived on a quiet cul-de-sac and the quote by Patrick Henry serve to illustrate the importance of autonomy in human behavior.

The need for **competence** reflects the fact that individuals want to interact effectively within their environment. If an activity provides the individual with a sense of competence, intrinsic motivation is facilitated. Thus, for example, if exercisers begin to attend a step-class and discover that they are never able to coordinate their actions with the rest of their classmates, they are likely to seek out another form of physical activity.

Finally, the need for **relatedness** reflects the fact that individuals want to feel connected to other people. When relatedness is perceived to be present, intrinsic motivation is facilitated. It is not surprising

that social experiences and social interactions were identified as among the most important motives for physical activity by both Willis and Campbell (1992) and Carron and Estabrooks (1999).

According to Deci and Ryan (1985), the various types of motivation are intimately related to perceptions of self-determination (see Figure 16-1). When self-determination is absent, amotivation exists. When an activity is undertaken for extrinsic motives, minimal perceptions of self-determination are present. At the extreme end of the continuum, complete self-determination is associated with the various manifestations of intrinsic motivation.

The schematic illustration of self-determination theory presented in Figure 16-2 is also intended to show that the type of motivation the individual possesses (i.e., extrinsic vs. intrinsic) influences the selection of activities, the effort and persistence devoted to those activities, and the affect experienced. The case of the individual informed by his or her physician to become active or be hospitalized provides a useful example. That person's motive is to follow orders and avoid negative consequences. Thus, perceptions of self-determination would likely be minimal, and his or her motivation could be best described as external regulation. Predictions from self-determination theory would be that persistence and effort could be a problem and that the affect associated with the physical activity would not be highly positive. Conversely, the case of the individual training for a marathon just to accomplish the feat also provides a useful example. That person has freely chosen to attempt the task. Therefore, perceptions of self-determination would be maximal. In this case, a prediction from self-determination theory would be that persistence and effort would be high and the affect associated with the activity would be highly positive.

Implications of Self-Determination Theory for Exercise and Physical Activity. The recurring motives associated with involvement in physical activity are to improve or maintain health and fitness (e.g., prevention of coronary heart disease), improve physical appearance (e.g., lose weight), experience a sense of enjoyment (e.g., have fun), enjoy a social experience (e.g., meet others), and obtain the psychological

autonomy   The desire to be self-initiating in the regulation of personal behavior.

competence   The desire to interact effectively within an environment.

relatedness   The desire to feel connected to other people.

176 SECTION FOUR   Models for Involvement in Physical Activity

benefits (e.g., reduced anxiety and depression). Many of these motives seem inherently intrinsic in nature including, for example, experiencing a sense of enjoyment, meeting others, and deriving psychological benefits. Thus, it could be predicted from self-determination theory that those individuals for whom these types of motives are particularly salient would not be at risk from an adherence perspective.

Conversely, however, motives such as improving health and/or physical appearance appear to be more extrinsic in nature. That is, individuals who hold these motives might consider exercise as a "must do" or "should do" type of activity. If so, self-determination theory would predict that adherence to programs of physical activity might be a problem. The critical factor, of course, is the individual's perception. Individuals who truly want to improve health and/or physical appearance might be intrinsically motivated toward accomplishment.

Research on Self-Determination Theory in Physical Activity Settings

Much of the earliest research into intrinsic and extrinsic motivation was carried out in laboratory, school, and sport settings. However, researchers have begun to assess the applicability of the theory in physical activity and exercise settings.

Applicability of Self-Determination Theory. In 1999, Li used self-determination as a conceptual framework to develop the *Exercise Motivation Scale*. After confirming the validity of the scale, Li used it to examine 598 male and female college students who varied in their frequency of exercise. Interestingly, Li found differences between males and females in underlying motivations for exercise. Females reported more intrinsic motivation to learn, intrinsic motivation to experience sensations, intrinsic motivation to accomplish tasks, integrated regulation, and identified regulation (see Figure 16-1 again). Frequent exercisers (i.e., individuals who were active 2 or more times per week) also reported higher levels of intrinsic motivation to learn, instrinsic motivaton to experience sensations, integrated regulation, and identified regulation than did infrequent exercisers (i.e., individuals who were active either one or no times per week).

Li (1999) also tested self-determination theory to determine how perceptions of competence, autonomy, and relatedness about physical activity were related to the various forms of motivation illustrated in Figure 16-1. He found that, consistent with what would be predicted from self-determination theory, perceptions of competence, autonomy, and relatedness were positively related to the three types of intrinsic motivation (i.e., to learn, to accomplish tasks, and to experience sensations) and negatively related to amotivation.

The Theories of Reasoned Action and Planned Behavior. A pivotal construct in the theories of reasoned action and planned behavior is intention (see Chapter 14); it has been found to be a reliable predictor of behavior. Is intention to engage in leisure-time physical activity (and actual leisure-time physical activity) influenced by perceptions of the degree of autonomy present in physical education classes? A sense of minimal personal control in physical education class might transfer to and influence both intention and actual leisure-time physical activity.

Chatzisarantis, Biddle, and Meek (1997) examined this issue with 160 adolescents (average age, 13.5 years). Amotivation was assessed by statements such as "I do not know why I take part in physical education." The researchers assessed the various types of motivation by asking the adolescents to indicate their level of agreement with statements about their participation, such as "because physical education is fun" (intrinsic motivation), "because I will get into trouble if I do not" (external regulation), "because I want to improve in physical education" (identification), and "because I will feel bad about myself if I do not" (introjection).

Chatzisarantis and his colleagues (1997) found that high scores on amotivation were associated with low scores on both intention and leisure-time physical activity. Interestingly, contrary to their predictions, they found that both autonomous and controlling forms of behavioral regulation in physical education classes were associated with both intention and leisure-time physical activity. They proposed that one reason for this finding might be that leisure time represents an environment that causes a shift in the perceived locus of causality from external to internal. "Such shifts can occur when important others who are involved with the motivation of behaviour support choice and do not pressure individuals to behave in particular ways" (Chatzisarantis et al., p. 357). It seems that school—including physical education—is a requirement. Therefore, adolescents attend. However, leisure-time activities are chosen on the basis of enjoyment and autonomy (Deci & Ryan, 1985).

As we pointed out in Chapter 14 in our discussion of the theory of planned behavior, attitudes and subjective norm are assumed to influence the individual's intention, and in turn, intention is assumed to influence behavior. Chatzisarantis and Biddle (1998) examined whether the degree to which individual attitude, subjective norm, and perceived behavioral control are perceived to be self-determined moderates in their influence on intention and physical activity behavior. Two groups of adults (mean age of 40 years) were tested: an autonomy group and a controlling group. The autonomy group endorsed the view that they were active more for reasons related to intrinsic motivation to accomplish tasks (e.g., do well in physical exercise) and intrinsic motivation to experience stimulation (e.g., feelings of enjoyment, excitement, fun). The controlling group, on the other hand, endorsed the view that they were active more for reasons related to external regulation (e.g., bad health) and introjected regulation (e.g., worrying about a health condition). Chatzisarantis and Biddle found that the autonomy group reported being involved in more leisure-time physical activities. Also, although there were no differences in perceptions of subjective norm (i.e., the degree to which important others

had an influence on activity), the autonomy group expressed more positive attitudes about physical activity, felt they had more behavioral control, and had stronger intentions to be active.

When the relationships predicted in the theory of planned behavior were tested for the controlling group and the autonomy group, an interesting pattern of results was obtained. For both groups, intention was found to predict leisure-time behavior. Chatzisarantis and Biddle (1998) pointed out that this result

> is expected especially when time [between intention and behavior] is left unspecified. However, only when behavioural regulation is autonomous [would individuals be] expected to keep engaging in tasks, and therefore to display stable motivation. When behavioural regulation is controlling, individuals [would be] expected to keep engaging in tasks as long as external controls are in effect. (p. 318)

Chatzisarantis and Biddle (1998) also found that for both the controlling and autonomous groups, attitude and perceived behavioral control were reliable predictors of intention to engage in leisure-time activity. However, differences were found in the influence of subjective norm. In the theory of planned behavior (and the theory of reasoned action), subjective norm reflects the individual's perception of social pressures to perform or not perform a particular behavior. Those social pressures arise through the influence of important significant others (e.g., family, friends, physician, priest) or groups (e.g., classmates, teammates, church members). For the controlling group tested by Chatzisarantis and Biddle, subjective norms were positively related to intention to engage in leisure-time physical activity. However, for the autonomy group, subjective norms were negatively related to intention.

These findings offer implications for practice and intervention (Chatzisarantis & Biddle, 1998). If people receive the message (implicitly or explicitly) from important others that they must engage in aerobic exercise because it is necessary—to lose weight, to feel good, or to be healthy, for example—the social influence could be viewed as controlling. As such, it would have a negative impact on intention to be

178 SECTION FOUR   Models for Involvement in Physical Activity

physically active (and ultimately on physical activity behavior itself). Conversely, if the message received is that physical activity can take many forms—walking, cycling, jogging, weight lifting, for example—and all are equally beneficial, the recipient is left with a perception of autonomy in terms of the path chosen. This perception of autonomy will have a positive impact on both intention and behavior.

Stages of Change and Self-Determination. Some of the most salient motives for involvement in exercise and physical activity are—at least on surface examination—extrinsic in nature. Thus, for example, improved fitness, health, or weight loss seem to represent motives that have their origin in either external regulation (i.e., the individual considers activity mandatory to avoid negative consequences), introjected regulation (i.e., the individual feels he or she should exercise), or identified regulation (i.e., the individual engages in an activity that is not enjoyable but is considered important). Mullen and Markland (1997) have suggested that although extrinsic motives may be a catalyst for individuals to become involved in activity programs initially, the focus is likely to change between initial adoption and subsequent adherence. This change of focus implies that a shift occurs in regulation over time and exposure from non-self-determination (i.e., external regulation) through limited self-determination (i.e., introjected regulation) to moderate self-determination (i.e., identified regulation) to complete self-determination (i.e., intrinsic motivation to accomplish tasks, experience sensations, and/or learn). Mullen and Markland used the stages of change in the transtheoretical model (see Chapter 15) as a framework to examine this possibility.

Males and females in their mid-30s ($n = 314$) were tested to determine where they fell on the stages of change continuum (see Table 15-1 for a description of each of the five stages). The degree of self-determination was also assessed using the *Behavioral Regulation in Exercise Questionnaire* (Mullen, Markland, & Ingledew, 1997a, 1997b). This questionnaire provides insight into the degree to which an individual is physically active for reasons of external regulation (i.e., I feel pressure from family/ friends to exercise), in-

People can have a number of motives for engaging in physical activity, including weight loss and personal appearance.
©PhotoDisc/Volume 76/Memorable Moments

trojected regulation (i.e., I feel like a failure when I haven't exercised in a while), identified regulation (i.e., I feel it's important to exercise regularly), or intrinsic motivation (i.e., I enjoy exercise sessions).

Mullen and Markland (1997) found that individuals in the first three stages—precontemplation, contemplation, and preparation—indicated less self-determination than did individuals in the action and maintenance stages. In short, as people progress across the stages of change, their behavioral regulation becomes more self-determined. Motives that have their basis in "ought to," "should," or "must" are replaced by motives that have their basis in "like to" and "enjoy." Mullen and Markland did provide a cautionary note, however. Their study involved a cross-sectional design, so it is not possible to determine whether "those in the later stages of change *became* more self-determined in the regulation of their exercise over time as they increased their stage of change, or whether they reached the later stages of change *because* they were more self-determined from the onset" (p. 358).

Carron–Hausenblas–Estabrooks:
The Psychology of Physical
Activity

IV. Models for Involvement
in Physical Activity

16. Motivational Theories
of Exercise and Physical
Activity

© The McGraw–Hill
Companies, 2003

PERSONAL INVESTMENT THEORY

Researchers have taken a variety of approaches in an attempt to better understand why people are or are not physically active and/or to increase physical activity in the general population. In one general paradigm, the focus has been on the nature of the *situation*. Thus, for example, in Chapter 11 we discussed a study by Brownell, Stunkard, and Albaum (1980) in which the nature of the situation was the principal factor contributing to physical activity involvement. The researchers placed, at a location where people could either take the stairs or ride an escalator, a sign showing a lethargic heavy heart riding up the escalator and a healthy slim heart climbing the stairs. That situational intervention had a substantial effect on the numbers of people choosing to use the stairs.

With another general paradigm, the focus has been on the nature of the *individual*. The stages of change concept that is the foundation of the transtheoretical model focuses on the individual and his or her psychological readiness to engage in physical activity. Thus, for example, in Chapter 15 we discussed a study by Cardinal (1999) that explored individual attitudes and behaviors about physical activity. Specifically, Cardinal investigated whether there are people who reach the termination stage—the final stage in the processes of change. Cardinal found that 16.6% of the 551 adults he examined could be classified within the termination stage—they had been continuously active for five or more years and had 100% self-efficacy in their ability to remain physically active for life.

The theory of personal investment, which was proposed by Maehr (1984; Maehr & Braskamp, 1986), uses a third general paradigm, one that is referred to as an *interaction* approach. In this paradigm, equal emphasis is placed on understanding the individual and understanding the situation. Personal investment theory is an integration of numerous theoretical models and propositions about human behavior.

Five assumptions represent the foundation of personal investment (Maehr & Braskamp, 1986):

- The study of motivation necessarily involves the study of behavior.
- Individual patterns of behavior reflect a personal investment.
- Choice of behavior (i.e., option taken) is important because behavior can take many directions.
- The meaning in a situation determines personal investment.
- The meaning in a situation and its origins can be determined and assessed.

What these five propositions are intended to reflect is that, as humans, we are constantly faced with choices: Take the elevator or use the stairs? Work out or watch television? Go for a run or lift weights? How do you choose to spend your time? What activities do you invest your time and energy in? According to Maehr and Braskamp, people who concentrate on the decisions they make when they are faced with these numerous diverse choices gain insight into the meaning they attach to an activity. In short, people make a personal investment in those options that have more meaning for them.

Components of Meaning

As Figure 16-3 shows, personal investment is influenced by meaning. Figure 16-3 also shows the three interrelated components, or general categories of factors, that in combination determine the meaning attached to various situations or activities. The three components are *sense of self, perceived options,* and *incentives*.

Sense of Self.   Maehr and Braskamp (1986) have defined sense of self as the individual's collection of thoughts, perceptions, beliefs, and feelings about who he or she is. Sense of self is considered to be a relatively stable disposition. Thus, for example, in terms of one aspect of your sense of self, you may perceive yourself to be a marathon runner. As part of that belief, you would likely feel that you put a high premium on fitness, that you work hard at it in order to compete periodically. This sense of self could be expected to remain relatively stable over time.

Within personal investment theory, sense of self is assumed to consist of four facets: social identity,

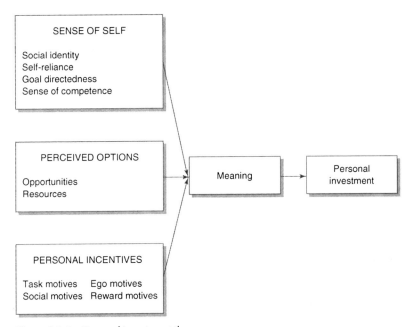

Figure 16-3   Personal investment theory.
Note. Based on Maehr, 1984, and Maehr & Braskamp, 1986.

self-reliance, goal directedness, and sense of competence. Social identity, as the terms suggests, represents the perceptions of the reference groups (i.e., significant others) to which an individual belongs or deems significant. Your sense of self as a marathoner would likely include belonging to that general category of people who place a premium on fitness, train regularly, and compete periodically in distance events.

Self-reliance represents the individual's perceptions of the origins of his or her destiny and degree of personal control present. This concept of self-reliance is similar in nature to the concept of self-determination. Do you as a marathoner perceive that the choice to train and compete periodically is yours to make?

Goal directedness represents an individual's ability to set realistic short- and long-term goals and behave accordingly. Competing periodically in marathons requires goal-directed behavior on your part. The concept of goal directedness is similar to a personality trait referred to as self-motivation that has been linked to adherence in exercise and physical activity programs (Dishman & Gettman, 1980; Dishman & Ickes, 1981).

Finally, sense of competence represents the subjective appraisal of one's ability to be successful in an activity. In our discussion of self-determination theory, we pointed out that individuals seek out activities or make choices or invest their time in those activities in which they exhibit personal competence. Similarly, they avoid activities in which they are incompetent. For you to train and compete in marathons, you would need a sense of competence.

Perceived Options. A second major contributor to meaning is perceived options (see Figure 16-3). Maehr and Braskamp (1986) have defined perceived options as the behavioral alternatives perceived to be available. In order for an individual to attach meaning to an activity, opportunities must be available to carry it out and resources available to overcome any potential barriers. The concept of perceived options is similar to the concept of perceived behavioral control from the theory of planned behavior (see Chapter 14). Again, the example of you as a marathoner is illustrative. You have many roles—student, family member, friend, competitor, and so on. It requires time and energy to carry out these roles effectively. Occasionally the requirements of one role may be in conflict with the requirements of another; that is, you need to train to be an effective marathoner, but you also need to study to be an effective student. What options are available—study/don't study, short/long/no training run? Any activity carried out because of a sense of necessity and not because it is perceived to be acceptable has minimal meaning and, as a consequence, is done with reduced motivation.

Personal Incentives. Personal incentives represent the motivational focus of the activity. According to Maehr and Braskamp (1986), there are four types of incentives or motivational orientations lying within two categories. Task and ego motives fall within the intrinsic category, whereas social and reward motives fall within the extrinsic category. Task incentives reflect a motivation to become involved in an activity for its own sake and/or to master the task. Maehr and Braskamp pointed out that task orientation could be of two types—task absorption and demonstration of competence. Involvement in exercise and physical activity for the sheer pleasure it provides is an example of the former, and training to accomplish some objective (e.g., run a marathon) would be an example of the latter. The concept of task incentives within personal investment theory is highly similar to the self-determination theory's intrinsic motives to learn, to experience sensations, and to accomplish tasks.

Ego incentives reflect motivation to compete and/or gain power. This motive has, as its basis, social comparison. People have an interest in comparing themselves against other people or against socially defined standards of excellence.

Social incentives are based on an individual's desire to affiliate with others and to enter into meaningful cohesive relationships. The concept of social

FIT FACTS

Does anxiety interfere with performance in endurance events?

There is no relationship between either precompetitive cognitive anxiety or precompetitive somatic anxiety and the performance of triathlon competitors.

(Hammermeister & Burton, 1995)

incentives is similar to the concept of relatedness within self-determination theory. A common recurring motive cited for involvement in exercise and physical activity is social experiences and social interactions (Carron & Estabrooks, 1999).

The fourth type of incentive listed by Maehr and Braskamp (1986), reward motives, represents a desire to be involved for social approval or financial benefits (in its development, personal investment theory was oriented toward the workplace). The three manifestations of extrinsic motivation within self-determination theory (see Figure 16-1) are closely related to the concept of extrinsic rewards.

Personal Investment in Exercise and Physical Activity

A considerable amount of research has investigated the specific concepts contained in personal investment theory. For example, we addressed questions about perceived motives for physical activity in relation to self-determination theory in this chapter. The relationship between perceived control (a construct similar to perceived options) and physical activity was addressed in Chapter 14. Here, we examine research by Duda and Tappe (1988, 1989a, 1989b, 1989c) that tested the complete theory of personal investment.

In one study, Duda and Tappe (1988) tested the theory with 47 older adults (average age, 65 years). The personal incentives that were measured included mastery, competition, social affiliation, recognition, health, coping with stress, and fitness. Remember the four components that constitute a

182   SECTION FOUR   Models for Involvement in Physical Activity

person's sense of self: competence, self-reliance, goal directedness, and social identity. Perceptions of general physical competence and perceived health status were used to reflect perceived competence. Psychometrically established tests were used to measure self-reliance and goal directedness, whereas social identity was represented through the activity level of close friends and loved ones. Maehr and Braskamp (1986) considered the concept of perceived options to be dependent on the degree to which incentives held to be important can be satisfied. Therefore, Duda and Tappe calculated an **incentive congruency measure,** which they defined as the difference between the emphasis placed on an incentive and the perceived opportunity to satisfy that incentive.

> **incentive congruency measure** The difference between the emphasis placed on an incentive and the perceived opportunity to satisfy that incentive.

Duda and Tappe (1988) found some support for personal investment theory. Involvement in physical activity was associated with both personal incentives and the degree to which the incentives were considered to be congruent with the focus of the program and sense of self. The incentive found to be most strongly associated with physical activity was recognition.

As Figure 16-3 shows, meaning is assumed to be influenced by sense of self, personal incentives, and social identity. In a second study, Duda and Tappe (1989c) examined whether the personal incentives and sense of self of physically active individuals vary on the basis of differences in age and gender. Male and females classified as young adults (25 to 39 years), middle-aged adults (40 to 60 years), and elderly adults (61 years and older) responded to a set of questions similar to those used in the 1988 Duda and Tappe study. Again, the researchers found support for personal investment theory in that both age and gender influenced the meaning associated with physical activity.

Summary

Motivation is the theoretical construct used to represent the selectivity, intensity, and persistence of behavior. Not surprisingly, therefore, it is a cornerstone of psychological theories of human behavior. Two theories that have been advanced to explain and predict physical activity and exercise behavior are the self-determination theory and the personal investment theory. The former is based on the premise that activities are more likely to be selected and maintained if they satisfy three psychological needs: competence, self-determination, and relatedness. Behavior occurs as a result of either three types of extrinsic motivation (external regulation, introjected regulation, identified regulation) or three types of intrinsic motivation (to learn, to accomplish tasks, and to experience sensations). The various types of motivation are associated with perceptions of self-determination, and perceptions of self-determination are associated with satisfaction and adherence.

Personal investment theory is based on the premise that people tend to focus their energy (i.e., invest in) those activities high in meaning. The meaning attached to a specific choice or activity is influenced by the individual's sense of self, personal incentives, and perceived options (i.e., the opportunities available to satisfy important incentives). Sense of self is derived from four components: social identity, self-reliance, goal directedness, and sense of competence. Similarly, four main types of incentives are possible: task motives, ego motives, reward motives, and social motives.

Research has shown support for both theories. Thus, both theories offer promise as a means of understanding behavior in the context of exercise and physical activity.

15 CHAPTER

Team Cohesion in Sport

KEY TERMS

Coactive sports
Conceptual model of team
 cohesion
Consequences of team cohesion
Determinants of team cohesion
Direct intervention approach
Direct measurement approach
Direction of causality
Group Environment
 Questionnaire
Indirect intervention approach
Indirect measurement approach
Interactive sports
Personal satisfaction
Social cohesion
Task cohesion
Team building
Team cohesion

Intuitively, athletes, coaches, and sport enthusiasts understand that there is more to athletic success than the collective individual skills of the members of a team. Sport psychologists refer to this extra team ingredient as *group* or *team cohesion*. Athletes have described the presence or absence of team cohesion in interesting ways.

Naturally there are going to be some ups and downs, particularly if you have individuals trying to achieve at a high level. But when we stepped in between the lines, we knew what we were capable of doing. When a pressure situation presented itself, we were plugged into one another as a cohesive unit. That's why we were able to come back so often and win so many close games. And that's why we were able to beat more talented teams.

(Michael Jordan, Chicago Bulls; Jordan, 1994, p. 23.)

We've got a funny chemistry here. It's a strange mixture of guys. They're all good guys; I don't have any personal problems with any of them. They are guys who have great talent and good dispositions, but the mix—something's not there. I can't really explain it other than it's a strange chemistry.

(Rob Murphy, Cincinnati Reds; Kay, 1988, p. 15.)

The first quotation was by Michael Jordan, arguably the best professional basketball player in the history of the game, describing how the Chicago Bulls played together as a cohesive unit to defeat more talented teams. The second quotation was by Rob Murphy, a relief pitcher on the 1988 Cincinnati Reds major league baseball team. After being picked to win the National League West in 1988, the Reds suffered a lackluster season. Murphy made his comment in an effort to explain how the talent-laden Reds could have performed so poorly on the field. He attributed it to a "strange chemistry," or what was likely a lack of team cohesion among the players.

The sports pages of local newspapers are full of examples of talented teams that failed to live up to expectations, or less talented teams that performed far above expectations. In sport, it is a well-established principle that a group of individuals working together is far more effective than the same individuals working independently of one another. On a basketball team, there may be several individuals capable of scoring 20 or more points a game. However, in the interest of team success, the coach may require that one or more of these athletes assume nonscoring roles. For example, a point guard has the primary responsibility of setting up plays and getting the offense started, while the power forward must "crash" the boards and get offensive and defensive rebounds. Athletes who play these specialized roles rarely score as many points as shooting guards or forwards. Yet, out of the desire to be "team players," these athletes accept less glamorous roles for the common good of the team. Thus, as a group or team evolves, a certain structure develops. This structure varies from group to group and situation to situation, but it is critical for team success.

When the Pistons won, I thought there might be hope yet for the National Basketball Association. A group of virtual unknowns who played together as a team beat a more talented team built around four superstars. How old-school can you get? There's an art to putting together a team that can compete with any other team. It isn't just a matter of having talent at each position, or matching up with other teams position by position. The players have to be able to play the game, to want to play together, to be willing to pick one another up and to be capable of making intelligent decisions.

(Oscar Robertson (2004) commenting on the Detroit Pistons' defeat of the Los Angeles Lakers in the 2004 NBA Championship series.)

Not only do members of successful teams have the ability to work together (teamwork), they also enjoy a certain attraction to one another. In this respect, it seems logical that teams composed of members who like each other and enjoy playing together will somehow be more successful than teams lacking this quality. In 1979, the Pittsburgh Pirates won the World Series. Their theme was "We Are Family," suggesting that they owed their success to this ability to get along and work together for a common goal. Ironically, the Oakland Athletics of the early 1970s and the New York Yankees in 1978 also enjoyed World Series success, but with well-publicized disharmony within their ranks.

As a social psychological topic, team cohesion ranks as a very important factor for enhancing team performance and feelings of satisfaction among members. It has evolved as a complex concept that requires study and additional research before it can be fully understood and appreciated. In the following sections, team cohesion will be discussed in terms of its defining characteristics, a conceptual model, its measurement, its determinants, its consequences, and its development.

15.1	CONCEPT & APPLICATION

CONCEPT Team cohesion is a multidimensional construct that includes both task and social cohesion.

APPLICATION When considering the development of team cohesion among members of a team, it is important that the coach differentiate between task and social cohesion. These two types of cohesion can be developed simultaneously in a team, or they can be developed independently of each other. It is possible to see an athletic team develop a high degree of social cohesion, yet not enjoy athletic success due to poor task cohesion.

Defining Characteristics of Team Cohesion

Albert Carron, a prominent sport social psychologist, defined group cohesion as "a dynamic process which is reflected in the tendency for a group to stick together and remain united in the pursuit of goals and objectives" (Carron, 1982, p. 124). Because an athletic team is a group, Carron's definition of group cohesion applies equally well as a definition for **team cohesion.** Intuitively, we know that team cohesion is the elusive ingredient that changes a disorganized collection of individuals into a team.

Fundamental to the study of team cohesion is the understanding of group dynamics. Members of a team or group begin to interact with each other the moment the group is first formed. Once a group is formed, it ceases to interact with outside forces in the same manner that a collection of individuals would. The team becomes an entity in and of itself. From a Gestalt perspective, the whole (group or team) is greater than the sum of its parts.

Over the past 20 years, research on team cohesion has made it clear that one must understand two basic concepts in order to understand the relationship between cohesion and team behavior. The first is the distinction between task and social cohesion, and the second is the distinction between direct and indirect measurement of cohesion.

Task and Social Cohesion

Task and social cohesion are two independent components of team cohesion. Failure to discriminate between the two can result and has resulted in hopelessly confusing results relative to the relationship between athletic performance and team cohesion. **Task cohesion** is the degree to which members of a team work together to achieve a specific and identifiable goal. We see task cohesion on display when a baseball team turns a double play, executes a hit-and-run, or completes a double steal. We see task cohesion on display when a basketball team runs a motion offense or sets up a full-court zone defense. We see task cohesion on display when a volleyball team executes the multiple-attack offense, or defends against the same.

Social cohesion is the degree to which the members of a team like each other and enjoy personal satisfaction from being members of the team. The independence of task cohesion and social cohesion was easily observed in the example of the world champion New York Yankees baseball team of 1978. This was a team that could turn the double play, hit the cut-off man, advance runners, and work together on the field of play better than any other team in baseball. Yet, this was also a team whose members did not like one another. Team members fought with each other, cliques were formed, and angry words were exchanged both privately and through the media.

If a study had been conducted on the 1978 Yankees to relate task cohesion and team performance, a very high and positive relationship would have been observed. Yet, if a study had been conducted to relate social cohesion and team performance, a very strong negative relationship would have been observed. If care were not taken to distinguish between the two different kinds of team cohesion in this example, confusing results would have been obtained. Such has been the case with numerous early studies on the topic of team cohesion and athlete behavior.

The Los Angeles Lakers of the National Basketball Association (NBA) provide a recent example of this paradoxical relationship. Before the break-up of the team in 2004, the tandem of Shaquille O'Neal and Kobe Bryant was instrumental in leading the L.A. Lakers to three NBA championships in five years. This feat was accomplished even though these two great athletes did not like each other (Broussard, 2004).

Direct and Indirect Measurement of Cohesion

Just as many early studies failed to differentiate between task and social cohesion, many also failed to differentiate between the two basic approaches to measuring team cohesion (Carron, 1980; Cox, 1985). The **indirect measurement approach** to assessing team cohesion tries to get at team cohesion by asking each team member how she feels about every other member of the team on some basic question (e.g., How much do you like the different members on your team?). Summed scores from team members would represent a measurement of team cohesion. The **direct measurement approach** to assessing team cohesion is direct in the sense that players are asked to indicate how much they like playing for the team (individual attraction) and how well they feel the team functions as a unit (group integration). Research using the indirect approach has generally failed to find a meaningful relationship between team cohesion and team or individual behavior. As with task and social cohesion, it is of critical importance that the approach to measuring team cohesion be reported, as results could vary greatly as a function of the approach. The indirect approach to measuring team cohesion is very rare in sport psychology research today.

A Conceptual Model of Team Cohesion

Building upon the distinction between task and social cohesion and focusing upon the direct measurement approach, Widmeyer, Brawley, and Carron (1985) developed the **conceptual model of team cohesion.** As illustrated in figure 15.1, the conceptual model is based on an interaction between the athlete's group orientation (social versus task) and the athlete's perception of the team. Task and social cohesion are relatively easy concepts to understand, given our discussion on their distinction. Conversely, perception of team is not quite so easy to understand. When an athlete conceptualizes team cohesion, is he thinking about the team as a collective whole (including himself), or is he thinking about his individual attraction to the team (he likes the style of play) and his individual

FIGURE 15.1 | Widmeyer, Brawley, and Carron's conceptual model of team cohesion.

Group orientation	Athlete's perception of team: Group integration	Athlete's perception of team: Individual attraction
Social	Bonding to the team as a whole to satisfy social needs (GI-S)	Attraction to team and team members to satisfy social needs (ATG-S)
Task	Bonding to the team as a whole to satisfy task completion needs (GI-T)	Attraction to team and team members to satisfy task completion needs (ATG-T)

Source: From Widmeyer, W. N., Brawley, L. R., and Carron, A. V. *The measurement of cohesion in sport teams: The group environment questionnaire.* Copyright © 1985, Spodym Publishers. Used with permission of the publisher.

| 15.2 | CONCEPT & APPLICATION |

CONCEPT The conceptual approach to looking at team cohesion takes into consideration task and social cohesion as well as the athletes' perceptions of the team.

APPLICATION The conceptual model takes into consideration the multidimensional nature of team cohesion. If the coach looks at team cohesion from a multidimensional perspective, it will be easier to understand the positive influence of team cohesion on athletic behavior. Social cohesion is different from task cohesion, and individual attraction to the group is different from group integration.

attraction to team members (they are good friends)? If he is thinking of the team as a unit, this is called group integration (GI). If he is thinking about his attraction to the team or to individual members, this is called individual attraction, or attraction to group (ATG). The combination of the two kinds of group orientation and two kinds of perception yields four different dimensions of team cohesion:

1. Group integration–social (GI-S)
2. Group integration–task (GI-T)
3. Individual attraction to the group–social (ATG-S)
4. Individual attraction to the group–task (ATG-T)

Measurement of Team Cohesion

A number of inventories have been developed for measuring team cohesion in sport. An incomplete list of inventories includes the Sports Cohesiveness Questionnaire (SCQ; Martens & Peterson, 1971); the Team Cohesion Questionnaire (TCQ; Gruber & Gray, 1981); the Sport Cohesion Instrument (SCI; Yukelson, Weinberg, & Jackson, 1984); the Group Environment Questionnaire (GEQ; Widmeyer, Brawley, & Carron, 1985); and the Team Psychology Questionnaire (TPQ; Partington & Shangi, 1992).

Of these five inventories, the **Group Environment Questionnaire** (GEQ) has been sport psychologists' primary inventory of choice over the last 15 years. The GEQ is composed of 18 items that measure the four team cohesion dimensions as illustrated in figure 15.1. Based upon the conceptual model of team cohesion, the GEQ devotes four items to measuring the GI-S dimension, five to the GI-T dimension, five to the ATG-S dimension, and four to the ATG-T dimension. Each item is anchored to an eight-point Likert Scale (1 = strongly disagree, 8 = strongly agree). Studies by Carron and Spink (1992) and Li and Harmer (1996) confirmed the four-dimension factor structure of the GEQ, while an important study by Schutz, Eom, Smoll, and Smith (1994) failed to confirm its factor structure. The Schutz et al. (1994) investigation did not call into question the four-factor conceptual model of team cohesion, but it did call into question the ability of the GEQ to accurately measure these four factors. Notwithstanding the results of this investigation, the GEQ has continued to be used extensively by researchers and practitioners. Recently, a French version of the GEQ has been developed (Heuzé & Fontayne, 2002).

Determinants of Team Cohesion

Carron (1982) proposed a sport-specific framework for studying team cohesion determinants and consequences. As illustrated in figure 15.2, the basic conceptual framework is composed of four classes of determinants and two classes of consequences. The basic notion is that there are certain factors that lead to or determine team cohesion, and certain consequences associated with having or not having team cohesion. In this section we

FIGURE 15.2 | Illustration showing determinants and consequences of team cohesion.

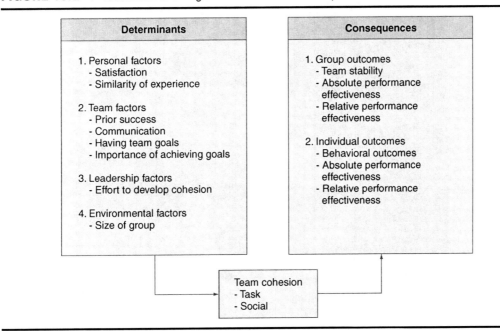

Source: From Carron, A. V. (1982). "Cohesiveness in sport groups: Interpretations and considerations." *Journal of Sport Psychology,* 4(2), 131. Copyright 1982 by Human Kinetics Publishers. Adapted by permission.

will focus attention upon the **determinants of team cohesion;** in the following section, upon the consequences of team cohesion.

In an important study reported by Widmeyer and Williams (1991), factors that determine team cohesion among female collegiate NCAA Division I golfers were investigated and reported. In this investigation, team cohesion was measured using the multidimensional GEQ. The results of this investigation revealed that each specific determinant shown in figure 15.2 was predictive of some aspect of team cohesion. The strongest predictor of team cohesion, however, was **personal satisfaction.** For intercollegiate golfers, the best way to develop team cohesion is by cultivating a personal feeling of satisfaction toward the team and team members.

Widmeyer and Williams' research is a benchmark study because it systematically studied the relationship between Carron's (1982) taxonomy of team cohesion determinants and team cohesion among intercollegiate golfers. Whether the specific findings of Widmeyer and Williams can be generalized to team sports such as volleyball, basketball, and football remains to be seen. Is personal satisfaction with the team as a whole and members generally as strong a predictor of team cohesion in basketball as it is in golf? This is an important research question, since team cohesion is generally believed to be of greater consequence in team sports than in individual sports.

Although the Widmeyer and Williams study was the most comprehensive investigation to date dealing with determinants of team cohesion, other studies have focused upon specific antecedents. For example, team stability as an antecedent of team cohesion has been studied by Donnelly, Carron, and Chelladurai (1978), with the general

A tremendous amount of task cohesion and coordinated play is required to execute the "multiple attack" in volleyball. Courtesy Ball State University Sports Information.

finding that team stability fosters cohesion. Similarly, research by Widmeyer, Brawley, and Carron (1990) suggests that team cohesion decreases as team or group size increases.

Communication among members of an interactive team is an important determinant of team cohesion (Eccles & Tenenbaum, 2004; Wickwire, Bloom & Loughead, 2004). As you will recall, effective communication was identified in chapter 3 as an important characteristic of successful leaders. Here we focus upon the athletes and upon the ways effective communication leads to cohesion

CONCEPT & APPLICATION

15.3

CONCEPT   The feeling of personal satisfaction with the team as a whole and members generally is the strongest predictor of team cohesion in intercollegiate golf.

APPLICATION   Other determinants of team cohesion, such as team success, group size, and interpersonal communication, are of small consequence in developing team cohesion compared to personal satisfaction. Golf coaches who value team cohesion should focus on developing a feeling of satisfaction among team members.

CONCEPT & APPLICATION

15.4

CONCEPT   Team cohesion is related to size and stability of a team or group.

APPLICATION   It is difficult to maintain team cohesion in teams or groups that are constantly changing and increasing in size. Coaches and leaders who wish to increase cohesion among members must avoid constant turnover and keep groups or subgroups relatively small.

among members, which leads to performance effectiveness. Wickwire et al. (2004) reported results of a qualitative investigation in which the athlete-athlete dyad in male international-level beach volleyball was studied. Of interest were identified factors and elements of the dyad that characterize the effective elite doubles volleyball team. Like doubles in tennis, doubles in sand volleyball requires superb athleticism and teamwork in order to be successful. Factors that emerged as being critical to good teamwork included mental strength, physical skill and strength, time with partner, personality traits, interpersonal development, and the ability to communicate verbally and nonverbally during play. The athletes identified communication and player cohesion as being codependent and equally important. One important component of team cohesion is shared knowledge, and the way that knowledge is shared is through communication (Eccles & Tenenbaum, 2004).

Consequences of Team Cohesion

Athletic Performance

Most research on **consequences of team cohesion** has focused upon performance. The primary question that has been asked is to what degree team cohesion leads to improved team or individual performance. This basic question is also reflected in figure 15.2, where performance is described in terms of individual and group outcomes. Absolute and relative performance effectiveness refer to the difference between winning or losing a contest, as opposed to performing better or worse than the last time. Having a team's performance reduced to a slash in the win or loss column is an absolute measure of performance effectiveness, whereas comparing a team's performance to how well it performed in the last outing is a relative measure of performance effectiveness. A similar dichotomy can be developed for the performance of individual sport athletes. From an absolute performance perspective, a golfer may not have won a golf tournament, but from a relative perspective, she may have improved her score significantly.

Research has consistently shown that a significant relationship exists between team cohesion and athletic performance (Carron & Dennis, 1998; Carron, Coleman, Wheeler, & Stevens, 2002; Grieve, Whelan, & Meyers, 2000; Lowther & Lane, 2002; Mullen & Cooper, 1994; Widmeyer, Carron, & Brawley, 1993). This observed relationship is much stronger when task cohesion as opposed to social cohesion is involved, and when interactive as opposed to coactive sports are involved. **Interactive sports** are those team sports, such as volleyball, basketball, and football, that require members of the team to interact with one another. **Coactive sports** are those activities, such as bowling, archery, and riflery, that do not require members of the team to interact with each other for team success.

A meta-analysis published by Carron et al. (2002) is very supportive of the cohesion-performance relationship. This is a very important study, as it shows the strength of the relationship between team cohesion and athletic performance in numerous situations and conditions from 1967 to 2000. For example, it shows relationships using all reported studies, as well as those that used only the Group Environment Questionnaire (GEQ). When the GEQ was used, the results show (a) a much stronger relationship between cohesion and performance for men compared to women, (b) a slightly stronger relationship for task cohesion compared to social cohesion, and (c) a much stronger relationship for subjective as opposed to objective measures of performance. It is generally believed that a stronger relationship exists between team cohesion and performance for interactive sports compared to coactive sports, but this is not entirely clear in the meta-analysis. The average effect size (measure of strength of relationship) is actually larger for coactive teams compared to interactive teams. It is likely,

however, that this is due to the small number of studies that looked at coactive teams.

An ethnographic study reported by Holt and Sparkes (2001) is interesting because 13 members of a male soccer team were studied across an entire season. The focus of this investigation was not upon performance but upon factors that are believed to lead to team cohesion. Specifically, the results of the study showed that the athletes improved across the course of the eight-month season in role acceptance, clear and meaningful personal goals, unselfishness, willingness to sacrifice for the team, and use of positive communication. These are all factors that are believed to contribute to team cohesion.

It is often difficult to find a measurable relationship between team cohesion and objective performance. This was generally true with a study reported by Bray and Whaley (2001) with high school basketball teams in terms of three of four subscales measured by the GEQ. However, it was interesting to note that the one significant relationship was between social cohesion and objective individual performance. It was further demonstrated that expended effort mediated the relationship. In other words, social cohesion leads to individuals' trying harder, which leads to increased basketball performance. So, even though social cohesion may not have a direct effect on improved performance, it may have an indirect effect through expended effort.

In the sections that follow, other consequences of team cohesion will be discussed. These include direction of causality for the cohesion-performance relationship, improving group self-efficacy, predicting future participation, homogeneity among starters and nonstarters, disruptive effects of self-handicapping, and team momentum.

Direction of Causality for the Cohesion-Performance Relationship

As was briefly mentioned above, numerous investigations have verified that a significant and positive relationship exists between direct measures of

CONCEPT & APPLICATION

15.5

CONCEPT Interactive sport teams, such as soccer, volleyball, and basketball, that enjoy high levels of task cohesion are more likely to experience performance success than equally skilled teams that are low in task cohesion.

APPLICATION It is especially important for interactive teams to work hard to develop task cohesion among members of the team. Coaches should

also encourage the development of social cohesion on interactive teams and both task and social cohesion on coactive teams, but these things are less critical to team success than task cohesion is for interactive teams. Coaches should use the GEQ or some other team cohesion measurement instrument of choice to monitor task and social cohesion of interactive team members.

---

team cohesion and performance in both individual and team sports. The issue of **direction of causality,** however, has been a difficult issue to resolve. Does team cohesion lead to or cause successful performance, or does successful performance lead to or cause high team cohesion? As you might guess, this is not a good "either/or" question. It is likely that high team cohesion leads to high performance, but it is also likely that successful performance leads to perceptions of team cohesion. The critical issue is which direction is the most dominant. We would like to think that the direction from team cohesion to successful performance is most dominant. Almost all athletes, however, have experienced the "halo effect" of success. When your team is winning, it is a lot easier to feel at one with your team and with your teammates.

> It was an easy season for me. . . . I'm a lot more comfortable right now . . . when you're winning everybody loves you. (Wesley Stokes, former University of Missouri–Columbia basketball player; Thompson, 2002)

The direction of the relationship between team cohesion and athletic performance has been a subject of discussion and academic debate for over 25 years. Initially, it was assumed that team cohesion leads to improved performance, but then a number of well-controlled studies started to suggest just the opposite, that performance leads to cohesion. Based upon the Carron et al. (2002) meta-analysis, it seems safe to say that a moderately

FIGURE 15.3 | Team cohesion leads to increased team performance, but increased team performance also leads to an increase in team cohesion.

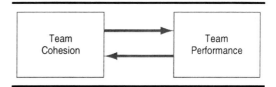

strong relationship exists between team cohesion and athletic performance regardless of direction of relationship, with the strongest relationships being observed when the two are measured concurrently. This relationship is illustrated in figure 15.3. It should be no surprise to anyone, however, that winning an athletic contest would lead to perceptions of increased cohesion among members and that losing a contest would lead to perceptions of reduced team cohesion (Boone, Beitel, & Kuhlman, 1997; Kozub & Button, 2000; Matheson, Mathes, & Murray, 1997).

Improving Group Self-Efficacy

The importance of individual self-efficacy in developing self-confidence and in skilled performance was introduced in chapter 5. Research by Kim and Sugiyama (1992) likewise points to the importance of group or team self-efficacy in helping teams

15.6 CONCEPT & APPLICATION

CONCEPT   The winning, and even more, the losing, of an athletic contest have a strong effect upon an athlete's perceived team cohesion. This effect may even be stronger than the effect that precompetitive team cohesion has upon team performance, but it in no way minimizes the importance of developing team cohesion in sport teams. Team cohesion, especially task cohesion, leads to improved performance of interactive team sports.

APPLICATION   It is useful to understand that winning or losing can influence perceived team cohesion, but the coach must not allow this information to reduce his efforts to develop team cohesion among members of an athletic team. Team cohesion does lead to improved performance of teams that are required to work together to achieve a common goal.

believe that they will be successful. Teams that have developed high levels of team cohesion tend to exhibit high levels of group efficacy as well. This effect is stronger for task cohesion than for social cohesion (Kozub & McDonnell, 2000).

Predicting Future Participation

For young athletes especially, it is important that the sport experience lead to the expectation of continued participation. Sport participants who exhibit high levels of social cohesion also exhibit high scores in the expectation that they will participate in sport during the following season. Thus, social cohesion is a predictor of the intention to continue sport involvement (Spink, 1995). This prediction is undoubtedly related to the further observation that high levels of team cohesion are related to lowered state anxiety (Prapavessis & Carron, 1996). Consistent with the McClelland-Atkinson model of motivation, individuals low in state anxiety are more likely to continue sports participation.

Homogeneity of Team Cohesion

It is not enough that starters alone exhibit high levels of team cohesion. Research indicates that homogeneity of team cohesion among both starters and nonstarters is an important predictor of successful team performance. Spink (1992) showed that successful volleyball teams are characterized by high levels of team cohesion on the part of both starters and nonstarters. Conversely, less successful

teams are characterized by a lack of homogeneity (agreement) in team cohesion between starters and nonstarters. This observation suggests that the coach must develop high team cohesion among all the members of a team, and not just the starters.

Moderator of the Disruptive Effects of Self-Handicapping

Introduced in chapter 14, self-handicapping represents the strategies athletes use to proactively protect their self-esteem by creating excuses for their performance in forthcoming events through adopting or advocating impediments for success. Typical excuses might include missing practice due to injury or illness, partying and loss of sleep, school commitments or distractions, and family commitments or distractions. If success follows, the athlete or athletes can always internalize (take credit for) the victory, but if failure follows, they will have numerous external explanations as to why they have failed. This behavior causes disruption in the athlete's preparation for competition, and is therefore referred to as *self-handicapping*. Research (Carron, Prapavessis, & Grove, 1994; Hausenblas & Carron, 1996) indicates that team cohesion has a moderating effect on the trait of self-handicapping. Athletes high on the trait of self-handicapping rated the severity of disruption associated with it as low when team cohesion was low, but high when team cohesion was high. There is something about being a member of a cohesive group that makes athletes sensitive to disruptions associated with self-handicapping.

CONCEPT & APPLICATION

15.7

CONCEPT In addition to increased athletic performance, there are numerous other positive consequences associated with increased team cohesion. These include collective self-efficacy, sports retention, sensitivity to disruptive effects of self-handicapping, psychological momentum, and mood.

APPLICATION Even if increased team performance is not a direct result of a coach's efforts to increase team cohesion, there are many other positive consequences associated with enhanced team cohesion. Coaches should work to increase the task and social cohesion among members of athletic teams.

Development of social cohesion is an important goal for an athletic team. Courtesy University of Missouri–Columbia Sports Information.

Effects of Team Cohesion on Psychological Momentum

Research by Eisler and Spink (1998) demonstrated, using high school volleyball players, that a high level of task cohesion is associated with perceived psychological momentum. As a psychological construct, perceived momentum was introduced in chapter 5. Here we learn that teams that enjoy a high level of task cohesion are more likely to enjoy the benefits of psychological momentum. There are times in an athletic contest at which the momentum seems to be in one's favor. For teams that are high in task cohesion, this perception of psychological momentum is likely to be more pronounced. Thus, we have another positive consequence of team cohesion.

Mood and Emotion

Athletes who belong to a cohesive team enjoy increased levels of positive mood, particularly in terms of vigor. Lowther and Lane (2002) observed that pregame measures of team cohesion are positively related to pregame measures of positive mood in male soccer players. Research also shows an association between task cohesion and directional state anxiety. Eys, Hardy, Carron, and Beauchamp (2003) measured competitive state anxiety in young athletes (soccer, rugby, field hockey) prior to a contest and task cohesion after the same contest. Using directional anxiety scores, the athletes were divided into two extreme groups, classified as viewing anxiety as being facilitative or debilitative to performance. The researchers then attempted to correctly classify the athletes as being facilitative or debilitative as a function of post game task cohesion measures. Results showed that athletes who perceived their anxiety to be facilitative to good performance tended to have higher task cohesion scores. Conversely, athletes who perceived their anxiety to be debilitative to good performance tended to be low in task cohesion.

Developing Team Cohesion

Given that team cohesion is an important characteristic of successful teams, how can it best be developed? In this section we will address that important question in three different ways. First, we will discuss the development of team cohesion as a process. Second, we will discuss team building as a way to develop team cohesiveness among team members. Finally, we will identify specific interventions calculated to enhance team cohesion.

Team Cohesion as a Process

Very early, Tuckman (1965) described four basic stages that a team must pass through in order to emerge as a cohesive unit. These four stages include forming, storming, norming, and performing. In the *forming* stage, the athletes experience the excitement of new relationships and getting together with teammates for a common goal or cause. In the *storming* stage, the athletes struggle with the frustrations of trying to learn a new team system and of getting acquainted with teammates with whom they may have little in common. During the *norming* stage, members of the team start agreeing upon common goals and establishing what the norms of acceptable and good performance are. Finally, during the *performing* stage, the team is ready to perform as a cohesive unit. As we look at these four stages of development, it should be clear that team cohesion should be at its lowest during the forming and storming stages. For this reason, if team cohesion is measured during one of these two early stages, one should expect it to be very low. This would be consistent with measuring team cohesion during spring training or some other preseason period of time. If you want to study the relationship between team cohesion and team performance, you should not assess team cohesion during the forming or the storming stage. The best time to measure team cohesion would be during the norming or the performing stage. If team cohesion were low during the performing stage, this could indicate that the team had not progressed as it should, and in reality might not be in the performing stage. Team building is a process that should be helpful for a team to emerge from Tuckman's four stages as a cohesive unit (Bloom, Stevens, & Wickwire, 2003).

Team Building

Team building is described by Newman (1984, p. 27) as a process to "promote an increased sense of unity and cohesiveness and enable the team to function together more smoothly and effectively."

Thus, team building is a process that should lead to cohesiveness among members of a team. In this regard, the entire March issue of volume 9 (1997) of the *Journal of Applied Sport Psychology* was devoted to the topic of team building. From this edition we learn that there are numerous approaches to team building. Here we will discuss three of these approaches. However, it is important first to point out that team building is supported by research. Using a physical challenges approach to team building, Ebbeck and Gibbons (1998) demonstrated that sixth- and seventh-grade physical education students could increase their perceived global self-worth, athletic competence, physical appearance, social acceptance, scholastic competence, and behavioral conduct.

Yukelson (1997) proposed a team building approach that he referred to as a direct intervention approach. In the **direct intervention approach,** the sport psychologist works directly with athletes and employees to empower them, through a series of educational seminars and experiences, to develop a shared vision, unity of purpose, collaborative teamwork, individual and mutual accountability, team identity, team cohesiveness, open and honest communication, and trust at all levels. Dunn and Holt (2004) reported on the effectiveness of a personal-disclosure, mutual-sharing approach to team building that would be direct in nature. Results showed that athletes increased in confidence, trust, and feelings of closeness to teammates.

Carron, Spink, and Prapavessis (1997) proposed a team building approach that they referred to as an indirect intervention approach. In the **indirect intervention approach,** the sport psychologist teaches coaches and managers to conduct team building with their athletes and employees. This particular team-building approach is delivered in four stages. The first three stages occur in a single workshop, while the fourth involves the application of specific interventions learned in the workshop. The four stages of this program include the introductory phase, the conceptual phase, the practical phase, and the intervention

phase. During the *introductory phase,* the coaches learn about the general benefits of group cohesion. During the *conceptual phase,* the coaches learn to conceptualize team cohesion as a direct result of the distinctiveness of the group environment, role clarity, conformity to group norms, cooperation, goal setting, and team sacrifices.

Finally, Smith and Smoll's (1997a) Coach Effectiveness Training Program (CET) is identified as an excellent team-building program. Recall that the CET program was first introduced in chapter 3, when we discussed leadership in sport. The purpose of the CET program is to teach coaches how to develop teams that have a positive team climate and to develop athletes who experience true satisfaction and feel interpersonal attraction to the team and team members. Thus, the CET program is an indirect team building program, in that the coach learns how to deliver the program to her own athletes.

Specific Interventions Designed to Enhance Team Cohesion

In the process of team building, specific interventions are learned that, if applied, will lead to increased team cohesion among team members. Ten specific interventions and strategies for developing team cohesion are listed below:

1. *Acquaint each player with the responsibilities of other players.*   This can be accomplished by allowing players to play other positions during practices. This will give them an appreciation for the importance of other team players. For example, a spiker in volleyball who complains of poor setting should be given the chance to set once in a while.

2. *As a coach or teacher, take the time to learn something personal about each athlete on the team.*   People will come to appreciate and cooperate with those who know little things about them, such as a girlfriend's name, a birthday, or a special hobby.

3. *Develop pride within the subunits of large teams.*   For example, in football, the various special teams need to feel important to the team and take pride in their accomplishments. For smaller units such as basketball teams, this may not be so critical. However, the team as a whole should develop pride in its accomplishments.

4. *Develop a feeling of "ownership" among the players.*   Individual players need to feel that the team is *their* team and not the coach's team. This is accomplished by helping players become involved in decisions that affect the team and them personally. Individual players need to feel that their voice will be heard.

5. *Set team goals and take pride in accomplishments.*   Individuals and teams as a whole must have a sense of direction. Challenging but obtainable goals should be set throughout the season. When these goals are reached, players should collectively be encouraged to take pride in their accomplishments and then set more goals.

6. *Make sure that each player on the team learns his role and comes to believe it is important.*   In basketball, only five players can be on the floor at one time. The process of keeping the other seven players happy and believing that they too are important is one of the great challenges of teaching and coaching. Each player on the team has a unique role. If players do not feel this, they will not feel they are part of the team, which will detract from team unity.

7. *Do not demand or even expect complete social tranquility.*   While it is not conducive to team cohesion to allow interpersonal conflicts to disrupt team unity, it is equally unrealistic to expect interpersonal conflicts to be completely absent. Anytime individuals are brought together in a group, there is potential for conflict. The complete elimination of any friction may actually suggest a complete lack of interest in group goals.

8. *Since cliques characteristically work in opposition to the task goals of a team, avoid their formation.*   Cliques often form as a result of (1) constant losing, (2) players' needs not being met, (3) players not getting adequate opportunities to play, and (4) coaches who promote the development of cliques through the use of "scapegoats" or personal prejudice.

9. *Develop team drills and lead-up games that encourage member cooperation.*   Many drills are designed solely for the purpose of skill development. Many other drills must be developed that teach athletes the importance of reliance upon teammates. For example, in basketball, drills that emphasize the importance of teammate assists could be emphasized.

10. *Highlight areas of team success, even when the team loses a game or match.*   Since we know from the literature that performance affects feelings of satisfaction and cohesion, the coach must capitalize on this. If a volleyball team played good team defense in a losing effort, point this out to them.

Summary

Group or team cohesion is defined by Carron as "a dynamic process which is reflected in the tendency for a group to stick together and remain united in the pursuit of goals and objectives." Task and social cohesion are two independent components of team cohesion. Task cohesion reflects the degree to which members work together to achieve a specific goal. Social cohesion reflects the degree to which members of a team like each other and enjoy being members of the team. Both a direct and an indirect approach have been used to measure team cohesion.

The conceptual model of team cohesion is based upon an interaction between the athlete's group orientation (social versus task) and the athlete's perception of the team in terms of individual attraction and group integration. The Group Environment Questionnaire measures four team cohesion dimensions and is based upon the conceptual model of team cohesion.

Determinants of team cohesion include personal satisfaction, team factors, leadership factors, and size of group. Consequences of team cohesion include team stability, behavioral outcomes, and absolute and relative performance effectiveness.

Relative to team and individual performance, research has consistently shown that task cohesion leads to enhanced performance in interactive teams. Based upon the Carron et al. (2002) meta-analysis, it seems safe to say that a moderately strong relationship exists between team cohesion and athletic performance regardless of direction of relationship, with the strongest relationships being observed when the two are measured concurrently.

In addition to increased athletic performance, there are numerous other positive consequences associated with increased team cohesion. These include collective self-efficacy, sports retention, sensitivity to the disruptive effects of self-handicapping, psychological momentum, and positive mood.

The development of team cohesion may be characterized as a process that passes through the four stages of forming, storming, norming, and performing. Team building is described by Newman as a process to "promote an increased sense of unity and cohesiveness and enable the team to function together more smoothly and effectively." Direct and indirect team-building intervention approaches were discussed. Finally, 10 specific interventions were identified that are instrumental in developing team cohesion in athletic teams.

Critical Thought Questions

1. When discussing team cohesion, why is it so critical to differentiate between task and social cohesion?
2. Why is the conceptual model of team cohesion so important to our understanding of this psychological construct?
3. Discuss the determinants of team cohesion illustrated in figure 15.2 relative to the 10 interventions for developing team cohesion. Are there similarities? Should there be?
4. Discuss the issue of direction of causality between team cohesion and athletic performance. Why is this an important concept to understand?

Glossary

coactive sports Activities, such as bowling, archery, and riflery, that do not require members of a team to interact with one another for team success.

conceptual model of team cohesion A model of team cohesion that is based on an interaction between an athlete's group orientation and the athlete's perception of the team.

consequences of team cohesion Outcomes derived from team cohesion.

determinants of team cohesion Factors that cause or determine team cohesion.

direct intervention approach The accomplishment of team building by working directly with the members of a team or group.

direct measurement approach A team cohesion measurement approach that assesses team cohesion by directly asking team members how much they like playing for the team and how well they feel the team functions as a unit.

direction of causality The issue of whether team cohesion causes an improvement in performance or a good performance causes an increase in team cohesion.

Group Environment Questionnaire A team cohesion measurement instrument designed to measure four dimensions of team cohesion.

indirect intervention approach The accomplishment of team building by teaching coaches and managers how to conduct team building with their athletes and employees.

indirect measurement approach A team cohesion measurement approach that assesses team cohesion by asking each team member how she feels about every other member of the team on some basic question.

interactive sports Team sports, such as volleyball, basketball, and football, that require members of a team to interact with one another.

personal satisfaction The contentment or enjoyment an individual derives from being a member of a sports team.

social cohesion The degree to which the members of a team like each other and enjoy personal satisfaction from being members of the team.

task cohesion The degree to which members of a team work together to achieve a specific and identifiable goal.

team building A process used to promote an increased sense of unity and cohesiveness and to enable a team to function together more smoothly and effectively.

team cohesion A dynamic process that is reflected in the tendency for a group or team to stick together and remain united in the pursuit of goals and objectives.

CHAPTER

7

The Sport Team as an Effective Group

Mark A. Eys, *Laurentian University*
Shauna M. Burke, *The University of Western Ontario*
Albert V. Carron, *The University of Western Ontario*
Paul W. Dennis, *Toronto Maple Leafs Hockey Club*

I'm humiliated, not for the loss—I can always deal with wins and losses—but I'm disappointed because I had a job to do as a coach, to get us to understand how we're supposed to play as a team and act as a team, and I don't think we did that.

—United States Men's Olympic Basketball Coach Larry Brown after losing to Puerto Rico in the preliminary rounds of the Athens 2004 Summer Games

Membership and involvement in groups is a fundamental characteristic of our society. We band together in a large number and variety of groups for social reasons or to carry out more effectively some job or task. Thus, each of us interacts daily with numerous other people in group settings—in the family, at work, in social situations, on sport teams. The result is a reciprocal exchange of influence; we exert an influence on other people in groups, and, in turn, those groups and their members have an influence on us. The following two examples illustrate just how powerful this influence can be.

In January 1980, Tony Conigliaro, a former Boston Red Sox baseball player, was driving with his brother when he suffered a massive heart attack—he experienced "sudden death." At least 6 minutes passed before CPR was administered and his heart was stimulated into activity. He remained in a coma for 4 days, and the prognosis for any significant recovery was bleak. A lack of oxygen to the brain for as few as 4 minutes can produce permanent brain damage. Also, people who are comatose for the length of time Conigliaro experienced are almost never able to walk, talk, or look after themselves totally again.

Conigliaro's family refused to believe the prognosis. They were at his side constantly, talking, encouraging, and providing love and affection. Slowly Conigliaro fought back, began to talk, and showed improvements that astounded his doctors. In fact, as Maximillian Kaulback, one of his doctors, stated, "This case is beyond science. . . . I wouldn't be surprised if someday it was proven that the input of the family in cases like this is significant" (as quoted in McCallum,

Mark A. Eys, Shauna M. Burke, Albert V. Carron, and Paul W. Dennis   **133**

1982, p. 72). The incident is powerful and moving; it also illustrates the importance of the family's positive influence—its love, concern, and physical and emotional support. The second illustration, however, shows another side of group influence.

In August of 2003, members of a high school football team in Pennsylvania attended a preseason camp. During the week of practices and team bonding, three members of the team were subjected to the common practice of hazing, a process of humiliating new members of the group. However, in this instance, the actions of the more senior members not only humiliated the freshmen but caused two members to seek medical treatment for their injuries. As a result, a number of spiraling events occurred that included the suspension of the team, first-degree felony charges for the perpetrators, and a media frenzy around the small community. Wahl and Wertheim (2003) described the situation:

> As the hazing inquiry intensified and the severity of the acts became more apparent, investigators from the criminal justice system . . . confronted an impenetrable wall of silence. The victims had spoken, albeit reluctantly, but no other players were willing to provide firsthand accounts. Nuwer says this is typical behavior: "Until you get to be about 25 years old, loyalty to the group is more important than moral qualms. We're more likely to agree as a group that we should turn on this victim than we are to confront one another."

These anecdotes show the dramatic influence groups can have on their members. In the Conigliaro case the influence was a positive one, whereas in the hazing case the influence was negative and destructive. The fundamental question is how groups can come to exert such influence. From a coaching perspective, insight into this issue could produce possible prescriptions for the development of a positive, productive sport group—an effective, cohesive team. In this chapter, both the nature of groups and group cohesion are discussed, and some suggestions for the development of effective groups in sport settings are offered.

The Nature of Sport Groups

Definition

As Carron, Hausenblas, and Eys (2005) note, "every group is like all other groups, like some other groups, and like no other group" (p. 11). What this means, of course, is that every group not only contains characteristics that are common to every other group but they also possess characteristics that are unique to themselves. The uniqueness or diversity among groups has led group dynamics theoreticians to advance a variety of definitions in an attempt to portray what a group is. With regard to sport groups, Carron et al. defined a team as:

> a collection of two or more individuals who possess a common identity, have common goals and objectives, share a common fate, exhibit structured patterns of interaction and modes of communication, hold common perceptions about group structure, are personally and instrumentally interdependent, reciprocate interpersonal attraction, and consider themselves to be a group. (p. 13)

A university basketball team can be used to illustrate each of these definitional components. Such teams are typically composed of 12 athletes (i.e., two or more individuals), all of whom consider themselves to be members of a group representing the university in intercollegiate competitions (i.e., common identity). Every team has explicit or implicit short- and long-term goals such as, for instance, winning upcoming games or eventually winning the conference (i.e., common goals and objectives). Success or failure in the achievement of these goals is experienced by the team as a whole (i.e., common fate). To increase the chance for team success, the coaching staff implements and emphasizes team offensive plays and defensive formations (i.e., structured pattern of interaction). In the heat of game competition, the athletes (or coaching staff) communicate various offensive or defensive options using either nonverbal communications or coded verbal communications (i.e., structured modes of communication).

Williams: Applied Sport
Psychology: Personal
Growth to Peak
Performance, Sixth Edition

I. Learning, Motivation, and
Social Interaction

7. The Sport Team as an
Effective Group

© The McGraw–Hill
Companies, 2010

134 Chapter 7   The Sport Team as an Effective Group

Over time, team positions become fixed, individual roles such as leadership become established, and common expectations for behavior develop (i.e., group structure). In order for the team to function effectively, team social gatherings and team competitions must be attended by a minimum quorum of athletes (i.e., personal and task interdependence). Because of the constant contact athletes have in a team context, friendships typically develop (i.e., interpersonal attraction). Finally, athletes on any team consider themselves to be members of that group (i.e., self-categorization).

It should be noted that the above characteristics are likely present *to some degree* on all sport teams. However, some characteristics will be more or less important than others and it is possible that others could be absent in certain contexts (e.g., it is not always a necessity for interpersonal attraction to be present for task-oriented groups to be successful; see Lenk, 1969). Regardless, on a sport team, coaches or leaders must facilitate the development of the sense of "we" and reduce the importance of "I." Associated with the development of a stronger sense of "we" is an increase in group cohesiveness.

Group Cohesion

Definition

Groups are dynamic, not static. They exhibit life and vitality, interaction, and activity. Their vitality may be reflected in many ways—some positive, others negative. For example, at times the group and its members may be in harmony; at other times, conflict and tension may predominate. Sometimes communication may be excellent between leaders and members, but at other times, it may be nonexistent. Also, commitment to the group's goals and purposes may vary over time. All these variations represent different behavioral manifestations of an underlying, fundamental group property that is referred to as "cohesiveness." Carron, Brawley, and Widmeyer (1998) proposed that cohesion is "a dynamic process which is reflected in the tendency for

a group to stick together and remain united in the pursuit of its instrumental objectives and/or for the satisfaction of member affective needs" (p. 213).

Cohesion has many dimensions or aspects—it is perceived in multiple ways by different groups and their members. It has been proposed (Brawley, Carron, & Widmeyer, 1987; Carron, Widmeyer, & Brawley, 1985; Widmeyer, Brawley, & Carron, 1985) that these multidimensional perceptions of the group are organized and integrated by individual members into two general categories (Figure 7-1). The first category, **group integration,** represents each individual's perceptions about the closeness, similarity, and bonding within the group as a total unit, set, or collection (i.e., it consists of "we" and/or "us" evaluations). The second, **individual attractions to the group,** represents each individual's personal attractions to the group, and more specifically, what personal motivations act to retain an individual in the group (i.e., consists of "I" and/or "me" evaluations). Both of these categories of perceptions about the degree of unity within the group are also assumed to be manifested in two principal ways: in relation to the group's *task* and in terms of the *social* aspects of the group. This conception of cohesiveness is depicted in Figure 7-1. As the figure

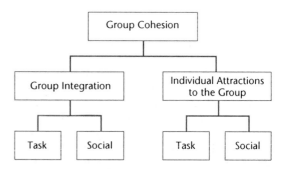

Figure 7-1 A conceptual model for group cohesiveness
Source: Brawley, Carron, and Widmeyer, 1987;
Carron, Widmeyer, and Brawley, 1985;
Widmeyer, Brawley, and Carron, 1985.

Williams: Applied Sport
Psychology: Personal
Growth to Peak
Performance, Sixth Edition

I. Learning, Motivation, and
Social Interaction

7. The Sport Team as an
Effective Group

© The McGraw–Hill
Companies, 2010

229

Mark A. Eys, Shauna M. Burke, Albert V. Carron, and Paul W. Dennis   135

shows, cohesion within sport groups is considered to have four facets: individual attractions to the group–task, individual attractions to the group–social, group integration–task, and group integration–social.

The Correlates of Cohesiveness

Because cohesiveness is multidimensional, it is associated with a wide variety of correlates or factors. Carron et al. (2005) have provided a framework to discuss the main correlates of cohesion in sport teams. As Figure 7-2 shows, one general category is referred to as *environmental factors,* which are situational. Cohesiveness in sport teams is related to aspects of the social setting, the physical environment, and various structural characteristics of the group. Characteristics of individual team members are also associated with the nature and amount of cohesiveness that is present; the category *personal factors* represents these correlates. *Leadership factors,* the third general category, are an acknowledgment that decision styles, leader behaviors, and leader–member relations are also related to team cohesion. The fourth category, *team factors,* represents the group-based aspects that are associated with a stronger bond, a sense of "we," and a commitment to the collective. In the following sections,

some of the main correlates within each general category are identified.

Developing a Team Concept: Correlates of Cohesion

Environmental Factors

Individuals who are in close **proximity,** who are physically close to each other, have a greater tendency to bond together. Physical proximity by itself is not always sufficient for producing cohesiveness, but being in close contact and having the opportunity for interaction and communication does hasten group development. Some situations in sport that ensure physical proximity among group members include having a specific team locker room, residence, or athletic therapy center. In youth sport situations, scheduling games that require the team to travel together in a bus or car is also beneficial. The important point is that group members should be placed in situations where interaction is inevitable.

A second situational factor associated with the development of cohesiveness is **distinctiveness.** As a set of individuals becomes more separate, more distinctive from others, feelings of oneness and unity increase. Traditionally, distinctiveness is achieved through team uniforms and mottos, by providing special privileges, or by demanding special sacrifices.

Many of the factors that make athletes distinct from the general population are taken for granted. These include year-round intensive training programs and reduced time for social activities or part-time employment. The coach should highlight such factors to develop a stronger feeling of commonality. Finally, emphasizing the sense of tradition and the history of the organization or team can contribute to the feeling of distinctiveness.

The team's **size** is also associated with the development of cohesiveness. Research by Widmeyer, Brawley, and Carron (1990) has shown that there is an inverted-U relationship between social cohesion and team size in intramural basketball teams. That is, moderate-sized groups

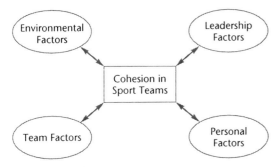

Figure 7-2 **A general framework for examining the correlates of cohesion in sport teams**
Source: Reprinted by permission from Carron and Hausenblas, 1998.

showed the greatest cohesiveness, and larger and smaller groups exhibited the least. Interestingly, the results of this study also showed that task cohesiveness decreases with increasing group size. Widmeyer and colleagues felt that this decrease could be attributed to the fact that it is more difficult to obtain consensus and task commitment in larger groups. In research by Widmeyer and Williams (1991) using only the travel rosters of women's NCAA golf teams, social cohesion did not vary with team size, although increasing team size was associated with increasing task cohesion. However, they only tested the four to five competitors on the travel rosters who were actually involved in the competition. The maximum team size among the teams examined was 12. Consequently, it is possible that the responses from the seven to eight golfers who were not on the travel rosters might have substantially altered the profile of the team's cohesiveness.

Personal Factors

A number of personal factors have been shown to be associated with cohesion. Arguably the most important personal factor associated with the development of both task and social cohesion in sport teams is individual **satisfaction.** Satisfaction is derived from many sources (Widmeyer & Williams, 1991). The quality of the competition is one element; having opportunities for social interactions with teammates is another. In order to feel satisfied, athletes also need to feel that they are improving in skill. Satisfaction also results from the recognition of others—parents, coaches, teammates, fellow students, the public. And, of course, the athlete's relationship with his or her coach is yet another potential source of satisfaction or dissatisfaction. When these elements are satisfying, cohesiveness is enhanced.

Another personal factor that has been shown to be related to cohesion is **competitive state anxiety.** Prapavessis and Carron (1996) found that athletes who perceived their teams to be higher in task cohesion seemed to experience less cognitive anxiety. They suggested that this might be the case because members of more cohesive

teams could experience less pressure to (a) carry out the responsibilities of the group and (b) satisfy other members' expectations of themselves. In addition, Eys, Hardy, Carron, and Beauchamp (2003) extended the above work and found that those athletes who perceived greater task cohesion were more likely to view their symptoms of both cognitive (e.g., worry) and somatic (e.g., sweaty palms) anxiety as facilitative (i.e., beneficial) and necessary for their competition.

The degree to which athletes engage in **social loafing** is another personal factor related to cohesion. Social loafing reflects "the reduction in individual effort when people work in groups versus when they work alone" (Carron et al., 2005, p. 250). Individuals feel they can reduce their effort in a group for a number of reasons. These include the fact that once more people take part in a task it is easier to get lost in the crowd and, thus, not expend as much effort. However, McKnight, Williams, and Widmeyer (1991) found that individuals who were members of swimming relay teams that were high in task cohesion were less likely to be social loafers.

Finally, other personal factors that are related to increased cohesion include a tendency to assume greater responsibility for negative events and outcomes (Brawley, Carron, & Widmeyer, 1987), greater commitment to the team or organization (Widmeyer & Williams, 1991), and an increase in sacrifice behaviors (Carron et al., 2005).

Leadership Factors

The interrelationships among the coach, the athlete, cohesiveness, and performance are complex. In a mutiny, for example, cohesion is high, the leader–subordinate relationship is poor (and the leader is excluded from the group), and performance from an organizational perspective is poor. One example of the complex interrelationship between coach, athlete, cohesiveness, and performance comes from a study by Widmeyer and Williams (1991). They had golf coaches rate the importance they attached to task cohesion, the importance they attached to social cohesion, and the number of techniques they used to foster

Mark A. Eys, Shauna M. Burke, Albert V. Carron, and Paul W. Dennis   **137**

cohesiveness. These measures were not related to their athletes' perceptions of the amount of team cohesiveness. In short, in the Widmeyer and Williams study, coaches were not crucial to the development of group cohesion.

Another example of the complex relationship arises when a leader is on the fringe of the group from the perspective of cohesiveness—this can produce problems. The perceptions a group has about itself, about other groups, and about nongroup members often become distorted with increased group cohesiveness. The group tends to be very favorable in its perception of its own members and to overvalue its own contributions, importance, and performance. Also, the group tends to undervalue the contributions, importance, and performance of other groups or nongroup members. This turning inward can lead to some difficulties for a new, formally appointed leader such as a coach. The new leader may not be readily accepted, and any proposed changes to existing practices may be met with resistance (Jewell & Reitz, 1981).

This situation is often encountered in sport when a new coach replaces a highly popular, highly successful predecessor. The group makes constant comparisons between the two leaders' personalities, methods, and so on. And because a cohesive group tends to overvalue its own membership and undervalue outsiders, the new coach will encounter initial difficulties in being accepted.

When people have ownership over a decision, they tend to support that decision more strongly. Consequently, the coach's *decision style* can have an influence on the level of cohesiveness within the team. Team members engage in behaviors more persistently, with greater intensity, and for a longer duration when they have had an opportunity to participate in decision making. In short, as Westre and Weiss (1991) found when they examined the relationship between coaching behaviors and the perceptions of team cohesion by high school football players, coaches who are viewed as engaging in more democratic behaviors will be more likely to have teams with higher cohesion.

Team Factors

When a set of individuals is brought together with the intention of performing as a group, cohesion can be influenced by a number of structural characteristics that emerge as the group develops (e.g., roles and norms), processes that take place between group members (e.g., group goals, communication), and group performance outcomes that occur throughout the duration of its existence. The emergence of these factors is inevitable and essential if the set of individuals is to become a more cohesive group.

Roles. A role is a set of behaviors that are expected from the occupants of specific positions within the group. Thus, when we think of the "role of a coach," a number of expectations for behavior come to mind: instruct athletes; set up the team's offensive and defensive alignments; communicate with parents, media, and the general public; organize practices; and so on.

Within every group there are two general categories of roles, formal and informal (Mabry & Barnes, 1980). As the term suggests, **formal roles** are explicitly set out by the group or organization. Coach, team captain, and manager are examples of explicit leadership roles within a team. Spiker and setter in volleyball; forward, guard, and center in basketball; and scrum half and prop in rugby are examples of explicit performance roles. The sport team as an organization requires specific individuals to carry out each of these roles. Thus, individuals are trained or recruited for these roles, and specific expectations are held for their behavior. **Informal roles** evolve as a result of the interactions that take place among group members. Some examples of the informal roles that often emerge on a sport team are leader (vocal or "lead by example" leaders), task booster (spark plug), enforcer, mentor, social convener, cancer, distracter, team player, star player, and comedian (Cope, Eys, & Beauchamp, 2007). In the case of informal roles, it should be pointed out that these can have a positive (e.g., mentor) or negative (e.g., distracter) influence on the team.

A variety of elements associated with athletes' roles determine how effectively they can be performed. One element is the degree to which athletes understand, or do not understand, what constitutes their role. The term **role ambiguity** is often used to describe this element of role involvement and is defined as the lack of clear consistent information regarding one's role (Kahn, Wolfe, Quinn, Snoek, & Rosenthal, 1964). Beauchamp, Bray, Eys, and Carron (2002) noted that it is important for athletes to understand four aspects with regard to their role: (a) the scope of their responsibilities or generally what their role entails; (b) the behaviors that are necessary to successfully fulfill their role responsibilities; (c) how their role performance will be evaluated; and (d) what the consequences are should they not successfully fulfill their role responsibilities. In general, previous research has shown that athletes who understand their roles better are more satisfied (Eys, Carron, Bray, & Beauchamp, 2003), experience less anxiety (Beauchamp et al., 2003), and are likely to view their teams as more cohesive (Eys & Carron, 2001).

A National Hockey League coach once observed that the worst thing that could happen to a team was to have its "enforcer" score a few goals in successive games. The enforcer would then begin to see himself as and prefer the role of goal scorer, to the detriment of the team as a whole. The roles that individuals are expected to perform should be clearly spelled out.

A second element of role involvement that has been shown to be related to group cohesiveness is the degree to which athletes accept their role responsibilities (e.g., Bray, 1998). It is beneficial to set out any contingencies associated with role performance. "We plan to use you as a defensive specialist only. If you cannot or do not want to play this role, you will probably get very little playing time this year." Role acceptance is also enhanced when the coach minimizes the status differences among roles. Thus, the success of the total team and the importance of all roles for team success should be continually emphasized. When all group members perceive that their responsibilities are important and make a contribution to the common good, they more willingly accept and carry them out.

A number of interventions, although not empirically tested, could potentially improve role clarity and role acceptance. One very simple intervention that serves to open communication channels and clarify roles is to arrange for individual meetings between the athlete and his or her coach. Another method is to utilize an effective goal setting program. Goal setting serves four important functions: it (a) directs the individual's attention and actions toward appropriate behaviors; (b) mobilizes and increases effort toward the task; (c) increases persistence in the task; and (d) motivates the individual to develop strategies and action plans to accomplish the task (Locke, Shaw, Saari, & Latham, 1981). All of these contribute to role clarity and acceptance.

Finally, other elements of role involvement that are extremely important to the group environment and are likely contributors to the cohesiveness of sport teams include **role efficacy** (i.e., athletes' beliefs about their capabilities to carry out role responsibilities; Bray, Brawley, & Carron, 2002), **role conflict** (i.e., athletes' perceiving others to be sending incongruent expectations; Kahn et al., 1964), **role overload** (i.e., athletes' having too many role expectations and/or being unable to prioritize them appropriately), and **role satisfaction** (i.e., how happy athletes are with their given role on the team). The applied practitioner or coach should be conscious of these role elements when working with sport teams.

Norms.   The presence of **norms** is also associated with increased cohesiveness (Gammage, Carron, & Estabrooks, 2001). A norm is a standard for behavior that is expected of members of the group. It may be task irrelevant or task relevant; in either case, a norm reflects the group's consensus about behaviors that are considered acceptable. The athletes' treatment of team managers (Gammage et al., 2001) or trainers is one example of a task-irrelevant norm. On one team the manager might be regarded and treated as little more than an unpaid servant; on another team he or she might be considered a member of the

Williams: Applied Sport
Psychology: Personal
Growth to Peak
Performance, Sixth Edition

I. Learning, Motivation, and
Social Interaction

7. The Sport Team as an
Effective Group

© The McGraw–Hill
Companies, 2010

233

Mark A. Eys, Shauna M. Burke, Albert V. Carron, and Paul W. Dennis   **139**

coaching staff. In both cases new team members quickly become aware of the standard of behavior considered acceptable in their interactions with the manager and begin to act accordingly.

In a sport setting, Munroe and her colleagues (1999) asked athletes to identify the types of norms that exist within their teams. What they found was that important norms existed in four different contexts. First, the two most important norms in the context of *competition* were that teammates put forth maximum effort toward the task and that they supported the other members of the team. These two norms also were the most relevant in the second context, *practice*. The third context for the existence of norms was the *off-season*. In this context the most relevant norms for members of sport teams were to continue training and development as well as maintaining contact with other group members. Finally, norms also were identified for social situations in which group members had expectations to attend social events (e.g., parties) and have respect for each other.

The relationship between the presence of group norms and the degree of group cohesiveness is circular. The development of norms contributes to the development of cohesiveness. With increased group cohesiveness there is also greater conformity to group standards for behavior and performance. A recently formed group has minimal influence over its members. But as the group develops and becomes more cohesive, adherence to norms for behavior increases. Failure to conform can lead to different sanctions or types of punishment. For example, the group can control the amount of interaction it permits members, their degree of involvement in decision making, and their accessibility to task and social rewards. Controlling the opportunity to interact and to influence the group is probably the most powerful sanction the group possesses. As a group increases in cohesiveness, its members place increasing value on social approval and the opportunities to interact with other group members. Therefore, they show an increasing tendency to adhere to the group norms and to give in to the group influence—even if that

influence is negative. Some examples of negative influence are the performance of deviant behavior (as in the case of the high school football team hazing incident) or the maintenance of an inappropriately low work quota (low standards for productivity).

One of the best-known, most heavily researched issues relating to task-relevant norms is the **norm for productivity.** One example of this occurs in industrial settings when the group establishes a level or rate of performance as acceptable and refuses to tolerate productivity above (rate busting) or below (malingering) that standard. Cohesion and the norm for productivity jointly influence group productivity and achievement. Traditionally it was assumed that there is a direct, positive relationship between cohesion and productivity: As the former increased, the latter was improved. Research in management science, psychology, and sport, however, has shown that the picture is not quite that simple. For example, when Stogdill (1972) reviewed 34 studies that had been carried out with a variety of different groups, he found that cohesiveness was positively related to performance in 12, negatively related in 11, and unrelated to performance in 11. According to Stogdill, the key factor that influences the relationship between cohesion and performance is the group's norm for productivity (Table 7-1). If group cohesiveness is high and the norm for productivity is high, performance will be positively affected (number 1). Conversely, if cohesion is high and the norm for productivity is low (number 4), performance will be low or negatively affected. When cohesiveness is low, groups with a high norm (number 2) will outperform groups with a low norm (number 3).

Another important aspect of group norms is their *stability*. It has been demonstrated experimentally that an arbitrary norm can persist for four or five generations after the original members have been removed from the group (Jacobs & Campbell, 1961). Thus, if a sport team develops negative norms, such as abusive behavior toward officials or other team members, a laissez-faire attitude toward training, or a reliance on

140 Chapter 7 The Sport Team as an Effective Group

Table 7-1 Interactive Effects of Group Cohesiveness and Group Norm for Productivity on Individual and Group Performance

		Group Cohesion	
		High	Low
Group Norm for Productivity	High	Best performance (1)	Intermediate performance (2)
	Low	Worst performance (4)	Intermediate performance (3)

individual versus team goals, those norms could persist over a number of seasons unless steps are taken to eliminate them.

Establishing positive group norms is extremely important in sport teams, particularly if an inappropriate norm is in place. One technique that has been used successfully is to enlist the formal and informal leaders of the group as active agents. If group leaders (in addition to the coach) accept and adhere to specific standards, other group members soon follow.

In some instances the group leaders may be resistant to change. This poses a problem because on sport teams the formal and informal leaders are usually the most highly skilled. If this is the case, the coach must decide how important the new standard is to the long-term success of the organization. In the event that the new standard is considered to be very important, the coach may have to release the resistant team members.

Group processes. Another important team factor that influences the development of a team concept and task cohesion is the interactive processes that occur among the members. One process is the establishment of *group goals and rewards.* In most group activities, including track and field, swimming, baseball, and even basketball, hockey, and soccer, there is an opportunity for the gifted individual competitor to obtain special recognition and rewards. This is inevitable. However, to ensure that a concept

of unity develops, the coach must emphasize the group's goals and objectives as well as the rewards that will accrue to the group if these are achieved. Individual goals and rewards should be downplayed.

Communication is another group process associated with increased group cohesiveness, but the relationship is circular. As the level of communication relating to task and social issues increases, cohesiveness is enhanced. And as the group becomes more cohesive, communication also increases. Group members are more open with one another, they volunteer more, they talk more, and they listen better. In short, the exchange of task information and social pleasantries increases with cohesiveness.

Performance outcome. As has been the case with so many other factors, the relationship between cohesion and performance outcome is a circular one. More specifically, cohesiveness contributes to performance success, and performance success increases cohesiveness. In fact, Carron, Colman, Wheeler, and Stevens (2002) conducted a meta-analysis to examine a number of issues related to the cohesion–performance relationship. A number of issues arose from their results. First, *both* task and social cohesion were positively related to performance and the relationships were cyclical (as mentioned earlier). That is, the strength of the cohesion to performance relationship was as strong as performance to cohesion. Second, there was no significant

Mark A. Eys, Shauna M. Burke, Albert V. Carron, and Paul W. Dennis   **141**

difference between the strengths of the task cohesion–performance relationship (i.e., effect size = .61) and the social cohesion–performance relationship (i.e., effect size = .70) although the latter was slightly greater. Finally, these relationships existed equally for interactive (e.g., volleyball) and coacting (e.g., track and field) sports and were present across the spectrum of skill and competitive levels, but seemed to be stronger in female teams. Overall, performance success is an important team factor for developing cohesion. Consequently, if it is at all possible, a coach should try to avoid an excessively difficult schedule early in a season.

Team Building

If everybody can find a way to put their personal agendas aside for the benefit of the team, ultimately they will gain for themselves in the long run. But I think what often happens is people think they have to take care of themselves first and the team second. Then the infrastructure breaks down and nobody's accountable. You have to sacrifice yourself for the good of the team, no matter what role you play on the team—whether you're playing 30 minutes or two minutes a game.

—*Mark Messier (as quoted in Miller, 2001, p. 152)*

As this quote by Mark Messier illustrates, the importance of cohesion in sport teams is recognized even by those who are best known for their individual prowess. Because it is critical for group development, group maintenance, and the group's collective pursuit of its goals and objectives, cohesion has been identified as the most important small group variable (see Golembiewski, Hilles, & Kagno, 1974). Consequently, at the core of any team-building program is the expectation that the intervention will produce a more cohesive group.

Coaches, either alone or with the help of a sport psychologist, invariably seek ways to build an effective team. It's not enough for the coach to proclaim to his or her charges, "Let's act like a team." Consequently, coaches or sport psychology specialists often engage in what is known as **team building.** As Carron and colleagues (2005) noted, team building can be defined as "team enhancement or team improvement for both task and social purposes" (p. 327). Thus, it would seem prudent for coaches and sport psychologists to implement certain strategies to foster team building so that athletes may have meaningful experiences that ultimately may lead to a greater sense of unity and cohesiveness.

However, sport is not the only physical activity domain in which team building has been shown to be effective. Research by Carron and Spink (1993) and Spink and Carron (1993) has shown that a team-building intervention program can have a substantial impact on perceptions of cohesiveness as well as on individual adherence behavior in an exercise context. In short, the group has a substantial stabilizing influence on its membership. Given that 50% of adults who initiate an exercise program drop out within the first 6 months (Dishman, 1994), this seems an important area for intervention. Thus, this chapter will conclude with suggestions for implementing a team-building protocol in both sport and exercise settings.

Owing to its distinct nature, the implementation of team-building interventions in sport and exercise settings is typically *indirect*. The coach/leader is generally the primary arbitrator of group goals, individual roles, and leadership style. As a consequence of this, all of the team-building interventions in these settings become more indirect as they must be filtered through the coach/leader in each instance.

One approach to team-building interventions adopted by Carron, Spink, and Prapavessis (Carron & Spink, 1993; Prapavessis, Carron, & Spink, 1996; Spink & Carron, 1993) involved the use of a four-stage process comprising an *introductory stage*, a *conceptual stage*, a *practical stage*, and an *intervention stage*. The purpose of the introductory stage was to provide the coach/leader with a brief overview of the general benefits of group cohesion. For example, in team building with sport teams, the relationship between

142   Chapter 7   The Sport Team as an Effective Group

perceptions of cohesiveness and enhanced team dynamics was discussed (Prapavessis et al., 1996). In team building with exercise groups, the introductory stage consisted of a discussion of the relationship between perceptions of cohesiveness and increased adherence to the exercise program (Carron & Spink, 1993).

The conceptual stage was used to accomplish three purposes: (a) to facilitate communication with the coaches/leaders about complex concepts (e.g., groups, cohesiveness); (b) to highlight the interrelatedness of various components of the team-building protocol; and (c) to identify the focus for possible interventions (Carron & Spink, 1993).

The purpose of the practical stage was to have coaches/leaders, in an interactive brainstorming session, generate as many specific strategies as possible to use for team building in their group. This was thought to be desirable for three reasons. First, coaches/leaders differ in personality and preferences; therefore, a strategy that might be effectively implemented by one coach/leader might not be by another. Second, groups differ, and coaches/leaders are the individuals most familiar with their groups. An intervention strategy that might be effective in one group might be ineffective in another. Finally, de Charms's (1976) origin-pawn research has shown that motivation is enhanced when individuals are given greater control over personal behavior. Thus, coaches and exercise leaders are likely to be motivated to employ various team-building strategies because they are given the opportunity to participate in the brainstorming session, and they have control over which strategies they use with their team or class.

Research by Carron and Spink (1993) and Spink and Carron (1993) in the exercise domain provides a good illustration of the type of activities characteristic of the practical stage. Carron and Spink encouraged fitness instructors to develop specific strategies to use in their classes. Table 7-2 contains examples of some of the specific team-building strategies identified by fitness leaders in the practical stage, as well as suggested strategies for coaches of sport teams.

In the intervention stage, the team-building protocols coaches or exercise leaders introduced and maintained in order to increase the level of task cohesiveness of the groups. One team-building intervention that was implemented in a sport setting used elite male soccer teams (Prapavessis et al., 1996). The coaches involved in the team-building intervention attended a workshop two weeks before the beginning of the season, at which the specific strategies for implementing a team-building program were established. Throughout the preseason and then during six weeks of the season, the coaches emphasized the team-building strategies. Perceptions of cohesiveness were assessed in the preseason and after eight weeks. No differences in cohesiveness were found, however, between the team-building, attention-placebo, and control conditions.

One possible explanation advanced to account for these results was that many sport coaches inevitably engage in team-building strategies on their own. That is, they establish goals and objectives, work to ensure conformity to group norms, facilitate role clarity and role acceptance, and so on. Also, in sport teams, cohesion is an inevitable by-product of group processes (e.g., communication), an evolving group structure (e.g., development of roles), and group outcomes (e.g., winning or losing). Thus, a team-building program in a sport team would most likely combine in an interactive way with ongoing concomitants of cohesion. The lack of research in sport on the impact of team building on cohesiveness makes it difficult to arrive at any definitive conclusions. Perhaps practitioners and researchers engaged in team building in sport might wish to consider the athletes' opinions on collective areas of concern (i.e., targets for team-building strategies). The applied example that follows highlights a protocol the Toronto Maple Leafs (of the National Hockey League) use to develop "team values" that enlisted and depended on the opinions of all team members. In addition, the inclusion of selected high-status members of the team (i.e., captains, co-captains) in implementing this team-building strategy was considered critical for its delivery.

Williams: Applied Sport
Psychology: Personal
Growth to Peak
Performance, Sixth Edition

I. Learning, Motivation, and
Social Interaction

7. The Sport Team as an
Effective Group

© The McGraw–Hill
Companies, 2010

237

Mark A. Eys, Shauna M. Burke, Albert V. Carron, and Paul W. Dennis   **143**

Table 7-2 Examples of Specific Team-Building Strategies for Coaches and Fitness Class Instructors

Factor		Examples of Intervention Strategies
Distinctiveness	Sport[a]	Provide the team with unique identifiers (e.g., shirts, logos, mottos, etc.). Emphasize any unique traditions and/or history associated with the team.
	Exercise[b]	Have a group name. Make up a group T-shirt. Hand out neon headbands or shoelaces. Make up posters and slogans for the class.
Individual positions	Sport[a]	Create a team structure in which there is a clear differentiation in team positions and roles.
	Exercise[b]	Use three areas of the pool depending on fitness level. Have signs to label parts of the group. Use specific positions for low-, medium-, and high-impact exercisers. Let them pick their own spot and encourage them to remain in it throughout the year.
Group norms	Sport[c]	Show individual team members how the group's standards can contribute to more effective team performance and a greater sense of team unity. Point out to all team members how their individual contributions can contribute to the team's success. Reward those team members who adhere to the group's standards and sanction those who do not.
	Exercise[b]	Have members introduce each other to increase social aspects. Encourage members to become fitness friends. Establish a goal to lose weight together. Promote a smart work ethic as a group characteristic.
Individual sacrifices	Sport[a]	Encourage important team members to make sacrifices for the team (e.g., ask a veteran athlete to sit out in order to give a novice athlete more playing time).
	Exercise[b]	Use music in aqua fitness (some do not want music). Ask two or three people for a goal for the day. Ask regulars to help new people—fitness friends. Ask people who aren't concerned with weight loss to make a sacrifice for the group on some days (more aerobics) and people who are concerned with weight loss to make a sacrifice on other days (more mat work).
Interaction and communication	Sport[d]	Provide opportunities for athlete input; create an environment that fosters mutual trust and respect so that athletes will feel comfortable communicating.[e] Have all players identify (on paper) why they want their fellow players on the team, then create a summary sheet for each player.
	Exercise[b]	Use partner work and have them introduce themselves. Introduce the person on the right and left. Work in groups of five and take turns showing a move. Use more partner activities.

[a]Bull, Albinson, and Shambrook, 1996

[b]Adapted from Carron and Spink, 1991; Spink and Carron, 1991

[c]Zander, 1982

[d]Yukelson, 1984

[e]Munroe, Terry, and Carron, 2002

144 Chapter 7 The Sport Team as an Effective Group

Example

Developing team values

In recent years, the Toronto Maple Leafs hockey team, a member of the National Hockey League, has engaged in several values-based team-building exercises. Values are beliefs that influence behavior and serve as guidelines to evaluate behavior (Crace & Hardy, 1997). A modified version of the Crace and Hardy intervention model was introduced to the Toronto Maple Leafs at the beginning of the 2005–2006 season. Although the model recommends that the players and coaches be introduced to the principles behind team-building interventions, it was felt that professional hockey players already had a clear understanding of what constitutes a functional team environment.

Thus, the session began with players divided into four groups of six, each table with a group leader who was one of the team's captains. The Player Development coach asked the leaders to discuss in their groups the important beliefs that would help guide their behavior and motivation for the upcoming season. After a 20-minute discussion, the group leaders reported three or four of their groups' most important beliefs. A general discussion ensued and the players collectively rank-ordered the beliefs. Following are the results:

Team Values Summary, 2005–2006 Season

1. *Team Toughness: Mentally and physically, never quit. Stick up for one another.*

2. *Team Speed: We must all take short shifts so we can wear down our opponents by the third period. We'll be able to win the close games if we can do this.*

3. *Team Defense: We can score, but in the past we've hung the goalies "out-to-dry." We need a commitment to play solid defense.*

4. *Work Ethic: On and off the ice strive towards your goal. Push yourself to be better.*

5. *Accountability: Being truthful and up front to your teammates. Don't make excuses. It has to be 24 players held accountable by each other and the coaches.*

6. *Respect: Respect must be earned. Respect each other's roles and what different players bring to the table, for example, goal scoring, checking, penalty killing.*

7. *Positive Attitude: We need to be more positive. No complaining about line combinations, defense partner and so on.*

8. *Loyalty: Don't cheat yourself or your teammates from your best effort. If you play 5 minutes or 20 minutes, work hard whenever you get the chance.*

9. *Leadership: There are 24 leaders in this dressing room, no passengers.*

10. *Commitment: Make the commitment to team concepts, systems, and off-ice conditioning.*

The 10 beliefs the players presented to the coaching staff were transformed into a plaque, and each player took ownership by signing his name to it. The plaque was mounted in the dressing room as a reminder of what the group valued as a team. Throughout the season, head coach Pat Quinn often referred to one of the values as a theme to begin his team meetings in preparation for an upcoming game. In addition, if the team was underachieving, he would target one of the belief statements. For example, if there was a lackluster effort after a period, the coach would refer to "loyalty," which the players had defined as not cheating themselves or their teammates from giving their best effort. The coach implied that they were letting each other down and not adhering to their own values. Such tactics would help motivate the players into giving a more concerted effort to achieve their goals.

Mark A. Eys, Shauna M. Burke, Albert V. Carron, and Paul W. Dennis   **145**

Summary

Groups are dynamic, not static; they exhibit life and vitality, interaction, and activity. Athletic teams are simply a special type of group. One important implication of this is that they are therefore subject to change, to growth, to modification, and to improvement. The coach is probably in the best position to influence change in a positive direction. To do this efficiently and effectively, it is beneficial to draw on the wealth of research information that has been developed over a number of years in management science, social psychology, sociology, and physical education. Given the influence that groups have on their members, a knowledge of group structure, group dynamics, and group cohesiveness is essential for coaches. This understanding will provide an excellent base from which to weld athletes into a more effective team.

Study Questions

1. Using Carron's definition of a group, briefly describe the six features that characterize groups.
2. Define cohesiveness. What are the four specific facets of cohesion?
3. List the four factors that contribute to cohesiveness and give one specific example of each.
4. Discuss the relationship of team size to group cohesiveness.
5. Describe the environmental, personal, and leadership factors that contribute to the development of cohesiveness.
6. Four team factors related to cohesion are roles, norms, group processes, and performance outcome. Distinguish between each of these factors and describe how the factors might be manipulated or modified to enhance team cohesion.
7. Give at least one example (using a sport of your choice or an exercise class) of a strategy that a coach, fitness leader, or sport psychologist to enhance group cohesiveness using each of the following factors: (a) distinctiveness, (b) individual positions, (c) group norms, (d) individual sacrifices, and (e) interaction and communication.

References

Beauchamp, M. R., Bray, S. R., Eys, M. A., & Carron, A. V. (2002). Role ambiguity, role efficacy, and role performance: Multidimensional and mediational relationships within interdependent sport teams. *Group Dynamics: Theory, Research, and Practice, 6* (3), 229–242.

Beauchamp, M. R., Bray, S. R., Eys, M. A., & Carron, A. V. (2003). The effect of role ambiguity on competitive state anxiety. *Journal of Sport and Exercise Psychology, 25* (1), 77–92.

Brawley, L. R., Carron, A. V., & Widmeyer, W. N. (1987). Assessing the cohesion of teams: Validity of the Group Environment Questionnaire. *Journal of Sport Psychology, 9,* 275–294.

Bray, S. R. (1998). *Role efficacy within interdependent teams: Measurement development and tests of theory.* Unpublished doctoral thesis. University of Waterloo, Waterloo, Canada.

Bray, S. R., Brawley, L. R., & Carron, A. V. (2002). Efficacy for interdependent role functions: Evidence from the sport domain. *Small Group Research, 33,* 644–666.

Bull, S. J., Albinson, J. G., & Shambrook, C. J. (1996). *The mental game plan: Getting psyched for sport.* Eastborne, UK: Sports Dynamics.

Carron, A. V., Brawley, L. R., & Widmeyer, W. N. (1998). The measurement of cohesiveness in sport groups. In J. L. Duda (Ed.), *Advancements in sport and exercise psychology measurement* (pp. 213–226). Morgantown, WV: Fitness Information Technology.

Carron, A. V., Colman, M. M., Wheeler, J., & Stevens, D. (2002). Cohesion and performance in sport: A meta-analysis. *Journal of Sport and Exercise Psychology, 24,* 168–188.

Carron, A. V., Hausenblas, H. A., & Eys, M. A. (2005). *Group dynamics in sport* (3rd ed.). Morgantown, WV: Fitness Information Technology.

Carron, A. V., & Spink, K. S. (1991). *Team building in an exercise setting: Cohesion effects.* Paper presented at the Canadian Psychomotor Learning and Sport Psychology Conference, London, ON.

Carron, A. V., & Spink, K. S. (1993). Team building in an exercise setting. *The Sport Psychologist, 7,* 8–18.

Carron, A. V., Widmeyer, L. R., & Brawley, L. R. (1985). The development of an instrument to assess cohesion in sport teams: The Group Environment Questionnaire. *Journal of Sport Psychology, 7,* 244–266.

Cope, C., Eys, M. A., & Beauchamp, M. R. (2007). *Informal roles on sport teams.* Paper presented at the Association for Applied Sport Psychology Conference, Louisville, KY.

Crace, R. K., & Hardy, C. J. (1997). Individual values and the team building process. *Journal of Applied Sport Psychology, 9,* 41–60.

de Charms, R. (1976). *Enhancing motivation: Change in the classroom.* New York: Halstead.

Dishman, R. K. (1994). *Exercise adherence: Its impact on public health.* Champaign, IL: Human Kinetics.

Eys, M. A., & Carron, A. V. (2001). Role ambiguity, task cohesion, and task self-efficacy. *Small Group Research, 32,* 356–372.

Eys, M. A., Carron, A. V., Bray, S. R., & Beauchamp, M. R. (2003). Role ambiguity and athlete satisfaction. *Journal of Sports Sciences, 21,* 391–401.

Eys, M. A., Hardy, J., Carron, A. V., & Beauchamp, M. R. (2003). The relationship between task cohesion and competitive state anxiety. *Journal of Sport and Exercise Psychology, 25,* 66–76.

Gammage, K. L., Carron, A. V., & Estabrooks, P. A. (2001). Team cohesion and individual productivity: The influence of the norm for productivity and the identifiability of individual effort. *Small Group Research, 32,* 3–18.

Golembiewski, R. T., Hilles, R., & Kagno, M. S. (1974). A longitudinal study of flexi-time effects: Some consequences of an O.D. structural intervention. *Journal of Applied Behavioral Science, 10,* 485–500.

Mark A. Eys, Shauna M. Burke, Albert V. Carron, and Paul W. Dennis   147

Jacobs, R. C., & Campbell, D. T. (1961). The perpetuation of an arbitrary tradition through several generations of a laboratory microculture. *Journal of Abnormal and Social Psychology, 62,* 649–658.

Jewell, L. N., & Reitz, H. J. (1981). *Group effectiveness in organizations.* Glenview, IL: Scott, Foresman.

Kahn, R. L., Wolfe, D. M., Quinn, R. P., Snoek, J. D., & Rosenthal, R. A. (1964). *Occupational stress: Studies in role conflict and ambiguity.* New York: Wiley.

Lenk, H. (1969). Top performance despite internal conflict: An antithesis to a functional proposition. In J. Loy & G. Kenyon (Eds.), *Sport, culture, and society: A reader on the sociology of sport.* Toronto, ON: MacMillan.

Locke, E. A., Shaw, K. N., Saari, L. M., & Latham, G. P. (1981). Goal setting and task performance: 1969–1980. *Psychological Bulletin, 90,* 125–152.

Mabry, E. A., & Barnes, R. E. (1980). *The dynamics of small group communication.* Englewood Cliffs, NJ: Prentice Hall.

McCallum, J. (1982). Faith, hope, and Tony C. *Sports Illustrated, 57,* 58–72.

McKnight, P., Williams, J. M., & Widmeyer, W. N. (1991, October). *The effects of cohesion and identifiability on reducing the likelihood of social loafing.* Presented at the Association for the Advancement of Applied Sport Psychology Annual Conference, Savannah, GA.

Miller, S. L. (2001). *The complete player: The psychology of winning hockey.* Toronto, ON: Soddart.

Munroe, K., Estabrooks, P., Dennis, P., & Carron, A. V. (1999). A phenomenological analysis of group norms in sport teams. *The Sport Psychologist, 13,* 171–182.

Munroe, K., Terry, P., & Carron, A. (2002). Cohesion and teamwork. In B. Hale & D. Collins (Eds.), *Rugby tough* (pp. 137–153). Champaign, IL: Human Kinetics.

Prapavessis, H., & Carron, A. V. (1996). The effect of group cohesion on competitive state anxiety. *Journal of Sport and Exercise Psychology, 18,* 64–74.

Prapavessis, H., Carron, A. V., & Spink, K. S. (1996). Team building in sport. *International Journal of Sport Psychology, 27,* 269–285.

Spink, K. S., & Carron, A. V. (1991, October). *Team building in an exercise setting: Adherence effects.* Paper presented at the Canadian Psychomotor Learning and Sport Psychology Conference, London, ON.

Spink, K. S., & Carron, A. V. (1993). The effects of team building on the adherence patterns of female exercise participants. *Journal of Sport and Exercise Psychology, 15,* 39–49.

Stogdill, R. M. (1972). Group productivity, drive and cohesiveness. *Organizational Behavior and Human Performance, 8,* 26–43.

Wahl, G., & Wertheim, L. J. (2003). A rite gone terribly wrong. *Sports Illustrated, 99* (24), 68.

Westre, K. R., & Weiss, M. R. (1991). The relationship between perceived coaching behaviors and group cohesion in high school football teams. *The Sport Psychologist, 5,* 41–54.

242

Williams: Applied Sport
Psychology: Personal
Growth to Peak
Performance, Sixth Edition

I. Learning, Motivation, and
Social Interaction

7. The Sport Team as an
Effective Group

© The McGraw–Hill
Companies, 2010

148   Chapter 7   The Sport Team as an Effective Group

Widmeyer, W. N., Brawley, L. R., & Carron, A. V. (1985). *The measurement of cohesion in sport teams: The Group Environment Questionnaire.* London, ON: Sports Dynamics.

Widmeyer, W. N., Brawley, L. R., & Carron, A. V. (1990). The effects of group size in sport. *Journal of Exercise and Sport Psychology, 12,* 177–190.

Widmeyer, W. N., & Williams, J. M. (1991). Predicting cohesion in a coaching sport. *Small Group Research, 22,* 548–570.

Yukelson, D. P. (1984). Group motivation in sport teams. In J. M. Silva & R. S. Weinberg (Eds.), *Psychological foundations of sport.* Champaign, IL: Human Kinetics.

Writing, Reading, and Researching in the Social Sciences

A Guide for Students

Dan Melzer
California State University, Sacramento

Contents

◔ An Overview of Social Science Writing, Reading, and Researching

◔ The Writing Process: Tips and Techniques for Social Science Students

◔ A Guide to Common Social Science Writing Genres

◔ Strategies for Reading Difficult Texts

◔ Researching in the Social Sciences: Collecting, Evaluating, Integrating, and Citing Sources

An Overview of Social Science Writing, Reading, and Researching

Social scientists use writing, reading, and researching to create knowledge about human behavior and human relationships through observation, hypothesis-testing, and theory. Social scientists like sociologists, anthropologists, and psychologists frequently use writing in their jobs and in their scholarship: abstracts, literature reviews, experimental reports, case studies, and ethnographies are just some of the kinds of writing in the social sciences. This guide will help you learn to use these different types of social science writing to communicate ideas and create knowledge. This guide will also help you with the writing, reading, and researching process, including research methods commonly used in the social sciences.

Sociologists, anthropologists, psychologists, criminologists, political scientists, and other kinds of social scientists all use writing to summarize and critique research articles, report on original research, and observe social groups. In every social science field, writers must define key terms, provide context by citing prior research, use research methods like interviews, surveys, and case studies, and connect their research to broader social theory. There are common genres (types of writing) you'll find in social science courses in any sub-discipline. This student writing guide focuses on some of the most common genres:

Abstracts: Summaries of the hypothesis, research methods, and results of a social science research article or book.

Literature reviews: Reviews of the important scholarly research on a specific social science topic.

Research reports: Formal research reports of social science studies.

Case studies: Reports of intense observations of an individual that are often used as examples or models.

Ethnographies: Participant observer studies that require prolonged observation and interaction with a specific group.

As you read this guide, it's important to keep in mind that each sub-discipline of the social sciences—and even each instructor within the same discipline—will have different purposes and expectations for writing. This guide can give you some useful guidelines and advice, but it's also important to understand what your instructor is asking for in his or her writing assignments.

The Writing Process: Tips and Techniques for Social Science Students

This section offers advice for all stages of the writing process: finding a topic, drafting and revising, and editing and proofreading. Everyone's writing process is different, and the stages of writing discussed in this section are more like a circle than a line: sometimes a social scientist will rethink her entire topic after doing more research, or come up with a new argument while revising a full draft. The important point is that social science research is complex and requires time for the writer to brainstorm, draft and revise, research, and edit. No researcher ever writes just one draft.

Finding a Topic

Sometimes your instructor will choose the topic for a writing assignment, and sometimes you will be able to choose your own topic. Whether you need to narrow a topic chosen for you or come up with your own topic, the following advice will help you find a focused topic you and your readers will find interesting.

> **Don't just choose a topic because it sounds easy or you can't think of anything else to write about.**

If the writer isn't interested in the topic, the reader won't be interested in the writing. Try to find a topic that you want to know more about, or that you already have a personal connection to. One way to brainstorm to find an interesting topic is to use an authority and interest list…

> **Use an authority and interest list to find a topic that you have a personal connection with.**

Without putting any pressure on yourself, come up with a list of 20-30 things that you are an authority on or have personal experience with. These could be hobbies, areas of expertise, academic areas, places you've lived, etc. Then come up with a list of 20-30 things you aren't familiar with but would like to know more about. After you've made these lists, brainstorm some social science topics related to your lists. For example, if "sports" was on your authority list, one topic for a sociology research paper might be "gender differences in women's and men's professional sports leagues."

> **Avoid topics that have already been written about extensively.**

The death penalty is a complex and interesting topic, but there has been so much written about it that a criminology student will have a difficult time finding something new to add. Your audience—including your instructor—might be less interested in reading about a common topic than a topic that has not been thoroughly researched and debated. Coming up with an original topic can be difficult even for experienced social scientists, but using an authority and interest list is one way to find a new angle or new area for research.

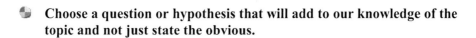

Choose a question or hypothesis that will add to our knowledge of the topic and not just state the obvious.

Most of your social science instructors will ask you to conduct original research. This doesn't mean that your study has to be ground-breaking and change the way social scientists view the world! It just means that you don't want to just repeat previous research or restate the obvious. For example, topics like, "Is crime is a problem in impoverished cities?" or "Are economic depressions a cause of homelessness?" are not interesting research questions because they state the obvious and don't add anything to our knowledge of the topic.

Narrow broad topics.

Because you are often writing about societies and cultures in disciplines like economics, anthropology, and political science, it's easy to choose topics that are so broad you could write an entire book on the subject. It's not bad to begin with a broad topic, but narrowing a topic down to a manageable size will help you focus your research and your writing. For example, the topic "studies about racial inequality in America" would be far too broad for a literature review assignment—you could spend years in the library collecting articles and books on such a broad topic. You could narrow this topic by location (racial inequality in large corporations), ethnic group (educational inequality faced by Native Americans), time period (racial inequality and voting in the 2004 election), or type (housing discrimination and race).

Prewriting

Social science writing is challenging, and it's a good idea to gather your thoughts, brainstorm, and do some rough, rough drafting when you're ready to write. This initial brainstorming is what writing teachers call "prewriting." The important point to remember when you're prewriting is to let the words flow. Don't put pressure on yourself to get it perfect when you're brainstorming. Get your thoughts on paper or on the computer and worry about organizing and editing later.

Dan Melzer: Writing, Reading, and Researching in the Disciplines: Student Guides

Student Guides

Writing, Reading, and Researching in the Social Sciences

Here are some tips for prewriting:

> ### 🌀 Use "freewriting" to loosen up and brainstorm.

Freewriting is a good technique for letting ideas flow and not getting blocked before you even begin. Think about your topic, and just start writing whatever comes to mind. Don't worry about grammar or organization…just write, write, write. Then read over what you've written and look for ideas or examples that may be useful in your first rough draft. You could also use freewriting to narrow a topic.

> ### 🌀 Use clustering to narrow topics or create a rough organization.

You can use clustering to narrow a topic, organize a first draft, or discover new topics or arguments. Clustering involves writing down your main topic and branching off from that topic to create related topics or sub-topics. Here is an example of clustering using a topic from the previous section of this guide, "gender differences in women's and men's professional sports":

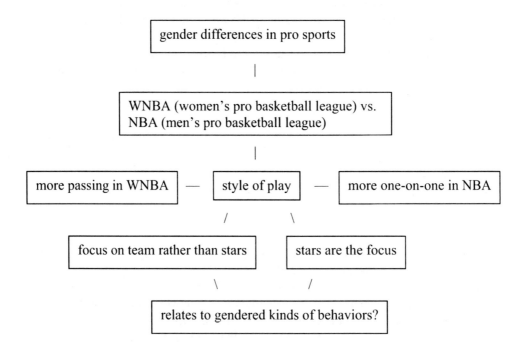

🌀 Tap into your prior knowledge of a topic.

Before you begin to research a topic and draft, write down everything you already know about the topic. Create a list of things you know or believe about your topic, or write a "quick draft." A quick draft is a kind of focused freewriting where you write a rough draft of an essay in one sitting without worrying about organization, spelling, grammar, etc. You may be able to use parts of this quick draft when you start your formal drafting process.

🌀 Create a list of questions you have about the topic

Let's say you are writing an anthropology research paper on wedding rituals in Mexico. Before you begin to write and research, create a list of questions you have about the topic. For example, What are the purposes of the rituals? How do they reflect the larger culture? What role do cultural gender differences play in the rituals?

Drafting and Revising

When you're writing an ethnography or a literature review or any complex kind of social science writing, it's easy to get overwhelmed when it's time to start writing the first draft. It's good to keep in mind that no one gets it right on the first draft. The following advice is based on this idea that writing is a process that requires a lot of revising.

🌀 Don't put pressure on yourself to get it perfect on the first draft.

Sometimes when we write for school we forget that no one is going to see that first draft but us. Think of your first draft like the first exploration of a place you've never been: it's "exploratory." Trying to get every sentence perfect or every idea complete and organized on the first draft makes the writing process much more difficult.

🌀 Start with what you're most interested in or confident about writing.

There's no rule that says that when you write your *first* draft you need to start with the introduction and then write in logical order from there. Let's say you're writing an experimental report for a psychology class, and you're most confident about writing the results section. You might write this section first, and then go back and write the lit review or methods sections.

🌀 Remember the differences between revising and editing.

Because social science writing is complex and no social scientist ever writes a perfect first draft, it's a mistake to think that revising means just editing sentences or looking for typos. Revising requires rethinking larger issues than just sentences and words. When you revise, don't be afraid to change the focus of your topic, question your theoretical perspective, move paragraphs, delete and add examples, etc.

🌀 Give yourself time to look at what you've written with a fresh eye.

When an instructor gives you a writing assignment, it's a good idea to get an early start and give yourself enough time to put down your rough draft for a day or two and then come back with a fresh eye. Every writer has a hard time getting some distance from what he or she has written, and if you give yourself some time between drafts, you'll have a more "objective" eye as a reader of your own writing.

🌀 Get feedback during the revision process.

Most social scientists believe that knowledge is socially constructed—that we make meaning by discussing and debating ideas with others. It makes sense, then, to get feedback on your writing before the final draft. Once you get involved in a topic it's difficult to get an "objective" eye on what you've written, so getting feedback from an outsider will give you a sense of what a reader would need to know more about, or what questions a reader would have for you. Asking your instructor to read a draft is one option. You could also seek out a classmate (or classmates) and share drafts. If your campus has a writing center or tutoring center, bring the assignment and your rough draft to get helpful feedback from an experienced tutor.

Editing and Proofreading

In writing for the social sciences, the content of your writing—your ideas and arguments, the quality of your research, your application and understanding of social theory, the value of the results of your research—will be what instructors pay the most attention to when they evaluate your writing. However, it's important to communicate those results clearly to your readers, and that requires editing and proofreading. Editing and proofreading involves revising sentences for clarity, correcting grammar and spelling errors, and finding typos. Experienced writers save editing and proofreading for the final stage of the writing process. However, social science writing is a specialized and complicated kind of writing, so don't be surprised if you need to devote much more time to editing and proofreading a research article review or experimental report than you would to editing a letter to your parents or an email to a friend.

Here are some tips for editing your final draft:

> **Read what you've written out loud.**

It's usually easier to *hear* run-on sentences or typos when you're reading aloud than it is to *see* them when you're reading silently, because you tend to fill in the blanks or skip over words when you're reading silently. Reading out loud can also help you hear your voice as a writer. If you're using too much jargon, or if you have too many long (or short) sentences in a row, you'll be able to hear this when you read out loud.

> **Read what you've written backwards, from the last word to the first.**

This might sound like an odd piece of advice, but it's an effective proofreading tool when you're looking for typos or misspelled words. This technique forces you to look at every word and not skim over a typo or misspelling. It's a good technique to use for the very final proofreading of your paper.

> **Give your final draft to a friend or classmate to edit and proofread.**

A social scientist submitting an article to an academic journal or a popular magazine will have an editor from the journal or magazine who makes sure that the final draft of the article is clean. Since experienced writers seek feedback from outside readers at all stages of the writing process, it makes sense for student writers to do the same.

A Guide to Common Social Science Writing Genres

The writing process I talked about in the previous section isn't always the same for every kind of writing assignment. In your social science courses, think of each new writing assignment as a different situation that will require you to think about the purpose, audience, and genre of what you're writing. "Genres" are kinds of writing that have evolved (and continue to evolve) over time to fulfill specific purposes within a discipline. Genres aren't set in stone: each discipline and even each instructor will have different expectations for abstracts, lit reviews, research reports, etc. The following advice about common social science genres provides some general guidelines, but it's also important to get a clear sense of your instructor's expectations.

Abstracts

Abstracts are one or two paragraph summaries of the hypothesis, research methods, and results of an article or book. You most often find abstracts at the beginning of articles in social science journals or in social science journal databases (most social science journals require authors to include an abstract with their articles). Abstracts allow readers to get a quick sense of the author's topic and the results of the research.

Here are some common features of abstracts:

- 200-300 words, usually one paragraph.

- Summarizes the central question or hypothesis, the research methods of collecting and analyzing data, the population studied, and the findings of the research.

- Written concisely and precisely, with no unnecessary words or flowery language.

- Includes any key words or concepts that are critical to the research.

- Written without your personal opinions on the topic: the goal is to summarize the article, not make evaluations. Readers should be able to draw their own conclusions about the value of the research, and you should avoid using "I feel" or "I think."

Notice the features listed above in this example abstract written by the authors of an article in the journal *Criminology*:

We examine the effect of alcohol consumption on an individual's risk of victimization for physical and sexual assault. Analyses of the National Violence Against Women Survey suggest that the frequency and amount of alcohol people consume has strong effects on their risk of victimization when drinking, but is not associated with their victimization while sober. This evidence suggests that drinking has a situational causal effect on victimization, and cannot be attributed to opportunity factors associated with drinking. This effect is particularly strong for men and young adults, who may be more likely to behave provocatively when under the influence. Victims of sexual assaults and men assaulted by their female partners are also particularly likely to be drinking.

The abstract begins with the authors' purpose for the study, then the research methods (analysis of a national survey), and the primary findings. The abstract also provides key terms such as "victimization" and "situational casual effect." Sentences are concise and the transitions from one sentence to the next are smooth.

Literature Reviews

This passage from a psychology course assignment provides a good overview of what the expectations are for a literature review:

> Your paper will be a literature review of a topic in cognitive psychology. A literature review is a well-organized overview and evaluation of the relevant research or findings related to your topic. I place emphasis on the words "overview and evaluation." You will be interpreting the available information and research findings and then drawing conclusions.

Sometimes your instructor will require a literature review as a separate assignment to give you practice exploring the research on a topic and looking for places where further research needs to be done, as in the example above. Sometimes a literature review will be part of a research report assignment (setting the context of your own study by discussing similar research on your topic). Whether given as a separate assignment or as part of a research paper, literature reviews are more than just summaries of prior studies. They also ask you to compare and contrast and make your own evaluations.

Here are some common features of literature reviews:

- Focused on a specific area of research (for example, the research on courtship rituals of a specific ethnic group or voting trends among the elderly in Florida).

- Must include the important studies of the topic, including books and journal articles.

- Compares research methods of the studies reviewed as well as results.

- Often ends with a statement about gaps in the literature or the need for further research.

- Organized either chronologically, by type of study, type of research method, or topic.

- More than just a summary of the research: also includes comparing and contrasting and your interpretation and evaluation of the research.

Case Studies

Case studies are reports of intense observations of an individual or a small group of individuals. Case studies can be used as evidence for a research report or they can be the focus of an entire writing assignment. If your instructor gives you a case study assignment, or if you decide to conduct case studies as part of a larger research project, you'll be practicing an important social science research method.

Case studies usually have the following features:

- Intense, prolonged, and structured observation of an individual or small group of individuals.

- Evidence about the subject under study from a variety of sources: observation, interviews, textual evidence, etc.

- Often used as an example or model for a larger argument or hypothesis.

- The observer attempts to keep a degree of detachment from the subject under study, unless the research is "participant observer" (see ethnography below).

Research reports

Research reports (which are often called experimental reports in psychology) are one of the standard genres for reporting the results of an original research study. The structure of a research report is a reflection of the way social scientists create knowledge: come up with an original topic and an interesting hypothesis, design a research project to explore the hypothesis, place the research in the context of similar studies and link it to broader social theory, describe the research methods, discuss the results and the significance of the results, and speculate on future research in the area studied.

Since research reports are one of the most complex social science genres, they tend to vary from discipline to discipline and instructor to instructor. For example, most instructors will expect a formal, detached style, which will give the sense of scientific "objectivity." Many social scientists have questioned whether "objectivity" is possible, however, and they have criticized the lack of acknowledgment of the role of the researcher in formal studies. This is another reason it's important to get a clear sense of the expectations of your instructor.

Despite some variations, most research reports have these shared criteria:

- An original and focused question or hypothesis drives the research.

- Follows research report format: title page, abstract, statement of the problem, the hypothesis or question, review of the literature on the topic, research methods, results/discussion, notes, references, appendixes.

- Use of academic, scholarly sources for context and support.

- Use of common social science research methods such as sampling, surveys, experiments, interviews, observation, case studies, etc.

- Use of quantitative information (statistics, charts, graphs) and/or qualitative information (observation, interviews, textual analysis, social theory).

- Includes tables and figures, when appropriate.

This assignment from a political science course will give you a sense of the expectations for a research report in the social sciences:

> This assignment involves reviewing the research that has been done on a particular subject, identifying a question that has been overlooked, designing some way to answer that question, using that method to investigate the answer, and reporting your results. Your method of investigation should be appropriate to your question; some possible research methods include administering a questionnaire, participant observation, archival research, content analysis, database analysis (there are, of course, many others). Your paper should include your literature review; statement of the question you are investigating and the rationale for investigating this question; a description of your research methods; an analysis of the data; and a discussion of your conclusions and their implications.

Ethnographies

Ethnographies are a kind of "participant observer" study. That means that rather than taking the stance of an objective, detached observer, the ethnographer interacts with a culture or group over a prolonged period and gathers data from careful and structured observation, interviews, sampling, surveys, etc. (what the ethnographer refers to as "fieldwork"). The ethnographer collects a lot of different kinds of information in order to achieve "triangulation." Triangulation means getting a variety of points of view and types of data in order to get richer, more valid evidence. Even with triangulation and prolonged observation, an ethnographer does not try to generalize about an entire group of people or an entire culture.

These are some features of ethnographies and fieldwork research:

- The researcher tries to understand the group or culture from an "insider" point of view, rather than posing as objective or detached.

- The researcher typically uses observation, interviews, sampling, surveys, or other research methods to triangulate the data and provide a rich description of the culture.

- The researcher typically comes up with research questions after immersing herself in the culture rather than before her observations of the culture begin.

- The style is much more descriptive and often more personal than other kinds of formal social science research.

This ethnography assignment from an anthropology course will give you a sense of the fieldwork research process:

Ethnography is the work of describing a culture. The essential core of this activity aims to understand another way of life. The first step of an ethnography is deciding what to study. Choose a social event or a situation that you would like to know more about and can observe in a reasonable amount of time

The second step of an ethnography involves thinking about the kinds of questions you would like to answer. Questions may be broad (Why do you do this? How do you do this?) or they may be focused (Why do people dress this way?). Research questions may change while you are doing fieldwork and you may not even know what they are until you are well into the process of collecting data, but it is important to remember that ethnographies tell the reader something about cultural values.

Strategies for Reading Difficult Texts

Because social scientists create theories and hypotheses about complex social issues and place their research in the context of prior studies, it's not surprising that the articles and books you read in social science courses are challenging. You can't approach an article in *Journal of Politics* or a book about educational theories the same way you'd approach reading a popular magazine or the newspaper. To understand social science texts, you need a set of strategies you can bring with you to your readings. What follows is some practical advice for reading difficult texts.

Advice for reading difficult texts:

Use "prereading" strategies to prepare yourself for reading a difficult article or book.

Prereading is a way to prepare yourself for your initial reading of a text. Think of it like reading a map before you make your trip: it prepares you for the road ahead by giving you clues about what to expect. If you're assigned an article from a scholarly journal, read the abstract and skim the major sections and the conclusions. If you're assigned a book, read the table of contents and the introduction before you dive into the book. For a textbook chapter, skim the headings and subheadings and look for a chapter summary before you begin.

🌀 Understand your purpose for reading before you begin reading.

If you are reading merely to prepare for a multiple-choice exam, your reading purpose might be to understand the author's main ideas, key terms, and important arguments and examples. If you are reading to gather information for a research paper, in addition to understanding the author's main ideas you'll want to think about your reactions to these ideas. If you are writing a literature review, your focus will be on a specific topic or area of research. Each of these are different purposes for reading, and require different reading strategies.

🌀 Annotate while you read to be an active rather than a passive reader.

Passive readers just read texts for information, but active readers question texts and think about their own responses to the author's arguments. Active readers read with a pen in hand, ready to underline key terms, circle places where they have questions, and jot down their own ideas and arguments. Another way to be an active reader is to use a double-entry journal…

🌀 Use a double-entry journal when you need to keep track of the author's main ideas and your response.

A double-entry journal is a kind of reading log. On a notebook or on the computer, make a journal with a line down the center. On one side of the line, record the author's key terms, research methods, and main ideas and results. On the other side of the line, write your questions and responses.

Here's an example of the beginning of a double-entry journal:

Author's hypothesis: class plays a greater role than gender in how people vote.	What other factors play a role in how people vote?
Research methods: case studies of 100 voters in Virginia.	I don't think this sample size is large enough to make generalizations.
Key term: "identification." How voters identified themselves in terms of social class.	Interesting that the majority of voters identified themselves as "middle class," but the researchers often labeled them differently.

🍂 **If at first you don't understand, read and read again.**

Just as successful writers never write just one draft but revise and revise, successful readers aren't afraid to reread when they don't understand a text. Speed reading might be a useful technique when you only need a few facts from a relatively simple text, but to fully engage complex social science texts, good reading is often slow reading and rereading. If you're struggling to understand a text, it's also helpful to seek out help from a classmate or your instructor.

Researching in the Social Sciences: Collecting, Evaluating, Integrating, and Citing Sources

Research is at the heart of the social sciences. Social scientists conduct research to support their hypotheses and they cite prior studies to place their work in the context of larger conversations and theories about issues in the social sciences. In your social science courses, you might be asked to conduct interviews, give surveys, observe cultures, review the scholarly literature on a social science topic, etc. Your research process will involve collecting relevant sources and evaluating those sources, conducting your own original research, integrating your research and outside sources in a written report, and citing sources within the body of your text and in a reference page.

| | |

Collecting Sources and Conducting Library Research

Library research is critical to social scientists. In order to find gaps in the research where original studies would be valuable, to provide support for their own research, and to connect their research to social theory, social scientists need to review prior research on their topics. That means finding articles in scholarly journals and books, which requires searching library databases and collections.

Here are some things to consider when you begin collecting sources:

🔹 **Social science research requires searching in specialized databases.**

Social scientists don't just get on the Internet and do a Google search when it's time to research a topic. Social scientists rely on databases that contain scholarly journals. Your library will have a list of these databases, which include general social science databases like *Social Sciences Index* as well as specialized databases for specific social science sub-disciplines, like *Anthropological Literature* and *Sociological Abstracts*.

🔹 **Keep track of key search words and use library databases to find relevant search words.**

Before you begin collecting sources, brainstorm a list of key words you might use as search terms. For example, if you were writing a research paper on the relationship between economic class and education, "class" and "education" would be two key words. But if you searched *Social Sciences Index* using just these two words, you would retrieve an overwhelming number of articles. Often the database you are searching will give you ideas for other key words, listed with each article you pull up. For example, "social class" and "socioeconomic factors" are two related key words listed in *Social Sciences Index* that might help you narrow your focus. Combining terms by using "and" also helps narrow searches ("social class and socioeconomic factors").

🔹 **Use the reference pages of the research you collect to find other relevant sources.**

When you find an article or book on the topic you are investigating, take a close look at the reference page to find more sources on that topic. It's also a good idea to pay attention to which studies in the area you are researching are cited the most, because these will be considered the most influential.

Evaluating Sources

The kind of sources you use will depend on the kind of genre you are writing, your purpose, and your audience. Most social science writing, however, requires you to cite scholarly sources. There are a number of advantages of scholarly sources:

Scholarly sources are peer reviewed.

This means respected researchers in the field review articles and book manuscripts before they are accepted for publication.

Scholarly sources focus on furthering knowledge rather than making a profit.

You will not find popular advertisements in scholarly journals. The audience is scholars in the field, rather than the general public.

Scholarly sources have strict research standards.

Writers of scholarly books and articles must cite the relevant previous research, conduct ethical research using accepted socials science research methods, and report their results accurately and fairly.

Scholarly sources rarely have an overt political agenda.

Most scholarly journals and publishers do not have an overt political agenda, and do not accept research they perceive to be biased or prejudiced. Of course, every publisher and every author has *some* agenda, so even scholarly sources must be given careful scrutiny.

Dan Melzer: Writing, Reading, and Researching in the Disciplines: Student Guides

Student Guides

Writing, Reading, and Researching in the Social Sciences

© The McGraw–Hill Companies, 2005

Evaluating Internet Sources

In many ways, the Internet makes life easier for researchers. A variety of valuable socials science resources are available online, from journal articles to government documents to entire books. But most websites aren't peer reviewed: anyone can post anything they want to the Internet, which means that much of what you get from the Internet won't be as useful as a resource for social science writing as scholarly articles and books will be.

You can and should use the Internet to find sources, but keep this advice in mind for evaluating Internet resources:

Use the Internet address to evaluate the source of the website.

Internet sites that end with ".com" are commercial enterprises. Even if they contain useful information, they are often trying to sell products or advertising space. Internet sites that end with ".org" are nonprofit organizations, and they can be a more reliable source of information than ".com" sites. Not all ".org" sites are reliable sources of information, however. Organizations that have overt political agendas, for example, may not be as reliable a source for statistics as scholarly articles and books. Internet sites that end with ".gov" (government sites) and ".edu" (education sites) tend to be the most reliable.

Avoid Internet sites that are not associated with a reliable and respected organization or individual.

You might find an interesting quote or some useful statistics on "Joe's Sociology Website," but your fellow scholars in the field of sociology will not trust that this is a reliable site. Information collected from websites associated with organizations, schools, and governments will be more useful and more reliable than pages posted by individuals, unless the individual publishing the website is a respected scholar in the field.

Try to find the original print source for any information you collect from the Internet.

Sometimes statistics, quotes, or other information posted on websites originally appeared in a book or scholarly journal. If the information from the original print source is available on the website, try to track down the print source and cite it directly, rather than citing the website. The information may be the same in print and online, but the print source will be seen as more reliable.

Integrating Sources

Integrating sources is one of the most difficult aspects of social science writing, but there are some general guidelines that can help you effectively cite sources. This section of this guide focuses on integrating sources in the body of your text, and the next section focuses on formatting the reference page.

There are different style manuals used in different social science fields: for example, ASA style (American Sociological Association) and APA style (American Psychological Association). Since APA is the most common style used in the social sciences, it's the style used in the examples in this section. One reason that APA is popular in the social sciences is that it highlights the year the source was published, which is a more important consideration in social science research than it is in most research in the humanities. In APA style, you cite the author's last name, the year of publication, and the page number or numbers that contain the information you're citing.

Advice for integrating sources:

Know when to quote directly from a source and when to summarize or paraphrase the information from the source.

Quote the exact words of a source only when you are citing a strong statement from the author or trying to capture the author's distinctive style, voice, or argument. Always put an author's exact words in quotes, and in APA style, include the year and page number.

Here's an example of a case where it is appropriate to use an exact quote to capture the author's voice:

Cohen argues that "the slippery slope of nuclear proliferation, with each side building bigger and deadlier weapons of mass destruction, leads us ever faster to our own destruction" (2005, p. 32).

Note that since you introduced the author ("Cohen argues..."), you don't need to include the author's last name in the parentheses. If you include the year and the name of the author in the sentence ("Cohen (2005) argues...") you only need to cite the page number in the parentheses. The parentheses are always placed outside the quotation mark, and the period is placed after the parentheses. If there is more than one author, use et al. (Cohen et al., 2005, p.32).

Summarize information from a source in your own words when you are citing facts and statistics.

Let's say you want to cite the following information from an article by Zuckerman:

The number of hours Americans work annually has dropped from about 2,700 at the beginning of the century to about 1,800 today; average life expectancy has gone up about 45 years to 80.

Although you could put this entire passage in quotes and cite it word-for-word in your essay, since the information is just a series of statistics, it would be more effective to simply summarize the information in your own words and cite the source. For example:

Social scientists such as Zuckerman (2003) argue that American life has vastly improved over the last hundred years: Zuckerman points out that Americans work 1,800 hours annually today, compared to 2,700 hours at the beginning of the 20th century, and life expectancy has increased forty-five years (p.59).

Avoid the "collage of sources" paper.

It's important to place your research in the context of prior studies, and to use information from scholarly sources to support your arguments. If you are conducting original research, however, it's also important to avoid creating a "collage of sources" that contains none of your own words, arguments, and research. Avoid paragraph after paragraph of quotes of someone else's words and ideas.

Don't just insert your sources; engage them.

Becoming a social scientist means entering the conversations going on about important debates in your field. Social scientists don't just mechanically drop sources into a paper; they enter a discussion with other scholars and their theories. Introduce sources, explain to your readers how sources support your argument, and engage in a debate with the scholars you cite. Think of research as a conversation.

Avoid plagiarism by citing any information you get from outside sources.

If you want to be a successful social scientist, you will need to establish the trust of your readers. If you use exact words and phrases from a source, it's important that you put these words in quotes and cite the source. If you get information or ideas from a source and put it in your own words, you still need to cite the source, both in the body of your text and in the reference page. You don't need to cite common knowledge (information that most of your readers will know from general sources), but you do need to cite any specific information or ideas you get from a source. Intentional plagiarism is a violation of academic honesty codes and a serious offense.

Preparing an APA Style Reference Page

The formatting style of the American Psychological Association, known as APA style, is the most common style used in the socials sciences. There are other style manuals that arc uscd in the social sciences (for example, American Sociological Association style), but since APA is the most common, this section focuses on creating a reference page using APA style. This guide to APA style is not meant to be exhaustive: if you are unsure how to cite a source in your reference page and cannot find an example of the type of source in this guide, refer to the APA style manual.

In an APA style reference page, you list all of the sources you cited in the body of your paper. The reference page is numbered and appears at the end of your paper. Following are the guidelines for formatting books, journals, magazines, newspapers, and websites in your reference page. Remember to organize the references in alphabetical order by the authors' last names.

A book with one author

Cite the author's last name, first initials, year of publication, title, place of publication, and publisher. If the book does not have an author, begin with the title, but do not use articles when you alphabetize (*A*, *The*, or *An*).

Schaefer, R.T. (2004). *Sociology: A brief introduction* (6th ed). New York: McGraw-Hill.

A book with more than one author

List all the authors in the order they're listed in the book, separated by commas.

Miller, P. M. & Wilson, M. J. (1983). *A dictionary of social science methods*. New York: Wiley.

An edited book

List the editor or editors, followed by (Ed.) or (Eds.).

Outhwaite, W. & Bottomore, T. (Eds.). (1993). *The Blackwell dictionary of twentieth-century social thought*. Cambridge, MA: Blackwell Reference.

A selection from an edited book or anthology

Cite the author and title of the selection, editor and title of the anthology, and page range of the selection.

Koslowski, P. (2002). Ethics of capitalism. In L. Zsolnai (Ed.), *Ethics and the future of capitalism* (p.p. 43-67). New Brunswick, NJ: Transaction.

Two or more works by the same author

List the works in order of date of publication, the earliest date first.

Dewey, J. (1916) *Democracy and education*. New York: MacMillan.

Dewey, J. (1938). *Experience and education*. New York: Colliers Books.

A government document

When no author is provided, use the government agency as the author.

U.S. Department of Education, National Center for Education Statistics. (2004). *Digest of education statistics 2003*. Washington, DC: U.S. Government Printing Office.

An article in a scholarly journal

Cite the author, year and month, article title, journal, volume and number of journal, and page range.

Thies, C. G. (2005, June). War, rivalry, and state building in Latin America. *American Journal of Political Science, 49* (3), 451-466.

A magazine article

Cite the author, year and month (and day if the magazine is published weekly), article title, magazine, volume, and page range.

Samuelson, R. (1995, May 22). Economics lesson. *Newsweek, 125*, 67.

A newspaper article

Cite the author, year, month, day, article title, newspaper, and page number.

Kinzer, S. (2004, December 26). Rethinking past American cultures. *The New York Times*, p. C1.

An online article or abstract from a database

Cite the author, year and month, article title, journal, volume and number of journal, page range, date the article was retrieved, and name of the database.

Weil, S. (2005, Winter). Child rearing in America: Challenges facing parents with young children. *Journal of Comparative Family Studies*, 36 (1), 155-156. Retrieved May 2, 2005, from PsycInfo database.

A website

Cite the author (or organization hosting the website), date the site was published or last updated, title, date retrieved, and website address.

U.S. Department of Justice. (2004, December). *Criminal offender statistics*. Retrieved April 22, 2005 from http://www.ojp.usdoj.gov/bjs/crimoff.htm#findings

A Note on Footnotes

Use footnotes when you want to offer further explanation to your readers without breaking the flow of your argument. Put superscript numbers at the points in your text you want to include footnotes. The footnotes should appear on a separate page after the end of the essay but before the reference page, titled "Footnotes" and double-spaced. Indent the first line of each footnote five spaces, and type the superscript number and then the note. Keep in mind that footnotes should not be overused: only include information you think will be truly helpful to readers.

APA Style Paper Format

Following are basic guidelines for formatting your paper in APA style:

- Use a standard 12 point font: Courier, Times, or Bookman.

- Include a title page with the title centered and a few lines below the title your name, the course number and title, the instructor's name, and the date. Number the title page.

- Use 1" margins except for the upper right-hand corner, which should include a short version of your title and page number on each page.

- For quotations of more than 40 words, indent each line of the quote (using block format) five spaces from the left margin. Do not indent from the right margin.

- Double-space throughout, including the abstract, footnotes, and references.

- Primary headings should be centered and all key words in the heading should be capitalized. Secondary headings should be italicized and flush against the left-hand margin.

- If your instructor asks for an abstract, it should appear on its own numbered page, entitled "Abstract," and placed just after the title page.

- Place tables, charts, graphs, and other visuals close to the place you refer to them in the text. Label each visual "Table" or "Figure" and number them consecutively (Figure 1, Figure 2).

- Place the reference page after the body of the paper (or the after the footnotes, if included) but before the appendices.

- Appendices should be placed at the end of the paper. Number and title each appendix using Roman numerals (for example, Appendix II: Interview Questions)

Chapter 1: In-Class Writing

This chapter provides the basics of writing. The in-class writing assignment can be anything from an essay question on a test to short response answers or reviews of readings. These kinds of writing assignments can be the most difficult: you don't have much time, you may not have notes, and it is hard to imagine the written page as a formal essay.

Here you will be able to learn all the parts and tools of effective essays. By incorporating these suggestions into your essays, your answers will be more complete and interesting. After reading this chapter you will understand how to:

- Anticipate your teachers' questions
- Answer questions with complete responses
- Use different kinds of sentences
- Organize your paragraphs
- Make transitions between paragraphs
- Incorporate all major parts of the essay into your papers
- Use different writing tools for better papers

As you progress to research papers and more formal writing, you should keep the parts of an essay in mind. They will help you craft a polished paper that will be impressive!

Practice

Often, in-class essays are timed. You may have an essay question on a final exam or on a standardized test. If you know how long you will have to write your in-class essay, practice by creating conditions similar to the ones you will experience on the exam. Read this chapter first and then:

- Sit down in a quiet place
- Write a question you want to answer (or take questions from your textbooks)
- Use a stopwatch or timer set to 45 minutes or an hour (or the amount of time you will have for your in-class essay)
- Write for the entire time. If you have an hour, you know that you have about 10 minutes per paragraph. Keep track of your progress
- Make sure you have included every part of the essay
- Did you answer the question? Is it legible? What would you do with more time? Where did you lose time? Practice as often as you need to in order to write a five or six paragraph essay in 45 minutes or an hour

1.1 In-Class Writing: Answering the Question

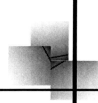

Anticipating Questions

Before you get to the test, you can know what your teacher might ask!

The most effective method for doing well on essay tests and other in-class writing is being prepared. Of course, being prepared means studying and completing reading assignments. But, being prepared also means knowing what a teacher might ask and how to answer it.

Questions your teacher asks usually fit into one of six categories.

1) **Knowledge:** define, list, name, recall, record, relate

   The first kind of response a teacher may look for is a knowledge-based response. Writing assignments that ask you to define cellular mitosis, for example, want you to use memorization skills to respond.

2) **Comprehension:** describe, discuss, explain, express, identify, locate, recognize, report, restate, review, tell, translate

   Question words found under comprehension ask you to pull information from a context. For example, you could be asked to identify the protagonist in a novel. You have to know both what a protagonist is and what happens in the novel.

3) **Application:** apply, demonstrate, dramatize, employ, illustrate, interpret, operate, practice, schedule, sketch, use

   Application questions require you to use information in a new way—that is, take it and use it in a new context. Using the concepts in the Declaration of Independence to argue for justice in a contemporary world conflict exemplifies this skill.

4) **Analysis:** analyze, appraise, calculate, categorize, compare, contrast, criticize, debate, diagram, differentiate, distinguish, examine, experiment, inspect, inventory, question, relate, solve, test

   Analysis questions are among the most common for in-class writing tests because these questions test your ability to think critically about a problem. Responding to analysis questions requires you to pull to knowledge from the class and usually necessitates drawing together multiple theories, ideas, and readings.

These categories were developed by Benjamin Bloom in 1956 and are known as

Bloom's Taxonomy.

Use the question words found next to each category to help you think about how to study.

What question words can you imagine appearing on a test? How would you answer them?

Search for more information about what kind of answers teachers are looking for by researching Bloom's Taxonomy.

5) **Synthesis:** arrange, assemble, collect, compose, construct, create, design, formulate, manage, organize, plan, prepare, propose, set up

   Synthesis questions ask you to create a new context for information you have learned. Creating a business proposal, for example, involves using the principles of your microeconomics course with an imaginary idea for a product or service.

6) **Evaluation:** appraise, assess, choose, compare, estimate, evaluate, judge, measure, rate, revise, score, select, value

   Evaluation questions are sometimes the most difficult because each evaluation question really wants you to use a system of values to determine an answer. The questions want you to bring educational, ethical, philosophical, or political science theories to a particular problem. Responding well to these questions means that you not only have to understand an issue, but you also must convincingly show your rationale for evaluation.

If you can keep these categories in mind, you will be able to approach any question with at least some idea of what kind of answer to give.

Answering the Question by Using the Question

Now that you know what might be asked, how do you answer the question?

Even prepared students get an unexpectedly bad grade on writing assignments sometimes.

Why?

Often, these poor marks are caused by a failure to actually answer the question. Failing to answer the question usually happens when a student gets on a tangent while writing.

Use this technique to avoid getting off track:

> Before you begin to draft your answer, take a piece of paper and write down a one or two sentence answer to the question that pulls from all the keywords in the question into the answer. You might even draw lines between the question and your brief answer to make sure you cover each part of the question.

> Keywords in questions are:
> - Question words (who, what, when, where, why, how)
> - Knowledge category words (apply, define, evaluate, etc.)
> - Number words (three examples, two poems, etc.)
> - Terms or issues the question asks about

Some examples of this technique:

Q. Using three different examples, discuss symbiosis.

A. Symbiosis involves two or more organisms living together in a more of less permanent relationship. Three examples include ants and aphids (mutualism), lice and people (parasitism), and egrets and cape buffalo (commensalisms).

Q. What is modernism, and how does T.S. Eliot's poetry exemplify this definition?

A. Modernism is a technique of writing that developed after World War I in response to the atrocities of war. Eliot's poems break with previous forms of poetry, are fragmentary, and portray seemingly desperate situations.

Now you have a map for your complete response. A complete response will involve an introduction, thesis, and supporting paragraphs. The brief answer you wrote may become the thesis in your more developed response. If your thesis is on target, your in-class essay will also be more accurate.

> When you are getting ready to write research papers, try using this technique to make sure your paper is on track.
>
> No matter how brilliant your paper may be, if it does not answer the question your teacher asks, it is not so good.

1.2 In-Class Writing: Patterns for Writing

Paragraph Patterns

Paragraphs are blocks of writing that you use to propel your papers forward toward answering the question your teacher has selected. Generally, every paragraph has these features:

- Indent first line
- A topic sentence
- Supporting sentences
- A concluding sentence
- A paragraph usually consists of **approximately five to ten sentences**
- An entire page should not be one paragraph
- Each paragraph should transition from one to the next

Topic Sentences
- Do not start a paragraph with a quotation
- Avoid "the purpose of this paper/paragraph/ etc."
- "According to ..." is not a good opening line for a paragraph (it may be useful for introducing a quotation later in the paragraph)
- Avoid: "I believe ..." "I think that ..." "In my opinion ..."

Topic sentences: These sentences tell your reader what the paragraph is about.

Supporting sentences: These sentences explain and justify the topic. They may include quotations.

Concluding sentences: These sentences have two functions: first they summarize what you have written, and second they help you make a transition between paragraphs.

Transition: This is the idea of "flow" in your paper. Each paragraph needs a bridge to the next one. This bridge is most easily formed by using a key word from the previous sentence that ended one paragraph in the first sentence of the following paragraph. You should also create a bridge from an essay's thesis to each paragraph's topic sentence by reusing key terms.

Paragraph patterns are easy: all you need to do is find an organizing principle for your supporting sentences. Here are a few organizational patterns you might try.

Argumentative Patterns:

General to particular / Global to local: Your first supporting sentence thinks globally about your issue, your next nationally, and your last one may consider the issue as it relates to your hometown.
Least important to most important: Consider organizing your support starting from minor benefits and building toward the single greatest benefit of your idea or position.

Descriptive Patterns:

Senses: Begin with what you want your reader to see, and use each subsequent sentence to incorporate a different sense until all five are included.

Right to left / Top to bottom: If a place or scene is important, try to describe it in order. Start from the right and progress across the stage, or begin with the ceiling and move down the wall until you describe the floor last.
Who, what, when, where, why, how: This pattern can be most useful in journalistic writing. Try to answer each of these question words in a sentence or two as you progress through your paragraph.
Chronological: Begin at a specific point in time, and develop your paragraph by going forward in time.
Simple to complex: Start with individuals or parts, and progress to a social or mechanical description.

Patterns for Quotations

Use any of the above organizational patterns when you are using quotations, but also keep these tips in mind:

✦ Do not start a paragraph with a quotation

✦ Do not end a paragraph with a quotation

✦ Always introduce your quotation

✦ Always explain your quotation

✦ Always, Always, Always, cite your quotation

Look at these sample paragraphs, and notice how and where they follow the advice on writing paragraphs:

Blues and Jazz music are America's most important exports. According to the Global Jazz Report, over three hundred cities in eighty countries have "American-themed" Blues and Jazz clubs (Fitzgerald 18). This kind of global exposure provides hundreds of young musicians from throughout the United States with opportunities to launch their careers as musicians in places as far-flung as Tokyo, Sidney, or Moscow. Hundreds of conservatories throughout the United States specialize in Jazz and Blues training. Verbena is the largest Mississippi Delta town without a conservatory to train and support young musicians.

The people of Verbena could profit immensely from global Jazz and Blues by opening a conservatory to attract talent to our city. Blues musician Johnny Monroe spoke of just this phenomenon:

> I respect Verbena, but there is no house in my home. I was born and raised in Verbena—I learned the blues in Verbena—but when I got my teeth, I needed more than milk. This is so with much of Verbena's young talent. Meat is in New Orleans and St. Louis. It could be in Verbena, too. (15)

If Johnny could find the support, his concerts and tours alone could double the revenue Verbena raises from tourism. [etc]

Topic Sentence: the reader expects this paragraph to discuss jazz and blues as an export and why they are significant.

Introduce Quotation

Cite Quotation (this is an example of MLA citation)

Explain the significance of your quotation.

Notice the progression from a global to local focus.

Transition word: notice how the word "conservatory" ties the two paragraphs together, but the topic sentence of the second paragraph begins a new idea.

Topic sentence: the reader expects this paragraph to discuss how Verbena can make money from a conservatory.

Block quotes are not in quotation marks, they are indented, and the citation goes after the period.

1.3 In-Class Writing: Parts of Every Essay

Parts of Every Essay

The first step towards turning in better written assignments is understanding what teachers are looking for in your writing. Every essay has certain parts that work together. These parts include:

- Introduction
- Hook
- Thesis
- Conflict
- Support
- Conclusion

These parts can apply to almost any essay that you are writing. Think of the parts as the skeleton of your paper. You must still "flesh" out the details, but this frame will help you hold your essay together. While you may want to adapt these parts of the essay for personal essays, the *Guide* will show you how to make them work in argumentative writing (writing where you have to take a position or convince someone that you're correct). The parts of the essay are expandable: using these same parts you can write a short five or six paragraph in-class essay, or with development and research you can expand these parts into a larger research paper.

It is sometimes helpful to think of an essay like a living organism—for it to thrive it must have all of its parts.

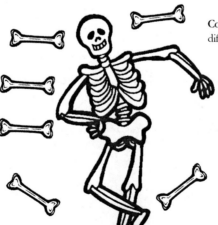

Introduction: the head of your paper contains the main idea which is called the thesis.

Support: the ribs, spine, arms, and legs hold your essay together, but they also function together so that your essay can do some hard work, such as convincing your reader about a certain point of view.

Conflict: the mouth can talk about many different points of view.

Conclusion: your footprint will leave a lasting impression—make sure your last steps are memorable.

Introduction

The introduction works with the Hook (the first few sentences of your paper) and the Thesis (usually, the last few sentences of your introduction) to form a complete picture of what your paper will be about; the introduction sets the tone (witty, scientific, academic, left or right of the issue, etc.) and prepares the reader for what's ahead.

The introduction is your first contact with readers. It is like a handshake when you meet someone: this first impression can make or break your paper.

A typical introduction can be as short as one paragraph in a short paper or in-class essay. More involved research papers, however, may require longer introductions to get the work done.

So, what is the work that an introduction should do in your essay?

You should use your opening paragraph(s) to introduce the terms and main ideas that you will be working with. Use the introduction to:

> - Establish the question at issue and the answer you propose
> - Establish importance of the question (why does your answer matter)
> - Define unfamiliar terms you will be working with
> - Situate your idea within current scholarship
> - Forecast the main points to be taken up

To help you plan your introduction think of these basic patterns:

The funnel introduction: starts with a broad overview of the subject, then "narrows down" to (focuses on) the specific topic, or issue, to be discussed.

The anecdotal introduction: starts with a brief story (usually factual) that illustrates and introduces the general subject, then "narrows down" (or focuses).

The bait and hook introduction: starts with some bit of information, or a dramatic scenario (factual or otherwise), to "catch" the reader's interest; then "narrows down" (or focuses).

The some-say introduction: Starts with a statement made by others (be specific—who are these others?), then replies—often to disagree, or to revise, modify, or extend the opinion on the table.

The deadlock introduction: points out incompatible opinions expressed by two or more people (or camps), or invokes a controversy going on, then undertakes to resolve the dispute—either by agreeing with one of the incompatible opinions and refuting others, or by offering a "new" opinion meant to supersede all others (or, simply to clarify something and/or advance the discussion beyond some sticking-point).

The selective introduction: starts by noting the various aspects of the topic (or issue) that could be taken up— ideally, this list should seem complete—and then zeroes in on one particular aspect as the "most important," or simply as the aspect you're best able to discuss. (This focuses the reader's expectations, and frees you from having to discuss everything that might seem relevant to the topic.)

Hook

The hook is the first chance you have to interest your reader. The hook should be the first few sentences of your introduction. When writing the first couple of sentences, consider this question: what do you offer that makes your reader want to finish the essay?

In the business world, if you don't "hook" your audience within the first few seconds, you've blown the deal. While your teacher is obliged to read your whole essay, you will get a much better grade if you can write so that he or she wants to read beyond the first sentences.

| **Do** something! Snag your reader with:
Thought-provoking statistics
An engrossing story
A significant personality's opinion
A paradox | **Don't** try these worn-out openers:
"According to Webster's Dictionary"
Jokes
"My paper is about" |

Consider the type of introduction you might want to write, then think about which type of hook might work best:

Statistics:

Using numbers to grab readers' attention is a tactic used all the time. Many news channels use this kind of information to frighten or shock people into paying attention. While it is best to use statistics responsibly, sensational numbers can hook readers.

> According to the Center for Global Warming, the Earth is heating up at a rate of 1°F each year. This statistic means that children born in Bangor, Maine in 2005 will need to ride camels to their first jobs by the year 2030.

Stories:

A brief narrative either from experience, from the news, or completely made up may set the tone for a paper and hook a reader with the unfolding drama.

> Imagine windswept sand dunes undulating in the distance. Two sun-scorched travelers struggle up one mound and down the next, tripping, coughing, and blinking back the powerful heat. This scene is not from the Sahara, but it could be a glimpse of Alberta, Canada before the century ends.

Important people:

We live in a world of experts. Interesting quotations from literary and/or scientific figures signal to readers that you pay attention to the same experts that they listen to.

> Kofi Annan recently condemned the United States' failure to sign the Kyoto Treaty. The US finds itself on a warming planet isolated from world opinion.

Paradoxes:

A paradox is a condition that posits two true ideas that seem as though they cannot exist at the same time. Offering to unravel a paradox can hook a reader because he or she will want to find the answer to a seemingly impossible condition.

> As our planet warms up, millions of people may be in store for winters colder than any other on record. Global warming may mean arctic temperatures for many. How can climate change be forecasted?

Thesis

The thesis is probably the single most important part of anything you write. All essays should have a clear one or two sentence thesis that lays out the plan of your paper. Think of your **thesis as a roadmap** for the reader: the thesis will dictate the path you take as you progress toward the conclusion. It will show your reader what stops you plan to make along the way.

> A THESIS is a concise map to your paper.

Hallmarks of a thesis statement:

If you are reading an essay and want to find the thesis statement, the following are some key sentence constructions you might want to look for:

- This paper will…

- The text [poem, short story, novel, play] does…

- The author of [title] illustrates…

Constructing your *own* thesis statement:

When you sit down to write an essay about a piece of literature, start with a general topic and move towards a thesis statement. As you fine-tune your thesis statement, keep these questions in mind:

- What assumptions do *you* have about the reader of your essay? (Or, what do you think the reader already knows?)

- What do you *want* your reader to learn about your subject?

- What does *your reader* expect to find in your paper?

- What is important about the subject/what does the subject do?

Bloom's Taxonomy

For a moment, let's return to Benjamin Bloom and his categories for different ways to learn a new concept. When writing a thesis, try to focus on the latter three categories. Look at the following examples:

- Knowledge (basic memorization of information)

- Comprehension (similar to paraphrasing; you can put information or instructions in your own words)

- Application (being able to use a concept)

- Analysis (compartmentalizing information; differentiation)

- Synthesis (putting together a pattern of meaning)

- Evaluation (judging the value of something)

Sample Thesis 1: In the poem "Leda and the Swan," Leda enacts revenge on Zeus by giving birth to two destructive women—Helen of Troy and Clymenestra. (This thesis attempts to *analyze* and *synthesize* an interpretation of the poem.)

Sample Thesis 2: Through a feminist reading, one could argue that Yeats gives Leda power despite her helpless position in "Leda and the Swan." (This thesis *applies* feminist theory to the poem in order to *evaluate* Leda's position.)

Sample Thesis 3: Yeats uses Leda to symbolize Ireland and Zeus to symbolize Britain in "Leda and the Swan" to suggest that Britain failed to realize the consequences of colonial power. (This thesis *synthesizes* the meaning of the poem by *evaluating* it in terms of Yeats' Irish Nationalist work.)

13

Conflict

Your interpretation, opinion, or idea should have valid differing points of view. These differing points of view are called counterarguments. Including counterarguments shows a balanced and well-researched position in your paper. Counterarguments also show that a conflict is involved in your paper.

All papers should demonstrate that a conflict is involved. If your essay cannot, logically, be argued from another side, then your topic is probably ineffectual. For example, arguing that schools should have more money is a no-brainer. No one would say they shouldn't have more money. However, arguing for a sales tax hike during a recession to increase school budgets is an idea that people might argue against. Conflict shows that people believe something is at stake in your topic and that they are willing to invest in a discussion of the topic.

Conflict in a paper may appear anywhere or even throughout the essay. Stating dissenting opinions and refuting them can propel a paper forward.

But there is a danger: your paper should mostly contain your voice and ideas— simply going back and forth with opponents' viewpoints will make your paper look weak and will take away from your argument. Instead try this:

TRY THIS

- Create a "con" section that contains the most salient points opponents might express
- Place this section between your introduction and the paragraphs that begin to support and explain your position
- Begin the "con" section by summarizing why the idea in your thesis might not work, continue with others' ideas that contradict your own, and then finish the "con" section by refuting opponents' ideas and returning to the idea of your thesis in the final sentence

A clear "con" section in your paper shows readers that you are aware of many opinions and that you are prepared to speak as an expert on the subject.

Conflict and Context

- A good "con" section should accurately and fairly portray differing ideas

- You should research and read others' opinions before trying to write the "con" section

- You may not need opposite points of view: if you are refining or revising an interpretation or idea, you may want to write your "con" section by contextualizing your idea by discussing how it relates to similar ideas

If you are too emotionally invested in a topic, you may not be able to give a fair appraisal of differing ideas. You might want to change your topic to something that you care about but that you can also think rationally about.

Recap: So far your essay may have two sections: The Introduction and the Conflict.

I. Introduction
    A. Hook
    B. Thesis
II. Conflict

Support

To convince a reader that what you are saying is correct, you need support. The majority of your paper should support your opinion, interpretation, or idea. Support can come in many forms. Some common ways of supporting your ideas are:

- Logos, ethos, pathos
- Interrogation
- Facts
- Expert sources

> The art of arguing has been studied since the time of the ancient Greeks. The Greeks found that a good argument established three qualities (what they found still holds true today!): logos, ethos, and pathos. They also discovered false logic as well: arguments that may sound good but are really empty.

Good Support:
- **Logos:** the use of logic—reasons and evidence used responsibly and free from fallacies—proves to your readers that you argue from a thoughtful position
- **Ethos:** the use of sincerity—common goals, shared beliefs, and earnest ideas—proves to your readers that the topic is something that matters and is important
- **Pathos:** identification with your readers' feelings. You should not sound threatening or irrational; rather, establish a shared interest in the topic that even your opposition would agree with

Bad Support:
Logical Fallacies—avoid these when you're arguing:
- **Ad Hominem**—Attacking the person—Do not say "the President is an idiot; therefore, we should vote against his tax bill"
- **Ad Misericordiam**—Appeal to pity—Do not argue with "think of the children/puppies/koala bears"
- **Ad Populam**—Appeal to the prejudices and emotions of the masses—Avoid these: "too much sex/violence on TV; the rich are like this; the poor are like this; the uneducated deserve what they get; etc"
- **Non Sequitor**—Doesn't follow—Do not make the illogical leaps: "She is beautiful, so she must not be smart"
- **Bandwagon**—Everyone is doing something—Don't say, "smart people believe in tort reform"
- **False Dilemma**—Simplifying a complex issue into an either/or decision—It's just not true: "Either we take away violent video games, or more teenagers are going to be sociopaths"

Interrogation: Interrogation is the process of questioning your topic. Try asking new questions, original questions about your topic. Can you approach the issue in a unique way, or are you asking the same questions everyone asks?

Facts: An argument is made stronger with facts. Make sure your facts come from reputable sources: Who would disagree with your data? Who sponsored the study you are using?

Expert sources: An expert source has credentials in the field of your inquiry. Good sources are those people who are readily recognized by most readers as important people in a field. These experts include: government officials, academics, and reputable authors. While researching your topic, find out who the most often referenced experts in the field are. Then, try to locate and utilize those sources, too. Use sources by **direct quotation** or **paraphrase**.

- **Direct quotation:** use sources in your paper by taking words accurately (word for word) from an original source. You must use quotation marks and cite in parenthesis and in a works cited page.

- **Paraphrase:** use sources in your paper by taking another person's words and condensing them and putting them into your own words. This approach may be useful for long or technical passages which may distract readers. Instead of quoting a whole paragraph, you may take the main points and put them in your own words. You still must cite in parentheses and on a works cited page.

15

Conclusion

The conclusion can be one of the most difficult parts of the essay to write—you've said it all already, right? One thing you can do is say it again: use the conclusion to summarize the main points in your essay. However, a good conclusion leaves your reader thinking about your essay. Go beyond just summarizing main points by using the conclusion to:

- **Predict** future applications or scenarios if your idea is or isn't followed
- **Forecast** directions for additional studies
- **Return** to the introduction

A good conclusion gives your reader something to think about: prediction and forecasting allows your reader to have a conversation about your paper.

A good conclusion also completes the paper. A good way to make your paper "feel" complete is to return to the introduction. If you opened your essay with a question or paradox, return to it in the conclusion and make sure that you can answer it.

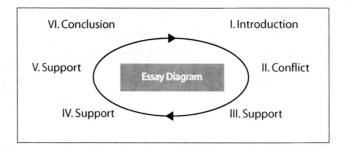

Use the essay diagram to think about your paper as you plan. In addition to taking your reader through main points, think about how to make your paper whole.

Be careful! Do not use the conclusion to start a new argument or assert a new claim. The conclusion is a place to review what you've already done; it is not a place to start something new.

> Recap: Your essay has four sections.
>
> Use these sections to plan your paper.
>
> I.   Introduction
>   A. Hook
>   B. Thesis
> II. "Con"
> III. Support
> IV. Conclusion

1.4 In-Class Writing: Developmental Tools for Every Essay

Development Tools for Every Essay

Sometimes it is hard to know what to say or what kind of example to give. In this section you will find many different techniques for filling in those paragraphs. Deciding on particular tools for sections of your paper will help your paper seem coherent. Tools help you develop the parts of the essay. Imagine the parts of the essay as if they were the highways between the beginning and end of your paper. The developmental tools help you decide where to stop along the way and what you'll do when you get there.

The tools you might want to use to develop your writing include:

- Argument
- Definition
- Description
- Illustration
- Narration
- Comparison and Contrast
- Cause and Effect
- Process
- Classification

Each part of your essay will require one or more tools to develop it. Your introduction may include a story (Narration). You may use cause and effect and illustration to develop the support paragraphs of your essay. When you plan your writing, try to think not only about what information you want to use in each part of the essay but also what tools you want to use to show or explain that information.

Tools also can be used to tie together different parts of an essay: for example, if you begin your essay with a story, then you should return to that story at the end— you may even want to try to tie the story to each supporting section. Depending on what question or problem you are trying to solve with your essay, different tools will be needed. As you write, make a note to yourself about which tools you are using and where you are using them—doing this will help you make your paper coherent.

Some papers may rely on one or two tools, and other papers will use a variety of tools in different places. Select the best tools to use based on the assignment you are given and the topic you are arguing. An in-class essay that asks you to describe a chemical reaction will probably need an extended use of "process" to describe the steps involved. However, a more involved research paper on the future of healthcare in America may use many tools to "illustrate" problems, "argue" a particular remedy, and even demonstrate a "process" for implementing that remedy.

Be Aware of Key Words in Assigned Topics

Read the question or topic you have been assigned carefully. Look for phrases that call for a particular tool to develop your answer.

Argument
Argue
Defend
Justify
Evaluate

Definition
Clarify
Discuss the meaning of
Define

Description
Provide details about
Describe

Illustration
Use examples of
List
Explain

Narration
Discuss the development of
Describe the history of

Comparison and Contrast
Detail the advantages/disadvantages of
Discuss similarities/differences between

Cause and Effect
Account for
Explain the consequences of
Discuss the influence of
Discuss why

Process
Show how
Explain how
Analyze

Classification
Discuss the components of
Analyze the types of

Argument

Argumentation is the art of persuading your audience to agree with you. To quickly review the concepts of *logos*, *ethos*, and *pathos* from section 1.3 **Support**, a supportable argument is built upon the concepts of sound, accurate, and specific evidence (*logos*); your credibility, reliability, and sincerity (*ethos*); and sensitivity to emotionally charged language (*pathos*).

Developing your paper through argumentation involves the use of **inductive** and **deductive** reasoning.

Inductive reasoning (from particular examples to generalization)

Inductive reasoning uses evidence, examples, and results from experiments to draw a conclusion or make a claim about a general phenomenon. Example:

Inductive reasoning relies on **inference**: other conclusions can be drawn from the same evidence. For example: Perhaps the city's equipment is up to date, but there is a manpower shortage, or the services are poorly managed.

- Fires burned three buildings last month (evidence)
- Ambulance response times are slow (evidence)
- Emergency services are falling behind (conclusion)
- The city should upgrade emergency equipment (proposition)

Deductive reasoning (from generalization to specific cases)

Deductive reasoning begins with a broad observation about a group, extracts an individual from the group, and then makes a conclusion based on this logic. Example:

Avoid hasty generalizations because they can lead to faulty conclusions.

- Watersheds near abandoned mines often have mercury in them (general premise)
- Nashobee pond is near an abandoned mine (specific premise)
- Nashobee pond may have mercury poising (conclusion)
- Nashobee pond should be regularly tested for contaminants (proposition)

In addition to using reasoning techniques, consider the insights the fields of rhetoric and psychology have brought to the art of persuasion.

Toulmin Logic

Stephen Toulmin developed a method for creating a strong link between your evidence and your thesis when you use argument in your papers. Consider these three categories:

- **Claim:** your thesis or proposal
- **Data:** evidence, facts, experts, observations
- **Warrant:** the underlying assumption that justifies going from Data to Claim

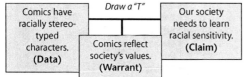

Comics have racially stereotyped characters. **(Data)** — *Draw a "T"* — Comics reflect society's values. **(Warrant)** — Our society needs to learn racial sensitivity. **(Claim)**

The less readily accepted your warrant, the more you need to back it up.

Rogerian Strategy

Carl Rogers came up with an idea that the point of argumentation is to **reduce conflict**.

1st: *Acknowledge* others' opinions and state your own.
"Although some think …, … is the case."

2nd: *Summarize* opposing viewpoints
"Opponents say…" "Some critics point out…"

3rd: *Present* in detail opposing viewpoints
"They cite … as evidence"

4th: *Grant* the validity of some of these points
"Granted, …"

5th: *Present* your own evidence
"Even so, …" "Nevertheless, …"

> By creating consensus, you make your argument easier to accept.

Fallacies: remember to avoid the logical fallacies of *ad hominem*, *non sequitur*, *ad misericordiam*, *ad populam*, bandwagon, and false dilemma arguments. See **1.3 Support** for more information.

Definition

Using definition to develop your paper does not mean quoting from the dictionary. Definition as a developmental tool for papers involves selecting a contentious word or concept and constructing a working definition in your paper.

Avoid the obvious: don't try to use widely held beliefs about a term; instead, be inventive and use an original or provocative definition. One technique for developing interesting definitions takes a term with a negative connotation and shows how it's really a positive force. Think about "disorganized"—can you imagine disorganization as a method of creativity, a way to spark new thoughts and unusual connections in the clutter?

Consider how these terms are fought over: How are they defined by opposing groups? How do these competing definitions complicate your understanding of the words?

Life	Gun Control	Discipline	Pornography
Right to Privacy	Evil	Love	Organic	Evolution
Healthy	Liberalism	Conservatism	Religion

You may also want to investigate how a word's meaning has shifted over time: sometime after the dinosaurs roamed the earth, "cool" meant "not warm." Eventually, "cool" came to also mean something like "popular" or "fashionable." Check out etymology dictionaries, and find out if your library carries an Oxford English Dictionary (OED)—these resources can help you trace the history of a word, but you will still need to develop your own working definition for your paper.

Description

Description is the use of vivid language to engage the five senses. Take a snapshot of a scene you are trying to set for your reader. Can you engage multiple senses?

- What visual details can you show?

- What textures can you feel?

- What can you smell?

- What sounds do you hear?

- What might you taste?

Description can draw your reader into the paper. Even in argumentative or analytical writing description lets your reader participate in events as you tell them. For instance, a pH lab at a local stream would benefit from a description of the plastic wrappers and smell of exhaust from passing trucks.

Pay attention to details such as color and shape when you are observing situations you might want use in your paper. Passages of your paper that rely on description will engage adjectives and adverbs to bring a scene to life. Compare these two sentences:

| The water was brown and dirty. | The murky brown water flowed slowly as sunlight made uneven rainbow-colored splotches on its oily surface. |

Which sentence describes the scene better? Description is a powerful tool that can place your reader at the scene of the action. Fill your reader's senses with the details you want him or her feel and see.

Illustration

Illustration is the technique of using examples to develop your paper. Use illustration to:

- **Depict a general situation:** if you are arguing about campus-wide apathy, an example from your dorm may make the point clear to readers

- **Make an abstract concept clear and concrete:** if you are trying to explain the difference between Modernism and Realism, examples of art in each category would make the point concrete

Illustration requires the use of markers to signal to your reader that an example is coming that will explain the point you just made. Try using these phrases before you use illustration:

- For example,
- For instance,
- In particular,
- Such as
- To illustrate,

While you may want to illustrate a point with a personal example, usually illustration relies on something that your reader could go see for him or herself. So, your aunt Betty's kitchen may not be the best illustration of a well-prepared chef, but Martha Stewart's TV kitchen would be a better example that readers could see for themselves.

Narration

Narration means storytelling. Stories in your paper may be made up, true, or personal, but regardless of the kind of story you tell, it must aid your thesis. Use narrative effectively by:

> **Stating** the point of the story—why are you telling the reader this story?
> **Limiting** your story to an incident or important event
> **Focusing** on the tension—where is the struggle or decision point in the story?
> **Keeping** verb tense and point of view consistent—do you use "I" to tell the story?
> **Organizing** the events of the narrative—can your reader follow what happens first and next?

You may use narrative techniques such as flashbacks and dialog to propel the stories you tell in your paper, but remember that in formal essay writing the point of the paper isn't the story: it's the thesis. Consider effective storytelling in these two passages:

Even a minor felony conviction is a life sentence.

Gray and bitter, the old man gathered his breath under the orange road construction vest—after years of rejection at offices and schools, he had surrendered to the fate of being a criminal even twenty years after he had served his time: he had many plans years ago, but a youthful prank gone awry ended forever his hopes to participate in the middle class.

Both passages assert a similar claim, but only one draws the reader into the detail and makes the reader want to know what happens. With a small narrative to return to throughout the paper, you can help keep your work unified and your reader alert by maintaining interest with a story—what happened to the man? What are his options? What were his plans? Even readers who disagree with your opinion about the topic will be drawn in by the story you are telling.

Comparison and Contrast

Show how two or more items are alike and how they are different through comparison and contrast. You can use this technique to:

- Show that one item is better than another
- Demonstrate that things that seem different are actually similar
- Explain that things that seem similar are actually different

Note that not every essay will ask you to both compare and contrast—you may decide to do one or the other.

Patterns for Comparing and Contrasting: <u>One then the Other</u>—Discuss several qualities of an item in one paragraph, and in the next paragraph compare or contrast those same qualities in another item.

I. Soap One
   A. Soap One price
   B. Soap One scent
II. Soap Two
   A. Soap Two price
   B. Soap Two scent

Patterns for Comparing and Contrasting: <u>Side-by-Side</u>—In a single paragraph show one point of similarity in two items, and in the next paragraph compare or contrast a different point.

I. Soap prices
   A. Soap One price
   B. Soap Two price
II. Soap scent
   A. Soap One scent
   B. Soap Two scent

Keep your purpose in your reader's mind—why are you comparing and/or contrasting these items? What is your reader supposed to learn? Try to be unexpected: if your comparison and contrast of two items confirms an opinion that is already widely held, it may not be effective.

Cause and Effect

Cause and effect develops answers to questions such as "why" and "what if": Why did the Gulf War happen? What if America had socialized medicine?

When used properly, cause and effect writing shows readers unexpected connections between people, events, and actions. You may work from a single phenomenon, such as the high divorce rate in the "Bible belt," and seek out causes that may explain the event, or you may work forward from the same phenomenon and discuss the effects of a high divorce rate in certain states, or you may do both (but be aware of the scope of your topic and the time and space you have to work on it).

Show cause and effect with these terms:	Avoid these terms:
Probably	It is obvious
Most likely	Clearly
It is probable	There is no doubt
One possible cause	Always
One overlooked effect	Never

Identifying causes and effects involves selectivity: Which events are more important to the paper you want to write? Which events are secondary? Which events do people think are involved but really are unimportant?

Process

Process is a method of developing paragraphs that explain to readers "how to" do something. You are giving **directions**. Consider these factors when using process to develop your writing:

1. What is your attitude toward the process? Is the process efficient as it is, or are you arguing for change?
2. What is the purpose of the process? Are you demonstrating how something is done or do you want your reader to try it him or herself?
3. What does your audience know? Explaining how enrollment works at your school to other college students will be very different than explaining enrollment to high school students visiting from Japan.
4. Use transitional words and phrases such as first, next, now, while, after, before, and finally.
5. If you use technical language, explain.

We've all had the experience of opening the "some assembly required" box: there are instructions, but they don't make any sense. This confusion results from poorly executed process writing. Don't let your reader end up with extra parts! Try to imagine explaining the process to someone who has never done it before: what should he or she be aware of? How can he or she know the process is going correctly?

Classification

Use classification to:

- Break a complex subject into component parts
- Divide a concept into parts
- Group different items or ideas under a single heading

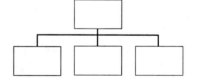

Classification involves taking a single topic and developing your essay by breaking that topic down to its component parts. Think of a grocery store: each aisle contains food, but the store is organized according to particular kinds of food such as dairy, pet food, produce, etc. These divisions often can be broken down further: there are fifteen kinds of butter in the dairy case, and you can find organic, whole, and skim milk in gallon, half gallon, and even individual containers.

Similarly, classification can take different ideas or objects and place them under a single heading. Communism and Christianity, for example, can both be classified as revolutions started by a book. Taking ideas that most people think are very different and showing how they are actually similar is a good way to generate interest in your paper.

Whenever you classify—whether you are taking a subject apart or putting ideas together—you should think of an organizing schema. What do all mammals have in common? Answering this question allows you to classify a completely unknown creature as a mammal if it meets the criteria. If you are dividing college courses into categories such as easy and hard, what are the hallmarks of an easy class? What makes a class hard? With this information your reader can use your classification to organize his or her own experiences.

An Essay Pattern for Beginners

An outline for a basic in-class essay would look like this:

PARTS

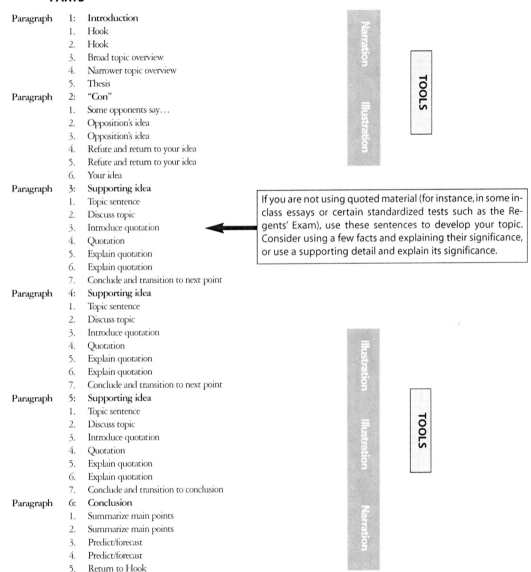

Paragraph 1: **Introduction**
1. Hook
2. Hook
3. Broad topic overview
4. Narrower topic overview
5. Thesis

Paragraph 2: **"Con"**
1. Some opponents say…
2. Opposition's idea
3. Opposition's idea
4. Refute and return to your idea
5. Refute and return to your idea
6. Your idea

Paragraph 3: **Supporting idea**
1. Topic sentence
2. Discuss topic
3. Introduce quotation
4. Quotation
5. Explain quotation
6. Explain quotation
7. Conclude and transition to next point

Paragraph 4: **Supporting idea**
1. Topic sentence
2. Discuss topic
3. Introduce quotation
4. Quotation
5. Explain quotation
6. Explain quotation
7. Conclude and transition to next point

Paragraph 5: **Supporting idea**
1. Topic sentence
2. Discuss topic
3. Introduce quotation
4. Quotation
5. Explain quotation
6. Explain quotation
7. Conclude and transition to conclusion

Paragraph 6: **Conclusion**
1. Summarize main points
2. Summarize main points
3. Predict/forecast
4. Predict/forecast
5. Return to Hook

> If you are not using quoted material (for instance, in some in-class essays or certain standardized tests such as the Regents' Exam), use these sentences to develop your topic. Consider using a few facts and explaining their significance, or use a supporting detail and explain its significance.

This basic outline is a typical six-paragraph in-class essay. Mastering this formula means you have a fundamental understanding of an in-class essay.

To make an "A" in many college courses, however, you must be able to go beyond this model. Rather than one paragraph for each topic, you may need several. The four basic parts of an essay do not change whether you're writing 3 pages or 300 pages, but how you develop each part must change.